**THE OFFICIAL RED BOOK**

# A GUIDE BOOK OF
# MORGAN
# SILVER DOLLARS

*Complete Source for History, Grading, and Prices*
*4th Edition*

## Q. David Bowers

Foreword by
**Leroy C. Van Allen**

**Whitman Publishing, LLC**
PUBLISHING SINCE 1934

www.whitman.com

© 2012 by Whitman Publishing, LLC
3101 Clairmont Road, Suite G, Atlanta, GA 30329

The WCG™ data grid used throughout this publication is patent pending. THE OFFICIAL RED BOOK is a trademark of Whitman Publishing, LLC.

Correspondence concerning this book may be directed to the publisher, at the address above.
ISBN: 0794836852
Printed in China

*Disclaimer:* Expert opinion should be sought in any significant numismatic purchase. This book is presented as a guide only. No warranty or representation of any kind is made concerning the completeness of the information presented. The author, a professional numismatist, regularly buys, sells, and sometimes holds certain of the items discussed in this book.

*Caveat:* The value estimates given are subject to variation and differences of opinion. Before making decisions to buy or sell, consult the latest information. Past performance of the rare coin market or any coin or series within that market is not necessarily an indication of future performance, as the future is unknown. Such factors as changing demand, popularity, grading interpretations, strength of the overall coin market, and economic conditions will continue to be influences.

*Advertisements within this book:* Whitman Publishing, LLC, does not endorse, warrant, or guarantee any of the products or services of its advertisers. All warranties and guarantees are the sole responsibility of the advertiser.

*About the cover:* In 1895, the Philadelphia Mint produced Morgan silver dollars in Proof format only—none were made for circulation. Only 880 coins were struck, making these some of the rarest and most highly valued coins in the series.

Other books in The Official Red Book® series include: *A Guide Book of Franklin and Kennedy Half Dollars; A Guide Book of Double Eagle Gold Coins; A Guide Book of United States Type Coins; A Guide Book of Modern United States Proof Coin Sets; A Guide Book of Shield and Liberty Head Nickels; A Guide Book of Flying Eagle and Indian Head Cents; A Guide Book of Washington and State Quarters; A Guide Book of Buffalo and Jefferson Nickels; A Guide Book of Lincoln Cents; A Guide Book of United States Commemorative Coins; A Guide Book of United States Tokens and Medals; A Guide Book of Gold Dollars; A Guide Book of Peace Dollars;* and *A Guide Book of the Official Red Book of United States Coins.*

For a complete catalog of numismatic reference books, supplies, and storage products, visit Whitman Publishing online at www.whitman.com.

# CONTENTS

# ABOUT THE AUTHOR

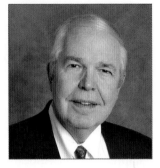

Q. David Bowers has been in the rare-coin business since he was a teenager in 1953. At present he is co-chairman of Stack's Rare Coins in New York and New Hampshire, and is numismatic director of Whitman Publishing, LLC.

Bowers is a recipient of the Pennsylvania State University's Distinguished Alumnus Award (1976). He has served as president of both the American Numismatic Association (1983–1985) and the Professional Numismatists Guild (1977–1979). A recipient of the highest honor bestowed by the ANA (the Farran Zerbe Award), Bowers was the first ANA member to be named Numismatist of the Year (1995), and he has been inducted into the Numismatic Hall of Fame at ANA headquarters in Colorado Springs.

Bowers is a recipient of the Professional Numismatists Guild's highest honor, the Founder's Award, and has received more honors from the Numismatic Literary Guild than has any other writer. In 2000 he was the first annual recipient of the Burnett Anderson Memorial Award, an honor sponsored jointly by the American Numismatic Society, the American Numismatic Association, and the Numismatic Literary Guild.

He is the author of more than 50 books, hundreds of auction and other catalogs, and several thousand articles in numismatic publications such as *Coin World* and *Numismatist*. He is an award-winning columnist for *Paper Money* magazine, and his "Joys of Collecting" column has run in *Coin World* for more than 40 years, making it the longest-running column by any author in the history of numismatics. He has written about Morgan and other dollars in hundreds of articles and catalogs and as part of several books, and his two-volume study *Silver Dollars and Trade Dollars of the United States: A Complete Encyclopedia* (1992) has become a standard in the field.

**Leroy C. Van Allen,** who wrote the foreword to this text, was coauthor with the late A. George Mallis of *The Comprehensive Catalogue and Encyclopedia of Morgan and Peace Dollars.* He has enjoyed the satisfaction of seeing his book go through four editions. Whenever varieties of Morgan dollars are discussed, Van Allen–Mallis (or VAM) numbers come to the forefront. In 2007 Van Allen received the American Numismatic Association's Lifetime Achievement Award. At present he enjoys spending his days in the restoration of antique and classic automobiles, and evenings at—what else?—enjoying rare coins. His enthusiasm is never ending.

# CREDITS AND ACKNOWLEDGMENTS

Sources and credits are given in footnotes, as appropriate, and in the text. See the bibliography for books used or recommended.

## RESEARCH, INFORMATION, AND OTHER HELP

**John W. Adams** provided certain information and granted permission for use of certain items from his study of American coin-auction catalogs. **John Babalis** furnished suggestions. **Pete Bishal** provided portraits of George T. Morgan. **Andrew Bowers** and **Wynn Bowers** helped with proofreading and suggestions. **Roger Burdette** supplied two letters regarding dollars of 1921 requested at the time by Waldo C. Moore, and shared information on Morgan dollar–related patterns. **Francis Campbell,** librarian of the American Numismatic Society, helped with information requests. **Jane Colvard** of the American Numismatic Association Library answered several urgent calls for the loan of reference materials. **Beth Deisher,** editor of *Coin World*, provided information from files regarding the 1962 Treasury release. **Michael S. Fey,** Ph.D., provided full use of information and photographs (by Tom Mulvaney) in *The Top 100 Morgan Dollar Varieties: The VAM Keys.* **Bill Fivaz** discussed die varieties and die-preparation processes, and helped in other ways. **Roberta French** worked closely with the author in aspects of transcribing and compiling research information and was essential in the project from beginning to end. **Wayne Homren** of the Numismatic Bibliomania Society helped publicize the project. **R.W. Julian** has been a long-time consultant on Mint history matters, and certain of his information has been used here. **Chris Karstedt** shared her extensive experience as a rare coin seller and auctioneer. **Melissa Karstedt** helped with proofreading and suggestions. **David Lange,** senior numismatist at the Numismatic Guaranty Corporation of America (NGC), helped with Photo Proof photographs and assisted in other ways. **Dwight Manley** contributed suggestions. **Pat Mullen** corresponded about an 1892 dollar. **Beth O. Piper** compiled price rarity data. **Melissa (Lamotte) Plasencia,** of Littleton Coin Co., helped in several ways. **Gary Schindler** corresponded about the Nevada State Museum. **J.T. Stanton** furnished information on die varieties. **David M. Sundman** made important suggestions, helped with proofreading, and (for chapter 8) contributed an essay on the buying of Morgan dollars. **Saul Teichman** provided several comments. **Anthony Terranova** shared his thoughts on the series. **Frank Van Valen** helped with proofreading and suggestions. **Stephanie Westover** provided photographs.

Our thanks to one and all, and also to the many other people whose articles, books, and other efforts are cited in the pages to follow.

## PAST INTERVIEWS

Over a period of years many people who were active in the market or were observers in the 1950s and 1970s were interviewed concerning hoards, including **Dean H. Albert, Stanley Apfelbaum, Ruth Bauer, Walter Breen, Rodger W. Bridwell, Dan Brown, Tom DeLorey, Joe Flynn Jr., John J. Ford Jr., Harry J. Forman, Larry** and **Ira Goldberg, Leon Hendrickson, John W. Highfill, Dean F. Howe, Robert Hughes, Robert Johnson, John Kamin, James F. Kelly, Abe Kosoff, Chet Krause, Julian**

Leidman, A. George Mallis, Steve Markoff, Dan Messer, Ed Milas, Wayne Miller, Maurice Rosen, Stephen D. Ruddel, Margo Russell, John Pancratz, James F. Ruddy, Hugh Sconyers, Jonah Shapiro, Benjamin Stack, and others, some of whose comments at length are given in the author's 1993 study, *Silver Dollars and Trade Dollars of the United States: A Complete Encyclopedia.*

Other interviews appeared in John W. Highfill's 1993 anthology, *The Comprehensive U.S. Silver Dollar Encyclopedia.* Such interviews are among the sources used in the compilation of hoard information.

## ILLUSTRATIONS (MAIN SOURCES)

The inventory and auction consignments in the possession of **Stack's Bowers Galleries** were sources for many photographs. **Liz Coggan** of J.J. Teaparty Coin Co. furnished several coins for illustration. **David M. Sundman** and **Stephanie Westover** provided many coin and historical photographs from the files of Littleton Coin Co. **Tom Mulvaney** took enlarged photographs used in *The Top 100 Morgan Dollar Varieties: The VAM Keys,* certain of which are used here by permission. Coin illustrations, actual size, of the obverse and reverse of various Morgan dollar dates and mintmarks are mostly by **Douglas Plasencia.** He also worked with the adjustment and editing of photographs supplied by others. Historical illustrations not credited are mainly from the collection of the author.

## CREDITS FOR THE FOURTH EDITION

In addition to the preceding: **Michael Casper** provided a private collection for photography that was used for the majority of the coin photographs of 1878 to 1921 issues. **Roberta French** compiled population reports. **Ash Harrison** assisted with VAM pricing. **Paul Herz Jr.** provided several suggestions. **Susan Novak** assisted with research and correspondence. **Nancy Oliver** and **Richard Kelly** provided revised information for the 1893-S mintage. **John Pack** provided information on several populations. **Vernon R. Padgett** reviewed past editions and provided numerous suggestions. **Paul Rynearson, Frank Van Valen,** and **Robin Wells** reviewed the book and suggested changes.

# FOREWORD
*by Leroy Van Allen*

Welcome to the wonderful world of Morgan silver dollars! David Bowers has written many superb coin books on various topics. Continuing this tradition, in this book he will introduce you to the collecting of this popular series and guide you in exploring its many exciting facets.

The Morgan silver dollar is presently one of the most widely collected of the U.S. coin series. It was not always that popular to collectors. For the first 84 years of its existence from 1878 to 1962, the Morgan dollar was shunned by the public and collectors. Minted as backing for Silver Certificates, they were generally unused by the public during these early years because they were bulky and heavy. They circulated mainly in the South and West. Most were held in the vaults of the Treasury Department even as late as the mid-1950s. They could be obtained from local banks at face value.

In 1962 the Morgan dollar was suddenly thrust into the numismatic limelight when bags of formerly scarce New Orleans "O" Mint dollars were released by the Treasury Department just before the Christmas holiday. At the same time, the rising price of silver bullion was rapidly approaching $1.29 per ounce, at which point the bullion value in a silver dollar would be equal to its face value.

By early 1964, collectors, dealers, and investors had cleaned out all of the Morgan dollars from the Treasury Department vaults. A market frenzy had quickly developed for Morgan dollars, and they were widely traded in bags, rolls, and individual pieces. Because of the Treasury Department hoarding of these coins from 1878 onward they are much more available in Uncirculated condition than their contemporary subsidiary coins. Their large size, beautifully detailed design, and availability have now catapulted them into one of the most widely collected American coin series.

The world of collecting Morgan dollars is vast, as explained in detail by Dave Bowers. There is the usual popular method of collecting by date and mint. This can be done by judicious buying of a combination of circulated and Uncirculated coins, which keeps the total costs down. At the other end of the cost spectrum is the expensive challenge of putting together a set of high-grade certified coins. Beyond a set of dates and mints, there are many specialized areas of collecting Morgan dollars which can open new avenues and challenges. A date series of one mint such as Carson City or New Orleans can be assembled. Collecting prooflike Morgan dollars with mirror fields can be especially rewarding because of their beauty, made possible by their 90% silver content and the preparation process of polishing the die fields.

Perhaps the most challenging area of Morgan dollar collecting is that of die varieties. This frequently requires the use of a hand magnifier for careful examination of minute details on the coin. However, a whole new world of collecting can thus be opened. Detailed examination of the coins coupled with knowledge gained from numerous specialized books on die varieties can be rewarded with breathtaking finds that are worth far more than a normal coin. Bowers points out some of his favorite die varieties, and beyond these, there are thousands of others to be found and bought.

Collecting Morgan dollars has changed dramatically since the 1960s when they first became collectible coins in a widely popular sense. Then, Morgan dollars were available only in uncertified form in 1,000-coin bags, 20-coin rolls, or individually from dealers' businesses, coin shows, coin clubs, auctions, or from individual collectors. No official grading standard or designation existed for Uncirculated dollars. Pricing and condition were in the eye of the beholder! One had to be physically present at auctions and coin shows to buy and sell coins. Communication was by telephone or letters by mail.

Slowly, the Morgan dollar bags and rolls became absorbed into the marketplace. Now, bulk holdings have all but disappeared. MS-60 and MS-65 Uncirculated grades were introduced in 1977, with the new Official ANA Grading Standards for U.S. Coins, with MS-63 introduced in 1980 and MS-64 in 1985. Then third-party grading and coin encapsulation was introduced in 1986 by PCGS, followed by NGC in 1987 and ANACS in 1989. The advent of the Internet and e-mail correspondence in the early 1990s dramatically speeded information exchange, provided web sites with extensive coin collector information, and introduced dealer web sites with coin sell lists and coin photographs. Coin Web auction sites were also introduced where coins could be viewed, bought, and sold without one's leaving home. The years from the late 1990s to the present time have seen the greatly increased availability of specialized coin books on select topics of collecting Morgan dollar die varieties. These books are carrying the die-variety collecting of Morgan dollars to new heights of popularity and coin values. It is indeed an exciting time to be collecting Morgan dollars, and David Bowers's book will give the knowledge to have fun and maybe also reap some profits!

**Leroy Van Allen**

# INTRODUCTION

Recently I was talking with Dwight Manley, a highly accomplished professional numismatist and businessman, who years ago in 1981, at the age of 14, was one of my students at the "All About Coins" class in Colorado Springs. The occasion was the Summer Seminar held by the American Numismatic Association, and about 20 people had signed up for my course. Dwight, barely a teenager, loved coins and, in the meantime, was busy with his schooling. Later, he did some serious thinking.

According to his biography, later printed in various places in connection with his coin activities (including supervising the sale of the SS *Central America* treasure as head of the California Gold Marketing Group, owning the finest known 1913 Liberty Head nickel and a gem 1804 dollar, and more), he credits me and the long-ago class for his decision to go into the rare coin business. The rest is history, and chapters in his life are still being written.

In my conversation of a few days ago I mentioned I was putting the finishing touches on a book about Morgan silver dollars for Whitman Publishing Company.

"Morgan dollars! I love them!" Dwight said. "No other coin can conjure visions of the Wild West, the shootout at the OK Corral, and other dramatic moments of history."

Well, I have no way of knowing whether, back in 1881, Wyatt Earp was carrying an 1881-S dollar in his pocket when he stopped by at the OK Corral in Tombstone, in Arizona Territory, but there is always the possibility. We do know that if Pawnee Bill, "Buffalo Bill" Cody, Billy the Kid, or Annie Oakley spent a dollar in the Rockies in the late 19th century, it was a dollar made of silver. Of such romantic (at least in hindsight and popular history) stuff, Americans cannot get their fill. This was the period of the Wild West, empire building, the Deadwood Stage, William Jennings Bryan's "Cross of Gold" speech, Scott Joplin down at the Maple Leaf Club in Sedalia, the French-chateau-style Cliff House overlooking the Pacific, society promenades in Saratoga Springs, the Pullman Palace Car, the five-cent cigar, and the silver dollar. All are everlastingly combined. A Morgan dollar is history in minted form, ready to come to life in the hands of an appreciative collector.

In time many Morgan silver dollars were spent and became worn out, including in such areas as Tombstone, where silver dollars were loved and paper dollars ignored. Similarly, neat little piles of dollars were seen at gaming tables in Rhyolite, Tincup, Silver Reef, Gillette, Bodie, Tonopah, and other places, some now ghost towns, others forgotten. In mercantile houses, banks, bordellos, and bistros in cities such as Helena, Cheyenne, San Francisco, and Denver, cashiers handled dollars in everyday transactions, never—or scarcely ever—pausing to see if below the eagle's tail on a particular coin there might be a tiny letter S or O, or the twin letters CC.

Minted from 1878 to 1904, and again in 1921, for no real reason other than a political boondoggle to provide a market for western mining and related interests (read: votes from citizens of the region), these pieces were anything but romantic at the time to the Treasury Department. Made in staggering, indeed frightening, quantities, they became a first-class nuisance. Vaults at the several mints were stuffed to their ceilings, and even a vast area of the Philadelphia Post Office was commandeered for storage, not to overlook a separate temple-like building set up in the Mint courtyard to store even more silver dollars, while in Washington the Treasury Building vaults had still more. Of course, what was their problem became our pleasure years later!

My own introduction to Morgan silver dollars came when I was a teenager in Forty Fort, Pennsylvania, in 1952. I began my lifelong fascination with old coins by learning that, marvelously, a 1909 Lincoln "penny" with an S below the date on one side, and the tiny initials V.D.B. on the other side, might be worth the munificent sum of $10! I scurried about to find one, or several, quickly. However, none were to be had. Soon, I read my copy of the *Guide Book of United States Coins,* 1952 edition, cover to cover, expanded my collecting interests to include nickels and dimes and other series, and went onward and upward. The going pay for doing odd jobs such as pulling weeds, cutting grass, or delivering drug store prescriptions by bicycle was 50¢ per hour, plus an occasional tip. Soon, my desires were greater than what I could afford.

Read these *Guide Book* prices from 1952 and weep: Uncirculated 1893-S Morgan dollar: $200. Proof 1895: $85. I could not afford either one.

Not too long afterward, I took to trading coins, first by exchanging duplicates, and then buying, in a small way, various coins at Wilkes-Barre Coin Club meetings and through newspaper advertisements, plus occasional attendance at the Empire State Numismatic Association coin shows and other events. My father, remarkably it seems in hindsight, loaned me $6,000 as an ante or business bankroll, but wanting to pay my own way, I gave him 3% interest on the money, the going rate at the time, although he made no such request.

My little enterprise grew, prospered, and in time became a fairly large business in the relatively small world of rare coin dealing as it was then. My first ANA bourse table was in Omaha in the summer of 1955, a show attended by an all-time record of 500 people.

Fast forward a few decades and lots of experiences, here I am today!

However, I still remember the times in the 1950s when banks in the Wyoming Valley, as the district around Forty Fort was known, would let me bring $1,000 in cash, from my inventory account, and give me a bag of 1,000 unsorted silver dollars. Such canvas bags were grimy, gray, stained, and always showed the marks of years of storage and handling.

Seeking to build my own set of Morgan dollars from 1878 through 1921 and Peace dollars from 1921 through 1935, and to acquire others for resale, I examined many thousands of coins. I never did find some of the CC coins (I think 1885-CC was considered to be the rarest back then), but most of the others came to hand, except, of course, a Philadelphia Mint 1895.

Typically, many of the Philadelphia Mint coins in a bag were Uncirculated, although rather dull and lifeless, and in sufficient quantities that they were annoying. In time I could identify certain dates and mintmarks of coins by simply looking at the obverse, and not checking for the mintmark, as Philadelphia, San Francisco, Carson City, and New Orleans coins for some dates had distinguishing "facial features." I never did see an Uncirculated CC coin, but early in my dealership bought from another dealer a bag of 1878-CCs and, on another occasion, a bag of 1885-CCs.

Before long I had a little business going with silver dollars. Way out in California, dealer Abe Kosoff (whose credentials included being the founder of the Professional Numismatists Guild) had one or perhaps several clients who liked to hoard bags of Uncirculated silver dollars. At that time, around 1955 and 1956, upon request local banks would order bags of "new" dollars from their regional Federal Reserve Banks. On the West Coast, Abe was able to find endless numbers of S-Mint dollars in bags, but none of Philadelphia (as to bags of CC and O coins, no one ever had any of those!). I was the logical East Coast connection for him, and his first check to me was for $16,000, for 15,000 silver dollars (15 bags) plus a $1,000 profit for me. Then we settled into a routine with a slightly higher margin, 10%. He would send me checks for face value plus 10%, and I would order the bags and ship them to him. This I did, and all parties were happy. Every time he bought a bag I made $100, which added up. This, to me, was a fortune!

All of this was before the great Treasury release of the 1960s, which plays the lead role in all modern accounts of Morgan silver dollars. In the meantime I eagerly sought old auction catalogs, reference books, and, in particular, the combined mother lode of all numismatic information: back copies of the *American Journal of Numismatics* (1866 onward), *The Numismatist* (1888 onward, although my set started with 1894), and *The Numismatic Scrapbook Magazine* (1935 onward). I skimmed them cover to cover, and paused to read, and reread, items of interest.

My first book, *Coins and Collectors*, was published in 1964 and became an instant success, selling quite a few thousand copies and going through several reprints. Later I wrote many more books, more than 50 by now. More than just a few included silver dollars either as a main subject—as in the two-volume *Silver Dollars and Trade Dollars of the United States: A Complete Encyclopedia*, and in a book I did on the 1804 silver dollar, the "King of American Coins," in 1999—or as a significant part of the narrative.

In the meantime, each week, without interruption, I have produced my "Joys of Collecting" column, earlier called "Numismatic Depth Study," for *Coin World*. Today this stands as the longest-running column by any author in all of numismatics. Apropos of this column, I was delighted to read this little blurb by Leroy C. Van Allen and A. George Mallis in their *Comprehensive Catalogue and Encyclopedia of Morgan and Peace Dollars* (origin of those Van Allen and Mallis, or VAM, numbers everybody uses to identify die varieties):

> In a series of articles in the "Numismatic Depth Study" column of the 30 October 1974 to 15 January 1975 issues of *Coin World*, Q. David Bowers traced the history of the Morgan and Peace dollars.
>
> These articles were very well written and covered in narrative form the development of the design, legislation affecting their coinage, production difficulties, Proof coin production, and patterns for both these series.

In closing these introductory remarks I refer you to the earlier and separately listed credits of the fine people who helped produce this book. In addition we all need to give a nod to those rascally politicians in Washington, DC, who in 1878 foisted upon the American public the Bland-Allison Act, which let forth a Niagara of silver dollars that no one needed or wanted!

We also need to thank Mint Director Henry R. Linderman, who in 1878 was in such a hell-bent fury to get silver dollars minted, immediately if not sooner, that this was done before either the designs or the die-making process had been perfected—necessitating a whole bunch of frustrating (to Mint people) and absolutely delightful (to later generations of numismatists) changes!

Further, we need to acknowledge the little-known George W. Rice, who in 1898 was the first to write a technical paper on Morgan dollar die varieties, then called "Bland dollars" by everyone. Rice was the intellectual ancestor of Howard R. Newcomb, Francis X. Klaes, Neil Shafer, the Van Allen and Mallis duo, Wayne Miller, and many others— enough scholars to create a substantial bibliography (to which please refer).

Today, here and now, I especially appreciate the truly wonderful wide world of collectors, dealers, and students who have been involved with Morgan dollars, either casually or deeply.

I hope that this book will contribute to your own pleasure and enjoyment of the series.

# INTRODUCTION TO THE THIRD EDITION

Welcome to the third edition of *A Guide Book of Morgan Silver Dollars*. Dressed up with a new and distinctive cover illustration, with the latest updates in market values and population figures, and color illustrations for the first time, this book is all set to be one of the most useful in your library!

In the two and a half years since the second edition was released, Morgan silver dollars of 1878 through 1921 have continued in the forefront of numismatic interest and activity. I am deeply appreciative for the many comments and nice reviews of the two earlier editions, and the impact they have had on our hobby.

Now, enjoy the third edition! Welcome to one of America's most fascinating series.

**Q. David Bowers**
**Wolfeboro, New Hampshire**

# INTRODUCTION TO THE FOURTH EDITION

Welcome to the fourth edition of *A Guide Book of Morgan Silver Dollars*. I am delighted but not surprised that this book has become a standard in the hobby community, and more than just a few enthusiasts have obtained one of each of the previous three editions. Of course, it is the subject of Morgan dollars that carries the trend, as these are far and away the most popularly collected American coins from the late 19th and early 20th centuries. As with previous editions, the fourth has the latest updates in market values, certification population figures (combining PCGS and NGC data), and color illustrations. I hope that this book will become a favorite in your numismatic library.

It seems that Morgan dollars improve with time, so to speak, and scarcely a year goes by without more devotees taking up this popular coinage series. Indeed, these dollars are at once historical, beautiful and, for the most part, readily obtainable in Mint State for very reasonable prices. If you are an advocate that "bigger is better," the large diameter of silver dollars makes them especially easy to study—in comparison to, say, half dimes! All American coins are interesting, but George T. Morgan's silver dollar is the king of the hill.

As you look through the following pages, enjoy the pursuit of your own collection. Thank you for being a reader.

**Q. David Bowers**
**Wolfeboro, New Hampshire**

# THE APPEAL AND CHALLENGE OF MORGAN DOLLARS

Today, in the early 21st century, Morgan-design silver dollars are far and away the most widely collected "classic" United States coins. Struck from 1878 to 1904 and then in 1921, these dollars were produced to the extent of hundreds of millions of pieces, far more than were needed in circulation or for any aspect of commerce of the era.

Created as a result of the Bland-Allison Act of 1878, one of the greatest political boondoggles of all time (at least from a numismatic viewpoint), such pieces were created simply to provide a market for western and other silver-mining interests. At the time, the international price of silver had been dropping sharply, and Uncle Sam was asked to provide a price support. The result is the vast panorama of coins available to collectors today.

In the early years, 1878 through 1904, four different mints were used to strike Morgan dollars: Philadelphia (1878–1904), Carson City (1878–1885 and 1889–1893), New Orleans (1879–1904), and San Francisco (1878–1904). Each of these mints has its own history, its own aspect of interest, its own excitement.

Without doubt, the Carson City Mint evokes images of the Wild West, gambling in the mining districts, and more—part of American tradition and drama, of course, but at the same time quite true. Today, many collectors focus on and enjoy these "CC" dollars, often available in sparkling, lustrous Mint State—like new!

The San Francisco Mint has its own story. The impressive new Mint building, made of granite, was opened in 1874. During the earthquake and fire of April 1906 it was the only structure in its district to remain intact. The coin presses in that facility struck many millions of Morgan dollars, most being very carefully made, with excellent sharpness of details.

New Orleans, way down south in Dixie, had its mint close to the levee guarding the city from the ravages of the Mississippi River. Coinage techniques were a bit different from those at San Francisco; minting was done in haste, and today this is evidenced by New Orleans dollars' often being weak at the centers—sloppy workmanship perhaps, haste perhaps—we will probably never know the details.

Philadelphia, the "mother mint," is where all dies were made, sometimes not quite right, with punching, mintmarks at crazy angles, and more, perhaps technically reflecting the loss of quality control, but for the numismatist yielding a garden of delightful varieties. Philadelphia also turned out a brilliant cascade of sparkling silver dollars by the millions. In

A brilliant, lustrous 1884 silver dollar struck at the Carson City Mint, and with the all-important CC mintmark below the eagle's tail. Such pieces, while plentiful and inexpensive, are highly prized by coin collectors today as tangible links to the romantic Wild West era.

addition, Proofs with mirrored surfaces were made there each year for collectors and sold at a premium. In 1895, the most desired year from a collector's viewpoint, there were 880 Proofs made, and today a choice example will bring tens of thousands of dollars.

While millions of Morgan silver dollars were paid out during the period of their manufacture and used in circulation, particularly in the mountainous areas of the West, a far larger part, amounting to hundreds of millions, remained stored in 1,000-coin bags in vaults. These were deep within the various mints, and when that space was exhausted, in other places as well. For example, the Philadelphia Post Office and the Treasury Building in Washington, DC, had storage areas stuffed with dollars.

Production of Morgan dollars ceased in 1904, then was revived in 1921. In the latter year Morgan dollars were soon superseded by a new design, the Peace dollar, after which they faded into history. Following the production of Peace-design dollars (1921–1935) there were no more made of the denomination until 1971, when Eisenhower-motif dollars made their debut, no longer of silver, but of a clad composition (although some 40%-silver pieces were struck and sold at a premium to collectors). These were made through 1978. Then followed Susan B. Anthony "mini-dollars" (1979–1981 and 1999), Sacagawea "golden dollars" beginning in 2000, and presidential dollars inaugurated in 2007.

From time to time after 1921, the Treasury Department paid out long-stored Morgan dollars when pieces were called for by banks in the West, by casinos in Nevada (prime users), and, in December, for use as holiday gifts. Every once in a while collectors would be delighted to find that a previously rare variety was now available at or near face value, sort of like finding treasure in the streets! And yet, because of the high face value of Morgan dollars and the general availability of certain varieties, such as the virtually impossible 1903-O (most leading dealers never even saw one in Mint State, let alone owned one), collecting such dollars was not popular.

All of this changed beginning in the 1950s, when several dealers began specializing in Morgan dollars, occasionally acquiring pieces stored in the San Francisco Mint, the Treasury Department, or elsewhere. Pages of the *Numismatic Scrapbook Magazine* contained many offerings of single coins and rolls. And yet, Morgan dollars were still second fiddle to series that were more plentiful, such as Indian and Lincoln cents, Buffalo nickels, and the like.

Gambling in Nevada, with silver dollars on the table. In the West, silver dollars were the coins of choice for a long time, and in some mountain states scarcely a *paper* dollar was ever used.

# THE TREASURY RELEASE

In November 1962 this changed. Bags of long-stored 1903-O dollars, considered to be *the* foremost rarity in the series, were brought out from a vault within the Philadelphia Mint that had been sealed in 1929, after bags of dollars had been shipped there from storage in the New Orleans Mint, which had long since ceased operation. In chapter 6 I give details of this amazing situation. Soon, these were the talk of the collecting community.

Word continued to spread about these fabulous dollars' being available, and banks across the nation sent requests to the Federal Reserve system, which in turn tapped coins stored at the various mints and elsewhere. During the next year, hundreds of millions of coins were paid out, singly, in small groups, and in sealed 1,000-coin bags to those who ordered them. In Washington at the Treasury Building, the cash window, so-called, paid out dollars to those interested, some of whom arrived with large bundles of cash to buy dollars, and wheelbarrows to cart them off! Occasionally a bonanza would be encountered with scarce or rare dates, for these coins had been stored there for decades, and no one had checked to see what dates and mints were involved. Again, see chapter 6.

By March 1964, the Treasury called a halt to the distribution, by which time only about three million silver dollars were left, as hundreds of millions were gone. Those three million, mostly stored in the Treasury Building in Washington, largely consisted of Carson City dollars, some of them quite remarkable—notably the 1884-CC, of which 1,136,000 were minted, and of which the Treasury found that it had about 85% of the original coinage on hand, in Uncirculated grade, in the original bags! How exciting! Again, this was like finding long-lost treasure, or going in a time machine back to the wild and woolly days of the West, to Carson City in an earlier era.

## MARKET DEVELOPMENT

For numismatists, the Treasury release of 1962 through 1964 was a godsend, a bonanza the effects of which are still felt today by anyone who collects Morgan dollars.

Today approximately 100 different date and mintmark varieties are considered to constitute a basic set from 1878 to 1921, and of these, more than half are readily available in Mint State for less than $100 per coin, many for *much less* than that. Only a handful are sufficiently rare as to cost more than $1,000 for a Mint State specimen.

Accordingly, with little effort, dozens and dozens of Morgan dollars from the various mints—Philadelphia, Carson City, San Francisco, and New Orleans—from the early

Circa 1903 photo of one small part of one vault in the basement of the Treasury Building in Washington, D.C. Shown are many bags of silver dollars, 1,000 coins per bag, each bag weighing about 57 pounds. In the foreground, against the other bags, are several (marked LAFAYETTE) that contain commemorative silver dollars. At the top are cases of $50 and $100 bills.

Sadly—or perhaps not, as the ramifications would be difficult to figure out—no numismatic inventory was taken of the Treasury's holdings. Years later, the same building yielded millions of Carson City silver dollars (which had been shipped there at the turn of the century). In the mid-1940s, dealer Aubrey Bebee heard a rumor that some Lafayette dollars, by then quite valuable, were stored in the Treasury Building in bags. Someone checked, and found that indeed they had been—until a few months earlier, when they'd been shipped away to be melted!

years plus the 1921-D (the Denver Mint struck Morgan dollars only in this year) can be acquired, arrayed before you, and enjoyed, for a nominal cost, numismatically speaking.

Remarkably, choice and gem Mint State Morgan dollars of the 19th century are much more available than are the basic coins of the realm, Indian cents, made during the same era, as Indian cents were not saved. Accordingly, anyone endeavoring to collect Indian cents by date sequence (such pieces were first made in 1859 and last in 1909) has to buy them one at a time, and not easily. There is no such thing as a mint-sealed bag of Indian cents, and there were no Treasury hoards. In contrast, there are enough Morgan silver dollars around that dozens of different dealers specialize in them, while only a handful make a point of featuring Indian cents.

Similarly, the numismatist seeking to put together a set of nickel five-cent pieces of the Shield and Liberty Head designs of the late 19th and early 20th centuries has a great challenge, and these have to be acquired one at a time, as there were no hoards to be tapped. As a reflection of the contrast, in 1887 the mintage of Liberty Head nickels for circulation amounted to 15,260,692. In the same year, the production of Morgan silver dollars for circulation was 20,290,700. Today, at least several *million* 1887 Morgan dollars exist, due to the Treasury hoard. Liberty nickels? Probably no more than a thousand or two Mint State pieces, all told, if even that many!

## YOUR COLLECTION

Although many Morgan dollars exist in quantity for you to contemplate and buy, others are scarce, sometimes frustratingly (but challengingly) so. One cannot simply write out a check and get a complete set of Morgan dollars, as some patience is required. There are enough around that the typical numismatist—not *you*, but the typical numismatist—can put together a Mint State set within a few weeks, perhaps excepting the 1893-S and 1901 (the two rarest in this preservation).

However, such a quickly formed set is apt to be a mixture of cats and dogs, so to speak, as although Morgan silver dollars are plentiful in many instances, their *quality* varies all over the place. Some Morgan dollars, the 1881-S for example, are readily available in gem Mint State, sharply struck, and with gorgeous eye appeal. No problem. Others, such as the 1891-O, are apt to be miserably struck and unattractive, and although they are not super-expensive, finding one can entail weeks or months of searching. Thus there is a challenge. The prevailing theme of this book is to share my own experiences with Morgan dollars and the guidelines for forming a truly beautiful collection, regardless of your budget—a collection containing coins that are nicer and more attractive than most others, but at no greater cost! This sounds impossible, but if you are a careful buyer it will happen.

This book is created for you, assuming that you would like to have a challenge. While, offhand, it might seem to be attractive to be able to write a check and buy a complete set of Uncirculated Morgan dollars all at once, or to put together a set within a week or two, in reality this is not the case. Human beings, particularly those with an intellectual turn of mind, love challenges. Indeed, that is what the entire field of hunting and fishing is about. Very few bass anglers would be even slightly interested in visiting a lake in which a bass without struggle grabbed onto a hook to be hauled in, and, a minute later, another bass did the same thing. There would be no golfers, no golf courses, no television networks devoted to golf, if with each game even a tyro could make the circuit in

18 strokes. And, no one would care at all about crossword puzzles if the answers were given along with the clues.

The thrill of the chase is what makes Morgan dollar collecting interesting and exciting, indeed all of numismatics a wonderful challenge and intellectual pursuit.

Within the approximately 100 dates and mintmarks of Morgan dollars there are enough challenges, enough variances, that your collection, as it grows, will be different from any other collection ever formed, as reflected by your own selection of sharply (hopefully) or weakly struck coins, perhaps interesting varieties of repunched mintmarks, or whatever.

## ROMANCE OF THE ROCKIES

At the same time, the pursuit of Morgan dollars offers other advantages. The history of the origin of the Morgan dollar, the development of the fabulous Comstock Lode in Nevada, the finding of silver in the Rocky Mountains in Colorado, and other slices of American life and endeavor are fascinating to read. Virginia City, Nevada, and Leadville, Colorado, both were born and lived because of silver, and, of course, the same can obviously be said for Silver Plume, Colorado (a tiny town tucked on the eastern slope of the Rocky Mountains not too far from Denver). Exploring many, or even one, of these silver towns can be a fascinating sidelight.

Silver dollars were the mainstay of everyday commerce in many areas of the American West—and if you enjoy history of this romantic era, you will especially enjoy the silver dollars with "S" (San Francisco) and "CC" (Carson City) mintmarks, as these coins were there when it happened and were part of the scenario.

## OPPORTUNITIES

In the field of buying and selling silver dollars, there are many interests and joys to experience. Go to a coin convention, and chances are good that many if not most of the dealer displays will feature Morgan dollars for sale, some of them offering cases full of them. You'll find some specialists in the series, likely including someone who would enjoy "talking Morgan dollars" with you if there is a lull in the buying and selling activity (which can sometimes be hectic). Dealers vary, and some could care less about outreach to newcomers, while others, if they have the time to do so, are more than willing to share their ideas and experiences. Diversity, I call it.

**Slot machines were everywhere in the West. The machine shown here, a Caille Musical Puck, dates from about 1903. At the top of the machine, the player inserted a coin into one of six slots, each of which represented a different color on the wheel. The wheel then spun around and stopped. If the right color had been selected, a cascade of coins emptied into the payout cup. In the meantime, the music box at the bottom of the cabinet played a tune. These machines cost only a few hundred dollars each and often paid for themselves in a matter of months. They required little attention, apart from the opening-up of the coin bin (accessible by key through a panel in the side or rear). (John Duckworth collection)**

Similarly, just about every auction sale of United States coins contains Morgan dollars, often many of them, presenting a panorama of opportunity.

"Nothing happens until someone buys something" is an old marketing axiom. And, it is always fun to acquire an object of desire—such as a sparkling, lustrous Morgan dollar just sitting there, silently giving you the message as you view it, "Buy me!"

Back home with a few Morgan dollars at hand, there are other pleasures to experience. As Lewis Carroll might have suggested, you can have a numismatic adventure through a looking glass. A handy magnifier of 4x or 8x (not a microscope, but something manageable) will reveal the surface characteristics of Morgan dollars, which can and do vary from year to year and even from mint to mint within the same year.

Such examination can develop into a specialty within itself. More than just a few collectors have become excited about small differences in die details, such as mintmarks that are slightly repunched. Indeed, the grand "bible" on this technical subject, the *Comprehensive Catalogue and Encyclopedia of Morgan and Peace Dollars*, by Leroy C. Van Allen and A. George Mallis, has gone through four large printings!

It is fun to examine the 1879-CC Large CC Over Small CC variety and see that the Mint tried to chip away or remove a small mintmark so that a larger one could be put in its place, the attempt being rather unsuccessful or even botched. Better success was achieved by converting certain Carson City Mint reverse dies to New Orleans dies, in the 1900-O/CC dollar. The last is certainly among the most fascinating of Morgan dollar varieties, and yet it is sufficiently plentiful and inexpensive that anyone can own an example.

Reading about Morgan dollars is fun. Buying them is great fun, too—even great sport. Remarkably, there are many truly rare coins available for "regular coin" prices—these being sharply struck or particularly attractive pieces, often in the minority, that are simply priced at market levels for ordinary pieces. For 90% or more buyers, buying a choice Mint State (MS-63 or MS-64) 1891-O dollar is a simple matter—just find one in a certified plastic holder, marked MS-63 or MS-64, and write a check. The price is more or less standard.

But, you can be different. You will know that among twenty MS-63 1891-O Morgan dollars in the market, perhaps only one is sharply struck (check the strands of hair on the portrait of Miss Liberty and the details of the feathers on the eagle). This is your coin! Tracking down a coin that is just right, a rarity in disguise, is called "cherrypicking."

Morgan silver dollars of 1878 through 1921: consider the possibilities. Excitement and challenge await you!

**Why the Morgan dollar was made: too much silver! Shown here is the Enterprise Mine in Aspen, Colorado, one of hundreds silver-mining sites in the Rocky Mountain district of Colorado—not to overlook lodes in** Nevada, Idaho, Montana, and elsewhere. Politicians were persuaded that good economic conditions for silver miners would also mean good times for the prairie states, and much of America west of the Mississippi River was behind the push that resulted in the Bland-Allison Act of 1878.

Casting ingots of silver in the refinery of the Colorado Smelting Company at Black Hawk, on the flank of the Rockies to the west of Denver. (*Harper's Weekly,* May 30, 1874)

# THE TRADITION
# OF SILVER DOLLARS

When Morgan-design silver dollars were first minted in 1878, such coins had a long-standing tradition. Dollars of other designs had been made as early as 1794, in the cradle days of the American nation, scarcely a decade after the end of the American Revolution.

Writing something truly meaningful as to the history of American silver dollars from the first year of issue, 1794, to the last (before the Morgan issues), 1873, in a few paragraphs is probably like trying to write a history of railroading in a few paragraphs, or the story of those who have lived in the White House, or a description of the progress of aviation in America, or aspects of South American politics, or whatever. It can't be done. Indeed, an entire book could be devoted to the subject—as I did at one time, with my 1993 effort, *Silver Dollars and Trade Dollars of the United States: A Complete Encyclopedia*, in two volumes, which devoted hundreds of pages to silver dollars before the Morgan series—probably about all you ever wanted to know, plus many things you never cared about.[1]

That said, in brief, the "silver dollar" of choice in the United States in the early years of the republic was the Spanish milled dollar, or eight-real piece, struck at various Spanish-American mints, with Mexico City predominating. Such coins were generally of good weight, contained full value of silver, and were the mainstay of world commerce, finding equal reception in the port of Canton in China, in New York City, or in Rome or Paris. The coin was about as universal as any ever devised, although the 1780-dated Maria Theresia (as some spell it, or Teresa or Theresa) dollar of the Levant, made over a long period of years but with the same date, furnished competition.

It may come as a surprise to know that these Spanish milled dollars were so popular, so essential to commerce, that they remained legal tender in the United States until 1860, by which time several mints in America had been making our own silver dollar coins.[2]

A Spanish-American milled dollar of 1734, struck at the Mexico City Mint, representative of the world's most popular coin for use in international trade. (**Guide Book of United States Coins**)

## THE SILVER DOLLARS OF 1794

In the United States, the Mint Act of April 2, 1792, provided for decimal coinage, the largest silver denomination being the dollar, equal in value to 100 cents. As a strong press was required to strike dollars, and none was on hand at the time, it was not until autumn 1794 that the first pieces were struck. At that time the mintage was slightly over 2,000 coins, but due to problems, none were struck with needle-sharp detail, and some were very weak, particularly at the lower left of the obverse and the corresponding part of the reverse. This was due in part to the inadequacy of the press and possibly in greater part to the fact that both die faces were not completely parallel. Some dollars were discarded as unsatisfactory, and 1,758 were retained to be passed into circulation.

Remarkably, the minting and distribution of the first 1794 dollars was done quietly and without any observance, ceremony, or press release. Nor is there a record of anyone's saving a coin as a souvenir. The Mint did not have its own collection (and would not until June 1838); the Smithsonian Institution was decades away from being formed; and there were no coin dealers in America, no reference books, no numismatic societies. Indeed, by the end of 1794, only a few different denominations of coins had been struck in Philadelphia—and a collection could have been kept in a little tray,

A silver dollar of 1794, the first year that this denomination was struck. In the autumn, 1,758 were released into commerce, without a single piece being saved by a numismatist—for coin collectors were few and far between at the time.

showing varieties of copper half cents of 1793 and 1794, cents of the same years (including several different major design changes in 1793), and a silver half dollar and dollar.

Silver half dimes, from 1794-dated dies, would not be struck until 1795—the year that United States gold coins were first made. Other denominations followed, such as the first dime and the first quarter dollar in 1796.

The silver dollars of 1794 were placed in the channels of commerce on a routine basis, and soon circulated far and wide. However, there were so few of them that scarcely anyone took notice. An exception was provided by the *New Hampshire Gazette*, published in Portsmouth, which had this to say on December 2:

> Some of the dollars now coining at the Mint of the United States have found their way to this town. A correspondent put one into the editor's hands yesterday. Its weight is equal to that of a Spanish dollar, encircled by Fifteen Stars, and has the word "LIBERTY" at the top, and the date, 1794, at the bottom. On the reverse, is the Bald Eagle, enclosed in an Olive Branch, round which are the words "One Dollar, or Unit, Hundred Cents."
>
> The *tout ensemble* has a pleasing effect to a connoisseur; but the touches of the graver are too delicate, and there is a want of that boldness of execution which is necessary to durability and currency.

At the time it was not at all unusual for sailing ships to leave American ports for expeditions of whaling, commerce, or other activity, and to carry aboard 10,000 or more Spanish-American dollars, typically stored in a secure place in the cabin area of the boat, not far from the room of the captain. Obviously, the entire coinage of 1794 United States dollars would have been but a tiny fraction of a typical ship's money. Thus, in the overall scheme of commerce they were not important. However, numismatically they were indeed important, and continue to be.

Today it is estimated that about 125 to 135 or so 1794 silver dollars exist, a handful in what can be called Mint State, but most showing evidences of circulation, and all of them, at least those I have seen in person or through illustrations, showing at least some signs of weakness. Many show planchet file marks (adjustment marks) as well. Ever since the cradle days of American numismatics in the mid-19th century, the 1794 dollar has been an object of desire.

# THE "KING OF AMERICAN COINS"

Dollars of the 1794 style were what are known today as the Flowing Hair type with Small Eagle reverse. Similar dollars were made, but in larger quantities, in 1795, by which time an appropriate press was on hand and pieces could be made of better quality and sharpness. In the same year the motif was modi-fied to the Draped Bust of Miss Liberty facing right, with a redesigned Small Eagle reverse; this style pro-duced in limited quantities from the end of 1795 until early 1798. In the latter year a new reverse, the Heral-dic Eagle style, was produced, and examples were struck through 1803, and into 1804.

Silver dollars struck in calendar year 1804, some 19,570 pieces, were from earlier-dated dies, most probably 1803. No 1804-dated dollars were struck, although anyone reading the *Annual Report of the Director of the Mint* would have thought that, indeed, 19,570 had been made.

This specimen of the 1804 silver dollar is believed to have been the one pre-sented to the Sultan of Muscat. Today it is treasured as the finest known exam-ple of the "King of American Coins."

Years later, in 1834, the Department of State desired to have the Mint make special presentation sets of coins as gifts to foreign dignitaries, most prominently the Sultan of Muscat and the King of Siam, with whom it was desired to establish trade relationships. In that era, foreign commerce was conducted by ships, and vessels from Portsmouth, Salem, Boston, New York, Baltimore, Charleston, and other ports sailed far to lands in which business connections had been formed or in which American traders found a favorable reception—such as the ports of Europe and South America, Bombay, Canton in China, and Batavia in Southeast Asia. Muscat and Siam remained terra incognita to American merchants, although ships of other nations regularly called there, and hopes were high that they would become important for the United States as well.

Along with such gifts as maps and wrought items of precious metals, coins of the United States would reflect the spirit of the nation. The Mint was contacted, and Proofs of current coinage were produced for the set, the denominations including the half cent, copper cent, silver half dime, dime, quarter, and half dollar, and the gold $2.50 and $5. By that time, in 1834, no silver dollars or $10 gold pieces had been struck at the Mint since 1804. Seeking to preserve historical accuracy, but not having dies on hand for the 1804 silver dollar and $10 piece, new dies were made up with these dates, and 1804 dol-lars and $10 gold eagles were included in the set. The Mint looked at records and assumed that silver dollars had been struck in 1804, as indeed they were, but current officers did not know that they bore an earlier date. Accordingly, in 1834, 1804-dated dollars were struck for the first time! Thus was generated a famous American rarity, made for presentation purposes in the 1830s, and later made (from a slightly different reverse die) as a delicacy for collectors, an issue known as the "King of American Coins."

# YEARS WITHOUT COINAGE

The reason that silver dollars were not struck at the Mint after 1804 is reflected by a situation later made official by this order, during the presidency of Thomas Jefferson, sent by James Madison, Department of State, to Robert Patterson, director of the Mint, under date of May 1, 1806:[3]

Sir:

In compliance of a representation from the director of the Bank of the United States that considerable purchases have been made of dollars coined at the Mint for the purpose of exporting them, and as it is probable further purchases and exportations will be made, the President directs that all the silver to be coined at the Mint shall be of small denominations, so that the value of the largest pieces shall not exceed half a dollar.

I am, &c.,

James Madison

Thus ensued a span of many years without dollars' being coined for circulation, as such coins were worth more abroad than in the United States. However, as noted, a few 1804-dated dollars were produced for diplomatic purposes in 1834.

# GOBRECHT SILVER DOLLARS

In 1836, steam-powered presses were employed for the first time at the Philadelphia Mint, replacing presses operated by hand (two men tugged on a long bar, weighted at the ends, to operate a screw press). In the same year a general revision began of the silver denominations. In that year 1,000 dollars of a new design by Christian Gobrecht, the Liberty Seated style with flying eagle reverse, were made on a steam press; they were unusual in that the edge was plain, rather than lettered (as on the earlier dollars) or reeded (as on later dollars). Gobrecht dollars, as they were called, were struck to the current standard of 416 grains total weight (including alloy).

The Act of January 18, 1837, reduced the authorized weight of silver coins, including the dollar, the last now being 412.5 grains, the standard maintained for a long time afterward, including through the entire Morgan dollar series from 1878 through 1921.

Silver dollars dated 1836 of the Gobrecht design were further struck to the extent of 600 pieces in early 1837, these to the new lower weight standard of 412.5 grains, and differentiated by having the dies aligned in a different position, both facing in the same direction, or *medal-wise*, as collectors know them (as opposed to being 180° opposite, as normal).

In 1839, 300 more Gobrecht dollars were minted for circulation, these with reeded edges, and with the design modified somewhat, so that now the obverse, which in 1836 had no stars, displayed 13 stars around the border, and the reverse, with 13 small stars and 13 large stars on the 1836 version, was now plain. Interestingly, both the 1836 and 1839 Gobrecht dollars were made with mirror Proof surfaces, intentionally, in the manner of pieces made for numismatists or presentation. However, they were intended for circulation, and nearly all went there. Some other Gobrecht dollars were minted from different die, edge, and metal variations in 1836, 1838, and 1839, and are properly part of the pattern series.[4]

The new silver dollar of 1836, designed by Christian Gobrecht, featured the Liberty Seated design on the obverse, and, on the reverse, an eagle "onward and upward" (per a Mint description of the time) in a field of 26 stars—one star for each state in the Union.

# LIBERTY SEATED SILVER DOLLARS

In 1840 the production of silver dollars for circulation began in earnest, and large quantities were struck, these having an adaptation of Gobrecht's Liberty Seated design for the obverse, and on the reverse a new motif featuring a perched eagle. In the first year 61,005 were minted, the odd five probably being set aside for review by the Assay Commission, a group of Mint and government officials as well as selected private citizens who met each year to review samples of the previous year's coinage, to ascertain that the precious metal denominations had their requisite amounts of silver and gold.

Liberty Seated dollars were struck continuously from that point forward, until 1873. In 1846 the New Orleans Mint became the first branch facility to strike silver dollars, at which time 59,000 were made, followed by additional coinages in New Orleans of 1850-O, 1859-O, and 1860-O. The first San Francisco Mint dollars consisted of 20,000 1859-S coins made especially at the request of San Francisco merchants, for use in the export trade to China. Beginning in 1870, the Carson City Mint struck limited numbers of dollars through the last year of the design, 1873.

Commencing in a significant way in 1850, gold became "common" on world markets in comparison to silver, this from the Gold Rush in California (which began to affect commerce in 1849) and, soon afterward, new gold strikes in Australia. No comparable finds of silver were made, and the historic ratio of the value of silver and gold, in which 15-1/2 units of silver were supposed to be worth one unit of gold, became disrupted, and silver achieved a higher value. A strange thing happened, and Liberty Seated silver dollars minted from 1840 through 1849, and common in everyday circulation, became worth more in meltdown value than face value, and many were simply converted back into bullion by exchange dealers and brokers seeking a profit.

During that era, silver dollars were not made on speculation by the Treasury Department or the mints, but were struck only when silver bullion was deposited by merchants or banks, and a request for the delivery of the silver in the form of minted dollars was made. Accordingly, in some years when requests were heavy, such as in 1842, mintages were large, in that year the total being 184,618. In contrast, in 1844, requests from depositors were low, and just 20,000 silver dollars were made. If anything, mintages were erratic. This situation is worth noting, for later when Morgan silver dollars were made, beginning in 1878, the government itself owned the silver, and mintages were much more consistent.

After 1850, merchants and banks no longer deposited silver bullion to get silver dollars for use in commerce, as more than a dollar's worth of silver was required to make each coin!

However, mintages of dollars continued, but for an entirely different reason: silver dollars remained very popular in the export trade, along with the more plentiful and, indeed, essential Spanish-American dollars noted earlier. In foreign ports silver dollars brought by American merchants were valued on their weight and silver content, and the denomination

A Liberty Seated dollar of 1872, San Francisco Mint (1872-S). Coins of this design were minted continuously from 1840 through 1873. After 1850 they were used in the export trade, and none were seen in domestic commerce. In 1866 the motto IN GOD WE TRUST was added to the reverse above the eagle.

stamped on them made no difference whatsoever. Thus, if an American silver dollar had $1.03 worth of silver in it, it was worth $1.03 in foreign markets. Accordingly, after 1850 silver dollars were made in fairly large quantities, but only for the export trade and in the manner indicated. Today, all Liberty Seated dollars are scarce, the early ones from 1840 through 1849 because of melting, and the later ones from 1850 through 1873 because most were exported.

From 1850 onward, no silver dollars were seen in stores, banks, pocket change, or anywhere else in domestic commerce. Ten years, then 20 years, passed, and still no silver dollars were used. By 1878, at the advent of the Morgan dollar, the denomination was strange to the typical American citizen. Most youngsters and even young adults had never seen one! After dollars became plentiful once again, in 1878, some popular writers, plus a few numismatists, referred to earlier coins of a previous generation as the "dollars of our daddies," pleasing terminology that appeared here and there in numismatic circles for many years afterward, indeed, until the early 20th century.

# TRADE DOLLARS

The Coinage Act of 1873 eliminated the standard silver dollar of 412.5 grains, and in its place launched a new denomination, the silver trade dollar. These weighed 420 grains each, silver plus alloy, and were specifically made for foreign commerce, with its characteristics prominently lettered on the reverse: 420 GRAINS, 900 FINE.

Trade dollars, made to compete head-on with the popular Spanish milled dollars, were an instant success with merchants in the export trade, and from 1873 through early 1878, millions were made. They were also legal tender in the United States, through an oversight in the legislation, and circulated widely, until July 22, 1876. On that date the legal tender status was abolished by decree, as by that time the price of silver had fallen sharply on world markets, and current trade dollars, as well as old Liberty Seated dollars, no longer had a full value of silver in them.

Trade dollars continued to be minted from 1876 until 1878 for the export trade, and then, possibly to prevent confusion, or for purely political reasons, the trade dollar was abolished when the Bland-Allison Act of February 28, 1878, provided for the Morgan silver dollar. No longer would silver producers in Nevada or in the Rocky Mountain districts wonder whether interested merchants would buy their bullion and have it coined for the export trade. Now, the United States government was their customer.

Ideal! Visions of profit danced in their heads. Prosperity, which had faded in the silver districts, was now just around the corner!

Trade dollars continued to be minted but only in Proof format for the numismatic trade through 1883, then a few quietly by Mint employees in 1884 and 1885, the last being rarities today, with estimated mintages of just 10 and 5 pieces, respectively.

Trade dollars of this design were minted from 1873 to 1878 for use in the export trade with China. They proved to be highly successful in competition with the Spanish milled dollar, the world trade coin of choice at the time.

# HARD TIMES IN THE SILVER DISTRICTS

As noted, the bustling silver centers of the West, especially in and around Virginia City, Nevada, had fallen upon hard times. Silver had become more plentiful than anyone would have imagined a decade earlier, and added to the production of domestic mines were vast amounts of metal from melted-down coins from Europe. Not enough was being converted into trade dollars, and the outlook for the silver industry was grim.

The works of the Yellow Jacket Silver Mining Company at Gold Hill, Nevada, in the heart of the Comstock Lode. Hundreds of silver mines dotted the American West in the 1870s and 1880s.

The "Silver Barons" of Nevada were licking their wounds, some comfortably nestled in elegant mansions in San Francisco, which offered more social amenities than the towns of Nevada. The days of prosperity were over. To be sure, silver trade dollars had been minted since 1873, but only on behalf of depositors who placed silver bullion with the mints and received trade dollars in exchange. There was no assurance that mintages of trade dollars for a given month at a particular mint would be high, low, or nothing. Thus, trade dollars offered no promise of a solution.

Now came the notion of having the federal government buy silver bullion for its own account, in effect to support the market. This would bring good times again to the several silver-mining states and territories in the West. Championing the cause in the mid-1870s was Representative Richard P. ("Silver Dick") Bland of Missouri. Politicians embraced the idea, and momentum increased in 1877 as more jumped on the band-

Mint Director Henry R. Linderman, trained as a medical doctor, chose a career with the Treasury Department instead. He hired young George T. Morgan to come to the Mint as an assistant engraver. A numismatist, Linderman counted among his possessions a rare 1804 silver dollar. (Library of Congress, LC-BH832-30769)

wagon. A strong silver market would benefit, by association, adjacent states, indeed just about everywhere west of the Mississippi River. Or so it was thought.

Henry R. Linderman, M.D., trained in the medical profession, had opted for a career at the Philadelphia Mint and had clerked there beginning in the 1850s, later rising to positions of importance. In 1878 he was director of the Mint. From the director's office (relocated to Washington from Philadelphia in 1873), he dictated policy for the main mint at Philadelphia, as well as the branches in Carson City and San Francisco. In New Orleans the large mint building first used in 1838 had stood idle since 1861, early in the Civil War. Soon, preparations would be made to refurbish the facility and bring it into operation.

Director Linderman was a very intelligent, astute man, and even a numismatist (a point of pride was his very own specimen of an 1804 dollar, the "King of American Coins"). In 1877 his book, *Money and Legal Tender in the United States*, still useful today, was published.

# THE BLAND-ALLISON ACT

On February 28, 1878, Congress passed the Bland-Allison Act over President Rutherford B. Hayes's veto. The legislation mandated that the Treasury Department buy $2,000,000 to $4,000,000 worth of silver bullion each month. The legislation was the brainchild of Representative Richard P. Bland of Missouri and Representative William B. Allison of Iowa. Hooray! Perhaps there was joy in the streets of Virginia City, Nevada. Hoopla in Leadville, Colorado. Jubilation in Carson City. I have not come across any specific accounts of such, but things were looking up for "Silver Barons" and hard-rock miners alike.

This remarkable legislation provided that the bullion be converted into standard silver dollars of 412.5 grains each (consisting of 90% silver and 10% copper). Profits on the difference between the face value of each coin and the cost of the silver bullion were to go to the government, not to the depositors of silver bullion (as had been the case with Liberty Seated silver dollars of an earlier era and also the recent 1873–1878 trade dollar). The new dollar contained 89 cents' worth of silver bullion. In coming decades, Uncle Sam would make over $100 million in profit coining these silver dollars—perhaps enough to compensate, at least in part, for all of the frustration involved, such as storing all of these nasty, annoying things!

Historian Neil Carothers wrote that the Bland-Allison Act was a wretched compromise, without a single redeeming feature, carrying with it the dangers of the wrong-ratio bimetallism without establishing the double standard. By it silver mine owners were bought off with a large market for silver, the bimetallists were deceived with a fictitious restoration of the double standard, and the single standard advocates were solaced with a last minute rescue of the gold standard when it appeared to be doomed. Its immediate effect was to add to the currency an unwieldy coin that had never circulated in the history of the country, too valuable for use as fractional currency, too bulky for large payments.[5]

Richard P. Bland, coauthor of the Bland-Allison Act of February 21, 1878. His name was attached to silver dollars for many years afterward, and the design by George T. Morgan was universally referred to as the *Bland dollar*, including in dealers' catalogs. (*Harper's Weekly*, March 24, 1894)

William B. Allison, a representative from Iowa, was the other lead sponsor of the 1878 bill that provided for the government to become the nation's largest buyer of silver bullion. (*Men and Issues of 1900*)

# Buying Silver Bullion in 1878

By the time the Bland-Allison Act was passed, on February 28, 1878, the Treasury Department had purchased quantities of silver bullion for lower-denomination coins, totaling 5,984,693 ounces at an average cost of $1.19879 per ounce.[6] In March, silver for dollars was purchased for the first time, on an as-needed basis. By September 30, some 17,925,702 ounces had been acquired at an average cost of $1.1747 cents per ounce. The Treasury paid $7,672,793 in gold coins and $13,384,576 in its newly minted silver dollars to buy the bullion. At this time, gold coins were not seen in circulation and traded for a slight premium in terms of paper money. Morgan silver dollars and paper money were exchangeable at par.

Once the initial euphoria passed, silver producers in Nevada, instead of being grateful for Uncle Sam's largesse in sopping up bullion in a sagging market, attempted a petty caper to get even more money than the current market price, stating that they not only wanted the

Silver miners and an impressive pile of silver ingots set up for a photographer at the Boston & Colorado smelter in Black Hawk, Colorado, in the late 19th century. Like as not, this metal was soon converted into silver dollars! A news item stated that the pile, which seems to have 30 ingots, was worth $45,000, probably an exaggeration.

London price for silver (this being the worldwide arbiter of value), but they also wanted to be paid extra shipping to represent the phantom cost of shipping bullion from London to the San Francisco Mint—never mind that the San Francisco Mint was just a few hundred miles distant, and the Carson City Mint scarcely a dozen miles away!

The Treasury rejected this outrageous proposal and geared up to make more silver dollars in Philadelphia, and to scale back plans for quantity mintage at San Francisco. Beaten at their own game, in July 1878 the silver producers agreed to sell bullion at the London net rate, and shipping charges were forgotten.

What the United States of America did *not* need in the late 1870s was another silver boom! The great silver empire in Nevada was experiencing tough times, and the metal was abundant in commerce—still precious, but less precious than a decade earlier. The silver market began falling apart early in the decade.

In 1878 the sleepy little town of Leadville, Colorado, more than 10,000 feet above sea level, was transformed almost overnight into one of the wildest bonanza cities in American history. What had been home to only a few dozen people now was crowded with thousands of fortune seekers. *Leslie's Weekly Newspaper*, published in New York, dispatched an artist-writer to

the site to document the high and (mostly) low life, and for several months the paper published illustrations and accounts like this one—the main street of the commercial district on a typical day.

# DESIGNING THE
# MORGAN DOLLAR

In 1876 Mint Director Henry Richard Linderman, anticipating that Congress would someday pass legislation for the coinage of a new silver dollar, set about creating designs. By this year the Liberty Seated motif had drawn great criticism from the public, and it was realized that a change was needed. Chief Engraver William Barber diddled with a few ideas at the time.

In 1877 the project went into high gear as it was realized that the authorization of a new silver dollar was a sure thing, or almost. Chief Engraver Barber, assistant engraver George T. Morgan, outside artist Anthony Paquet (who had been on the Mint staff earlier), and possibly the chief engraver's son, Charles Barber, began work in earnest. The half dollar denomination was selected as the test bed for what would be well over two dozen different varieties of designs and die combinations. Then, when the dollar became a reality, Linderman was sure that "the designs for the same can be selected from those above referred to, and considerable time saved in commencing its coinage."[1]

## REVIEWING POSSIBLE DESIGNS

Early in 1878 there came a hurry-up call for finalizing a new motif to use on the dollar, as it was proposed that silver purchases begin almost immediately. Following the pattern coinage of half dollars (mostly) and dollars in 1877 (three by Barber), and a few pattern dollars made early in 1878 by Barber and Morgan, it was time to select a winner.[2] Mint Director Henry R. Linderman had done his homework, and all was in place.

After news about a forthcoming silver dollar gained circulation in early March, various comments appeared concerning what it should look like, although the Treasury is not known to have released any information about the design. The *Cincinnati Commercial* gave this tongue-in-cheek suggestion:[3]

> We do not want a Wall Street silver dollar coined, but a people's silver dollar—a Mississippi Valley dollar—a dollar with an eagle on it, whose right wing shall fan Washington city, while his left wafts the dust along the streets of San Francisco, and his tail spreading over Hudson's Bay, while his beak is dredging the mud islands from the stream between the jetties at South Pass.

On February 21, 1878, Linderman, at his office in Washington, wrote to Superintendent James Pollock at the Philadelphia Mint, after having reviewed patterns made by Chief Engraver William Barber and his assistant, George T. Morgan, noting in part: "Morgan and Barber both show high skill and artistic taste. I selected the one with the lowest relief [requiring the] lightest power to strike." This was the Morgan design. Neither the Mississippi Valley nor South Pass could be found as part of the motif!

On February 25, Morgan wrote to Linderman, "Today I delivered to Supt. Pollock an impression in silver from the dollar dies with alterations as directed by you."

Again, Linderman wasted no time, and on February 28, the same day that the Bland-Allison Act was signed into law, the director asked Superintendent Linderman to prepare new silver dollar dies for use at the three mints then in operation (Philadelphia, Carson

City, and San Francisco). Then on March 1, Linderman wrote to Pollock, "Commence at once the preparation of silver dollar blanks to your full capacity. Get working dies ready as soon as possible and commence striking. The full force of the Engraver's Department will be applied to the preparation of silver dollar dies."

Chief Engraver William Barber created several different pattern dollar designs in 1876, of which this is one (variety Judd-1467).

Within a week at least a few Morgan dollars had been struck, as evidenced by the delivery of two Proofs to the Mint Cabinet on March 7, 1878.[4] However, none had been made in quantity by that time. In fact, on February 28, Linderman had written to Pollock, "You will instruct the coiner to hand you the first piece struck and the second piece, with a certificate of their being the first and second pieces struck, and transmit the pieces and certification to me."

On March 12, three coins were delivered for President Rutherford B. Hayes, Secretary of the Treasury John Sherman, and Director of the Mint Henry R. Linderman respectively, plus 300 other specimens. These were all of the 8 Tail Feathers design.[5] As to whether a few had been made as specimens or test pieces before March 12, this is not beyond the realm of logic—so that all would be in order, and there would be no surprises as on the 12th there would be people on hand to watch the event.

# GETTING READY FOR PUBLIC DISTRIBUTION

The *New York Semi-Weekly Times*, March 12, 1878, contained this item datelined March 7, before the first dollars were struck:

> Washington, March 7.—In reply to numerous inquiries as to how the public may obtain the new dollars from the government, Secretary Sherman today issued a circular stating that, for the present, these dollars will be issued only in payment for silver bullion and in exchange for gold coins, dollar for dollar.[6]
>
> Parties desiring silver dollars can obtain them by depositing gold coin with any Sub-Treasurer of the United States. Numerous applications for the new coins have been received from bankers and others at New York, and one party has already deposited with the Sub-Treasurer at that city $25,000 in gold for exchange in silver dollar pieces. Secretary Sherman thinks that the first 10,000,000 of the new dollars will be issued at par in gold until the new coins become so plentiful that they will have to be issued in the ordinary course of business.
>
> They will not be generally disbursed by the department for current obligations, the Secretary not feeling at liberty to use them until the amount coined is sufficient to furnish all alike without discrimination; nor does he deem it expedient at present to exchange them for United States notes, or to use them in payment of the interest on the public debt until the amount coined is sufficient to enable him to do so impartially. The silver certificates will soon be ready for issue, and are of the form of bank notes, engraved in the best manner, and printed on bank-note fibre paper.[7]

# AN ACCOUNT OF THE FIRST STRIKING

A newspaper account told of the genesis of the "Morgan" dollar, although at the time the identity of the designer was not important enough to merit mention:[8]

THE FIRST DOLLAR: It was coined yesterday afternoon at 3:17.

Philadelphia, March 11. There had been no announcement of the time for beginning the coinage of the new silver dollars at the Mint, so it was by accident that your correspondent, dropping in at 2 o'clock this afternoon, was the only press representative there to see the first of the new coinage made. The dies were finished soon after noon, and the first pair was placed in the largest coining machine, used for double eagles.

A little time was spent and a half dozen planchets spoiled before the dies were exactly adjusted. Then Albert Downing, foreman of the coining room, put a polished planchet under the press, and, giving the wheel a single revolution, the first dollar was stamped. It was removed by hand, and critical examination made of the developing flaws, the pressure was readjusted, and another was put in.

Ten more were then coined, but the eleventh was found to be defective, and this, as well as the first, was at once defaced and returned to the melting room. The first twelve having been struck on polished planchets, were removed by hand, to prevent indentation, and each enclosed in an envelope numbered to show the order of coinage. The first goes to the President, and the second to Secretary Sherman. The first was struck at 3:17, and at 3:35 the steam was turned on and the dollars began merrily clanking into the box at the rate of eighty a minute.

Tomorrow two more pairs of dies will be finished, and another machine put to work, turning out $150,000 of the new shiners a day. The dies for the San Francisco and Carson mints will be ready then, and will be forwarded at once. The first delivery will be made on Thursday. The Secretary has as yet made no orders for the first issue of the new coinage, but it is believed that it will be issued only for gold coins, because it will command the same price readily.[9]

Orders are already in for millions from store-keepers who want them for advertising purposes.[10] Whatever silver finds its way into the Treasury will be promptly paid out for the purchase of bullion for coining purposes.

# "WHAT THEY SAY" ABOUT THE NEW DOLLAR

*Harper's Weekly* in its issue of March 30, 1878, reviewed comments noted elsewhere in the press:

The design of the new silver dollar, of which we give an engraving, is very neat and graceful; but the motto, "In God We Trust," retained from previous coinages, is the subject of a great deal of good-natured bantering. The *Christian Union* suggests that the words, "Forgive us our debts," ought to be added. *The New York Mail* thinks the 412 1/2-grain men will "find hereafter that there is no reciprocity in the sentiment."

Another paper, quoting the motto, adds, "With abou't 8% off."[11]

The *Cincinnati Commercial* alone of the newspapers we have seen treats the subject in a spirit of serious fault-finding, painful to witness in so staunch an advocate of the new dollar. Speaking of the design, that journal remarks: "We cannot say the art of it 'makes us feel to rejoice.' The eagle, we understand, was drawn by an Englishman. We should think so, too, from appearances. It doesn't seem to resemble the bird of our country. In fact, we are afraid the thing is a British grouse. There is also an absurd prominence given the 'In God We Trust,' which is a new thing in our coinage.

**The first Morgan silver dollar, as made in March 1878, from designs by George T. Morgan. In the eagle's tail, the feathers numbered eight, but soon the dies were modified to show just seven feathers.**

The words should be, 'One hundred cents.'" But that, as the *Hartford Courant* justly remarks, "would be more of a whopper than the other."

# The American Journal of Numismatics

In April 1878 the *American Journal of Numismatics*, published by the American Numismatic and Archaeological Society,[12] gave this view and detailed description, which was widely read by dealers and collectors of the time:

> THE NEW DOLLAR. The recent action of Congress on the remonetization of silver has given employment to the officers of the Mint. Indeed, that or some similar course had been anticipated, and two designs have been under consideration: one by Mr. Barber, who has been for some time the designer of the Philadelphia Mint, the other by Mr. George T. Morgan, a young gentleman, formerly a pupil of Mr. Wyon, the engraver in the Royal Mint, at London, but since October 1876 in the employ of our government. The description of the accepted design, which was that made by Mr. Morgan, is as follows:
>
> Obverse: A large head of Liberty to left, with the Phrygian cap and a wreath of wheat and cotton leaves and full flowing hair, partially covered, of course, by the cap. Above the head is the legend E PLURIBUS UNUM the circle being completed by 13 stars; while the year of mintage, as in the old pieces, is placed at the bottom of the coin.
>
> Reverse: The eagle with wings "displayed," somewhat like that on the National Arms; olive branch in its right talons, and arrows in the left, below which is a laurel wreath; immediately over its head is the motto in Old English letters, In God We Trust, completing the circle, ONE DOLLAR.
>
> The Barber design will be sought after by coin collectors as a specimen piece. The obverse is in some respects similar to the Morgan design, there being, however, the absence of the Liberty cap and wreath. The motto IN GOD WE TRUST is placed on this side in Roman capitals, while the motto E PLURIBUS UNUM is in the reverse in Old English. In our judgment the Barber dollar is far superior to the one adopted.

The editor also added his opinion of the new coin:

> The long line of monstrosities issued from the United States Mint, certainly receives its crown in the new dollar. The ugliness of the piece adds another wrong to the original one of dishonesty: To ask the European bondholder to take this!

Why does not the "Dollar of our Daddies" appear in the exact design of 1794–5?[13] Before the question was half written, instinctively came the answer, that shame naturally prevented the authorities from reproducing an honest dollar.

In the same issue the *American Journal of Numismatics* reproduced various press clippings under the title "Opinions on the New Dollar":

Public opinion on the taste and design of the new dollars, as represented by the newspapers, is divided, but with a large preponderance against them. We have noticed no commendation of the eagle; the head of Liberty is more generally praised, especially the arrangement of the hair, and the wreath, which is novel.

The *Sunday Republic*, of Philadelphia, greatly admires the obverse; it says:

"The head of Liberty is chaste and beautiful, and, in an artistic sense, is considered the best executed head that has ever appeared upon United States coin. It is so well distributed as to be susceptible of easy work under the die, and altogether will certainly reflect credit upon both the designer and the government. . . . It was taken from life, and is a fair type of the beauty of one of our Philadelphia ladies, the model having been a young lady who is a teacher in one of the public schools in the Fifteenth Section, and who naturally objects to having her name published."

Whether this is true we know not, but the *Boston Advertiser* says, "It has been well remarked that the great prominence on the cheek and chin of the goddess of Liberty is truly emblematic."

The *New York Evening Post* suggests that "If the emblem is to be perfect, the goddess should be represented as wearing a paper collar, that kind of a collar being typical of the advanced civilization of the day, as well as illustrative of the profound regard that the great majority of the silver party have for paper itself."

Many other papers ridicule the coin severely. The eagle comes in for the most abuse; one sarcastically compares this design of the "Bird o' Freedom" to a hen.

The *Philadelphia Record* says: "Mr. Barber's eagle looks as if it was just recovering from a severe spell of sickness, or that it had been disturbed in its meditations by some unruly schoolboys. Mr. Morgan has a good idea of America's proud bird of freedom, and his original design showed an eagle with wings that nearly enveloped the whole coin. Its wings were so large that Dr. Linderman, no doubt, feared it might get loose and fly off, so he ordered its wings clipped. In this position it will appear to the public. In its talons is a dart, containing only one feather at the tip of the barb. The director ordered more feathers, so that the barb would present a ship-shape appearance, and not be liable to fly off lop-sided.

"The head of the Morgan eagle is very poor, and the wings are badly managed. The Barber design shows the eagle with wings as if just unfolding for flight. The motto furnishes the text for many quips, especially from those papers which denounced the 'silver delusion.'"

# REFLECTIONS OF THE OCCASION

Thus, on March 11, 1878, less than two weeks after the legislation passed, the first silver dollars left the high-speed coining presses, employing motifs by George T. Morgan.

Perhaps if coinage for circulation had not been so rushed, finessing of Morgan's design would have been done. As it was, during the next year a number of modifications were made to the regular design, including changing the number of tail feathers in the eagle from eight to seven, making the breast of the eagle more rounded, and a few other refinements.

The selection of any design created by Morgan is curious, as it was the prerogative of the chief engraver, in this instance William Barber, to design at least the obverses of new motifs for coins of the realm. Assistant engravers were usually relegated to doing finishing work, or creating items apart from coin motifs, such as medals. However, in this instance, Morgan was the fair-haired choice of Mint Director Henry Linderman, himself a numismatist, who thought that Barber lacked talent.

President Rutherford B. Hayes (extreme left) and his Cabinet, with secretary of the Treasury John Sherman to his left. Sherman served as secretary of the Treasury from 1877 to 1881. Later a senator, he gave his name to the Sherman Silver Purchase Act of 1890. Hayes received the first Morgan dollar struck at a ceremony at the Philadelphia Mint on March 12, 1878 (never mind that a few others had been struck privately earlier, including two placed in the Mint Cabinet). In time, Hayes found the superabundance of unwanted silver dollars to be annoying, and made some smart remarks to the effect that the government should get rid of the pesky coins. (*John Sherman's Recollections*, 1895)

## THE BASINING PROCESS

Now, for some technical aspects, a window on why all of those different varieties exist among silver dollars of 1878, the raison d'être for many who have pursued the specialty of collecting coins of this date.

It was realized by March 11 that for the effective bringing up of the design of the Morgan dollar, the dies needed to be "basined," this being a process in which each die was held against a curved zinc receptacle, a basin about seven inches in diameter, charged with lens-grinding compound and liquid. The basin was slowly revolved, and in the same manner that fine telescope mirrors were ground, the working die gained a gently curved face.

While all dies were made in Philadelphia at the time, Director Linderman asked Superintendent Pollock to send instructions for die preparation and basining to the branch mints. At the time each of these mints had its own machine shop. Chief Engraver Barber sent a memorandum to Pollock, giving the opinion that "the new silver dollar dies from the new hubs will not basin on any specific basin but require three different grades . . . a matter of some pains and skill to use of long practice. I hesitate to put the task on the Western mints which have not had the experience."

Probably for this reason, shipment of the first 8 Tail Feather dies was not made to the branch mints at the time.

The practice of basining, or dishing of the die face, is what gave certain varieties among dates and mintmarks of Morgan dollars a prooflike or "deep mirror prooflike" (DMPL) surface, and thus the procedure had more than casual numismatic consequences.[14]

# COUNTING FEATHERS

During the second week of production of the new silver dollars Director Linderman came to Philadelphia to meet with the officials and engravers Barber and Morgan. He directed that new hubs be made for the obverse and reverse to slightly reduce the relief of the designs, to facilitate coinage, and that the number of tail feathers in the eagle be changed from eight to seven, as earlier birds on coins were said to have had an odd number of feathers, as evidenced by one central feather that was longer than the others.

Chief Engraver Barber, in a memorandum to Superintendent Pollock, March 25, stated that work on the new hubs had commenced even during Linderman's visit, and the work had just been completed. Further, and of numismatic importance today, "New dies from this hub will be ready about the 2nd of April, but I can enter this hub into the dies—fifty in number—made from the old hub, and have these ready this week."

Thus dies were made by impressing the new 7 Tail Feathers hub over existing impressions from the 8 Tail Feathers hub, creating reverses that coined the "Doubled Tail Feathers" varieties. On the April 26 the new dies were being used in the coining room.

The preceding scenario would seem to isolate the making of 1878 8 Tail Feathers dollars to the period from March 12 to March 25, assuming that on the 26th no old dies were being employed.

Coinage deliveries were as follows:

Week ended March 16—233,200
Week ended March 23—416,100
Week ended March 30—352,000

Pattern 1877 Judd-1516 half dollar (by assistant engraver George T. Morgan), featuring the portrait of Anna Willess Williams. This motif was later used on the regular-issue silver dollar of 1878.

The first Morgan dollar style as made in March 1878 from dies designed by George T. Morgan. In the eagle's tail the feathers numbered eight, but soon the dies were modified to show just seven feathers.

The eagle on the first Morgan dollars had eight tail feathers (top). Soon, however, someone suggested that real eagles had an odd number of tail feathers; as a result, the die was retooled to give the eagle seven feathers (bottom). The difference was scarcely noticeable to the casual user of silver dollars, but to Director Linderman it was important.

As of the latter time, 1,101,500 dollars were struck, with some figure over 649,300 (the total for the first two weeks) reflecting the 8 Tail Feathers coinage.

On April 8, 1878, the first dies were sent to the Carson City and San Francisco mints, these being of the new 7 Tail Feathers variety.

Further refinements, minor in nature, were made, as reflected in this letter from Morgan to Linderman, April 17, 1878, noting in part:

> In the hubs on which I am now at work, I am most carefully attending to all the points where I have noticed improvements can be made either in appearance or in the working of the coins. When the coins were first made, the reverse border was broader and heavier than the obverse.
>
> In the hubs now being used I tried to get the border equal in width by lessening the reverse. The hub, however, expanded more than usual in the hardening and made the reverse narrower than the obverse border. I shall get the borders equal and slightly heavier than they are now.
>
> The reverse dies now fill up quickly while striking the coin. I am finishing this hub so that I believe this filling will be avoided. I noticed that some places in both dies are apt to get rubbed too low in the polishing. I have softened both the original dies and deepened these places.
>
> I notice that the part of the cheek coming opposite to the wing of the eagle is still the last to come up when the dies have sunk a little. I shall cut down both the cheek and the wing . . . I shall have these hubs finished next week, and we shall proceed to use them as soon as finished.

This correspondence is interesting in that Morgan, assistant to Barber, communicated directly with Linderman in Washington.

To this point, all reverse dies had the top arrow feather parallel to the shaft of the arrow (PAF). In time, numismatists would refer to these 7 Tail Feathers dies with PAF as the "Reverse of 1878."

A modified die, with slanting top arrow feather (SAF), was in progress by Morgan. On May 11, Director Linderman wrote to Superintendent Pollock:

> Mr. Morgan told me impressions of the die from the new hub may be struck on Tuesday next. In order that I see if the border alteration is [satisfactory] please send a specimen as soon as struck.

On May 16 Pollock sent a sample coin, noting that he expected that "no more alterations will be made and that we will issue a coin uniform and creditable to the Mint." On the next day, Morgan wrote directly to Linderman:

> We have made two pairs of dies from the new hubs for the silver dollar and tried them in the coining presses. I understand that you have received a piece from these dies.
>
> I report that the reverse dies worked well both on the basin and in the presses, an improvement in both cases on those used before. You will notice the border is now broader.
>
> The obverse dies worked well in the presses. . . . The failing on the cheek which we almost always saw before now disappeared

**Parallel Arrow Feather (PAF) and Slanting Arrow Feather (SAF) varieties, as defined by the appearance of the uppermost feather.**

entirely on these dies. The obverse dies, however, do not go on the basin satisfactorily. They could be finished by hand or put on another basin, but as there will not be any difficulty in making a slight change in the hub so that the dies could be rubbed down on the same basin as heretofore, I have softened the hub with this view.

When hardened I propose to make two more dies and test them again. If you think the reverse is now satisfactory in appearance . . . we could take this hub into general use. I beg to say that we have now in stock nearly 100 pairs of dollar dies.

This communication is important numismatically as it reveals that although the new SAF reverse with slanting top arrow feather had been made (called today the Reverse of 1879 by numismatists), there were still many old Reverse of 1878 PAF dies on hand. As it developed, these would be used intermittently in the next two years, probably with no one paying any particular attention to them.

# MORGAN AND THE "BLAND DOLLAR"

The *Philadelphia Record* included this interesting account of the birth of the "Morgan" dollar, once called the "Bland" dollar (from the Bland-Allison Act):[15]

In the early part of 1876 the Treasury Department opened communication with the Royal Mint of England for the purpose of procuring the services of an expert designer and engraver, whom it was desired should come to this country and take a position in the Philadelphia Mint. As a result of these negotiations a clever young man named Morgan was sent over here. He engaged accommodations with a very estimable lady, Mrs. Eckfeldt, on Mount Vernon Street, above Sixteenth. He announced his business as being employed by the Treasury Department, and stated that he was engaged to make a design for a new dollar, and immediately proceeded to turn his apartment into a workshop.

At the same time Mr. Morgan was engaged in his labors to produce something which would startle the country, Mr. Barber, the chief designer at the Mint here, was hard at work upon the same subject. For weeks and months Mr. Morgan toiled on, failing to produce a design which was satisfactory to himself. His attention at first was given to the reverse side, and eagles in various attitudes appeared, but at last he designed a copy of the great American bird which pleased him. This was not the one which appears on the coin now, but was larger, and the wings longer. An afterthought occurred, when the wings were clipped, the bird reduced in size, and the one which holds a position on the reverse side of the dollar of the daddies[16] was adopted as the proper design.

While engaged in his labors, Mr. Morgan visited the Academy of Fine Arts for the purpose of brightening up his ideas, studying American art. He was acquainted with the English and the Continental schools, but, as his work was to be Americanized, he desired to make it thoroughly so. He made the acquaintance of Mr. Thomas Eakins, an artist of no little reputation, and this soon ripened into a warm friendship. Their interests being identical, to Mr. Eakins was communicated many of the thoughts of the foreign artist regarding the work on hand.

Mr. Morgan desired to present as the principal figure on the coin a representative head of the American female beauty. His first inclination was to make a fanciful head of a Goddess of Liberty or something of that sort, which would be pleasing in its appearance and yet have no real significance. A couple of designs of this sort were made, but did not come up to the expectations of the artist. Then it was determined that the head should be the representation of some living American girl, who should sit while the artist sketched her features. But where to procure such a lady was a question which bothered Mr. Morgan. He examined the countenances of the young women who make it their business to pose as models for the artists at the Academy, and among the large number he could find none who suited his purpose. He went to the Women's School of Design, but in all his sketchings and casts there examined he could find nothing which accorded with his views. Then the services of his newfound friend, Mr. Eakins, were called in, and that gentleman induced a young lady friend of the family to sit as the model for Mr. Morgan. This lady is the one whose face is now stamped on the coin of the country, and whose identity therefore becomes a matter of historical record.

The posings took place at the residence of Mr. Eakins, on Mount Vernon Street, below Eighteenth, in this city, where the lady was initiated into the difficulties and mysteries of art. It was a question for a long time as to just what form the head and its ornamentation should consist of. Large caps were made to represent the Goddess of Liberty and all sorts of things. The position was rather trying to a young lady who had never sat before. The designer is represented to have said that the profile of the miss was "the most perfect he had ever seen in England or in this country." After four or five sittings, tracings sufficient to proceed with the work had been secured, and Mr. Morgan dismissed his model.

The person whose features form the design on the Bland or Standard Dollar, is a very estimable and modest young lady. Her name is Miss Anna W. Williams, and she resides at No. 1023 Spring Garden St., Phila.

## MORE ABOUT MORGAN

As to whether Miss Williams was actually the inspiration for the Morgan dollar there have been some questions raised by numismatic researchers. However, had she not been, it is likely that engraver Morgan would have said so, for many newspaper and magazine accounts were written about her posing. However, Morgan may have modified her features and adapted elements from other sources as well, as many engravers have done. On November 1, 1876, early in his experiments with heads of Miss Liberty, he wrote to Director Linderman, noting that he made some models and, "I have taken one to the Mint today for reduction—I have entered as a student at the Academy of Fine Arts—where I am making a profile study from a Greek figure which I feel will be useful in finishing the head of Liberty. I shall endeavor to get studies in nature for the Eagle."[17]

George T. Morgan, as depicted in a directory, circa 1904. Designer of the 1878 "Bland dollar," today called the "Morgan dollar," he came to America from England in 1876 to work as an assistant engraver at the Philadelphia Mint.

Early in 1877, Morgan wrote that he had been working on the portrait of Miss Liberty, noting that he had been "making more of the cap and less of the hair."[18] He also related that he had been looking at the coins of other countries for ideas.

One of the great ironies concerning Morgan is that during his lifetime the dollar he designed was nearly always referred to as the "Bland" dollar. No less a numismatist than F.C.C. Boyd wrote, in 1940:[19] "He is remembered for having designed and executed the once famous 'Bland Dollar.'"

Compounding the irony is that rare coin catalogers, makers of albums, and writers of the early 20th century, before 1950, often referred to the 1892 through 1916 silver designs by Charles Barber, each with the engraver's initial B on the neck of Miss Liberty, as the "Morgan" dime, quarter, and half dollar!

George T. Morgan was born in Birmingham, England, in 1845. He studied art and engraving in his early manhood and exhibited much talent. In the early 1870s he was awarded a scholarship to the South Kensington Art School, where he remained for two years.

In 1876 in America, Mint Director Henry Richard Linderman felt that current coinage designs were unsatisfactory. He also believed that Chief

**QUARTER DOLLARS**

**Barber, Liberty Head or "Morgan" Type**

Like other silver coins of this type the quarter dollars minted from 1892 to 1916 are erroneously called "Morgan quarters." They were designed by Charles E. Barber.

**In the first half of the 20th century, Morgan's name was often applied to Charles Barber's designs. In the first (1947) edition of the Red Book, R.S. Yeoman corrected the popular misusage.**

Engraver William Barber was underqualified, or overworked, or both.[20] Besides, Barber, with the consent of management, also operated a private engraving business within the Mint. Linderman expected that Barber would retire soon, so as to devote more time to private business, and take his son Charles with him. Charles, also of uncertain artistic talent, assisted his father.

In spring 1876 Linderman wrote to Charles W. Fremantle, deputy master of the Royal Mint, London, to see if an expert engraver could be secured in England, noting in part:

> Could you find us a first class die-sinker who would be willing to take the position of Assistant Engraver at the Mint at Philadelphia? We would like a man who could produce a finished hub, and if he understood modeling and also bronzing it would make him more valuable to us. We could pay about $8 per day to a person of proper qualifications. If you know of such a one who would be likely to answer our purpose, I will be glad if you will place me in communication with him.

Fremantle's reply included:

> My enquiries as to an Assistant Engraver lead me very strongly to recommend for the post Mr. George Morgan, aged 30, who has made himself a considerable name, but for whom there is not much opening at present in this country. I send a letter from him, to which you will of course reply as you may think best, but I may perhaps just say that looking to Mr. Morgan's real talent, I do not think that he wishes to make conditions which are in any way unreasonable, and that I am convinced you would not find in him any inclination to take undue advantage of such privilege in regard to private work & as you may see fit to concede to him.

I may add that he is personally agreeable & gentleman-like, & particularly modest and quiet in manner, so that he would be likely to make an agreeable colleague. You will judge of his qualifications by the work he is sending you, & I can only say that I shall be sorry if we lose him from this country, while I make no doubt he will be a valuable acquisition to yours, both officially and as an artist. It has of course occurred to me that you may think Mr. Morgan too good for the place you have to offer, but I have a strong opinion that he ought not to be lost to you on that account, & that you will do well to secure his services.

The enclosed letter from Morgan included this information, among other details:

I am familiar with the engraving of coin dies, having for several years, assisted Messrs. J. S. & A. B. Wyon. . . . I think I may say that I have a good knowledge of design and modeling. I served an apprenticeship to the die sinking at Birmingham. From Birmingham School of Art I successfully competed for a scholarship at South Kensington. . . . During my studentship I obtained medals and prizes for models of heads from life [and] figures from life and antique.

Morgan was hired and came to the United States in the same year. His advent was strongly resisted by Chief Engraver Barber and his son Charles. Both men made life sufficiently uncomfortable for Morgan that for a time he worked off-premises in a rooming house near the Mint.

As related earlier, he enrolled as a student at the Academy of Fine Arts, and in due time became acquainted with Thomas Eakins, a well-known Philadelphia artist. Eventually he designed the Liberty head and eagle for certain 1877 pattern half dollars, the same motifs being used for the 1878 silver dollar.

William Barber died at his post in 1879, and later the same year his son Charles was appointed as chief engraver. By that time former Mint Director Henry R. Linderman, the champion of Morgan, had passed away. After Charles E. Barber died, on February 18, 1917, Morgan became chief engraver, a post he held until his death on January 4, 1925, at his home at 6230 McCallum Street, Germantown, Pennsylvania. Morgan was survived by his widow and three children: Phyllis Morgan, Leonard P. Morgan (a chemist at the U.S. Assay Office in New York City), and Mrs. C.M. Graham.

Morgan had worked as an engraver for 48 years at the Mint, a remarkable tenure.

# MINTING PROCESSES

## MAKING DIES
### ART OF THE ENGRAVER

Morgan silver dollars were struck using two working dies, an obverse and a reverse. At the mints where they were used these were often called a face die and a tail die, although these terms are not popular in numismatic circles now.

Early in the procedure leading up to the manufacture of working dies for striking coins, a model was created by an engraver, in this instance by George T. Morgan. This consisted of the motifs or illustration features. Models were large, to permit them to be worked on easily, and sometimes measured a foot in diameter or more. The obverse model portrayed in raised relief the image of Miss Liberty, as interpreted by Morgan by the study of the facial features of kindergarten teacher Anna Williams. He likely added modifying touches, perhaps inspired by other coins, sculptures, or his own ideas. The reverse model was of a wingspread eagle holding an olive branch and arrows. Possibly the wreath was part of the model as well.

Morgan's models were probably made in wax, although various substances were used by different artists, based on preferences. When completed, a wax model was coated with graphite and immersed in an electrolytic bath. By electrodepositation a mirror image of the model was made in copper, with the features recessed, and called a galvano. By further transfer, a positive galvano would be made. The large model, now with a hard surface, was placed on a portrait lathe, or reducing machine. This device consisted of a stylus with a pointed tip that traced over the contours of the model, up and down or level, as the model was very slowly rotated, much in the manner that a phonograph needle moves up and down in a slowly spiraling path, except that the slow spiral on the Janvier machine starts at the center and continues to the rim.[1] A mechanical arm connected to the stylus was directly connected to another arm that had a tiny rotating cutter at its end, and cut away at a soft steel blank, the end of a cylinder. The position of the secondary arm could be adjusted to reduce (or enlarge) the design of the model to any diameter required. For the Morgan dollar, the reduction was to dollar-size, the same size as the finished coin.

### THE HUB DIE

The result was an incuse or recessed image of Miss Liberty (or the eagle) on the face of the newly created die, called a hub.

This hub was then given to the engraver, who, using magnification, studied its features carefully. If some details of Miss Liberty's portrait did not transfer properly, or a few lines or details required strengthening, this would be done by hand, using engraving tools.

A metal compass or scribe was placed at the center, and tiny circles were scratched around the periphery, to serve as guide lines. Then, the letters in E PLURIBUS UNUM were added by hand, one by one, as were the dots between the words. A single

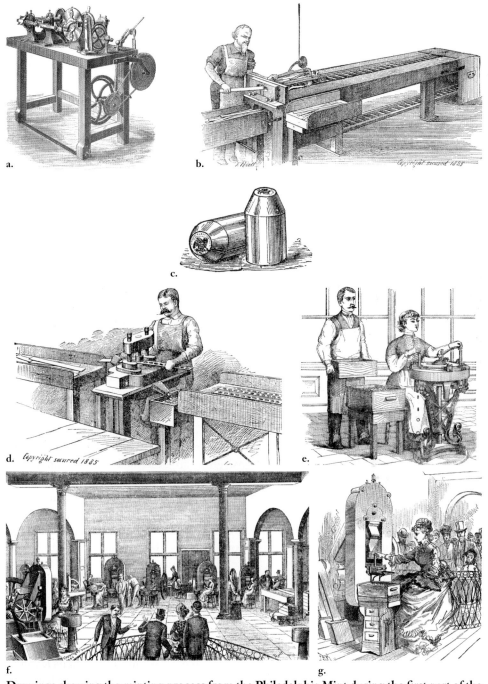

**Drawings showing the minting process from the Philadelphia Mint during the first part of the Morgan-dollar era: (a)** Janvier-style transfer lathe; **(b)** the drawing bench; **(c)** typical dies used for coinage; **(d)** worker cutting planchet disks from a strip of metal; **(e)** the milling machine; **(f)** coining room ca. 1885; **(g)** a coining press in use. (A, c, and g: George C. Evans, *Illustrated History of the United States Mint*, 1892; b, d, e, and f: A.M. Smith, *Visitor's Guide and History of the United States Mint*, 1885)

punch was used to add stars to the left and right, taking care to space them regularly. Dentils (toothlike projections inside the rim, adjacent to the field) were then added by machine. The die was then finished by light grinding and polishing, to remove the raised burrs that rose around the letters and other features as metal was displaced. The result was a hub die with all of the features of a finished coin except for the date.

## Master Dies

The hub die was then hardened. The next step was to impress, using a powerful hydraulic press, the hub die into a soft steel cylinder, creating another die, this with the design in raised relief—appearing as a finished coin, but still without a date. Many such dies were created, and were designated as master dies, or, sometimes, master hubs. Nomenclature has varied over the years.

The master die was then hardened. Other master dies were made, so as to have a small supply on hand.

## Making the Working Dies for Coinage

The *working dies* for coinage were prepared by slowly and powerfully impressing a hardened steel master die into the face of a soft cylinder of steel. The impressions from the master die, which were in relief or raised in the master die (as on a finished coin) were transferred directly into the working die, becoming recessed or incused in the working die. This was done for both the obverse and reverse.

## Adding the Date to a Die

Afterward, separate punches were used to add other features. For the obverse, a four-digit logotype with the entire date, such as 1886, was separately punched into the working die, positioning the punch by eye, thus resulting in some variations of placement. In some instances a little "dash" in the field a short distance above the border dentils helped set the position. Today, within a given common date for which many different dies were used, there are interesting variations. These are described in detail in the book for the technician and dedicated specialist in die varieties, *Comprehensive Catalogue and Encyclopedia of U.S. Morgan and Peace Dollars,* by Leroy Van Allen and A. George Mallis. Generally, the positions in a date can be differentiated by determining the distance of the first digit, 1, from the neck of Miss Liberty to its left, and also by the distance of the first digit of the logotype, 1, to the dentils below. The final digit, 6 in the case of an 1886 logotype, can also be measured by its distance from the dentils.

Usually, just one four-digit logotype punch was used on Morgan dollar dies for a given year, but there are a few exceptions, as noted later in the present text.

Sometimes, indeed often, a date logotype was punched into a die with multiple blows of a hammer or mallet, with some slight jiggling occurring between blows, giving what is called a repunched date, or slight doubling of the figures, sometimes all of them, sometimes just one or two. If a date logotype was punched in with two strong taps, and jiggled or slightly misaligned between the two hits, the second hit would sometimes obliterate much of the first, and no repunching would be seen. Other times, by chance it would seem, perhaps just one or two digits would show repunching.

## Adding the Mintmark to a Die

The Engraving Department kept on hand a supply of letter punches for use in adding mintmarks. These were of different sizes to suit different diameters of coins. Generally, a large-diameter coin such as a silver dollar or gold $20 would use the largest size of mintmark punch, while a dime or a gold $2.50 would use the smallest size.

It was usually the job of an assistant engraver to add the mintmarks. It is easy to envision that while Chief Engraver William Barber was performing executive functions and designing an occasional pattern for one denomination or another, assistant engraver Morgan was kept busy with date and mintmark punches.

While certain size mintmarks were intended for certain denominations, the use of punches was casual, and sometimes to add an O mintmark to a dollar die a large punch would be used, or a medium-sized one, or, rarely, a small (called "micro" by numismatists) punch would be employed. Some mint letters were short and wide, others were thin and tall. In 1878, a small C punch was punched twice to create a CC mintmark. In 1879 and later, large C punches were used for CC. New Orleans O mintmarks were sometimes elliptical (usually called "oval" in catalogs—never mind that oval means egg-shaped, or smaller on one end!) and other times round or nearly so. Sometimes the central opening was wide, and other times it was but a narrow vertical slit.

The engraver eyed the die to see where the mintmark went, then placed the punch in that position—below the wreath ribbon—and tapped the punch with a hammer. The punch was held by hand, not in a jig, and as a result, many variations were created. Some mintmarks were high and close to the ribbon, others were lower. Some were centered, more or less, while others were noticeably to the left or right. Often, a mintmark would be tilted slightly. In some instances, a large mintmark was punched over a smaller one, such as two CC punch impressions on a die on which small CC impressions had been made earlier.

In 1884 the elliptical O mintmark used from 1879 onward was replaced with a small round (or nearly so) O mintmark, both varieties being used in 1884, and the small round mintmark used thereafter, until 1904, plus some variations such as a "micro" O used from time to time, probably a mintmark intended for quarter dollars. It is fun to put "micro" mintmarks in lower-case letters, and perhaps I should write cc as well as CC and micro o; others have done this.

Of special interest to collectors are major "goofs" in mintmark placement. On one curious 1895-S die the S mintmark was first punched horizontally, on its side. The error was realized, and another impression was made in the correct position. This variety, VAM-4 (for Van Allen and Mallis), is highly prized today.

The 1882-O/S die was created when an S mintmark was overpunched with an O. Why this was done remains a mystery today, as in 1882 the New Orleans Mint needed dies as did San Francisco. Perhaps the engraver had finished a "run" of San Francisco dies, had no mintmark-less dies nearby, and needed a few New Orleans dies quickly. Who knows? At least three different O/S dies were made that year, so there must be some logical explanation. Or, similar to the details, no doubt fascinating, that will never be learned regarding Holmes's giant rat of Sumatra, we will just have to keep guessing.

## HARDENING AND BASINING

The working die was then hardened. The heating and cooling treatment in the hardening and softening (annealing) processes sometimes resulted in scale or rough spots on the face of a working die.[2] The working-die-in-progress was then taken to a machine to be *basined*, as described earlier. While some dies for branch mints may have been basined at Philadelphia, many if not most were basined, or given extra basining, at the branch mints, as each had a machine shop.

Depending upon the fineness of the grit used in the zinc receptacle, and the length of time of basining, working dies acquired surfaces ranging from smooth and clean, to slightly polished (creating what we call semi-prooflike coins today), to more polished (prooflike), or even further, to impart a deeply mirrored surface (deep mirror prooflike, or DMPL, is the term used today).

Although details are not known to have been recorded, it is likely that DMPL coins were made by simply leaving a working die in the basining machine for an overly long time, no doubt inadvertently. This may be reflected (pun) by the fact that more proof-like coins were made in New Orleans than at any other mint, and the New Orleans Mint produced coins more casually, often downright sloppily, in comparison to the careful work usually done at Carson City and San Francisco, and sometimes done at Philadelphia.

If during this transfer process there was a slight jiggling, a doubled die was produced. Such a working die showed doubling of some details, often very slight, such as the ear of Miss Liberty or a few letters in the inscriptions. In American numismatics the most famous example of such is the 1955 Doubled Die Lincoln cent. Most often in the Morgan dollar series, die making was done precisely, without any doubling.

## HUB CHANGES

From time to time the hub die, from which working dies were made, was modified, as in the earlier discussion involving 8 Tail Feathers in March 1878, replacing the hub with 7 Tail Feathers, and, in the same year, varieties with parallel top arrow feather (PAF) and slanting top arrow feather (SAF).

In 1900 the hub die was slightly modified, a change being less detail in the breast feathers of the eagle, plus a few other differences. Some working dies from 1900 and the immediate following years show the later hub impression over the earlier one, a super-technical distinction, but one of interest to those who follow the Van Allen–Mallis text.

In 1921, for the final or stray coinage of Morgan dollars that year, after none had been made since 1904, completely new hubs were created, but of the same basic design. The 1921 dies and dollars were a strange breed of cat, with no basining to the dies and with other differences—explained later in the text.

# MAKING AND PROCESSING THE PLANCHETS

## THE PLANCHET STRIP

Each Morgan silver dollar was struck on a blank disk or *planchet*, being a circular piece of metal cut out from a long strip. At the mint, silver was refined, brought to the proper statutory requirement of 90% silver and 10% copper (with some other trace metals permissible with the copper), creating pieces that were, in technical terms, .900 fine, or 9/10 pure. The copper was employed to add strength. Similarly, gold coins were made with 10% copper alloy.

The silver metal was then cast into long ingots, which were then run through a rolling machine consisting of polished, heavy steel cylinders spaced a certain distance apart. On the first rolling the thickness of the silver ingot would be reduced, then on a subsequent rolling the strip would be run through again, with the rollers more closely spaced together, making it thinner yet. Then another rolling, then another, until the correct thickness was obtained. At the same time, the other dimensions of the strip increased as the thickness decreased.

Finally, to achieve exact thickness, the planchet was given a coat of grease and was pulled through a drawing bench, which had a thin rectangular opening. Sometimes the edges of the opening would leave little streaks on the strip, which, if not later flattened out during the coining process, would create what are known today as planchet striations.

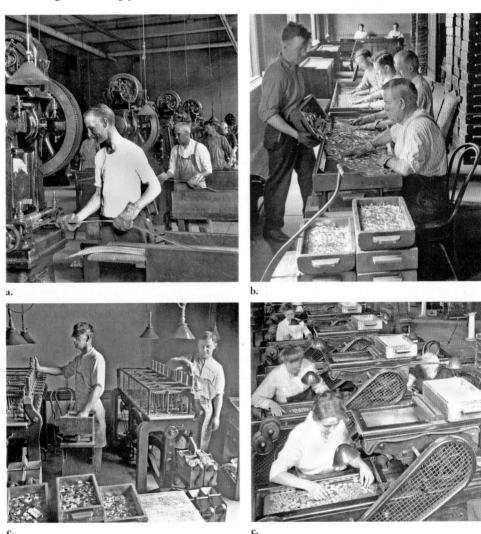

**From planchet strip to finished coin, ca. 1903: (a)** Cutting planchet discs from a strip of metal. By 1903, more-powerful equipment was in place, but the strips were still fed by hand. **(b)** Mint workers inspecting each planchet ready for coining and removing any that were imperfect. As a result of this and an inspection of the finished coins, very few misstruck or imperfect Morgan dollars ever left the Mint—to the chagrin of modern-day collectors of error coins! **(c)** Automatic weighing machines, first employed for $5 gold planchets in the 1880s. More machines were acquired, and by the time the third Philadelphia Mint was in operation in October 1901, all planchets for gold and silver coins were inspected in this manner. **(d)** Finished coins being inspected prior to being placed into bags for shipment. By this time, a typical Morgan dollar was apt to have many nicks and marks from handling within the Mint.

## CUTTING, MILLING, AND FINISHING

The planchet strip, cut down to a narrow width, was then fed by hand through a mechanical punch, much the same as a cookie cutter. Flat disks, perfectly round, were created.

The planchets were then washed, rinsed, and dried, to remove grease and other dirt. They were run through an automatic weighing machine that rejected any that did not meet tolerance, this being plus or minus 1.5 grains on the 412.5-grain standard planchet. Planchets that were slightly overweight could be adjusted by filing. Lightweight planchets were returned to the melting pot.

The silver disks were then run through a milling machine, sometimes called an upsetting machine, in which they were fed between two rollers more narrowly spaced than the width of the disk, and rotated while passing through the machine, with a roller on one side and a curved flat part on the other side. The edge of the planchet was then forced, developing a raised rim.

After appropriate washing and annealing, the last being a heat treatment to soften the planchets and make them easier to strike, they were ready to be put into a coining press. By this time a typical planchet had been run through a cleaning device and jingled with other planchets, and while bright and sparkling, was apt to have many surface nicks and contact marks, plus, sometimes, die striations from the earlier drawing machine process.

The planchets were heated, then slowly cooled, to make them softer and easier to strike. Afterward they were bathed in dilute sulfuric acid to remove discoloration, rinsed, and dried, the last sometimes by tumbling them with sawdust.

# MINTING MORGAN DOLLARS

## STRIKING THE COINS

By the time a planchet was ready for use, it was of the proper weight, had a raised rim, and was bright and clean, although any contact or other marks were still present.

Accordingly, they were of a standard weight, within the 1.5-grain tolerance. If the dies in the press were spaced ever so slightly farther apart than needed to bring up every detail in the deep part of the dies, then there would be no problem if a slightly overweight planchet was used. There was more than enough space that was not used. In general, the New Orleans Mint adopted this procedure, which prolonged die life and made operations simpler.

On the other hand, if the dies were spaced precisely so to bring up every little element of the design, sometimes problems occurred with overweight planchets, such as those at the upper limit of tolerance, and in any event the operation had to be more closely managed. In general, the San Francisco Mint and the Carson City Mint used dies closely spaced, an extra effort that present-day numismatists can appreciate.

## THE COINING PROCESS

Boxes of planchets were then brought to the coining room and placed in front of a coining press. An attendant then fed blank planchets into a vertical brass tube attached to the press. Mechanical fingers grabbed the planchet from the bottom of the tube, and moved it laterally into a space between the obverse and reverse dies, the reverse being at the bottom of the press, or in the anvil position, and the obverse being at the top, or in the hammer position. Around the planchet, after it was dropped into place, was a circular ring with indentations, in which the planchet would become squeezed, thereby causing raised ridges (reeding) on the edge of the Morgan dollar.[3]

The two dies came together, squeezed or struck the planchet, and the metal flowed downward into the reverse die, upward into the obverse die, and into the collar die, all at the same time.

In instances in which a coin was "lightly struck" (a misnomer, as the term refers to die spacing; not to the pressure applied by the press, which was constant no matter what the die spacing), certain details, particularly at the center, did not come up fully.

When the top and bottom dies were placed in the press before the coining process began, the press was turned slowly, by hand on the flywheel, until the top (or hammer) die descended to meet the bottom (or anvil) die, with a small space in between, representing the distance or depth the top die was to reach. Both top and bottom dies were then secured firmly in position by metal chucks. When a planchet was put into the press, the top die would come down and hit the planchet, continuing downward to the set depth, and then return upward. The depth was to be sufficient that the metal in the planchet would be squeezed into the dies and the collar.

As earlier noted, if the depth was optimum, the metal was squeezed as to fill the deepest recesses of the die, which on the Morgan dollar included the high points of Miss Liberty's hair and ear at the center, and on the reverse, the breast of the eagle. If the depth of the top die stroke was slightly short of optimum, the die recesses would not be completely filled, as was often done at the New Orleans Mint.

Accordingly, when wide die spacing was used, certain areas of the planchet were not obliterated by die details, it tended to retain its original characteristics—the features of the planchet before it was fed into the coining press. These sometimes included planchet striations from the drawing bench, or even nicks acquired during the planchet washing and cleaning process.

In 1902 the *Annual Report of the Director of the Mint* stated that the pressure required for stamping a silver dollar was 160 tons, and 90 coins per minute could be made. The speed was an optimum figure, and every now and then the presses had to be stopped to tend to the dies, or if a problem developed.

Die surfaces often varied. A die newly put into a press could have a normal or smooth finish to its face, but not a polished look. Others could be lightly polished from the basining process. Still others could be deeply mirrorlike.

Sometimes, dies were used to strike hundreds of thousands of coins, pounding away minute after minute, hour after hour, creating a frightful noise (press attendants often wore earplugs). Other times, the dies were retired early—possibly because there were ample extra dies on hand, or the coiners wanted to preserve the quality of their products.

When a die was used past the 100,000 mark or so, it developed wear and stress marks in its face, from the flow of metal and simply from use. Coins struck from tired dies show grainy surfaces, sometimes with ridges or flow marks, and not with deep luster.

Treasury records reveal that from 1878 to 1904, 1,198 pairs of dies were produced for Philadelphia Mint coinage, and at the Philadelphia Mint, 222 pairs were made for Carson City, 1,231 for New Orleans, and 898 for San Francisco.

Dividing these numbers into the mintage figures from each facility produces a figure of 217,679 coins per die pair from the Philadelphia Mint, 62,441 from Carson City, 151,208 from New Orleans, and 121,930 for San Francisco. These numbers factor into the *quality* of coins produced, especially toward the end of a die's life. However, die spacing in the coining press was as important, or even more so, in the producing of quality impressions. As precise as they appear to be, these production figures are of necessity approximate, as obverse and reverse dies were not retired at the same time. Moreover, by law it was necessary to stop using obverse dies at the end of a calendar year, even if they were serviceable or had not been used, whereas reverse dies, not bearing any indication of date, could be employed later.

## Pausing to Reflect

Over a period of years, certain of the described processes varied. Within a given year, procedures at the different mints varied. It is easy to see if any one of the processes was rushed—such as the preparation of planchet strip, the cutting, annealing, cleaning, or anything else—different qualities would result.

It is no wonder that as you study the "personalities" of the different dates and mintmarks of Morgan dollars—and personalities they have indeed—you will come across so many different aspects of quality, sharpness, mirror surface or lack thereof, brightness or dullness, and so on!

And, let's not forget the idiosyncrasies, sometimes delightful from a numismatic viewpoint, from the process of hand-punching dates and mintmarks.[4]

## Counting and Packing

After a coin was struck in a press it was mechanically ejected into a rectangular box. In time, other silver dollars were heaped on it. Afterward the coins were taken to another location, spread out, and reviewed by women who picked out any error coins, such as misstruck or clipped pieces. The approved dollars were then dumped into another box and taken away.

Next they were run through a mechanical counting device, sometimes putting further marks on the surface. Some counting machines put toothlike marks on the surfaces of coins. Then they were put into a canvas "duck" bag in quantities of 1,000 pieces weighing about 57 pounds, sealed, tossed on a cart, and transported to either a vault within the Mint, or one at another location. For shipping to other locations, bags were packed in barrels. By this time a typical coin in a bag might be severely bagmarked.

As early as the first year of coinage, 1878, it was realized that all of the dollars being minted would not be needed for commerce, and, accordingly, they were viewed as simply a commodity, such as a sack of potatoes or a sack of coal.

Packing bags into wooden barrels for shipment to locations outside the Mint. At the destination, such as a bank, the heavy barrels were easy to roll along the ground, whereas boxes or crates would have required special handling.

# STORING AND INVENTORYING DOLLARS

Once tossed into a vault, the dollars remained, often with dozens or hundreds of other canvas bags on top. At regular intervals, the coins would be taken out and counted, sometimes again by mechanical devices (putting more marks on them), sometimes by hand. This was necessary for accounting and inventory purposes, often at the end of the Treasury Department's fiscal year (which ended on June 30), and other times when there was a change in political administration.

It is likely that the typical Morgan dollar in storage was physically counted, or tossed about in a bag, at least once a year, sometimes more often, over a very long period of time. Finally, someone came up with the brilliant idea of putting bags in a vault and then sealing the vault in its entirety. An example was provided by the sealed vault in the Philadelphia Mint, in which New Orleans silver dollars and others were placed in 1929, and then forgotten. When unsealed, in 1962, the vault yielded the fantastic treasure of super-rare 1903-O Morgan dollars as mentioned earlier, thus igniting the great treasure hunt that extended to March 1964.

Sometimes the bags became damp, causing the coins to discolor, or at least the surfaces of coins in contact with the surface of the bag. When opened years later, some of this discoloration was indeed quite beautiful, delicate colors of the rainbow. Wayne Miller, in his 1982 study, *The Morgan and Silver Dollar Textbook*, gives color illustrations of pieces that captured his interest or fancy. Many bags rotted and fell apart, and the coins had to be rebagged.

However, most silver dollars remained fairly dry and with surfaces intact, except for perhaps very slight natural toning, yielding pieces that, for example, were sparkling and brilliant in the 1960s, when they first were viewed by numismatists during the great Treasury release.

There are many stories concerning the counting and storage of Morgan dollars, and severe space problems encountered in the 1880s and 1890s, usually mentioned each year in the *Annual Report of the Director of the Mint.* Indeed, some years the storage of Morgan dollars seem to be the problem of problems, completely overwhelming anything else going on in the coinage realm. Occasionally there were mysteries, the extent of which we will never know, but exemplified by the finding of large steel washers, dollar sized, in one bag opened years later. Apparently during an audit process, some sharpie substituted these washers and pocketed nine silver dollars to spend.

Even the president of the United States recognized the problem early on, when Rutherford B. Hayes (recipient of the first Morgan dollar minted on March 12, 1878) commented, in 1880: "We have minted 72 million silver dollars and we have spent a lot of dough trying to keep them in circulation, but they keep coming back. The people don't want them. I think we should melt 700 of them and make an Aztec Calendar for General John W. Foster."[5] While the inside joke about Foster (ambassador to Mexico and an enthusiastic supporter of the silver-buying program) was soon forgotten, the problem of dollars lingered.

# THE FIVE MORGAN
# SILVER DOLLAR MINTS

## INTRODUCTION

From the first year of the Morgan silver dollar, 1878, to the last, 1921, five different federal mints were used to strike the coins:

**Philadelphia Mint:** 1878–1904, 1921. No mintmark.
**San Francisco Mint:** 1878–1904, 1921. Mintmark S.
**Carson City Mint:** 1878–1885, 1889–1893. Mintmark CC.
**New Orleans Mint:** 1879–1904. Mintmark O.
**Denver Mint:** 1921. Mintmark D.

The following paragraphs give a brief history of each.

## THE PHILADELPHIA MINT

The first federal coinage facility to go into operation was the Philadelphia Mint, constructed in 1792, following cornerstone laying on July 31. Director David Rittenhouse was in attendance, and it is possible President George Washington may have been as well. This operation, consisting of several buildings, was employed for decades.

The first Philadelphia Mint was destroyed in 1911 by Frank H. Stewart, a numismatist who operated the Stewart Electric Company, and who wrote a history of the Mint. Stewart felt that he needed the real estate to expand his company. A recent book by Joel Orosz and Leonard Augsburger, *The Secret History of the First U.S. Mint*, explores Stewart's actions and possible motivations in detail. Stewart's own history of the Mint still stands as an important reference.

On July 4, 1829, the cornerstone was laid for the second Philadelphia Mint, in a ceremony in which some silver half dimes, not coined since 1805, were struck to be included in the cornerstone (the Mint employees worked in the early hours of the morning of July 4 to do this; later, quantities of half dimes were made for circulation). The new Mint was ready for occupancy in January 1833, with assaying, refining, planchet preparation, and coinage equipment in place, along with related offices for supervisors and for the director, and a special section for the Engraving Department.

The first Philadelphia Mint. Erected in 1792, it remained in use continuously through 1832. (Painting by Edwin Lamasure, 1914)

Built in the Greek Revival style, extremely popular in America at the time, the second Mint was used through 1901. During that time the Mint saw many evolutions and changes, including the production of new designs, the introduction of steam-powered coinage presses in 1836, the beginning of the Mint Cabinet in 1838, and more.

By 1878 the Philadelphia Mint was operated by a *superintendent*, as it had been since 1873, while the director of the Mint, a separate position, did business from an office in the Treasury Building in Washington, DC, and oversaw operations of the Philadelphia Mint as well as its branches. Prior to 1873, the director had his office at Philadelphia and also attended to the affairs of that mint, as well as cor-

The second Philadelphia Mint as it appeared in the late 19th century. This building was first occupied in 1833, and from then until 1901 it was the main or "mother" mint. The engraving department was housed here, and the facility made dies for all the mints.

responding with superintendents of branch mints. While coinage laws were made by Congress, signed by the president, and facilitated by the Treasury Department, it was the director of the Mint who made nearly all of the operating decisions.

Over a period of time in the late 19th century, many innovations were introduced at the Philadelphia Mint, including, relevant to Morgan dollars, automatic devices for weighing planchets and counting coins. In 1891 the first electric motors were used to drive the presses and most of the machinery. In time, steam power became obsolete. As the demand for coinage grew, primarily for the cent and nickel (not struck anywhere but Philadelphia), as well as for large quantities of gold double eagles and other denominations, the Philadelphia Mint simply needed more space. Already the vaults had been stuffed to nearly overflowing, and thousands of bags of silver dollars had been stored in other places, such as the United States Post Office in the same city and in a steel vault, quite resembling a miniature Greek temple, set up in the yard of the Mint.

Designs were made for a new facility, the third Philadelphia Mint, which was built, and in October 1901 occupied for the first time. The building was used through the late 1960s, and within its halls Morgan dollars were made from 1901 to 1904, and again in 1921. George T. Morgan remained assistant engraver from his hiring in 1876 until the death of Chief Engraver Charles E. Barber in 1917, after which Morgan became chief engraver, a post he held until his passing on January 4, 1925. His office was in the Mint.

The second United States Mint, abandoned for coinage in 1901, was put up for bids, finally sold, and wrecked, so the land could be used for other purposes. The six Ionic columns on the front were salvaged for use on another structure. The third Mint, operated from 1901 to 1969, still stands in Philadelphia today but is used for other purposes. Today, coinage is conducted in the fourth Mint, on Independence Square.

Facility for refining gold and silver at the Philadelphia Mint in 1903. The standard for dollars was 90% silver and 10% copper.

The third Philadelphia Mint was first used for coinage in October 1901. The facility remained in use for the rest of the Morgan-dollar era, 1921, and beyond, until in 1969 it was superseded by the fourth Philadelphia Mint at another location.

# THE SAN FRANCISCO MINT

The San Francisco Mint, opened for business in 1854, has a generous measure of romance attached to it, as it was set squarely in the middle of the greatest bonanza city, the wildest of all metropolises, during the Gold Rush.

In the first year the coinage was limited to gold denominations, primarily $20 pieces, of which 141,468 were made. In that year and also in 1855, private minting firms were still operating in the city.

Other denominations made at the San Francisco Mint in 1854 included the gold dollar (1,632 pieces), the quarter eagle (246), half eagle (268), and eagle (123,826). As can be readily imagined, the quarter eagle and half eagle are prime rarities today, with only slightly more than a dozen known of the former, and, believe it or not, just three of the half eagle, the last being an American classic.

The first San Francisco Mint, which actually had been built earlier as a private coinage facility for Moffat & Company, was cramped and poorly ventilated. From time to time workers fell ill, and in any event, being employed there was anything but pleasant.

In 1870 the cornerstone was laid for a new mint—large in size and containing the latest innovations—this in anticipation of vast quantities of silver and gold continuing to arrive from the Comstock Lode and elsewhere. Although the Carson City Mint in Nevada was but a very short distance from the Comstock Lode, political considerations intervened; the mint was unpopular with mine owners and refiners, and the business was directed to San Francisco. In 1874 the second San Francisco Mint opened for business, and would remain in operation until the late 1930s, when replaced by the third San Francisco Mint, a modern-design structure resembling perhaps a penitentiary, but no doubt suitable for keeping away unwanted visitors.

At the San Francisco Mint, Morgan dollars were first struck in 1878, and from that time they were continuously made through 1904, and again in 1921. In general, the coining press operators paid careful attention to their duties, were proud of their work, and turned out coins that were usually quite sharp and visually appealing. Quite a few of the San Francisco Mint Morgan dollars went into circulation soon after they were struck, as dollars were popular in the mountain states of the West, and San Francisco was the main supply. In Montana, Wyoming, Colorado, Utah, and Nevada, paper dollars were hardly ever seen, and silver dollars ruled the day—for grocery purchases, stakes in card games, and many other things in everyday life as well as in sporting activities. Perhaps, unlike the coiners in New Orleans, the employees of the San Francisco Mint knew their silver dollars would be used and appreciated by a wide slice of the general population. Whatever the reason, the output was excellent, and today certain issues stand as models of Morgan dollar excellence, the typical 1881-S being an example.

The San Francisco Mint in the early 20th century.

# THE CARSON CITY MINT

In 1859 two prospectors, Patrick McLaughlin and Peter O'Reilly, discovered a silver deposit on Mount Davidson at Washoe, in Nevada Territory, on land claimed by Henry Tompkins Paige Comstock. The latter sold his interest, but his name remained on the deposit, which was found to be huge, the Comstock Lode. In the next several years the district was developed, and Virginia City was built and became the epicenter of activity. The newspaper of record in the community was the *Territorial Enterprise*, under the editorship of Samuel L. Clemens (Mark Twain), who in time achieved great fame and became a giant of American literature. One of Twain's many stories told of a potential silver mine that had been "salted" so that naïve investors could inspect the site and see for themselves the valuable silver ore. Unfortunately, one of the perpetrators of the intended fraud melted down some regular Liberty Seated silver coins into little lumps to strew here and there around the mining area, but part of the reverse design of a coin wasn't completely melted away and was seen by one of the investors!

Although the San Francisco Mint had been operating since 1854 and furnished a depot for gold (in particular) and silver bullion, the citizens of Nevada wanted their own mint. Appropriate legislation was passed through Congress, and the town of Carson (as it was generally called) was selected, later to be known as Carson City, but nearly always referred to as Carson in *Mint Reports* in the early years of its operation. A beautiful stone building was erected in what was essentially a very quiet community, about 15 miles from the center of silver-mining activity at Virginia City. In the latter place there were many silver operations, the largest and most impressive of which was the Gould & Curry Mine, complete with refining and smelting facilities and grandly appointed offices, the last decorated with gardens and sculpture. Quite a scene this must have been! Abe Curry, an owner of that business, was appointed to be the superintendent of the Carson City Mint. The move was stupid, or wise, depending on one's point of view.

Curry had many political and business enemies, and some of them simply did not want to send their silver to Carson City to be minted under his direction, but instead preferred to ship it to San Francisco at a distance. Accordingly, while the San Francisco Mint produced vast quantities of Morgan silver dollars from Comstock Lode metal, the production at Carson City was much smaller. The negative side of this, perhaps from the overall viewpoint of government efficiency (although efficiency is certainly not a word that can be used in connection with federal mintage of silver dollars), the appointment of Curry was unfortunate, as the Carson City Mint was underutilized. However, from a numismatic viewpoint, it may have been fortunate, for many scarce and rare coins, objects of numismatic desire, were created! Indeed, this was true from the first year of coinage, 1870, onward.

By 1878, Curry was long gone as superintendent of the Carson City Mint, and James Crawford was in his place. However, San Francisco still tended to be favored, as evidenced by production that year: of the

The Carson City Mint. Opened in 1870, it coined Morgan silver dollars from 1878 through 1885 and again from 1889 to 1893. Each bore a CC mintmark on the reverse. (Library of Congress, HABS NEV, 13-CARCI,20-1)

1878-CC dollars, 2,212,000 were struck, compared to 9,994,000 of the 1878-S. In the next year, 1879, there were 756,000 1879-CC dollars made as opposed to a flood of 9,110,000 1879-S dollars.

Production of Carson City dollars seems to have been accomplished in a workmanlike manner, and today most of the coins from this romantic western mint are well struck, and more than just a few have deep mirror prooflike surfaces. As noted in the preceding chapter, the coiner at the Carson City Mint retired the dies long before they showed stress marks or excessive wear. Production of dollars continued in Carson City through 1885, then was stopped, to resume in 1889 and continue through 1893. During that span the silver coinage consisted nearly entirely of silver dollars (except in the first year, 1878, in which dimes, quarters, half dollars, and trade dollars were also struck), and gold coinage of the denominations of $5, $10, and $20, with the double eagle being by far the most popular.

After coinage operations ceased in 1893, the Carson City Mint was kept open as an assay and refining facility, but was referred to as a mint in reports until 1899. In that year some reverse dies with the Carson City mintmark were converted to New Orleans dies by partially effacing the CC mintmark and punching an O mintmark in the same place, as by that time it was realized that no more dollars would ever be made in Carson City. Thus was created the 1900-O/CC dollar.

After the turn of the century, long-stored silver dollars were moved by railroad car from Carson City to the Treasury Building in Washington, DC, where they were put in vaults, and mostly (but not completely) forgotten, to achieve their finest hour in 1964 when vast quantities of sparkling Carson City dollars came to light, including hundreds of thousands each of the previously rare 1882-CC, 1883-CC, and 1884-CC. In 1942 the Carson City Mint building became the Nevada State Museum, which it is today. On view is a coining press, some cancelled dies, and other exhibits relating to the numismatic tradition of this facility.

Today, Carson City Morgan dollars occupy a special affection, a special place in the hearts of collectors. Although the 1879-CC is rare in comparison to demand, and the 1889-CC is even more so, the majority of Morgan silver dollars from 1878 to 1885, and again from 1889 to 1893, can be acquired in Mint State for reasonable cost.

# THE NEW ORLEANS MINT

In 1835 Congress passed legislation for the establishment of three branch mints to supplement the production that up to that time had taken place only at Philadelphia. Selected were Dahlonega in Georgia and Charlotte in North Carolina, both located near goldproducing areas. The third mint was to be set in New Orleans, not a source of precious metals, but one of America's most important ports, a depot for the receipt of precious metals from elsewhere, especially silver from Spanish America. The city was a key spot for distributing coins throughout the Mississippi River Valley, at the time constituting much of what was known as the American West.

A very large facility was constructed, far exceeding in size those at Charlotte and Dahlonega. Coinage commenced in 1838, and consisted of silver half dimes and dimes of the Liberty Seated design. In addition, from 1838-O dies an estimated 20 half dollars were created early the next year; these became rarities.

The first silver dollars, of the Liberty Seated design, were minted at New Orleans in 1846, the quantity being 59,000. Virtually all were placed into commercial circulation, and not even a specimen was saved for the Mint Cabinet (established in Philadelphia in June 1838). After that, additional Liberty Seated dollars were struck for 1850-O, 1859-O, and 1860-O.

The New Orleans Mint, opened in 1838 as one of three branch mints (the others being in Charlotte, North Carolina, and Dahlonega, Georgia), struck Morgan silver dollars continuously from 1879 to 1904. This view is from the early 20th century.

In New Orleans in 1861, early in the Civil War, troops representing the State of Louisiana seized the Mint, after which it was occupied for a short time by Confederate forces. Certain silver and gold bullion on hand was used up in the striking of some half dollars and double eagles, after which the Mint closed. In 1862 New Orleans was liberated by Union troops, and remained in Union hands afterward, but the coin presses remained silent. Finally, in 1878, long after the war, it was decided to reopen the Mint. Extensive repairs and updates were made, and in 1879 coinage resumed, consisting of Morgan silver dollars primarily, but also a small number of gold eagles (1,500) and double eagles (2,235). Morgan dollars were struck at New Orleans each year from 1879 through the end of the early coinage in 1904. In 1909 (the last year of coinage at New Orleans), only dimes, quarters, half dollars, and a limited number of gold half eagles were struck at this facility. The following year, mintage ceased, although the building continued to be used for storage and other purposes. The building still stands today.

Regarding Morgan silver dollars, many millions were struck there, but most were simply bagged and tossed into storage vaults. Coins were made with little attention to quality, and the dies in the presses were spaced slightly farther apart than they should have been. As a result the metal in the planchets did not flow into the deepest recesses of the dies. Accordingly, it is the rule, not the exception, that for many dates of New Orleans dollars there are flat areas at the center of the obverse and the center of the reverse. Among the worst of the bunch is 1891-O, but some other dates can certainly give a typical 1891-O competition for getting the booby prize.

Today, finding a sharply detailed New Orleans Morgan dollar is generally more difficult than locating those from Philadelphia, Carson City, or San Francisco, and therein lies a fascinating challenge.

# THE DENVER MINT

On the Morgan silver dollar stage, the Denver Mint plays but a bit part, producing coins only for part of the year 1921, and at no other time. However, the single Denver Mint product, the 1921-D dollar, each with a very small D mintmark, is significant.

In 1862 the federal government purchased the private mint operated by Clark, Gruber & Company, bankers who had come to Denver from Leavenworth, Kansas, and who had struck gold coins there in 1860 and 1861, of the denominations of $2.50, $5, $10, and $20, the two larger values being distinguished by each having a view of Pikes Peak—not at all what the actual mountain looked like, but symbolic nonetheless.

The intention of the government was to operate the facility as the Denver Mint, and in Treasury records from that point onward, including the *Annual Report of the Director of the Mint*, it was consistently referred to as the Denver Mint. However, no coins were ever struck there under federal auspices.

Beginning in 1904 a new mint was erected on a different site, and in 1906 it was opened for business. At the time it was the most modern in America, a state-of-the-art facility. At first, silver and gold coins were struck there, each with a D mintmark, then beginning in 1911, Lincoln cents, and in 1912, nickel five-cent pieces.

The Denver Mint earned high accolades for efficiency of production, and quantities of other coins struck there tended to be large, although not necessarily higher than that of the other operating mints during a given year.

Today, the same Denver Mint building is still used and is a vital part of coin production. The facility is somewhat larger, having undergone expansion in 1937.

**The Denver Mint, opened for coinage in 1906, struck Morgan silver dollars for only one year, 1921.**

# TREASURY HOARDS
# AND OTHER QUANTITIES

## FAST AND FURIOUS MINTING

Before the calendar page for December 1878 was torn off to reveal January 1879, well over 20,000,000 Morgan dollars had been struck at the Philadelphia, Carson City, and San Francisco Mints. When figures were combined, more silver dollars had been struck in the months of 1878 than had been made of all earlier silver dollars combined, from the first year of the Flowing Hair dollar in 1794, to the last year of the Liberty Seated dollar in 1873! In 1879 the New Orleans Mint would join in production, and in that year the number of dollars made at all mints crossed the 25 million mark.

The specter and then the reality of a great glut arose, and yet silver kept pouring into the mints and by federal mandate had to be converted to coins. Thousands and thousands of "cartwheels," as some called them, were produced, put into cloth bags, and stored. Those needed for actual commerce, such as in the mountain states of the West, took up some small percentage, but the majority remained useless and a first-class nuisance. In the description of various Morgan dollars by year in the present text, the worsening problem is described as it developed.

In 1890 the Sherman Silver Purchase Act mandated the purchase of more silver and replaced the Bland-Allison Act of 1878. The *Annual Report of the Director of the Mint, 1894*, included this:

> Further legislation by the United States, still more favorable to silver, was enacted by the Act of July 14, 1890, which provided for the purchase of 54,000,000 ounces annually, the estimated production of our domestic mines. The effect of this act was to cause a temporary advance in the price of silver, but the high price could not be maintained owing to the largely increased output by the silver-producing countries of the world, and the price commenced to decline in September 1890, and continued to do so.

The Trade Dollar Recoinage Act of March 3, 1891, provided that silver trade dollars, whose legal tender status had been repudiated on July 22, 1876, and which were now worth only bullion value, be melted and coined into silver dollars. In addition, there were other sources of silver flowing into the mints each year, including the recycling of worn and mutilated coins. Then, in 1904, the supply ran out.

After the coinage of Morgan dollars stopped in 1904, hundreds of millions remained in storage. Most of these were Mint State, but quite a few were also lightly worn, pieces that had been in circulation for a short time, but had been returned to banks or, in New Orleans, even to the Mint. In

Senator John Sherman of Sherman Silver Purchase Act fame (here shown in the library of his home) had served earlier as secretary of the Treasury under President Rutherford B. Hayes, 1877–1891. (*John Sherman's Recollections*, 1895)

the meantime, the public used paper money, including Silver Certificates, a special class of paper money instituted in 1878 and produced in large quantities beginning in 1886, under which provisions each paper dollar was backed by one silver dollar held by the Treasury. A $100 Silver Certificate was backed by 100 of the same coins, and so on. The rules for the issuance of these dollars made it mandatory that large quantities remain in storage,

To be sure, some paper money was used in the Rocky Mountain states in the late 19th century. An example is this rare $1 bill bearing the imprint of the Missoula (Montana) National Bank and the personal signatures in ink of cashier Kennett and president Higgins.

The bank was chartered on May 14, 1873. Just 2,100 of these $1 bills were issued, and today there are so few in existence that they could be counted on the fingers of one hand. Apparently, the local citizenry did not want to be bothered with paper dollars, for all of the bank's later bills—running into tens of thousands—were of higher denominations!

and had there been a request for them for circulation, any withdrawals beyond a certain amount would have been denied. Not to worry, no such demand ever arose.

# THE PITTMAN ACT

In 1918 the Pittman Act was passed, whereby silver dollars were melted for their bullion, and under a complex arrangement, much of the bullion was sent to India. The strategy was complex, but it was felt that this would help keep the price of silver as well as gold bullion lower on world markets. The price had been rising as an effect of the World War and uncertain economic conditions. In one fell swoop some 270,232,722 silver dollars were reduced to molten metal.[1] Still, untold millions remained. No accounting was kept of the dates and mintmarks of dollars melted, thereby introducing a major mystery for numismatists who later contemplated the situation.

In time, well after 1918, it was found that certain Morgan dollar dates and mintmarks were much rarer than mintage figures suggested. A prime candidate was the 1903-O dollar, struck in New Orleans to the extent of 4,450,000 pieces, but for which pieces were hardly ever seen in circulation, and Mint State coins were so rare that they were considered to be classics. In fact, in 1941 when B. Max Mehl, the Fort Worth, Texas, dealer offered the W.F. Dunham Collection at auction, one of the pieces specifically showcased in the catalog was the 1903-O dollar rarity. It was logical to presume that millions of them had been melted in 1918.

Another candidate for Pittman Act destruction was the 1895 Morgan silver dollar. Mint records indicated that 12,000 circulation strikes were made, plus 880 Proofs. The trouble was that no one had ever seen an Uncirculated coin. Where did they all go? Apparently, within the Mint it was known that no circulation-strike dollars had been made bearing the date 1895, as soon thereafter dealers plainly stated that only Proofs had been struck. However, the enticing quantity of 12,000 circulation strikes continued to appear year after year in summary accounts in the *Annual Report of the Director of the Mint.* Every once in a while, in cases of one-upmanship, a dealer or collector might say, "I have actually seen an Uncirculated, not Proof, silver dollar of 1895." Others could only listen in awe.

Long afterward, in the 1990s, researcher Henry T. Hettger, in an article in the *Rare Coin Review*, effectively demonstrated that no dollars bearing this date had been made for circulation, and that the figures applied to those bearing the date 1894. Still later, in the National Archives, Roger W. Burdette found information that when the Assay Commission met in early 1895 to review samples of the 1895 coinage, there was one Philadelphia Mint silver dollar on hand, and it was a Proof.

Today as you read these words, the melting under the Pittman Act still has its mysteries, although others have been answered by later events, such as the Treasury Release of 1962. However, that is ahead of the story.

## Amazing, but True

As only the United States government can do, no sooner had hundreds of millions of dollars been melted under the Pittman Act, when it was decided that more silver dollars should be coined, in order to act as backing for Silver Certificates. Indeed, the Pittman Act had provided for this, and no new legislation was needed.[2] Accordingly, in 1921 over 85 million additional Morgan dollars were struck. The logic of this escapes just about everyone, but must have been clear to politicians at the time!

After 1921, long stored Morgan dollars remained in storage at the Philadelphia, Denver, San Francisco, and New Orleans mints, although later in the decade many of those stored in New Orleans were shipped to Philadelphia to be held. Beyond that, a vast area in the lower level of the Treasury Building in Washington, next door to the White House, was devoted to the storage of Morgan silver dollars. To the flood of Morgan dollars came millions more coins of this denomination when Peace type silver dollars were first struck beginning in December 1921, continuing intermittently through 1935.

As before, silver dollars continued to circulate in the American West and were a common sight in Wyoming, Idaho, and other places, but a tradesman in Boston could go a year without taking one into his cash register.

The First National Bank of Pocatello, Idaho, shown here in a postcard view from the 1920s, no doubt had bags of silver dollars in its vault. In Idaho scarcely a paper dollar was ever seen—just the opposite of the situation in New England's banking and commercial practice at the time.

Whenever this or another bank wanted to replenish its supply of silver dollars the cashier sent a request to the nearest Federal Reserve Bank, and bags of 1,000 coins would be delivered. Some banks put silver dollars up in 20-coin paper rolls, but most handled them loose or in bags.

## Carson City Dollars Are a Surprise

### The Depression Years

In the 1930s numismatics became especially popular in the United States. Although the Depression was in full force, hobbies provided an alternative to boredom, and leisure-time activities prospered—including the working of crossword puzzles, playing miniature golf, camping and fishing, assembling jigsaw puzzles, and collecting coins. Hobby shops opened in many towns across the United States, and a few were even devoted to the sale or rental of wooden puzzles.

Of course, someone who was unemployed could not collect coins effectively, but enough people had incomes or assets that in autumn 1935 and for much of 1936 a fantastic boom took place in the field, when commemorative coins became all the fad, and the prices of some issues multiplied overnight.

In 1934, Wayte Raymond launched his *Standard Catalogue of United States Coins*, and his popular "National" brand albums, the last providing circular openings in cardboard panels, protected on both sides by clear slides. Others made albums, including so-called penny boards, or open sheets of cardboard, with openings in which Indian cents, Lincoln cents, Liberty nickels, and other popular lower denominations could be gathered and displayed.

## THE CASH WINDOW

From August 21 to 28, 1937, the annual American Numismatic Association Convention was held in Washington, DC, with more than 200 people in attendance. The weather was less than ideal—days of stifling heat followed by days of downpour.[3] During the course of events a few conventioneers visited the Treasury Building and at the cash window bought for face value some "old" silver dollars. However, nothing was numismatically notable.

In 1938, apparently by chance, in the continual paying out of silver dollars a few bags of long-stored Carson City dollars were reached in the vaults. These sparkling coins, dated in the 1880s, were casually paid out at the cash window. Harry X Boosel, a young man who worked for the government in Washington since 1936, got word of the little CC mintmarks on these coins and hastened to learn more.[4] At once delighted, surprised, and grateful for the opportunity, Boosel took money he could spare and bought a few hundred coins, which at the time had market values of $5 to $10 each. He then mailed postcards to ANA members per their published addresses in *The Numismatist*, and to other collectors. A selection of CC dates was offered for $2.25 per coin, with the extra 25¢ for postage and handling.

Later, he recalled:

> I was swamped with orders. Quite a few people wrote to say they didn't believe the offer to sell coins for two dollars each was legitimate, and that I was pulling some kind of a fast deal like Frank Dunn did when he distributed Boone commemorative half dollars.[5] However, it became known that I was selling very nice dollars, and for a couple of years I did a great business.[6]

At the Treasury Building employees did not examine coins in the vaults to seek rare dates, nor would they fill specific requests. Payouts of silver dollars were the luck of the draw, and in addition to prized Carson City dollars, Boosel received quite a few ordinary Philadelphia Mint coins, some worn, which he turned back in. Not long afterward, the supply of CC coins seemed to run out, and in time the situation was forgotten.

The Treasury Building as it appeared in the late 19th century. Hundreds of millions of Morgan silver dollars were stored in its vaults, until the great rush to buy them years later, from 1962 to 1964. (Bureau of Engraving and Printing vignette)

## More Collectors

In 1935 the *Numismatic Scrapbook Magazine* was launched by Lee F. Hewitt, at which time there was only one other monthly publication, *The Numismatist*. The latter was the magazine of record for the American Numismatic Association, but not a spirited front-line periodical for the typical collector. Hewitt, ever with an eye for an interesting story, spiced the *Scrapbook* with all sorts of fascinating fillers, notes of rare varieties found in circulation, and more. Soon its circulation handily eclipsed that of *The Numismatist*. Along the way the *Scrapbook* introduced many to the hobby of coin collecting. The Whitman Publishing Company, then located in Racine, Wisconsin, entered numismatic book sales by the first edition of the *Handbook of United States Coins*, by Richard S. Yeoman, 1942. The *Handbook* listed wholesale prices paid by dealers. By that time Whitman had been selling "penny boards" and other holders for several years.[7] In 1946 the *Guide Book of United States Coins*, also by Yeoman, made its debut with a cover date of 1947, and gave retail or market prices. Both books went on to be published annually and to be the best-sellers in their respective fields. In time, expanded lines of albums and books were added.

Then in 1952 came *Numismatic News*, created by Chet Krause in Iola, Wisconsin, which started as an exchange for subscribers who ran classified advertisements. In coming decades Krause Publications would become an empire, with several dozen different hobby periodicals under its wing, and would produce many reference books. Chet has been a fine friend of mine for a long time, and every now and again we'll get together for a nice dinner and discussions about the "good old days" of numismatics. Of course, the present days are fine, too!

In 1960 the first weekly coin periodical, *Coin World*, was launched by Sidney Printing and Publishing Company in Sidney, Ohio. By 1960 coin collecting had been very popular for a long time, and tens of thousands of numismatists seriously followed the hobby. *Coin World* became a dazzling success, far exceeding the most optimistic expectations of its founder.

Morgan silver dollars were not in the mainstream of collecting in the 1950s due to their high face value and the unavailability of certain "impossible" rarities such as the 1903-O and the Proof-only 1895, but still they had a strong following. Several dealers specialized in dollars, and in Omaha, Nebraska, Aubrey and Adeline Bebee filled many want lists for the series, while in Salt Lake City, Utah, Norman Shultz did the same thing. Several other dealer specialists could be mentioned. Harry Forman, who entered the coin business in 1955 in Philadelphia, took an early liking to silver dollar bags and bought and sold them with regularity, a typical price being $1,050 plus shipping. The market was not large, and the premium remained remarkably low for common varieties. However, a somewhat rare $1,000 bag of 1885-CC dollars cost a few hundred dollars more. I remember well the times.

## On the Roulette Tables

Over a period of time, dollars continued to come from storage in various facilities operated by the Treasury Department, including vaults at the mints. Each year in December there was a call for dollars for use as gifts, a popular tradition. In the meantime, in Reno, Nevada, and later in Las Vegas as that city was developed, casinos depended upon silver dollars for use on the gaming tables, gold coins having been withdrawn after 1933.[8] Countless bags of Morgan dollars were shipped to Nevada, opened, and used on the gaming tables for roulette, poker, and craps. Although there were a few slot machines with dollar slots, the quarter denomination was the highest in popular use.[9]

Sometimes casino owners with a numismatic interest would get a bag with Carson City or San Francisco mintmarks, and toss them aside as a private reserve, popularly called a stash. In a memorable visit to Las Vegas in the 1960s, Amon Carter Jr. took me to two casinos owned by acquaintances, and I was allowed to see the bags of silver dollars kept by each. The owners were numismatically aware and, in fact, had on hand the latest edition of the Red Book.

# THE GREAT TREASURY RELEASE

## THE SCENE IN 1962

First, a view of the hobby in 1962: By that time the rare coin market was in a boom period, indeed a frenzy, spurred by the popularity of *Coin World* (which at one point achieved over 150,000 circulation), the fascinating 1960 Small Date Lincoln cent that captured the imagination of the public, and the investment success of the low-mintage 1950-D nickel. Within the past two years coins had come to the forefront as an investment. News media took an interest, publicity and exciting news seemed to be everywhere, and hundreds of thousands of people joined the ranks of collectors, never mind that most could not pronounce *numismatist*.

Tens of thousands of newcomers became more serious and, indeed, could say *numismatist* with great facility and ease, and subscribed to various coin-collecting periodicals. However, most were more casual, simply satisfying themselves with purchases at coin shops and flea markets. Coin stores sprung up as if by magic, like mushrooms after a summer rain, and just about every medium-sized town had one or more, quite like the situation in the 1990s with sports card shops.

To learn what a coin was worth, nearly everyone relied on the *Guide Book of United States Coins*, popularly known as the Red Book. Listed were all U.S. coins, including Morgan dollars. The last were priced in several grades, including simply Uncirculated. There were no choice, gem, or MS number listings.

Each summer when a new edition of the Red Book appeared, collectors would review their albums and dealers their inventories, and make notes of increased values. For more than just a few collectors, the Red Book was a one-volume "library," the only reference they used. However, for others, additional pricing information would be obtained from retail advertisements and auction results.

## NUMISMATICS TURNED UPSIDE DOWN!

Now to the excitement mentioned briefly in chapter 1, the most pivotal event in generations:

In early November 1962 the coin collecting hobby was tranquil, sort of, although everybody kept an eye on the 1950-D nickel, like watching the lead horse in the Kentucky Derby. However, apart from ever-increasing investment interest and the gathering of new faces to numismatics, collectors kept collecting and dealers kept dealing.

Then something happened.

Similar to the song "The World Turned Upside Down," popular during the American Revolution, the events of late November changed numismatics to the extent it would never again be the same.

At first one, or perhaps a few, 1903-O silver dollars were found in Philadelphia, as part of the holiday payout of coins. Then more. Then a deluge! While occasionally a worn 1903-O would be found among mixed dollars, these were anything but: they were brilliant, sparkling, and looked as if they had been made yesterday! Or even made this morning! Or even a few minutes ago! They appeared to be, indeed, *brand new*.

Cataloging $1,500 each in the Red Book, these coins were the treasure of treasures in the Morgan dollar series, the Holy Grail. Although by 1962 I could not possibly count all of the 1793 copper cents, 1856 Flying Eagle cents, Gobrecht silver dollars of 1836 through 1839, and 1879 Flowing Hair $4 gold stellas that had passed through my hands, to mention just several popular rarities, I had never owned an Uncirculated 1903-O dollar. In fact, I had never even *seen* one.

However, I had handled a number of circulated ones, these being valuable and always a pleasure to buy and sell. In fact, a few months earlier I had sold a lightly worn but rare and expensive 1903-O dollar to a good customer (who later became quite upset, stating that I had "inside information" that in November Mint State coins would be released!—oh, well).

## CAPERS AND OTHER 1903-O DOLLAR EVENTS

Harry Forman, Johnny-on-the-spot in the Morgan dollar bag and roll business, and ever alert for opportunities, was early in the game. Forman, knowing that all sorts of chicanery and misrepresentation could occur (as, after all, these were great rarities, cataloging $1,500 each in the Red Book, and hardly anyone had ever owned one), thought to alert others he knew. Phone calls were made, and I was among the recipients. Dealers in turn informed their clients. The news was exciting, and the story was eagerly spread. All was positive: virtually no one had an Uncirculated coin at the time, and just about everyone wanted to buy one, or a roll of 20, or even more.

One enterprising, or perhaps *unscrupulous* would be a better word, person bought a bunch of 1903-O dollars and hopped on a jet plane for London, hoping to sell them to dealers there who would find them to be very valuable, simply by looking in the Red Book. Then and now, numismatics is a universal hobby, and to an extent American coins are popular in England, Germany, Japan, and other places—not as much as in the United States itself, but still bought, sold, and traded with regularity. Spink & Son and B.A. Seaby, Ltd., the two leading retail dealers in London, did a lot of business with Americans. Apparently, they were victimized and paid "old prices" for these rarities, which now, even if bought at a wholesale dealer price, could only be sold at a wipeout loss.

While newspapers and television covered the drama in the early days of the release, it took a while for the information to be confirmed and published in numismatic journals. In the meantime many collectors and dealers were in the dark as to what happened from a coin collecting viewpoint, as popular stories often omitted numismatic details.

## YOU ARE THERE: THE SCENE IN 1962

If you had been a subscriber to *Coin World*, this is what would have greeted you on the first page of the issue of December 14, 1962, the newspaper's first reports on the bonanza, by which time the editor had done a lot of checking and had conducted interviews in an effort to learn the facts:[10]

## MINT RELEASES SILVER DOLLARS
## SCARCE DATES TAKE PLUNGE

### New Supply Affects Market
### Mint Vaults Yield Coins From Four O-Mint Years

The 1903-O silver dollar emerged from the deep recesses of the Philadelphia Mint last week along with other scarce date silver dollars. . . . Quantity release of scarce date silver dollars from the Philadelphia Mint in late November—including the 1898-O, 1902-O, 1903-O and the 1904-O—has sent prices of the heretofore rare coins plummeting to a fraction of their current catalogue valuation.

The 1903-O dollar, listed in the *Guide Book* at $400 each in Extremely Fine condition, and $1,500, Uncirculated, has dropped to a range of $13 to $15.

The 1904-O dollar also dropped to $4 to $7.50 each: it was previously listed at $350 in Uncirculated condition. The 1902-O is cataloged at $7 Extremely Fine and $35 Uncirculated. Now it is advertised at a $4 to $7 range Uncirculated. The same new valuation—up to $7—was placed on the 1903-O silver dollar. Previously it was listed at $1,500 Uncirculated.

Coin dealers across the nation who hastily adjusted their prices in relation to the new supply expressed little surprise at the break in the silver dollar market and felt that release of the rare date dollars was inevitable. They also predicted they would eventually stabilize into prices in line with their respective mints.

The Bureau of the Mint releases silver dollars regularly from a stockpile of dollars dating from the 1800's, held in the deep recesses of the Philadelphia Mint. On November 25 Miss Eva Adams, director of the Mint, said a Christmas supply was being distributed to the Federal Reserve banks across the country. She said there would be nine million more than in 1961, and 14 million more than in 1960.

First reports of the availability of scarce date silver dollars came from the East—it was reported that "hundreds of bags" had been distributed to banks in New York, New Jersey, Pennsylvania, Michigan, and Maryland. A Bureau of the Mint spokesman said it was not possible to give figures on the current release of dollars because supply to the Federal Reserve banks is on a continuous procedure basis.

"We release silver dollars without regard to dates," a Bureau of the Mint spokesman said as he described storage processes of the dollars in vaults. "Although we spot-check the bags, there is no pre-occupation with numismatic valuation." "In fact," he said, "this is against Mint regulations." Mint rules to combat numismatic interest by its personnel were stiffened in 1957. They read: "Coins shall not be reviewed for numismatic value." The Mint spokesman said he believed these same regulations were sharply enforced at Federal Reserve Banks, too.

Bags of silver dollars are stored at the Philadelphia Mint from the 1800s and 1900s (a total of over 102 million silver dollars are held here or at the main Treasury in Washington as backing for Silver Certificates). They were shipped to Philadelphia from sister Mints, from Sub-Treasuries no longer in existence, and some never left the Philadelphia Mint. The bags contain both circulated and new dollars—some have never been opened, others contain a mingled quota of new and circulated coins.

Bulk of the dollars was stored in 1921; there is no member of the Mint staff living, Mint officials believe, who supervised the operation. Records are also considered inadequate, and it is believed that as the dollars poured in from Baltimore, New York, Cincinnati and other Sub-Treasury points, they were weighed and deposited into compartments without any special system.

The large vault, capable of holding $140,000,000 is divided into small compartments, each holding from $3 to $7 million at the most. A committee of Mint personnel from other offices, and a Philadelphia Mint representative oversaw the procedure of a joint seal on the bags. This eliminated the impossible task of counting each and every dollar—which would consume months and months—for the required annual settlement. Instead the number of bags could be inventoried.

"Upon demand, (when there is an indication of a need for silver dollars) we go down the line and start paying them out," said the Bureau of the Mint spokesman. "There is a spot check, tattered bags are replaced, of course, and some coins are declared unfit for circulation.

"These are cast aside to be melted. Others are suitable for immediate release; others require cleaning," the Mint official said. Bags cannot be opened without a Mint director's representative present.

What is the future of the silver dollar in America—the coin which was last struck in 1935?

"We have over $100,000,000 on hand—we are not likely to run out in the future!" The Mint spokesman smiled.

Front page of the December 14, 1962, issue of *Coin World*, bringing the first news of the silver-dollar bonanza to its readers. The news had been circulating furiously by telephone, letter, and other means since mid-November. When this article went to press, the price of the 1903-O, valued at $1,500 a few weeks earlier, had dropped to about $13 to $15 (and would eventually go as low as $3 to $4 on the resale market).

A related story in the same issue of *Coin World*:

## DEALERS TAKE DOLLAR DROP IN GOOD STRIDE

Most coin dealers were philosophical about the drastic silver dollar decline if they had heavy stocks of the scarce dates affected by the new release.[11] They were aware such a thing could happen but they took a chance.

Many converted it into a demonstration of customer good will and good faith. They advised their customers of the new status and returned funds if orders for 1898-O, 1902-O, 1903-O, and 1904-O were received at the high prices. Some furnished 1903-O's without charge to customers who had the coin high on their "want list." There was a scurry to change advertisements to conform with the new prices.

A similar incident was recalled by several dealers involving the 1885-CC silver dollar a few years ago. At that time it dropped from $100 to $5 per coin when a flood of them hit the market. However, the supply was absorbed, and the 1885-CC has climbed back to $15 EF and $25 Uncirculated. Other silver dollars have been similarly devalued from time to time.

## The News Continues to Spread

By mid-December the story had been widely circulated in the popular media and other numismatic periodicals, and the treasure hunt was on! Just about everybody salivated at the idea of getting a $1,500 coin for face value. Thousands, then millions of other Morgan dollars were taken out of storage in the Philadelphia Mint. Some were from the same vault, sealed since 1929, that had contained the marvelous 1903-O dollars. Very soon, more rarities emerged in the form of hundreds of thousands of sparkling 1898-O and 1904-O dollars, varieties that had been worth several hundred dollars each, but even at that level were not easily found.

Then other long-hidden New Orleans dollars of other dates, Carson City dollars, Philadelphia dollars, San Francisco dollars—in no particular sequence.

At any given time the finding of silver dollars was the luck of the draw. If you had taken $10,000 in cash (later, that "cash" had to be in the form of Silver Certificates) to the Treasury Building in Washington in late 1962, or had asked your bank to order 10 bags of dollars through the Federal Reserve System, there was no telling what you would get. While some people got bags of CC dollars and others bags of 1903-Os, most received mixed assortments of worn Morgan and Peace dollars, or bags of unwanted Philadelphia Mint dates such as 1886 and 1887. Those who were lucky enough to buy 1903-O dollars by the thousands were able to turn a nice profit. Although the market value went down, down, and down some more, and finally touched bottom at around $3 to $4 per coin, the coins remained worth a premium over face value.[12] Today the 1903-O is listed normally among many silver dollars, not the commonest, but not at all in the category of being scarce or rare. Most collectors are not aware of its former aura and glory. Can you imagine the thrill of owning one of these? Here, indeed, is the great rarity of years past, but now a treasure available for a very reasonable price. Every time I see a 1903-O dollar I think of the great Treasury release of 1962—the numismatic equivalent of finding gold in the street! I was there when it happened.

On the other hand, there were so many 1898-O and 1904-O dollars found, especially the latter, that these could be bought for a few hundred dollars above face value, per 1,000-coin bag.

## Scrambling for Dollars

Reserves were tapped at other mints, at other government facilities including the Treasury Building in Washington, and at banks all across America. Month after month, the scramble continued. Amidst the frenetic activity there was a great deal of uncertainty and hesitation. By that time it was realized that all bets were off, and that silver dollars previously rare might all of a sudden become common. There were more than just a few speculations that the long-missing 12,000 1895 Philadelphia Mint dollars had turned up in a vault in Philadelphia, or in New York, or someplace else—rumors were a dime a dozen. The market got a case of the shivers, and some varieties that were scarce or rare but had not shown up yet did not sell particularly well, as there was a fear that they might become common tomorrow.

From the outset I found the situation to be very exciting, and over a period of time I kept notes concerning events and my observations of them. From my own perspective, one of the most fascinating experiences I had was the buying of a few 1,000-coin bags of unsorted Liberty Seated dollars, such pieces comprising but a very tiny part of the Treasury release of the time. I arranged a tabletop grid and wrote down the dates from

1840 to 1873, and the mintmarks, and then arranged them into piles like poker chips. When a pile grew large—and 1847 was the most plentiful early date and 1871 the most common of the later ones—I would take them away and start a new pile. Great fun!

In the early 1990s I took some of my notes, did other research, spent a lot of time with books and publications in my library, and with the help of many others, eventually turned out the two-volume study *Silver Dollars and Trade Dollars of the United States: A Complete Encyclopedia.* I did many interviews with dealers and collectors who had been on the scene of the Treasury release. This one, from John J. Ford Jr., is especially interesting, and if you have not read it before, I hope you will agree that his recollections are unique.

## John J. Ford Jr. Remembers the 1960s

John J. Ford Jr., partner in New Netherlands Coin Company in the 1960s, told of his experiences with the silver dollar releases of the era:

> With [my wife] Joan I went up to the Concord resort in the Catskill Mountains in February 1963—it was the week before Washington's birthday. We went up on a Saturday and came home on a Sunday a week later, but the whole time I was there I spent most of my time either skiing, eating, or talking to Harry J. Forman (of Philadelphia) on the phone about silver dollars.
>
> Harry of course was a source for the mint bags of Morgan dollars, and we had done a tremendous amount of business with him in late November, all of December 1962 and part of January 1963. He had called me up early in November of 1962, I guess it was the 17th or the 18th, and he wanted to know if I could sell him any 1903-O, '04-O, '98-O silver dollars Uncirculated, which at that time were considered rare coins, particularly the '03-O. I guess he was buying them from various places, and wanted to know if I had any.
>
> I asked him what was going on, and he said he had a large quantity of these rare dates. The next three weeks were hectic. Harry was selling these coins by the bag to individuals, some of whom would then go to Europe or the rural areas of the United States and sell them to people who had Guide Books and thought they were very valuable. There was a lot of gouging. In particular, I understand the first guys who arrived in Europe made a fortune burying Spink's and Seaby's. By the time the situation stabilized—I guess the first week of December—I came up with the brilliant idea of sending out postcards to our entire mailing list telling them that we had bags available and so forth.
>
> To avoid using the New Netherlands name, we sent them in the name of Werner Amelingmeier, who was running Ford Numismatic Publications. We sent out 7,000 or 8,000 postcards and return reply cards, and soon we were selling bags at the rate of maybe 15 to 20 bags a day. These were Federal Reserve bank-sealed bags of silver dollars, all which were Unc., and all of which had a little hole in the bag burned with a cigarette. [A supplier with access to the Federal Reserve bank vault] would get permission to take a cigarette in there, and he'd burn a hole in the bag and then he put his eye up to the hole and put a flashlight on the other side of the bag to illuminate through the canvas the other side of the bag, enough so he could see the front of one coin and the back of another to find out the date and the mint and to see if they were all BU [Brilliant Uncirculated].
>
> Then based on what the date and mint was, he'd pay the guys $50 or $100 and they'd go to the cash room and he'd pay up and he'd take all the bags out of there. . . . The

dollars went into Harry's hands. As fast as we would get orders, we would call Harry, and he would drive up in his Cadillac, which looked like a rocket ship because the rear end of it was about touching the ground and the front wheels were barely touching the ground. With all the weight he had in the trunk and the back seat of the car, even a Cadillac would tip.

He'd bring these bags up and then have to schlep 'em up in the elevator from where he parked I don't know. He carried them up; we [New Netherlands Coin Co.] were on the fourth floor. Harry would carry up two at a time, and when he arrived, I'd run down and help him. Each bag weighed about 60 pounds, so we must have been in fairly good shape then. We'd pile these up on the floor, then figure out what went to whom, and the next morning or the next afternoon we'd schlep 'em back down to Railway Express and park the truck downstairs opposite the entrance to the building. And Charles Wormser and I—well, Wormser had a dolly; he couldn't carry these bags—we'd take the bags down, and send 'em out Railway Express. The buyers had to pay the Railway Express charges.

How many silver dollars did we handle at the time? I remember at one point we figured that we handled about 140,000 1881-S dollars alone, and nearly all of these were prooflike. This amounted to 140 bags. I had to laugh a few years ago when some guy told me how rare 1881-S prooflikes were!

I estimated that we handled about 20 bags a day, five days a week, for about a month and a half. We handled a lot of other coins besides 1881-S, but I have forgotten the dates. Many were shipped by us, but many were sent out by Amelingmeier, who had a Ford car dealership in Lynbrook, New York, called Ted Rowland, Inc. We were doing a tremendous business, but after about two months, the thing tapered off to next to nothing because everybody was in on the act.

In fact I had just gotten rid of the last of the 1893 dollars that I had bought with Ralph Lathrop in 1952. That was the bag I found when I was walking downtown with Ralph J. Lathrop. He always carried a large amount of cash in his pocket. We were going down Broadway, and there was an Eisenhower campaign procession coming and some motorcycles, and so we ducked in a side street and found we were in front of the Federal Reserve Bank. I said to Lathrop, "Let's go in and see if they've got any coins."

And we went in and Lathrop said, "Hey, got any silver dollars that are brand new? I'll give them as gifts." The guy said, "Oh, we got lots of silver dollars; I think some of them are brand new." So, he came back with a bag, and Lathrop gives him $1,000 cash. I give him a $5 tip for carrying them upstairs and everything. This was from the cash room at the Federal Reserve Bank of New York. We took them back to Ralph's apartment, we opened them up and spread them out on the floor, and they're all 1893-Ps. So we went through them, and I found recut dates, I found a couple of die varieties, and I called up Wormser and said, "How many do you want for stock?" And Charles said, "How much are they going to cost me?" I said, "A dollar apiece." Charlie said, "I'll take 100," or 150, whatever. I took out nice gemmy ones, rolled them up in paper towels or napkins, and took them to the office. We were selling them for years afterward for $2, $3, $4 apiece. Whenever I see some guy rave about how rare the 1893-Ps are I have to laugh because I had 1,000 of them. And who cares?

I didn't go after any other coins at the Federal Reserve. There was not enough demand for the coins at the time. Besides, we had just bought the Roebling estate, and we had six 1796 silver dollars, 25 '98s—we had coins all over the place. Our capital was stretched beyond belief because there were so many rare coins and collectible coins available. To buy Morgan dollars in 1952, even for face value, and beg people to buy them for $2 was a pain in the neck. They were so common.[13]

## MARKET PREDICTIONS

Other dealers had their own experiences—no two of them alike. There were enough silver dollars around in enough different and diverse hiding places that each situation was unique.

More than just a few dealers and collectors thought that the Treasury release was the beginning of the end—and that these former rarities would remain as common as all get-out, the market would become super-saturated, and, at the end, there would be no more buyers. For this reason, and also as bags of silver dollars tied up a lot of capital, nearly everyone sold bags as soon as they were received.

It was fun while it lasted, many thought. Soon, Morgan dollars would be forgotten, and dealers could go back to selling coins that remained popular, such as low-mintage 1950-D nickels, Proof sets, and other popular items.

## SILVER DOLLARS IN HIDING

The Treasury Department kept track of silver dollars stored in bulk, by quantity, not by dates and mintmarks. The figures below show the record from 1958 through autumn 1963. Of these dollars, most were of the 1878 through 1921 Morgan design, but many millions were also of the 1921 through 1935 Peace type:[14]

**1958**—On hand on January 1: 219,000,000. Withdrawn during year: 16,300,000.

**1959**—On hand on January 1: 202,700,000. Withdrawn during year: 20,400,000.

**1960**—On hand on January 1: 182,300,000. Withdrawn during year: 21,100,000.

**1961**—On hand on January 1: 161,200,000. Withdrawn during year: 31,100,000.

**1962**—On hand on January 1: 130,100,000. Withdrawn during year: 36,100,000.

**1963**—On hand on January 1: 94,000,000. Withdrawn during year (partial): 59,000,000.

Although these figures were not widely circulated, it is obvious that the Treasury vaults would soon be empty!

In autumn 1963 Uncirculated bags of these dollars were being found in California, Nevada, and Montana: 1879-S, 1880-S, 1881-S, 1882-S, 1883-O, and 1884-O. In Colorado and Wyoming, these bags were being paid out: 1878 (7 Tail Feathers), 1879, 1880, 1881, 1881-S, 1884-O, 1887, and the 1900. These were nearly, but not quite, the end of the line in bulk distribution of original bags of dollars.

In the meantime, bags of 1921 Morgan dollars remained plentiful, including at the gaming tables in Nevada, but few coin collectors or dealers wanted them. Often, those in search of bags of dollars would say, "except for 1921-P," it being common to add a "P" after the date of Philadelphia Mint coins, even though they bore no mintmark.

## All Gone! (Almost)

By March 1964 the supply of silver dollars held by the Treasury Department in Washington was nearly exhausted, this after paying out coins day after day at the cash windows, sometimes to people who had waited in long lines, some with wheelbarrows to carry what they obtained. On March 13, a business associate of Charles Slade II, a prominent rare coin dealer in Orlando, Florida, visited the Treasury Building in Washington and exchanged $20,000 in Silver Certificates for twenty 1,000-coin bags of dollars. At the cash window bags currently being delivered consisted of mixed worn pieces, retrieved from circulation and sealed by the Treasury Department prior to 1920.

These were then shipped by air to Slade. On the 14th, after he had looked through 18,000, he composed a form letter and sent it to a list of active buyers, stating what scarce varieties he had found:

| | | |
|---|---|---|
| 1878-CC (62 pieces) | 1890-CC (28) | 1896-S (25) |
| 1878 8 TF (14) | 1891-CC (20) | 1897-S (about 40) |
| 1879-CC (9) | 1892-CC (13) | 1898-O (about 60) |
| 1880-CC (7) | 1892 (12) | 1898-S (about 80) |
| 1881-CC (4) | 1892-S (48) | 1899 (3) |
| 1882-CC (5) | 1893 (10) | 1899-S (about 60) |
| 1883-CC (14) | 1893-CC (8) | 1900-S (about 120) |
| 1884-CC (2) | 1893-O (26) | 1901-S (about 120) |
| 1885-S (21) | 1893-S (2) | 1901 (10) |
| 1886-S (10) | 1894 (2) | 1902-S (29) |
| 1887-S (6) | 1894-S (26) | 1903-O (5) |
| 1888-S (2) | 1895-O (42) | 1904-O (about 80) |
| 1889-CC (1) | 1895-S (17) | 1904-S (about 100)[15] |

Although there is no way of knowing with certainty, the preceding list may well represent what dates and mintmarks among scarcer issues that might have been turned in at banks or other places in the years just prior to 1920, and bagged for storage.

One of the perplexities of numismatic history is that while the mintages of coins are well documented, and, of course, there is no end of listings of offerings and auctions in the marketplace, it is difficult if not impossible to ascertain the mix of dates and mintmarks of coins in circulation at a given time. Believe it or not, one can only guess at the answers of such questions as:

What varieties of coins, and their grades, might be found in the cash register of a grocery store in 1910?

Ditto for the dates and mintmarks of silver dollars on a roulette table in Las Vegas in 1955.

Ditto for the bagful of coins turned in at the end of the day by a streetcar conductor in St. Louis in 1900. Or 1915. Or any other year.

Of course, the unknown is always interesting, and worn silver dollars keep their secrets well!

## A Marvelous Turnabout

On March 26, 1964, not long after Slade bought 20,000 coins, Secretary of the Treasury Douglas called a halt to the payout. The vaults of the Treasury Building in Washington had been stripped of their silver dollar contents, and now all were gone. Not completely all, as several thousand bags still remained—pocket change, so to speak, from the situation a few years earlier. By this time most other reserves, such as in banks, were mostly depleted.

As all of this evolved, a marvelous situation occurred, a turnabout in the mind-set of nearly everyone. Although the supply of Morgan silver dollars in numismatic hands multiplied many times over as millions of Morgan and also Peace silver dollars were distributed, the demand more than made up for it, and although no figures are available, if the supply outside of vaults increased a hundredfold, the demand increased a thousandfold!

Now that the Treasury had run out, or almost, a feeling of relief came over the numismatic community. At long last, collectors and dealers could breathe easily and take stock of the situation. There were no more vaults waiting to be tapped, no more hoards waiting to come to light, no more surprises.

If in the summer of 1964 a certain silver dollar was scarce in Mint State, it was a cinch that the dollar would remain scarce and in time become more valuable, as there were no more to come on the market. However, there were some lingering doubts. Did some casinos in Nevada, or silver dollar dealers in Montana, or investors have caches of still-rare dates that they did not want to reveal—intending to keep them scarce?

Meanwhile, the *Coin Dealer Newsletter* had been launched in 1963, and before that a series of Teletype machines had been set up to link dealers. Trading activity was fast and furious, everybody wanted Morgan dollars! Peace dollars were in demand as well, although that series, with just 24 pieces of various dates and mints 1921 through 1935, was not as much in the mainstream.

## A SPECIALTY GAINS STRENGTH

By the summer of 1964 at least a few dozen dealers had made Morgan dollars their specialty. Later, some banded together to form the National Silver Dollar Roundtable, which held meetings and conventions and gave awards. What was once a niche became a foundation stone, an essential part of numismatics.

A number of alert enthusiasts set about writing down their observations, with Leroy C. Van Allen and A. George Mallis, a distinguished Massachusetts collector, collaborating on the study of minutely different die varieties, and Wayne Miller writing a memorable book with an overview of Morgan dollars year by year, date by date, sort of a precursor to the volume you are now holding in your hands, but differently styled and arranged. In time, other authors jumped in, and a virtual library of Morgan dollar references was created, including one written by Mike Carter on the date 1921 alone.

In the meantime silver dollars were the focal point of the rare coin market, remaining popular year after year. After all, there were no other old United States coins that could be bought for low prices in Mint State. These elements combined to make Morgan dollars super-attractive to just about anyone. It was easy to fall in love with them.

## UNBELIEVABLE!

In the late 1970s the market was (fill in your own word) either *wrecked*, or *enhanced*, or *perturbed*, or *restructured*, or? No two people will agree on whether what happened was beneficial, or something best forgotten. The coin market was hot, on fire, dynamic. All bets were off, and the slow days of a few years earlier, a normal cycle, were all but forgotten. In the limelight were the two most famous of all precious metals, gold and silver, not necessarily coins, but bullion in a market as hot as a firecracker![16]

These elements were becoming increasingly hard to find and expensive to refine and produce, and existing supplies would soon run short—or so the prevailing philosophy ran. Books and brochures were written on the wonderful aspects of investing in gold and silver, seminars were held across the United States and elsewhere, and predictions were rife. The price of bullion went up and up and up. Among the catalysts for this were the Hunt brothers of Dallas, who figured that silver in particular was vastly undervalued, and by purchasing bullion itself as well as calls and warrants, they invested untold millions of dollars in what was expected to yield a fantastic profit. And, they were right, as the price kept rising.

At the same time the world was experiencing an energy crisis, made worse by increasing uncertainty in the Mideast, especially in Iran. Domestically, many were confused, uncertain, and fearful of the future. One of America's greatest corporations, Chrysler, was in danger of going belly-up, and only a bailout by Congress saved it. The consumer price index rose 13.3% in 1979, the greatest increase in 33 years. Interest rates rose, confronting Americans with the specter that, soon, citizens would not be able to afford homes, everyday living expenses, or much of anything else! Jimmy Carter, although he was much admired as a fine, charismatic human being, did not have the "smarts" to manage the economy, many thought. Gold and silver beckoned as an everlasting, enduring refuge. The Golden Rule was parodied: He who has gold, rules. As to silver, down in Dallas the Hunt brothers, backed by an oil fortune, bought as much silver as they could, and purchased options and futures on still more. And, what a great insight—as they watched silver go up, and up, and up some more!

Citizens all across America emptied their piggy banks, dresser drawers, and other storage areas. To the melting pot, not to the coin album, went untold quantities of Mercury and Roosevelt dimes, Washington quarters, Liberty Walking, Franklin, and early Kennedy halves, and Morgan and Peace silver dollars. These were coins that were in grades such as VF, EF, AU, or even Mint State, but whose meltdown value was more, often much more, than their numismatic value.

At that level there was no numismatic demand, or very little, and many tons of coins were melted. I believe that many tens of millions of Morgan dollars were also melted, perhaps more than 100,000,000 of them. Such super-common issues as lightly worn Philadelphia dollars from the 1880s, the 1921 Morgans, and others were not worth nearly as much to collectors as they were to silver refiners—as such coins could be melted for $25 or more, later on the long side of $30, following the market price of silver as an ounce crossed the $40 mark.

Just about every coin shop in the United States had a scale on the front counter and a mechanical counting machine, to quickly service people as they came in with dimes, silver dollars, and other things, plus tableware and art objects, that had been kept on hand for years—but now were valuable. At coin conventions the air would be rattled every few minutes by the chink-clink-zip sound of electric counters at a dealer's table over there, now in another part of the room, and then in a corner—never ending, morning until night. Gray canvas bags of silver piled up.

The stars and planets must have come together precisely in alignment, or perhaps everyone's tea leaves were in a certain arrangement. The fever pitch continued. More accurately, the continually rising price of silver and gold generated more excitement and took along with it much of the rest of the market. Besides, more than just a few dealers had comfortable next eggs built on profits in dealing in gold and silver bullion. One of them, in Wisconsin, let me know before our sale that he had his eye on the Garrett Collection specimen of 1804 dollar we were auctioning for the Johns Hopkins University—as it would look nice on exhibit, and would certainly impress the people in the town where he lived! (The coin eventually brought $425,000 and was taken home by another bidder.)

Then came reality. The price of silver bullion peaked on January 18, 1980, in London (the main trading center) at $49.50 per ounce, followed a few days later on the 21st by $850 per ounce for gold, values that have not been seen since!

Well, the market continued on its momentum for a while, but prices drifted lower, eventually the Hunts ran into financial difficulty with their "corner" on silver, the "greater fool theory" stopped working, and no more investors came along who were willing to pay increasingly higher prices. The value of silver and gold collapsed. And, what about coin values? Did they collapse?

Yes and no. The values of common, worn Morgan dollars bit the dust, as did all other common, worn silver. Few if any numismatists were hurt, as they were not buyers of, for example, EF 1921 Morgan dollars when they were selling for $25 to $30 or more to be melted down.

In time, all Morgan dollars that had a claim to being choice Mint State, or rare, recommenced their upward price march, and soon record levels were attained.

## BUILDING THE SILVER DOLLAR HOBBY

Collectors continued to enjoy adding Morgan dollars to their albums coin-by-coin, and dealers enjoyed buying and selling them. In time, the silver peak of 1980 was forgotten. Probably not one in five of this book's readers was collecting back then—and this scenario may represent new information.

A decade later in Broken Arrow, Oklahoma, John W. Highfill solicited contributions from several dozen dealers, writers, and observers of the numismatic scene, and in 1993 published a compendium of what he had received, under the title *Comprehensive U.S. Silver Dollar Encyclopedia*, a volume crammed with personal experiences, predictions, comments, data, and more—sort of a family scrapbook of the silver dollar.

In the years since, Morgan dollars have matured and have become a foundation of the hobby as we know it. Countless 19th-century dates and mintmarks are still available in Mint State for nominal prices, creating a constant stream of newcomers interested in the hobby, some coming through numismatic circles, others through promotions on television, and still others in different ways. It seems that a sparkling, brilliant Morgan dollar from the 19th century has irresistible appeal, and even more so, if that is possible, if its reverse bears a mysterious CC mintmark!

## THE FABULOUS "CC" REMAINDERS

Oh, yes! What about those bags that did remain in Treasury vaults after Secretary Dillon called a halt to payouts on March 26, 1964? An inventory was taken of those still on hand, about three million coins, which were known to have included a lot of Carson City bags held back, but no one knew the mix of dates involved. In time the Treasury released an inventory, and it was found that there were many of some dates, such as hundreds of bags of 1884-CC, and hardly any of others—such as 1889-CC, 1890-CC, and 1893-CC.

What to do with the silver dollars? Dealers and others jockeyed for position as the Treasury Department sought or at least listened to potential partners in the private sector to assist in the sale. Paramount International Coin Corporation (Englewood, Ohio), for one, endeavored to use its certain connections in Washington to put the distribution its way, via Paramount official Michael V. DiSalle, a former governor of Ohio who in the 1940s had served as head of the Office of Price Administration (issuer of ration coupons and tokens) in Roosevelt's administration.

Meanwhile, the letters-to-the-editor columns of *Coin World*, *Numismatic News*, and other hobby periodicals were filled with other thoughts. Some suggested that these millions of coins be melted, to increase the rarity of those held by collectors and also to obviate the problem of distributing them. Others suggested different methods of distribution by auction or fixed price.

## THE GSA SILVER DOLLAR SALES OF THE 1970S

Finally, on December 31, 1970, President Richard M. Nixon signed legislation authorizing the sale of these silver dollars through the General Services Administration (GSA). On December 6, 1971, custody of the dollars was transferred to the auspices of the GSA. The coins, in storage at the U.S. Bullion depository in West Point, New York, were reviewed by representatives from various organizations, publications, and the private sector. The best part of a year was subsequently spent in the sorting, evaluation, and packaging of the coins by the GSA.

The first group of dollars was distributed on October 31, 1972, through what was planned to be a series of five mail-bid sales, the last taking place on June 30, 1974. Although President Nixon lent his name to advertising these coins as sound investments, the public reacted mildly, and sales were anything but spectacular.

At the conclusion of the fifth mail-bid sale, nearly a million coins remained without buyers. More suggestions were brought forth, and finally in March 1979, President Jimmy Carter signed legislation authorizing the GSA to sell the remaining pieces, hoping that by now a new group of buyers could be found. Another series of mail bid sales was planned, complete with restrictions as to minimum bids, quantities that could be ordered, and so on. The first auction was to take place on February 8, 1980. However, at the time the market for silver bullion was very volatile due to speculation by the Hunt brothers and others, and minimum bids and evaluations could not be sustained. Unlike the earlier sales, the distribution in 1980, ending in July of that year, met with great investor and speculative interest, plus many complaints and problems. However, finally all of the silver dollars were gone.

The dollars were packaged in sealed plastic containers, larger than but somewhat similar to the "slabs" popularized by the Professional Coin Grading Service in 1986. These large Carson City holders, with the coins mounted against black backgrounds, were viewed as too large and clumsy for convenient transportation and mailing, and many were broken out of the holders, so as to be more conveniently stored or for the coins to be placed into albums. In 1987 the Numismatic Guaranty Corporation of America introduced its holders, a slightly different format. This precipitated a great penchant for "cracking out" coins from the government-issued holders, so that they could receive numerical grade designations from ANACS, PCGS, or NGC, often sharply increasing the value of the coins, particularly if a high number could be obtained.

Year after year dealers and collectors continued to break coins out of the GSA holders. However, beginning early in the 21st century a demand arose for Morgan dollars still in the GSA holders, themselves becoming collectible, what with expanded distribution of coins on eBay and other venues. Somehow, a coin in an official GSA holder had a "pedigree" that was not available with a coin in the holder of a private service (ANACS, NGC, or PCGS). In January 2003 NGC revealed an innovation, a service whereby coins still mounted in GSA holders could separately receive an NGC certification.

# HOW MANY EXIST TODAY?

## ESTIMATING QUANTITIES

In this book I have given estimates or approximations of the number of coins believed to exist today. These have been derived from many sources, including Treasury reports, dealer and collector notifications of bags or single coins observed, and, by extrapolation, the published figures of ANACS, NGC, and PCGS.

Regarding the survival of Mint State coins, original mintage figures are of little help. Of the 1901 Morgan dollar, 6,982,000 were struck for circulation. From this prodigious quantity, I estimate that fewer than 1,500 coins exist today in any Mint State level, and at the gem level, MS-65 or finer, no more than 25 exist, and even this figure may be too generous, for only 6 have been certified as being so fine.

Then consider the 1884-CC dollar, of which 1,136,000 were coined, or about one-sixth of the quantity for 1901. By logic, some might think that if 1,500 Mint State 1901 dollars are estimated to survive, then one-sixth of this amount, or perhaps 250, would survive of 1884-CC. However, it is a fact—not an estimate, not a guess—that precisely 962,638 Mint State 1884-CC dollars were found in the vaults of the Treasury Building in Washington in 1964 and that in following years each and every one was sold at a premium to interested collectors and other buyers. By the way, so far only about 56,000 Mint State 1884-CC dollars have been certified by NGC and PCGS combined, or about 5% of the Mint State coins we know are in existence.

These figures are telling for several reasons. Today, more than just a few people worship the "population reports" of the leading certification services. However, the above demonstrates that while useful—I can say with certainty that about 56,000 1884-CC dollars exist in plastic holders bearing the imprints of these fine services—they do not have much relevance at all to the quantities actually in existence. Actually, only one 1884-CC dollar in 16, from the Treasury release, has been certified. I wonder how this fact reconciles with the opinion of many that population reports are the answer to all questions concerning rarity. Think about it.

For Proof coins the situation is simpler. If 880 Proofs were struck of the 1895 dollar, it is logical that most survive today, as they were sold to numismatists who paid a premium for them. The situation of spending or melting, as with the 1901 dollar that is surprisingly very rare in Mint State, is not relevant to Proofs. Probably 70% to 80% or so of all Morgan dollar Proofs still exist.[17]

## MORE ABOUT CERTIFIED POPULATIONS

While I am at it, here are a few more thoughts about population reports.

For purposes of illustration, here is a hypothetical Morgan dollar, date 18xx. Although I have no way of knowing, suppose that from information concerning hoards, from interviews with dealers, and from observations, I make estimates as to how many are really out there. At the same time, for the current market price I have checked advertisements and auction results, and population reports have furnished the numbers certified:

**Good to AU:** 250,000 in existence. Current market value for VG-8, $15. Certified in that grade, 25 coins.

**MS-60 to MS-62:** 100,000 in existence. Current market for MS-60, $40. Certified in that grade, 100 coins.

**MS-65:** 3,000 in existence. Current market value for MS-65, $2,000. Certified in that grade, 500.

Although coins in Good to AU exist to the extent of 100,000, only 25 coins in VG-8 have been certified, and relatively few others in this range, up to AU-58, have been certified either. The reason is that the certification cost, usually $10 to $20, is too expensive in terms of the market value.

Even in MS-60 the coin appears rare, for the same reason.

However, in MS-65, the coin is more plentiful, per the reports. Now, nearly everyone realizes that an MS-65 is more valuable, and justifiably so—but few are aware that the percentage of lower grades certified is usually tiny in comparison to the total numbers out there.

We have seen that for the 1884-CC in Mint State, only 1 in 16 coins has been certified, and this is for an ultra-popular Carson City coin.

Returning to our hypothetical 18xx coin of which 3,000 exist, and which in MS-65 grade is worth $2,000, and for which 500 have been certified: have 500 *different coins* been certified? Likely not, as such a valuable coin may have been submitted multiple times. Perhaps only 200 to 300 *different* specimens are involved.

The answers are elusive, but it is worth giving careful thought to population report figures and adding grains of salt, as appropriate. Another aspect is that population report figures never get smaller. If today there are 500 certifications, perhaps 10 years from now the number will be 1,000 or 1,500. In the course of doing population estimates for this book I checked the reports published by NGC and PCGS and was amazed how dramatically the number of gem coins, MS-65 to MS-68, has grown from what it was in, say, 1990. This is due to resubmissions as well as "grade inflation." Many coins that were graded MS-63 years ago have "graduated" through resubmissions to become MS-64 or even MS-65. Indeed, that is what the resubmission game is all about.

In some areas of numismatics, perhaps including Proof Morgan dollars of high value, in which the same coin is often resubmitted, sometimes several times, the "population" may someday exceed the mintage! Actually, instead of *population* reports, lists of coins certified should be called *submission* totals.

Not too long after PCGS, NGC, and ANACS began grading in 1986, 1987, and 1989, respectively, an investor paid over $100,000 to buy the only Proof Morgan dollar of any date certified as Proof-68. He held on to it for some time, then tried to sell it at a profit, but by then others had been certified in that grade. Now, dozens have been certified at lofty levels. Of course, the coins themselves do not become any more plentiful. It is only the population numbers that continually inch upward.

Consider that fact that if 962,638 Mint State 1884-CC dollars were found in the vaults of the Treasury Building in Washington in 1964, nearly all of these must exist today. No one would have thrown one away! Consider that only about 56,000 have been certified. Now, based upon population reports, how many exist? You know the answer.

DMPL coins, the certified populations of which are given in the date-by-date analysis, are a special case in themselves. For the 1878 8 Tail Feathers, the combined populations of NGC and PCGS coins are as follows: DMPL-60, 7; DMPL-61, 30; DMPL-62, 91; DMPL-63, 111; DMPL-64, 79; DMPL-65 or higher, 6.

An uninformed reading of the above might suggest that most DMPL coins of this variety are DMPL-62, and that relatively few are DMPL-60. In reality, there are probably 10 times more DMPL-60 coins around, but the bagmarks make them so unattractive that there is little market for them, and few have been certified.

By the way, I am simply trying to encourage thinking on your part. Population reports are, indeed, useful in their own way, if you understand them. If there are two different dates of San Francisco Mint dollars, and in MS-65 grade there are 100 certified of one of them and 1,000 of the other, then you can be sure that the first one is much harder to find and is even rare on the market.

## EXISTENCE VERSUS AVAILABILITY

The existence of a certain quantity of Morgan dollars is one thing; availability at a given time might be another. Large numbers of coins, including rarities, often simply disappear into safe deposit boxes, library shelves, and other places, and are tightly held for a long time.

In his 1982 study, *The Morgan and Peace Dollar Textbook*, Wayne Miller mentioned that in recent years he had "examined at least a dozen fully gem 1884-S dollars." Today, I suggest that if you were to look up the highest auction record you can find for an MS-65 1884-S, and offer to pay double that if you can buy 10 pieces totally, you will not spend a cent. Indeed, I would be surprised if you were offered any more than one, two, or three coins.

One of the mysteries of numismatics is that there are a lot of coins "out there" that we in the dealer or collector community do not know about.

Also, the frequency of appearance of some coins, even classic rarities, is apt to vary widely. As of summer 1979, no 1787 gold Brasher doubloon had been offered at auction for many years. A generation of coin collectors had come and gone without having had the opportunity bid on one. Then, within the space of a few months, two different pieces came on the market!

In 1921 B. Max Mehl advertised the forthcoming sale of the James H. Manning Collection, stating that it had an 1804 silver dollar, the first to be auctioned in over 15 years. But in the next year, 1922, he had another, the Ten Eyck specimen. In modern times there have been enough offerings of 1804 dollars at auction that scarcely a year or two elapses without at least one opportunity to bid. As only 15 specimens of the 1804 dollar are known to exist and no new specimens have come to light since the 19th century, and as several are held in museums, is it not strange that they are more plentiful in the auction room now than they were a century ago? The answer is that many buyers do not hold on to coins for very long. In contrast, years ago many varieties were placed in collections to remain there for a decade or longer.

Morgan silver dollars are, like many things, where you find them. For most dates and mintmarks there are enough around that you can pick and choose—which I hope you will do. Being a connoisseur is part of the fun, and in the long run it will make your collection worth more. However, for certain rarities—and a gem 1884-S dollar is an example— while it might be fun to read about the good old days when a bunch of them were on the market, now the appearance of just a single coin would be an important occasion, and careful thought must be given to the opportunity presented.

# WAYS TO COLLECT
# MORGAN SILVER DOLLARS

## FIRST, SOME BASICS

### THE MORGAN DOLLAR DESIGN

From 1878 to 1921 the same basic design was used on all Morgan silver dollars, although there were several modifications, as you already know.

On all coins, the obverse features the portrait of Miss Liberty facing left, E PLURIBUS UNUM and stars surrounding, and the date below.

The reverse illustrates a wingspread eagle at the center, holding in its talons an olive branch and arrows. In God We Trust in Old English letters is above its head. A wreath surrounds the lower part of the eagle. Around the border of the coin is UNITED STATES OF AMERICA / ONE DOLLAR, the last with a star to each side.

The edge of the coin is reeded, usually having from about 180 to 190 reeds (the VAM text gives reed counts for each variety, a tribute to the patience of the authors).

### DIFFERENT REVERSE "TYPES"

From the outset of coinage in 1878 there was dissatisfaction with certain aspects of the coin, with the first significant modification, called "types" by many, being the changing of tail feathers in the eagle from eight to seven, creating the coins known today as 8 Tail Feathers and 7 Tail Feathers. The changes were made in the hub die, and by transfer, subsequently in working dies. The first die with 8 Tail Feathers is thus the first type in the series and is known as Reverse A. Then followed three others, some discussion of them being given the earlier account of the initial coinage of Morgan dollars in March 1878, and the months afterward.

Several obverse modifications were made as well, but scarcely any notice is taken of them today, except by specialists. The reverses are important, however, for descriptions of certain silver dollars in the 1878 through 1880 date range, including major varieties listed in the Red Book. The reverse types are reviewed here.[1]

**Reverse Type A: 8 Tail Feathers.** Eight feathers in eagle's tail. Parallel top to topmost arrow feather on reverse. Eagle's breast flat (not rounded). Used only on Morgan dollars struck early in 1878 at the Philadelphia Mint. *Nomenclature:* 8 Tail Feathers.

**Reverse Type B: 7 Tail Feathers, Reverse of 1878, Parallel Arrow Feather (PAF).** Seven feathers in eagle's tail. Parallel top to topmost arrow feather on reverse. Eagle's breast flat (not rounded). Used on most dollars of 1878, all 1878-CC, most 1878-S, some 1879-S, some 1880-CC. Nomenclature when used to describe dollars dated 1878: 7 Tail Feathers, Reverse of 1878 (PAF). *Nomenclature when used to describe certain dollars dated 1879 and 1880:* Reverse of 1878 (PAF).

**Reverse Type C: Reverse of 1879, Slanting Arrow Feather (SAF).** Slanting top to topmost arrow feather on reverse. Eagle's breast rounded. Used on some 1878, some 1878-S, all 1879, all 1879-CC, all 1879-O, most 1879-S, all 1880, most 1880-CC, all 1880-O, all 1880-S, all 1881 to 1904. In 1900 Reverse C was slightly altered, now with a larger space between the eagle's left wing and the eagle's neck and, most important, shallow definition of the feathers on the eagle's breast. This modified style was used on some but not all dates and mints of dollars 1900 to 1904, at the same time certain varieties were employing the earlier version, and still others had the working die made by impressing the modified design over the earlier design. The VAM text gives details. *Nomenclature:* Reverse of 1879 (SAF).

**Reverse Type D: Reverse of 1921, Parallel Arrow Feather (PAF).** Parallel top to topmost arrow feather on reverse. Eagle's breast flat (not rounded). Details in low relief. Copied from Reverse B, but not well detailed. Used on all 1921, 1921-D, and 1921-S Morgan dollars. *Nomenclature:* No particular popular designation, as all 1921 dollars are the same.

# Collecting by Date, Mintmark, or Variety

Now, to ways of collecting:

What to include in a basic set of Morgan dollars has no official definition. However, the following list is a good guide to dates, overdates, mintmarks, overmintmarks, and reverse types. Only in the past generation have overdates, overmintmarks, and reverse types become popular, especially since their listing in the Red Book. However, not all numismatists opt to include them. I, for one, would not bother with all of the 8/7 varieties of 1880-CC listed in that book, but you might find them to be fascinating. On the other hand, I could not live without having basic tail feather varieties of 1878 in my collection if I were assembling a set.

## A Basic Collection of Morgan Dollars

The following varieties constitute a basic collection and suggested list based upon my opinions and experience. Of course, some of the listings can be easily enough ignored, if desired, and you can form a collection with just one of each date and mintmark—no feather differences, overdates, overmintmarks, or reverse types. Selected annotations may be of interest:

**1878 8 Tail Feathers**—Struck only in early 1878. The even number of feathers was considered to be a design error, and modifications were made soon.

**1878 Doubled Tail Feathers** (earlier called 7 Over 8 Tail Feathers)—Multiple dies with traces of under-feathers. At least four under-feathers must show to be qualified as Doubled Tail Feathers.

**1878 7 Tail Feathers, Reverse of 1878 (PAF)**

**1878 7 Tail Feathers, Reverse of 1879 (SAF)**—This variety, although very important, is not widely known except to specialists. It is, however, listed in the Red Book.

**1878-CC**—All have Reverse of 1878 (PAF).

**1878-S**—All have Reverse of 1878 (PAF).

**1879**—All have Reverse of 1879 (SAF).

**1879-CC**—All have Reverse of 1879 (SAF). Key date among the early Carson City dollars 1878–1885. The 1879-CC with Large CC Over Small CC is not widely collected as a separate variety, as most

numismatists desire only one example of this rare issue.

**1879-O**—All have Reverse of 1879 (SAF).

**1879-S**—Reverse of 1878 (PAF). Probably less than a third of the 1879-S dollars are of this style.

**1879-S**—Reverse of 1879 (SAF).

**1880**—All have Reverse of 1879 (SAF). Some dies are over 1879, but the overdates are not bold; these are of technical interest. Most numismatists are content to own just one 1880 dollar.

**1880-CC, Reverse of 1878 (PAF)**—Possibly all dies are over 1879, with traces of the under-digits ranging from slight to distinct. Most numismatists are satisfied with just one 1880-CC dollar with Reverse of 1878 (PAF).

**1880-CC, Reverse of 1879 (SAF)**—Possibly all dies are over 1879, with traces of the under-digits ranging from slight to distinct. Most numismatists are satisfied with just one 1880-CC dollar with Reverse of 1879 (SAF). Collecting comment as preceding.

**1880-O**

**1880-S**—All have Reverse of 1879 (SAF). Some dies are over 1879, but the overdates are not bold; these are of technical interest. Again, most numismatists are content to own just one 1880-S dollar.

**1881**—All from 1881 through 1904 have Reverse of 1879 (SAF), and thus there is no need to make note of this feature in catalog descriptions.

**1881-CC**

**1881-O**

**1881-S**

**1882**

**1882-CC**—One of three Carson City issues for which hundreds of thousands were in the Treasury hoard.

**1882-O**

**1882-O/S**—Odd overmintmark variety.

**1882-S**

**1883**

**1883-CC**—One of three Carson City issues for which hundreds of thousands were in the Treasury hoard.

**1883-O**

**1883-S**—First of the San Francisco issues to be rare in high Mint State grades.

**1884**

**1884-CC**—One of three Carson City issues for which hundreds of thousands were in the Treasury hoard.

**1884-O**

**1884-S**—Even though some 3,200,000 were struck the 1884-S is a rarity in Mint State, as most were placed into circulation at or near the year they were struck. Only a few were in the Treasury hoard.

**1885**

**1885-CC**

**1885-O**

**1885-S**

**1886**

**1886-O**—Despite a large mintage of 10,710,000 coins, the 1886-O is a rarity in Mint State, as most were placed into circulation at or near the year they were struck. Only a few were in the Treasury hoard.

**1886-S**

**1887/6**—The overdate is not bold, and not all collectors desire to add this variety.

**1887**—Highest mintage figure in the early (1878–1904) series, 20,290,000.

**1887/6-O**—Same comment as under 1887/6.

**1887-O**

**1887-S**

**1888**

**1888-O**

**1888-S**

**1889**

**1889-CC**—By far the rarest of the Carson City Morgan dollars.

**1889-O**

**1889-S**

**1890**

**1890-CC**

**1890-O**

**1890-S**

**1891**

**1891-CC**

**1891-O**

**1891-S**

**1892**

**1892-CC**

**1892-O**

**1892-S**

**1893**

**1893-CC**—The majority of Mint State pieces are extensively bagmarked, a negative distinction that is also true of the 1895-S issue. Last year of coinage operation at the Carson City Mint.

**1893-O**

**1893-S**—With a production of 100,000 pieces this has the lowest circulation-strike mintage in the Morgan dollar series. Important key date in any grade, a major rarity in Mint State. Only a few dozen Mint State pieces were in the Treasury hoard.

**1894**

**1894-O**

**1894-S**

**1895**—Struck only in Proof format, and to the extent of just 880 pieces. By far the rarest Morgan dollar date, although not collected by some, who can achieve completion of a collection of *circulation strikes* by not having an 1895.

**1895-O**—This is the only date/mintmark issue in the Morgan dollar series for which no quantity is known to have been part of the Treasury hoard dispersed in 1962 through 1964. Common in low grades, exceedingly rare in choice Mint State.

**1895-S**—The majority of Mint State pieces are extensively bagmarked, a negative distinction also true of 1893-CC.

**1896**

**1896-O**—Despite a large mintage of 4,900,000 coins, the 1896-O is rare in Mint State today. Most were placed into circulation at or near the year they were struck. Only a few were in the Treasury hoard.

**1896-S**

**1897**

**1897-O**

**1897-S**

**1898**

**1898-O**

**1898-S**

**1899**

**1899-O**

**1899-S**

**1900**

**1900-O**

**1900-O/CC**—First of the overmintmarks to be discovered in the Morgan series, and the most prominently defined.

**1900-S**

**1901**

**1901-O**

**1901-S**

**1902**

**1902-O**

**1902-S**

**1903**

**1903-O**—Considered to be the rarest of all branch mint Morgan dollars in Uncirculated grade, until 1962 when many long-hidden bags were released by the Treasury.

**1903-S**

**1904**

**1904-O**

**1904-S**

**1921**—The highest mintage by far in the Morgan dollar series: 44,690,000. This and other Morgan dollars of 1921 were struck from a modified design with shallow definitions.

**1921-D**—First and only Denver Mint Morgan dollar. Tiny D mintmark.

**1921-S**—Tiny S mintmark.

## COLLECTING PROOF MORGAN DOLLARS

While at first consideration it would seem natural to collect Morgan dollars in Proof format by date sequence, in actuality there are very few who do this. Years ago, before mintmarks became popular, collecting Proofs was the rule—in an era in which dates were the be-all and end-all, and mintmarks were scarcely noticed. Today, few collectors can resist the appeal of a wide panorama of branch mint coins being available for low prices.

The idea of having Proof coins for the Philadelphia Mint dates and Mint State or other coins for the branch mints is not popular either, possibly because the appearances do not match—although it can be said that the appearance of Deep Mirror Prooflike (DMPL) circulation strikes does not match the luster of most Mint State pieces either.

The rule of thumb is that most who collect Morgan dollars by date and mintmark sequence opt for circulation strikes. Even when Proofs are more available and much less expensive than Mint State coins (an MS-65 1901 dollar is many times more costly than a Proof-65 of the same date), the search for Mint State coins persists.

Given the lack of interest in a mix-and-match situation, that leaves the time-tested arrangement of forming a Proof set on its own—just as numismatists were apt to do a century ago.

Proofs were made of each year 1878 to 1904, with several reverse varieties within the year 1878, these being 8 Tail Feathers, 7 Tail Feathers with Reverse of 1878 (PAF), and the nearly impossible 7 Tail Feathers with Reverse of 1879 (SAF). Otherwise, the list is simply one for each year. A few Chapman Proofs, or true mirrored Proofs, were made in 1921, and are very rare. Under each year in the date-by-date analysis, Proofs are discussed together with rarity ratings and market values.

The majority of Proof Morgan dollars encountered today are apt to be hairlined, these not being too objectionable on selected specimens Proof-65 or finer, but often fatal to eye appeal for Proof-60 to 62 examples. While most Proofs are sharply struck, beginning about 1888 and continuing for several years, many are weak at the centers. Proofs from 1902 to 1904 inclusive have bright or "polished" portraits, rather than frosty, due to an unexplained change in the preparation of Proof dies.

Over the years only a few truly high-quality sets of Proof Morgan dollars 1878 to 1904 have been formed (forgetting for the moment about the "impossible" 1921). If you embark on this pursuit, get set for a great challenge. Among Proofs, true quality is often much harder to find than for circulation issues, as you do not have the opportunity to review 10, 20, or more pieces in a short time to make a selection.

However, a finely matched set of high-grade Proofs can be a joy to own.

## DIVERSE COLLECTIONS

If you are collecting United States coins by design types, then you need just one Morgan dollar of 1878 through 1921 to be "complete." Enough said. Not quite, really, for buying just one Morgan dollar would deprive you of all of the fun you could have!

Collecting Carson City dollars by date has been popular for a long time. These coins have their own niche in romance and legend and possess a magnetic attraction, unlike specialized collections of other mints.

A set of such coins would have one each of 1878-CC, 1879-CC, 1880-CC, 1881-CC, 1882-CC, 1883-CC, 1884-CC, and 1885-CC, then a jump (as none were made in the interval) to 1889-CC, 1890-CC, 1891-CC, 1892-CC, and 1893-CC.

A "collection" of Denver Mint Morgan dollars would be easy enough to complete, as there is just one coin—the 1921-D. However, I doubt if it would provide much excitement.

Although I am not aware of anyone having done this, you could pick a special era, such as the presidential administration of William McKinley (1897–1901), and collect silver dollars of that span. Somehow, this lacks pizzazz, as perhaps, numismatically, this is not often done. This reminds me that in various collecting pursuits across the wide field of possibilities, techniques do differ. Stamp collectors enjoy "topical" collecting, such as stamps depicting birds, or sailing ships, or palm trees. While some coin collectors have narrowed in on presidential portraits, such as coins depicting Washington, I don't know of anyone who goes after bird coins, or palm tree coins. Come to think of it, P.B. Trotter Jr., a Tennessee banker, once collected coins depicting ships, and an architect friend in New York City enjoys coins and medals showing buildings. More properly, some do collect by topics, but it is not a main avenue in the hobby.

A few people have put together grading sets of Morgan dollars, showing different states of wear and preservation from Good-4 on up. Probably, these are more useful for informational purposes than for the enjoyment of collecting.

Patterns by George T. Morgan can be a challenging and exciting pursuit, although all are scarce and some are very rare. While I was writing this book, Edward J. Linkner, M.D., who was a contributor to my 1993 *Encyclopedia*, reminded me that such patterns are one of his specialties.

Collecting by different specialized die varieties is another possibility, and chapter 9 is devoted to this. In the meantime, let's examine the marketplace first.

## INFORMATION AND COINS GALORE

Today, in the early 21st century, it might seem at quick glance that anything anyone ever wanted to know about Morgan silver dollars is available. The Internet, the weekly *Coin World* and *Numismatic News* papers, plus the weekly *Certified Coin Dealer Newsletter* and *Coin Dealer Newsletter* market guides, plus auctions, plus dealer price lists constitute a flood of data concerning market valuations. In the meantime, the advent of widespread certified grading by PCGS in 1986, followed by NGC in 1987 and ANACS in 1989, has resulted in millions of Morgan dollars' being neatly encapsulated, marked with a grade such as MS-63, MS-65, or whatever.

With certified grading taking the place of individual knowledge on the subject, and with so many price quotations available, it would seem that there is little to do to build a set of Morgan dollars except to write checks. For some buyers this is indeed true. Today, anyone with a sufficient checking account balance could within a few days place orders for 90% or more of the different Morgan dollar dates and mintmarks from 1878 through 1921, in grades of MS-63 or better. After that there would be some patience required to track down elusive issues such as 1886-O, 1892-S, 1893-S, 1896-S, and 1901, but even these can be obtained in time, perhaps the 1901 being the last acquired, although for this particular Philadelphia Mint issue a Proof can be obtained without much difficulty. Although the 1895 Proof is rare, and just 880 were minted, I could probably make some telephone calls and have 10 to 20 in my office next week.

That said, what else is there to know?

Plenty!

In any market, coins can always be bought in haste. The more sellers there are, and the more price information available, the easier it is to do so. Quickly, one can amass an accumulation, even called a *collection*, but the quality of such may be another matter indeed.

I suggest that you form a *special* collection, one of extremely high quality. The challenge, and perhaps for the minus part for those who want instant gratification, is that some patience is needed even to acquire "nice" examples of common dates and mintmarks, and for some issues a lot of patience is required. The great reward for you is that in most instances this high quality will cost you no more than others are paying for ordinary, indeed sometimes ugly, coins!

It is true.

I share with you some of the guidelines I have found to be useful, plus basic information about grading, coin surfaces, and related matters.

## GRADING BY THE NUMBERS

The importance of grading is simple: it is a major determinant of value. For that reason alone (although there are others), grading is essential.

In general, in numismatics the higher the grade of an item, the more valuable it will be. The rule is not inviolable all across the hobby, but within the series of Morgan dollars I am not aware of any exceptions. In case you wonder what exceptions might exist elsewhere, I mention just two, but could give other illustrations: In the numismatic byway of obsolete paper money produced during the early 19th century, most brand-new, crisp Uncirculated notes are not worth as much as well-worn ones. This is because many notes were left over and not used in commerce, and were not signed by a bank's officers (cashier and president). Those that were signed and used are worth more! Now, isn't this strange? A Morgan dollar that was paid out by a bank and used is not worth as much as one that was held back as a remainder! However, trade dollars chopmarked by bankers and used in commerce in China have a strong collector following.

Time was when grading of coins was casual, including in the cradle days of Morgan dollar production. During the era of Morgan dollar minting from 1878 through 1921, there were no readily accepted grading interpretations, let alone standards. One person's Proof could be another's polished AU, and what was Extremely Fine to one seller might be Uncirculated to another. Although the term *Mint State* was used now and then, *Uncirculated* was the preferred word. There were no minute separations.

Within the Uncirculated category, sometimes a piece would be called nicked, marked, with a scratch, or with some other problem, including being haymarked (an early term for "hairlined"). Particularly attractive pieces might be called choice or gem, with no particular rule. What might have been gem to one numismatist was not necessarily gem to another.

# GRADING AND
# THE MARKETPLACE

In the late 19th century, collectors and dealers realized that in the absence of being able to visit a coin shop or attend an auction in person, it would be very useful to have some sort of standardization to facilitate the buying and selling of coins from a distance. Over the years many grading ideas were advanced, including one in *The Numismatist*, February 1892, compiled by Joseph Hooper, which used Roman numerals on the following scale. "Coins are graded as to condition, and the following terms thereto apply," noted the writer, who then gave a list ordered by Roman numerals:

    I. Mint Brilliant Proofs, or first strikes on planchets, especially prepared for numismatic purposes.

    II. Mint Proofs, on ordinary prepared planchets. Brushing Proofs produces what is termed "hay marks" and should never be adopted, the sale value being lowered. Later collectors have sometimes referred to these as "hairlines."

    III. Uncirculated, showing no abrasion or wearing of the reliefs, scratches, nicks or indentations. A coin may be Uncirculated and yet not have the sharp impression of the first strike as the dies tire, widen in sinkages, and lose their sharpness, gradually, in so much that the later impressions have often been mistaken for die varieties, more especially where the same dies have done long service for a large issue.

    IV. Extremely Fine.

    V. Very Fine.

    VI. Fine. Below this condition, unless in extreme rarities, we would not recommend the bidding on at auction sales.

    VII. Very Good.

    VIII. Good. The latter conditions as described in the sales are often disappointing, the terms applied misleading, until understood, being used by dealers to describe a certain state of preservation.

    IX. Very Fair.

    X. Fair.

    XI. Poor.

    XII. Very Poor.

Like the roller-coin press, Esperanto, the *Spruce Goose*, and the Townsend Plan, the idea did not catch on, and no catalog offered an "1885 silver dollar, Mint Proof II." Or perhaps the idea of numerical grading was ahead of its time.

## GRADING KNOWLEDGE ESSENTIAL FOR SUCCESS

Although many columns of print were devoted to the subject of grading in publications such as *The Numismatist* and the catalogs of dealers, at the turn of the 20th century the ability to grade was considered to be one of the assets of a successful numismatist, the result of training, experience, and a lot of looking. This seemed reasonable enough, for then, as now, someone learning to catch trout had to master the intricacies and pleasures of fly casting, an adventurer seeking to climb Half Dome in Yosemite Park would need to know how to use pitons, how to rappel with ropes, and other techniques, and anyone wanting to drive a car needed to master the various skills of shifting, basic car maintenance (such as tire repairs), and the rules of the road.

So it was with numismatists. Anyone with money to spend on coins, and who wanted a semblance of good value for the price paid, needed to know the difference between Fine and Extremely Fine, between Proof and Uncirculated, between Very Fine and About Uncirculated. I rather imagine that if a well-moneyed, well-intentioned numismatist went into the Philadelphia coin shop of the Chapman brothers in 1900 and said, "I don't want to learn anything about grading. I will simply believe what I see written on coin envelopes and in auction catalogs," he would be dismissed as some sort of a nut. Really. Learning to grade was part of the hobby.

Although beginners wished that there would be a magic pill to help them along, those at the game for some time considered grading technique to be enjoyable, part of what numismatics was all about—and, anyone skillful at it was able to attend a coin convention and pick out bargains that uninformed people or even dealers might not spot. This was part of the thrill of the hunt, the fun of the game.

As a side note, by the late 20th century, when grading had become divided into many categories, books had been published and seminars held. I never heard the slightest complaint from an *experienced numismatist*. Emery May Holden Norweb, John Jay Pittman, Eric P. Newman, Kenneth E. Bressett (editor of the Red Book), and, I believe, *just about everyone else who had enjoyed the hobby for years*, always formulated their own opinions based on experience, with no books necessary. None of these people relied on someone else to do the grading for them.

## MARKET PRICES RISE

Returning to the early 20th century, as time went on, and the coin market gained momentum and strength—propelled forward by the commemorative boom (1934–1935), the popularity of the *Standard Catalogue of United States Coins* (the first regularly issued price guide for the hobby, launched by Wayte Raymond in 1934), and the popularity of albums, holders, and folders—prices rose. More and more people became attracted to the hobby of numismatics. Every once in a while there would be a quantum jump in interest, perhaps such as the Michael F. Higgy Sale held in 1943 by Abe Kosoff, which was a pivotal point, conducted during World War II, when cash was common, commodities were scarce, and dollars were looking for a place to land. In some instances prices in the Higgy Sale brought double, triple, or even greater multiples of *Standard Catalogue* listings. A report of the "record breaking" prices, from *The Numismatist*, makes interesting reading today, for the values of these once-high-priced coins are for the most part 100 times or more today:

> The Michael F. Higgy Collection of rare coins was sold at the Numismatic Gallery, 42 E. 50th Street, New York, on September 10 and 11, for a total of over $30,000. Many outstanding dealers and collectors were in attendance, and brisk bidding resulted in many record breaking prices.
>
> A 1796 half dollar sold for $210, and an 1802 Proof silver dollar for $250. A $3 gold Proof of 1877 sold for $300, a 1793 cent went for $170, an 1856 cent brought

$110. A $50 gold piece of Augustus Humbert dated 1852 went to a private collector at $600, a cent dated 1792 went for $390, a $4 piece brought $340.

## SHELDON'S MARKET FORMULA

In 1949, Harper Brothers published *Early American Cents*, by Dr. William H. Sheldon, a long-time numismatist. The text dealt with large copper cents of the years 1793 through 1814 exclusively, and endeavored to give the reader every bit of information desired about each die variety, with some things explained to a fare-thee-well. Sheldon came up with a market formula based on numbers. Each die variety within that range, and there were over 200 of them, was assigned a Basal Value, determined by its rarity and popularity. A very common large copper cent back then might have a Basal Value of 50¢ or $1, while a rare variety might have a Basal Value of $5 or so. Then, with current market values in mind in 1949, Sheldon came up with a scale of grading numbers that, if multiplied by the Basal Value, would yield the current price of a coin.

The numbers were designed to fit the market, and that is how the scale of from 1 (Basal State, so worn as to be virtually unidentifiable) to MS-70 (Gem Mint State) came to be. The theory was that a particular coin with a basal value of $5, if in VF-20 grade, was worth $5 times 20 or $100.

As strange as it may seem today, in 1949 there was not a great premium—not a great "stretch"—on the price of Mint State coins as opposed to, say, EF or AU. Indeed, in Sheldon's era the typical copper cent in MS-60 was worth twice one in VF-30, at least in many instances.

To many if not most casual observers, numbers are scientific, whereas adjectives are fuzzy. If a coin was described as VF-30, that was easy to understand, certainly better than Fine-12, but not as good as EF-40. On the other hand, such terms as Extremely Fine, Very Good, Very Fine, About Uncirculated, and so on, tended to be obscure, and without doubt a newcomer to the hobby might think that a piece described as Very Good might be better than one called simply Fine, and the same person would have no clue as to whether About Uncirculated was more desirable or less desirable than Extremely Fine.

For Mint State Sheldon had just three separations: MS-60, or basic Mint State; MS-65, or gem; and MS-70, equal to perfection, the last being an ideal standard, much as 18 strokes would be a perfect accomplishment for a round of golf. Not long after 1949, numismatists started using the numbers to describe series besides 1793 through 1814 cents, particularly later large copper cents of 1816 through 1857 (none were coined in 1815), copper half cents of 1793 through 1857, and American colonial and state copper coins.

## PRECISION WANTED

Then, during the crazy, hectic market days of the 1960s, sparked by the launching of *Coin World* in 1960, the discovery of the 1960 Small Date Lincoln cent, and other factors, plus, of course, the Treasury release of silver dollars beginning in November 1962, the market became white hot. Prices of just about all coins rose, and as pieces achieved high values and as hundreds of thousands of newcomers came into the field, there was an increasing demand for precision grading.

Aha! The Sheldon numbers fit the bill exactly, as they appeared to be scientific. However, by that time Uncirculated coins were described far beyond basic Mint State and gem Mint State. There were *sliders*, referring to a low-grade Uncirculated coin with scuffing or rubbing, actually probably AU; there were choice coins; there were choice plus coins; gem coins were offered here and there; as were super gem coins; and on and on.

Soon, dealers and collectors took matters into their own hands, and by the mid-1970s it was not unusual to see coins graded as MS-61, MS-62, MS-63, MS-64, MS-65, MS-66, MS-67, MS-68, MS-69, and MS-70, sometimes with one or two pluses added or one or two minuses, as MS-63++. If this seems improbable to present day readers, all you need to do is to secure a copy of *Coin World* or *Numismatic News* from the mid-1970s and see for yourself.

## THE ANA GRADING SYSTEM

The American Numismatic Association decided to get into the grading game. It set up a Grading Committee, and in 1977 published *The Official ANA Grading Standards for United States Coins*, largely supervised by dealer Abe Kosoff, and compiled by Kenneth E. Bressett, of Whitman Publishing Company, editor of the *Guide Book of United States Coins* and successor to Richard S. Yeoman. I wrote the general introductory material. At first, the ANA Grading system mirrored the Sheldon system, more or less, but in successive editions intermediate grades were added, such as MS-60, MS-63, MS-65, MS-67, and MS-70, then the full range of Mint State possibilities.

The following is the ANA Official Grading System:[1]

### OFFICIAL ANA GRADING STANDARDS
#### Morgan Dollars 1878–1921

**MINT STATE—Absolutely no trace of wear.**

**MS-70 Uncirculated:** A flawless coin exactly as it was minted, with no trace of wear or injury. Must have full mint luster and brilliant or light toning.

**MS-67 Uncirculated:** Virtually flawless, but with very minor imperfections.

**MS-65 Uncirculated:** No trace of wear; nearly as perfect as MS-67 except for a few additional, minute bagmarks or surface mars. Has full mint luster but may be unevenly toned. Any unusual striking traits must be described.

**MS-63 Uncirculated:** A Mint State coin with attractive mint luster, but noticeable detracting contact marks or minor blemishes.

**MS-60 Uncirculated:** A strictly Uncirculated coin with no trace of wear, but with bag marks and other abrasions more obvious than for MS-63. May have a few small rim mars and weakly struck spots. Has full mint luster but may lack brilliance, and surface may be spotted or heavily toned.

MS-65                    MS-60

Circulation-strike silver dollars were all placed in mint bags of 1,000 coins. Subsequent handling of bags caused bagmarks and abrasions on virtually all coins, which should not be confused with circulation wear. Full mint luster and lack of any wear are necessary to distinguish MS-60 from AU-58.

**ABOUT UNCIRCULATED—Small trace of wear is visible on highest points.**

**AU-58 Very choice:** Has some signs of wear: hair above eye and ear, edges of cotton leaves and bolls, high upper fold of cap; high points of eagle's breast and tops of legs. Weakly struck spots are common and should not be confused with actual wear.

**AU-55 Choice:** *Obverse:* Slight trace of wear shows on hair above ear, eye, edges of cotton, leaves, and high upper fold of cap. Luster fading from cheek. *Reverse:* Slight trace of wear shows on breast, tops of legs, and talons. Most of the mint luster is still present, although marred by light bagmarks and surface abrasions.

**AU-50 Typical:** *Obverse:* Traces of wear show on hair above eye, ear, edges of cotton leaves, and high upper fold of cap. Partial detail is visible on tops of cotton bolls. Luster is gone from cheek. *Reverse:* There are traces of wear on breast, tops of legs, wing tips, and talons. *Surface:* Three-quarters of the mint luster is still present. Surface abrasions and bagmarks are more noticeable than for AU-55.

**EXTREMELY FINE—Very light wear on only the highest points.**

**EF-45 Choice:** *Obverse:* Slight wear on hair above date, forehead, and ear. Lines in hair are well detailed and sharp. Slight flat spots are on edges of cotton leaves. There are minute signs of wear on cheek. *Reverse:* High points of breast are lightly worn. Tops of legs and right wing tip show wear. Talons are slightly flat. Half of the mint luster is still present.

**EF-40 Typical:** *Obverse:* Wear shows on hair above date, forehead, and ear. Lines in hair well detailed. Flat spots are visible on edges of cotton leaves. Cheek is lightly worn. *Reverse:* Almost all feathers gone from breast. Tops of legs, wing tips, and feathers on head show wear. Talons are flat. *Surface:* Partial mint luster is visible.

| AU-50 | EF-40 | VF-20 |

**VERY FINE—Light to moderate even wear. All major features are sharp.**

**VF-30 Choice:** *Obverse:* Wear shows on high points of hair from forehead to ear. Some strands visible in hair above ear. There are smooth areas on cotton leaves and strands visible in hair above ear. There are smooth areas on cotton leaves and at top of cotton bolls. *Reverse:* Wear shows on leaves of wreath and tips of wings. Only a few feathers are visible on breast and head, but they show clearly on right wing.

**VF-20 Typical:** *Obverse:* Smooth spots visible on hair from forehead to ear. Cotton leaves heavily worn but separated. Wheat grains show wear. *Reverse:* Some leaves on wreath are well worn. Breast is smooth, and only a few feathers show on head. Tips of wings are weak but lines are complete.

**FINE—Moderate to heavy even wear. Entire design is clear and bold.**

**F-12:** *Obverse:* Hairline along face is clearly defined. Lower two cotton leaves smooth but distinct from cap. Some wheat grains merge. Cotton bolls are flat but the two lines in each show clearly. *Reverse:* One-quarter of eagle's right wing and edge of left wing are smooth. Head, neck, and breast are flat and merge. Tail feathers are slightly worn. Top leaves in wreath show heavy wear.

**VERY GOOD—Well worn. Design is clear but flat and lacking details.**

**VG-8:** *Obverse:* Most details in hair are worn smooth. All letters and date are clear. Cotton bolls are flat, and leaves merge in spots. *Reverse:* One-half of eagle's right wing and one-third of left wing are smooth. All leaves in wreath are worn. Rim is complete.

**GOOD—Heavily worn. Design and legend are visible but faint in spots.**

**G-4:** *Obverse:* Hair is well worn with very little detail remaining. Date, letters, and design clearly outlined. Rim is full. *Reverse:* Eagle is worn nearly flat but is completely outlined. Design elements are smooth but visible. Legend is all visible; rim is full.

**ABOUT GOOD—Outlined design. Parts of date and legend are worn smooth.**

| F-12 | VG-8 | G-4 |

**AG-3:** *Obverse:* Head is outlined with nearly all details worn away. Date is readable but worn. Legend merges into rim. *Reverse:* Entire design partially worn away. Rim merges into legend.

## NOTES AND COMMENTS (ANA GRADING)

Portions of the design are often weakly struck, especially on the hair above the ear and on the eagle's breast for dollars from 1878 to 1904.

A flat-breast eagle reverse design was used for 1878-S, CC and some 1878, 1879-S and 1880-CC issues. These tend to show more breast feathers in each grade than the round-breast eagle design.

New Orleans issues are often found weakly struck, particularly above the ear on the obverse and the eagle's breast on the reverse. Dates most prone to such weakness are 1887 to 1897.

The three 1921 issues, particularly the 1921-S, are often softly struck on the eagle's breast feathers and lower wreath on the reverse.

Some of these dollars have a prooflike surface. (This should be mentioned in any description of such pieces, but the coins should be graded independently of their prooflike quality.) The following test is commonly accepted to determine this quality in such pieces: Place the coin upright at the end of a clearly printed ruler. If the printed lines are observably reflected at a distance of 1" to 2", the surface is called *semi-prooflike*. At 2" to 4" it is termed *prooflike*. Beyond 4" is *deep mirror prooflike*.

The prime focal areas are as follows: on the obverse, the face, neck, and field in front of Liberty; on the reverse, the eagle's body and wings, and the fields to either side of and above the eagle.

Secondary focal areas are as follows: on the obverse, the cap and field behind Liberty's head, and the date and field to right; on the reverse, the legend and denomination, and the outer periphery.

## DETAILS FOR MS-60 TO 70 (ANA GRADING)

**MS-70**—*Contact marks:* None show under magnification. *Hairlines:* None show under magnification *Luster:* Very attractive. Fully original. *Eye appeal:* Outstanding.

**MS-69**—*Contact marks:* One or two minuscule, none in prime focal areas. *Hairlines:* None visible. *Luster:* Very attractive. Fully original. *Eye appeal:* Exceptional.

**MS-68**—*Contact marks:* Three or four minuscule, none in prime focal areas. *Hairlines:* None visible. *Luster:* Attractive. Fully original. *Eye appeal:* Exceptional.

**MS-67**—*Contact marks:* Three or four minuscule, one or two may be in prime focal areas. *Hairlines:* None visible without magnification. *Luster:* Above average. Fully original. *Eye appeal:* Exceptional.

**MS-66**—*Contact marks:* Several small, a few in prime focal areas. *Hairlines:* None visible without magnification. *Luster:* Above average. Fully original. *Eye appeal:* Above average.

**MS-65**—*Contact marks:* Light and scattered without major distracting marks in prime focal areas. *Hairlines:* May have a few scattered. *Luster:* Fully original. *Eye appeal:* Very pleasing.

**MS-64**—*Contact marks:* May have light scattered marks, a few may be in prime focal areas. *Hairlines:* May have a few scattered or small patch in secondary areas. *Luster:* Average. Full original. *Eye appeal:* Pleasing.

**MS-63**—*Contact marks:* May have distracting marks in prime focal areas. *Hairlines:* May have a few scattered or small patch. *Luster:* May be original or slightly impaired. *Eye appeal:* Rather attractive.

**MS-62**—*Contact marks:* May have distracting marks in prime focal and/or secondary areas. *Hairlines:* May have a few scattered to noticeable patch. *Luster:* May be original or impaired. *Eye appeal:* Generally acceptable.

**MS-61**—*Contact marks:* May have a few heavy marks (or numerous light) in prime focal or secondary areas. *Hairlines:* May have noticeable patch or hairlining over surfaces. *Luster:* May be original or impaired. *Eye appeal:* Unattractive.

**MS-60**—*Contact marks:* May have heavy marks in all areas. *Hairlines:* May have noticeable patch or continuous hairlining throughout. *Luster:* May be original or impaired. *Eye appeal:* Poor.

## GRADING CERTIFICATION SERVICES

In 1986 David Hall and several associates banded together the Professional Coin Grading Service, whereby anyone could submit United States coins to PCGS and, for a fee, get the opinion of the graders on the staff. The coin was then hermetically sealed in a plastic holder, permitting both sides to be seen, and containing a label with a specific grade, such as MS-63 or whatever.

Soon thereafter, in 1987, John Albanese formed the Numismatic Guaranty Corporation of America (NGC).

Today, PCGS is a division of Collectors Universe, and is located in Santa Ana, California (mailing address in Newport Beach); NGC is owned by Mark Salzberg and associates, with David Lange as chief numismatist, and is located in Sarasota, Florida.

Several other commercial services have seen success, but few issue population reports, and they are not studied here. With permission, the data compiled by market leaders PCGS and NGC have been compiled herein.

## BEYOND THE NUMBERS

Since 1970 James F. Ruddy's *Photograde* guide, illustrating circulated pieces, has been a great aid, indeed the first such pictorial reference. The ANA Grading Standards are also fine and quite useful for circulated grades. A recent addition to the literature is *Grading Coins by Photographs*, now in its second edition.

However, in the Mint State category one runs into difficulty, as no one wants to count bagmarks and nicks on a silver dollar, and if you did, how could you determine whether 173 medium size bagmarks were better or worse than 27 large ones? There are so many variables that it boggles the mind.

In order to be scientific, a grading system should be capable of precise definition. Then, with specifications at hand, two intelligent numismatists, widely separated and not in consultation with anyone else, should be able to replicate the findings, and each come up with MS-61, or MS-64, or whatever. If one person in Hailey, Idaho, comes up with MS-61, and another using the same standards in Vero Beach, Florida, grades the same coin at MS-63, or even MS-62, then the standards are not scientific.

## MORGAN DOLLAR VARIABLES

For the typical Morgan dollar, the obverse, with the cheek of Miss Liberty in high relief and exposed to contact, tends to be graded a point or two less, if evaluated separately, than does the reverse. The reverse has many elements to protect the field, and no single smooth, high area to showcase bagmarks.

Further in the Morgan dollar series, the surface of a coin can accentuate or hide the presence of bagmarks. A prooflike coin or, even more dramatic, a deep mirror prooflike (DMPL) coin, can look as ugly as sin if it is peppered with bagmarks, although it might be in the same technical grade (say, MS-63) as a lustrous, frosty Morgan dollar, which can have excellent eye appeal and be well worth owning.

Complicating matters still further is that in the absence of precise scientific standards on which all agree, the subject of evaluating coins is left to interpretation, or indeed in some instances to the imagination. Further, over a period of time, the interpretations have "stretched," and it is my opinion and that of many others that in numerous instances what used to be MS-65 years ago is MS-66 or MS-67 today, for some coins.

This escalation of grades has resulted in a situation such that today, in the early 21st century, there are many Morgan dollars graded on the long side of MS-65, such as MS-66, MS-67, or MS-68. Recall my earlier comment that in population reports of the grading services years ago in 1990, such pieces were few and far between.

## REALITY CHECK

Back in 1976, which is ancient history for many present-day collectors of Morgan dollars, Wayne Miller wrote this in *An Analysis of Morgan and Peace Dollars:*

> The flaw in all grading systems is this: After one has assigned a numerical rating to a coin, embellished it with the grandest adjectives, or compared it (always favorably) to other specimens of the same date, THE COIN IS STILL WHAT IT IS. Even the beginning collector will not accept a gem rating for a coin which is poorly struck, heavily abraded, or lackluster. Eventually the coin must be judged by its own merits . . .
>
> No grading system, however inclusive in detail or excellent in design, should ever be substituted for common sense, or utilized as a crutch to avoid the seeking out of all the information necessary to learn how to grade coins accurately. NO GRADING SYSTEM WILL BE RELEVANT TO A PERSON UNTIL HE ACQUIRES SOME VERY BASIC DATA AND SKILLS.

These words are just as true today as they were when written a generation or so ago. And yet, most buyers indeed grasp for crutches, and cannot exist without them, such crutches being the grades applied by others, however well intentioned.

## CROSSOVERS AND UPGRADES

Per the comments of Wayne Miller, a coin is what it is. If a coin is in a certified holder marked "MS-65," I as a long-term dealer may look at it and think it is only MS-63 or MS-64, or I might think it's undergraded and is MS-66. Who knows?

However, I do know that if you take 100 specimens of a given Morgan dollar variety— say, an 1883-O in MS-63, certified—and place a piece of masking tape over the grade indications on their holders, and pass them around among the leading dealers and graders in the country, opinions will vary all over the place. There is absolutely no way that everyone will agree that each coin is MS-63.

As I have mentioned in my writing in *Coin World* and in books, perhaps the most dramatic indication of varying opinion is the symposium conducted by Barry Cutler, at the time legal counsel for the Federal Trade Commission. At a forum he held at an American Numismatic Association Convention he addressed the audience on the subject of certified coins and wide variations in grading, even among recognized experts. He stated that as a test he took a particular coin—it happened to be a 1908 double eagle—and showed it individually to nearly a dozen different people who earned their livelihood by grading coins as employees of grading services. The expert opinions of this particular coin ranged all the way from AU-58 to MS-64.

Another thought-provoking episode occurred a few years ago at my office in New Hampshire. On a particular day a number of America's biggest names in rare coin dealing were on hand to inspect rarities in a tremendously important upcoming auction. As it happened, Dr. Richard A. Bagg had on hand a large group of certified double eagles as part of a consignment sent in for a future sale. He picked out one each, certified as MS-60, MS-61, MS-62, MS-63, MS-64, and MS-65, put a piece of masking tape over the grade indications, and labeled them in no particular order from A through F. He then passed them around to the dealers, with a sheet of paper, asking them for the grade evaluation of each. At the same time, Beth Piper, a long-term staff numismatist, but not at all a dealer in the buying and selling sense, asked if she could try her hand at guessing as well.

When the tape was removed and the results were compared, it was Beth who came closest to the grades marked on the holders, although no one, including Beth, got them all "right."

Certifying a coin as MS-63, or MS-64, or MS–anything else, does not mean that I will personally agree with that certification, that you will, or that another given numismatist will. Grading was, is, and always will be a matter of opinion.

This brings me to the subject of "upgrades." With grading being an art, not a science, and opinions varying, it is often the situation that a coin can be resubmitted to the grading service that graded it in the first place, or sent to another grading service, and receive a higher label on the holder when it is reinspected.

Take, for example, a hypothetical Morgan dollar rarity that is worth $2,500 in MS-64 grade and $5,000 in MS-65 grade. Also suppose that the cost to have the coin certified is $20. It seems obvious that if your coin is labeled MS-64 and worth $2,500, it is a good gamble to send it in once, twice, or even 10 times at $20 per shot, to see if sometime along the way it gets upgraded to MS-65!

Recently, an astute numismatist, a Harvard physicist by education, expressed amazement at this: in order to generate fee-generating behavior by owners of already-certified coins, some services will evaluate them for an upgrade without requiring that they be removed from their holders, eliminating the risk of—perish the thought—downgrades.

# Advice to the Serious Collector (You!)
## The Search for Quality

Most if not all of the pricing sources for Morgan silver dollars—coin papers, the Internet, market guides, auction listings, and the like—simply give basic information such as date, mintmark, and a grading number. Nothing more. True, for a particularly elusive issue, such as an 1889-CC in, say, MS-64 grade, a cataloger may wax poetic and regale the prospective purchaser with a paragraph or two of prose. Scarce dates and rarities always command attention, and deservedly so.

However, beyond date, mint, and grade, the aware, intelligent buyer can find more, *much* more. Throughout the course of the pursuit of numismatics in America, the greatest collections have been obtained by numismatists who have carefully considered each coin acquired, not only its grade and price, but, beyond that, aspects of *quality*. For a Morgan silver dollar, there are multiple aspects of quality, and the connoisseur will wish to consider each one.

## A Tale of Two Coins

Some varieties of Morgan silver dollars are usually seen with every detail sharply defined, even under magnification. The 1881-S is a good example. The majority show excellent definition of the strands of Miss Liberty's hair at the center of the coin, above the ear, and, on the reverse, the feathers of the eagle's breast—these two points, obverse and reverse, being the areas that for some issues are weakly struck or even flat. Further, examination of a typical 1881-S will reveal good detail in the dentils (toothlike projections around both borders), the edges of letters, the leaves in the wreath on the reverse, and other aspects.

In contrast, the 1891-O Morgan dollar, perhaps the most casually or sloppily struck of all issues, is often seen flat at the center, with little detail in Miss Liberty's hair above the ear, and with many breast feathers obliterated.

Using these two examples, it is seen that when you seek an 1881-S silver dollar, while it pays to be particular, the quest will not be difficult. Given the opportunity to view a dozen MS-65 examples, chances are that nearly all would be satisfactory to own.

Not so for the 1891-O, as you might imagine. First of all, finding a dozen pieces together at one time would be difficult, as this issue is considerably scarcer than the 1881-S, and the pieces are widely scattered. It pays to be fussy, to be a cherrypicker (a term popularized by Bill Fivaz and J.T. Stanton). Certification holders are of no help. An 1891-O dollar described as MS-63 (PCGS) or MS-65 (NGC) or MS-62 (ANACS) gives no indication at all as to whether the piece is as flat as a pancake, or whether, marvelously and exceptionally, it possesses great detail.

Moreover, the typical seller of Morgan dollars could care less, and little or no effort is made to address the aspect of sharpness, simply because 99% of the buyers out there don't care!

My hope is that you will be in the 1% who *do* care. The beauty part is that in the absence of information in the marketplace, cherrypicking can yield coins that are head and shoulders above what other people are acquiring for their collections, often for the same prices you are paying for quality.

When the time comes to sell your collection, a display of carefully chosen, sharp, and attractive Morgan dollars will be worth a special presentation and auction catalog, and if past is prologue, the prices you receive will be significant premiums above what others will get for ordinary pieces.

## Evaluating Sharpness

To evaluate sharpness, the first thing is to check my remarks in this category under each date and mint in the appropriate pages of this book, to see whether the quest will be simple or arduous. That done, you are forewarned, and if you are ordering coins by mail, not examining them prior to purchase, it becomes a simple matter to say, "Send me the 1891-O only if the hair strands on the obverse and the eagle feathers on the reverse are sharp." Of course, your order might be canceled forthwith! Some dealers do not want customers who are too informed! Eventually, however, you will find a nice one.

Over the course of time the basic hub dies for the Morgan dollar were changed several times. The reverse was altered in 1900, and what Van Allen and Mallis and many others call the C4 reverse, in standard use after that time (but with some earlier hubs employed on occasion), does not have the eagle feathers as sharp as on earlier dates. The feathers are there, to be sure, but are not crisply defined *in the die*. Accordingly, a slightly different mindset must be adopted when purchasing Morgan dollars of the 1900 through 1904 years.

In 1921 entirely new hubs were made up for the Morgan dollar, in somewhat shallow relief, and lacking much detail. The result is that the typical 1921, 1921-D, or 1921-S Morgan dollar is apt to be rather "flat" in appearance, not at all with the almost three-dimensional effect of earlier issue. Again, the characteristics can be studied, and within the context of the 1921 Morgan dollar nice examples can be obtained.

## DIFFERENT MINTS, DIFFERENT SHARPNESSES

During the early span of Morgan dollar mintage, 1878 through 1904, production took place at the Philadelphia, Carson City, New Orleans, and San Francisco mints. In their time Morgan dollars were used in circulation mostly in the American West, rarely in the Midwest or East, but sometimes in the South. To reiterate a comment made earlier, the study of Morgan silver dollars reveals that as a handy rule of thumb, pieces struck at Carson City and at San Francisco are much sharper than those made at New Orleans, and often sharper than those made at Philadelphia. The vast majority of New Orleans dollars were minted, run through a counting machine, tossed into bags, and stored, per the minting and storage descriptions given earlier. One might imagine that the workmen at Carson City and San Francisco, knowing that many (but hardly most) of their coins would be going into circulation, had justifiable pride in what they did, while those in New Orleans could not have cared less. Of course, this is conjecture, but the New Orleans pieces do present the greatest challenge in the search for sharp pieces. Philadelphia coins vary.

While general rules can be stated for sharpness of a particular issue, such as the typical 1881-S being well detailed and the typical 1891-O having areas of flatness, in practice the obverse and reverse of each variety should be studied separately. Also, for a given specimen there can be weakness on the hair strands at the center of the obverse, but very sharply defined eagle feathers on the reverse. Look at the obverse first, and if it passes muster, then look at the reverse. Usually, when only one side is lightly struck, that side is the obverse.

## ASPECTS OF LUSTER

The surface quality of Morgan dollars varies widely, from deeply lustrous and frosty with lots of almost three-dimensional "flash," to dull, insipid, and lifeless. The quality and depth of the luster depends upon several considerations.

If a die is normally finished and placed in a press, and pieces carefully struck from it, the early impressions are apt to be very frosty. However, as a given die pair continued in use, and tens of thousands were struck, or even more, the surfaces tended to become grainy and dull. Sometimes they were given new life by relapping, but often they were simply allowed to be used and used some more, turning out coins that are not numismatically appealing. The number of coins struck from a die pair depended on circumstances. The entire issue of the 1893-S dollar, 100,000 pieces, was struck from a single pair. Those made early in the production run are more attractive than those made later, although for this particular issue, a rarity in Mint State, there is little opportunity to view multiple pieces at the same time.

## Semi-Prooflike to DMPL

As noted earlier, during the basining process some dies were sufficiently polished that they quite resembled full Proofs. These are called deep mirror prooflike (DMPL) by the grading services today. Other dies are slightly prooflike, a combination of luster and mirror qualities. Different terminologies, not standardized, range from semi-prooflike, to prooflike, to deep prooflike, to deep mirror prooflike, sometimes with the word *cameo* added to denote frosty motifs and inscriptions against the fields.

As dies were prepared separately, it is often the instance that an obverse die would be prooflike, even DMPL, while the reverse die would be only partially prooflike or even deeply lustrous; in other words, of a completely different quality. Or, the reverse may be mirrorlike, and the obverse frosty.

Although at the outset a prooflike Morgan dollar would seem to be a very desirable item—better than one that is frosty—and a DMPL piece might seem to possess a heavenly aspect of desirability, in practice this is not always the case.

Sometimes the mirror surface is not particularly attractive or is dull, and other times the contrast with the lettering and devices is not sharp. If the devices are deeply lustrous and frosty, set against DMPL fields, then a great coin is on hand, if it is in high grade and shows few if any bagmarks. This is the catch, as prooflike coins serve to emphasize contact marks, and if a DMPL piece was jostled about in a bag in storage it might receive so many marks as to be almost disfigured, while the same number of marks on a frosty-surface coin would be largely hidden and not particularly noticeable today.

The search for DMPL coins of *quality* is especially important, as, at least to my way of thinking, a DMPL coin in, say, MS-62 grade is apt to have so many marks that it can be as ugly as a toad. In such an instance I would much rather own a regular MS-62 with a frosty surface. You can be the judge, as always, as you are the buyer.

To revivify dies that had developed graininess or stress marks, they were sometimes rebasined (*relapped* is another term), imparting a prooflike surface to them, or, in other instances, restoring the luster. However, worn details, such as edge dentils, were not made sharp.

## Brilliant Coins, Toned Coins

Silver alloy is chemically active, and just about any silver coin in existence in numismatic hands, including any and all Proof coins from the 19th century, tended to acquire natural toning, often quite attractive. There is no such thing, to my knowledge, as a fully brilliant or "bright" 19th-century Proof coin, the brilliance including all aspects of the obverse and reverse as well as the edge. Such coins have been dipped to remove the toning.

However, scarcely ever is a coin described as "1889 Morgan dollar, Proof-67 fully brilliant, full 'white,' dipped to remove toning." Instead, you might see (with some hyperbole added), "1889 Morgan dollar, amazing super-gem full 'white' and brilliant.

Awesome!" Incidentally, while expertly dipping a coin once or twice might be okay (see details in the *Photograde* book), repeated dipping will dull the surface. Ugh!

On the other hand, Morgan silver dollars struck for circulation, and placed in bags of 1,000 coins each, and stored, when opened years later (such as in the 1960s) indeed yielded pristine, brilliant, frosty pieces—full original brightness and luster, including on the edges—an exception to the rule. No such counterparts of coins with full original brightness exist among Barber or Liberty Seated dimes, quarters, and half dollars of the Morgan dollar era, as these were never part of hoards. Any fully brilliant Liberty Seated or Barber coin has been dipped or treated sometime in its career. This is not necessarily undesirable if done professionally, as noted above. Indeed, now in the early 21st century, several people offer worthwhile conservation (their term) services.

That said, it is often the case that brilliant Morgan dollars taken from bags have a few spots, or areas of dullness, or even milky white spots caused from dampness. It is a normal and acceptable procedure to carefully "dip" such a coin to restore its brilliance, but with the caveat that if this is done repeatedly, a coin will become dull and unattractive. Indeed, in many series other than Morgan dollars, the repeated dipping of, say, Proof Barber half dollars by succeeding generations of numismatists, has spoiled many otherwise beautiful pieces. The nicest of all Liberty Seated and Barber dimes, quarters, and half dollars are those that were preserved in cabinets decades ago, and not touched by their owners, such as from the Garrett and Clapp (Eliasberg) holdings dating from the 19th century. On the other hand, other coins in numismatic hands have been cleaned repeatedly, including those in the Mint Cabinet. Not even careful conservation can restore a deep mirror surface to a Proof that has been etched by repeated dipping, or to a once-lustrous Mint State coin that has been cleaned repeatedly.

## A Deadly "Misadventure" in Coin Cleaning

Years ago most popular numismatic periodicals carried advertisements for products, some employing acids or abrasives, for making coins brilliant and thus "more valuable."

Perhaps the last words (pun intended) on coin cleaning are these from the August 1921 issue of *The Numismatist*:

> J. Sanford Saltus, an international figure in the numismatic world, died suddenly at the Hotel Metropole, in London, on June 24. . . . His body was discovered lying on the floor, fully dressed, by one of the hotel maids. . . .
>
> A verdict of "death by misadventure" was rendered by the coroner's jury. The evidence at the inquest disclosed the fact that on the day before his death he had purchased a small quantity of potassium cyanide for the purpose of cleaning some recent purchases of silver coins, and retired to his room. Shortly afterward he ordered a bottle of ginger ale.
>
> A glass containing the poison and a glass containing the ginger ale were found side by side on the dressing table, and it is believed that while interested in cleaning the coins he took a drink of the poison in mistake for the ginger ale. Potassium cyanide, although one of the most deadly poisons, is frequently used by collectors in cleaning coins, as it will have the desired effect when other methods fail.

Potassium cyanide was used by collectors (as Saltus) and dealers alike to make dull coins "brilliant" and to remove tiny hairlines and scratches, by etching away a few microns of the metal surface.

## NATURAL OR "ORIGINAL" TONING

Atmospheric contact with Morgan silver dollars as well as surface contact by other materials, such as cloth in a bag or cardboard in a coin holder, will in time impart a toning, sometimes objectionably called tarnish, to a coin's surface. Particularly beautiful are pieces that were stored in the 1930s onward in "National" and related albums, consisting of cardboard panels faced on the front and back by clear slides. The sulfur in the cardboard acted on the coins, from the edges inward, giving them a rainbow or "halo" toning, sometimes encompassing a palette of beautiful and vibrant colors. Many Morgan dollars kept in bags had part of the coin touching the cloth exterior, which imparted toning, particularly if the cloth became damp, while other parts of the coin were partially overlapped by other pieces in the bag. Such coins can have a just one area toned, sometimes a rainbow color, while other areas are brilliant. Still other Morgan dollars can be splotchy, stained, or otherwise unattractive.

The preceding types of coloration are what might be called natural toning in numismatic circles, never mind that coin albums may or may not be "natural." A number of years ago I had a dollar-sized silver medal, freshly minted, and of no particular rarity, which I casually put in the top drawer of a newly acquired oak table. The piece was forgotten, and a few years later I looked at it, and the reverse had the most gorgeous delicate electric blue toning I have ever seen! The obverse, face up in the drawer, had very light toning, also attractive. Whether this toning should be called natural, or not, is left up to the imagination.

However, toning acquired deliberately and quickly, by chemical means, is generally referred to as artificial toning. If *detected*, artificial toning is considered to be undesirable. The methods of toning coins artificially have been mentioned here and there in numismatic articles, on the Internet, and elsewhere, and include coloring with chemicals, "cooking" pieces in a frying pan, coloring them with iodine or other fumes, and so on. One enterprising collector acquired a bunch of old albums, put coins in them, and successfully accelerated the "natural" toning process by heating the holders—again, you can be the judge as to whether such toning is natural or artificial.

Discussions of toning are the numismatic equivalent of how many angels can dance on the head of a pin—there are no particular right or wrong answers, no generally agreed upon conclusion as to when natural toning ends and artificial toning begins. However, I can say that wizards with chemistry can do wonders with coins, and turn out absolutely gorgeous pieces. Some such artists are called coin doctors, in a derisive context.

# PROOF MORGAN DOLLARS

## PROOFS FOR COLLECTORS

Each year at the Philadelphia Mint, 1878 through 1904, Proof strikings were made for sale to collectors and other interested buyers. A few additional Proofs may have been made in 1878 for ceremonial purposes. In each instance, Proofs were sold as part of silver coin sets, the contents of which varied according to the other denominations being made at the time.

An 1878 silver Proof set contained a dime, twenty-cent piece, quarter dollar, half dollar, silver dollar, and trade dollar. A 1904 silver Proof set contained a dime, quarter dollar, half dollar, and silver dollar.

No record has been found of Proofs' having been deliberately struck at Philadelphia in 1921, although it is believed that a few may have been made to the order of local dealer Henry Chapman, these being called Chapman Proofs today. Indeed, in 1921, Chapman advertised Proofs in *The Numismatist*. In addition, some pieces with slight prooflike surfaces, struck from dies with many minute striations, have been marketed as Zerbe Proofs, but it is unlikely that such were made as Proofs, as they are not deeply mirrorlike, and Farran Zerbe, a leading numismatist of the era, would hardly have accepted them as such. Indeed, during the preparation of this book, several experts agreed; one, Saul Teichman, stated that the "Zerbe Proof" nomenclature is probably from the imagination of the late Walter Breen,[2] who was fond of creating historical scenarios, often with fascinating details, when facts were scarce.

Proofs were struck from deeply polished dies, at slow speed on a special press, using specially prepared planchets. Most are cameos with frosted designs and lettering set against the mirrored field, but all of 1902 to 1904 were made from dies in which the portrait of Miss Liberty was polished in the die—perhaps by an employee unfamiliar with the process. In any event, such pieces lack contrast.

The striking of Proof coins was supposed to be needle-sharp, for such coins were sold at a premium and represented the finest impressions of their kind. However, some were made with the dies spaced slightly too far apart, showing some flatness near Miss Liberty's ear and on the eagle's breast. The individual Proof listings year by year in this book explain such variables.

## BRANCH-MINT PROOFS

Were any Proof coins ever struck at the branch mints? Wayne Miller may have said it all, or most of it anyway, in 1982 in his highly important study, *The Morgan and Peace Dollar Textbook*: "Of all the specialized areas of numismatics none is more rife with misinformation, speculation, hyperbole, controversy, etc., than branch mint Proof Morgan dollars."[3]

Basically, this question is posed: If a branch mint Morgan dollar has fully deep mirrorlike fields, excellent contrast against frosty or satiny devices, and a reasonably decent rim (not nicked or showing mishandling), is it a Proof?

The answer is that although ever since the 1880s some branch mint dollars have been called Proofs, the writer is unaware of any original documentation supporting the specific striking of Proofs. Again, from Miller: "The most extensive discussion thus far . . . is in Walter Breen's book on Proof coinage. Breen discusses the possibility of no fewer than 12 different dates of branch mint Proof Morgans. He also provides detailed information regarding the events which occasioned their striking; estimates of total mintages; locations of known specimens; etc. However, much of Breen's information is based on conjecture. . . . Of the specimens which he himself has examined, none are described in detail."[4]

And yet we are all fans of branch mint Morgan dollars that to the eye appear every bit as nice as a Philadelphia Mint Proof!

The problem lies with the fact that many different date and mintmark varieties were struck with deep mirror prooflike (DMPL) surfaces in the ordinary course of business, simply because highly polished dies were employed to strike them.

In the absence of facts, many have elected to designate branch mint coins with Proof characteristics as specimen strikings or simply as DMPL. However, the certification services have labeled a few as Proofs. Are they Proofs? Aren't they? I leave you with these questions to ponder.

# IN THE MARKETPLACE: BUYING MORGAN DOLLARS
## GETTING STARTED

Few people reading this book will have unlimited budgets so as to be seriously interested in collecting one of each date and mintmark in superb gem grade. Even past cabinets such as the Bodway, Lee, Miller, and other memorable holdings, or the finest-of-the-fine set that went on tour through the efforts of PCGS, could hardly be replicated today— regardless of the amount of money on hand to spend. Some pieces simply are not available, at least not in a combination of high grade, sharp strike, and attractive luster.

You do not have to formulate a plan immediately. Take your time. Read. Contemplate. Ask around. Think. And then buy.

Although it might defy logic, it is a fact of life that most people, myself included, buy something first, then learn about it second, especially when entering a new field of endeavor. No doubt most specialists in large copper cents of 1793 through 1814 bought one or two at first, became fascinated with them, then endeavored to learn more. Same for specialists in double eagles or commemoratives, or any other series. Harry W. Bass Jr., the greatest student of gold coin varieties the numismatic field has ever known, knew nothing about technicalities when he first started. And, there was a time that J. Hewitt Judd did not know much about pattern coins, although he probably owned a few.

Buying coins and appreciating their history and characteristics go hand in hand. I doubt if there is a single owner of this book who will read it from cover to cover, and then go out to buy his or her *first* Morgan dollar!

While buying something expensive without knowing the details can prove to be a mistake later, in the Morgan silver dollars of 1878 through 1921, this risk is minimized. I suggest that to get your feet wet you indeed buy a handful of Morgan dollars—take your pick of dates and mints—but in each instance acquire pieces that are sharply struck and with nice luster, so they will not need to be upgraded later. Ideal candidates include several varieties of the first year of issue, 1878, among which can be found very interesting feather details; a gem 1881-S (easy enough to find); a lovely MS-63 to MS-65 (depending upon your budget) 1903-O; and one of the three varieties of the 1921, the last date from dies quite different from those used earlier.

Along the way, start to learn more about Morgan dollars. Or, add to the learning you already have.

## SETTING GOALS BY FORMULA

With so many Mint State Morgan dollars in the marketplace, if you become enchanted with the series it would be a mistake not to buy as many nice Mint State coins as you can afford, as there is a great satisfaction in ownership. Granted, a well-worn VG-8 or even a VF-20 1881-S silver dollar costs very little. However, as there are well over a million Mint State 1881-S dollars in existence, of which tens of thousands are gems, and as the price is quite low, it makes sense to buy a gem.

Over a period of time I have made the following suggestion, which has had merit to more than just a few people:

If you have several tens of thousands of dollars to spend on your Morgan dollar set, then begin buying as many different gem (MS-65) pieces as you can, up to a certain value per coin, say, $1,000. This will give you a large array of different dates and mint-marks. Many coins will cost you far less, just a fraction of $1,000. Then, beyond that, for the dates and mints you are missing, buy every MS-64 you can up to a price of $1,000. Again, many will cost far less. The $1,000 figure is simply the maximum. Then every MS-63 to fill in remaining dates, as far as you can at the $1,000 level. By the latter time you will be down to relatively few pieces that you need. Then, one by one, you can review their availability and prices—such as the 1889-CC, the 1893-S, and the Proof-only 1895, and select what grades you would like to acquire. Perhaps the mintmark varieties could be obtained in VF or EF grade, while the 1895 could be acquired in Proof-63, the last being priced into five figures, but desirable as a key to the series.

I rather imagine that the preceding $1,000 entry level will reflect more than a typical reader would like to spend, so the alternative is attractive and easy: lower the threshold. Pick a figure per coin, such as $200, $300, or $500. Also, be flexible as to Mint State grade, and pick pieces that range from MS-63 to MS-65. If desired, stick strictly to MS-63, at which level for just $200 per coin quite a few varieties can be obtained.

Along the way, cherrypick for quality, a situation just as important for an MS-63 as for MS-64 or MS-65.

The object is that no matter what your budget, your collection will have a nice spread of Mint State coins, including all of the more readily available varieties.

## TAKE YOUR TIME

Another goal worth setting is this: pace yourself, do not rush. The book now in your hands contains much information and a goodly amount of advice as to the challenges involved and how to go about facing them, conquering them one by one. You will find that some dates and mints are as common as can be, with mintages over 10,000,000, and priced very low in the market, but that the typical piece is apt to be a dog—take an Uncirculated 1889 Morgan dollar as an example. Take your time for this one, and although you will be offered many, it might be that one that is "just right" does not come along for many months or even more than a year.

In the collecting of any numismatic series, it is always more enjoyable if pieces are added on a regular basis, not all at once. If you start your collection of Morgan dollars today and spend a year or two gathering it, you will enjoy it much more than if you go to a coin show this afternoon, and by this evening return with miscellaneous quality examples of 75 of the different dates and mintmarks.

## ENJOY BY LOOKING

Another goal worth setting that will cost you nothing but can multiply your enjoyment is this: as you acquire pieces, and every once in a while after you own them, study them carefully. Yogi Berra said, "You can see a lot by just looking." Perhaps a numismatic expansion of this would be "You can learn and enjoy a lot by just looking."

A low-power magnifying glass of 4x or 8x is ideal, I have found, as it will reveal such differences as date and mintmark positions, repunchings, and the like (a microscope would be overkill). Even the basic elements of the design are worth looking at carefully—the various botanical things on the head of the obverse portrait above and to the right of the word LIBERTY, the cap that Miss Liberty is wearing (a Phrygian cap, so called—the ancient Greek liberty cap of freedom, similar to that used later on the Barber silver coins of 1892), and other details.

Then there are other inconsistencies, interesting features, and the like. Why is the motto "In God we trust" in lowercase Old English letters on the reverse, when this style of lettering is used nowhere else, including in the motto E PLURIBUS UNUM? I don't know the answer, but perhaps an explanation has appeared in print somewhere. Regarding the other motto, why is it so dominant on the obverse, while on many if not all other coins it is in an inconspicuous position or is missing altogether? I bet that half of today's graduating high school seniors do not know what E PLURIBUS UNUM means.

## IN THE FOOTSTEPS OF PROFESSIONALS

The following commentary was created for this book by David M. Sundman, president of Littleton Coin Company, and a fine friend for many years. David shares my interest in numismatic history.

### Selecting Morgan Dollars for Your Collection
#### *by David M. Sundman*

Even though you are putting together a Morgan dollar collection of only about 100 different coins and are dealing with "experts," it is very important to be selective. Our numismatists annually purchase more than 200,000 Morgan dollars for our retail customers, and we are very selective—we look at our retail inventory as a collection that must be of consistent quality. Many dealers can make a one-time sale, but to achieve customer loyalty one must deliver a combination of quality and value. Indeed, Dave Bowers's own business success over many years has been based upon doing just that. The precepts he sets forth in this book are those he follows himself, and we follow them as well.

Here at Littleton Coin Company we spare no effort. To find 200,000 coins that fit our quality standards, we might examine half a million or more coins—and this is after our suppliers, often other dealers, have made their own reviews!

What are we looking for? Regardless of the date, the mintmark, or the grade on the holder, the number-one thing is "eye appeal." Ideally, the coin's surfaces should be original. Avoid coins that have been cleaned or polished (unless you really need to fill that space in a hurry, and won't mind spending money to upgrade later). For a circulated coin, you want light- to medium-gray coloration, with no major scratches. Don't forget to examine and grade the rim around the field, along with the edge—the *third* side of the coin. Rims and edges count! (Unfortunately, if a coin is in an older certified holder, the edge cannot be seen, and sometimes the rim is hard to see clearly.) Obviously, MS-60 Morgans (which are technically "new") are going to be bagmarked to varying degrees—but their eye appeal is still critical to present enjoyment and future value. Avoid dollars with heavy fingerprints, or that seem to have been hit by every other coin in the bag of a thousand along the way!

Eye appeal is even more important in the Uncirculated grades, with luster being especially desirable. Look for a coin with "life" to it. Avoid coins with a dull, washed-out look. If you like toned coins, look for transparent, light toning, where you can still see the details and surfaces clearly.

Quality of strike is also important. With lower-grade circulated coins, striking is not an issue; but it is very critical in higher circulated and all Uncirculated grades, and even more so for certain dates that are notoriously poorly struck. Certain issues (often from the New Orleans Mint) are so difficult to find well struck that you will have to compromise, unless your budget and patience are unlimited. However, even among these, by being selective you can acquire pieces that, if not optimal, will be far nicer than the average.

In short, seek coins that will please you every time you look at your collection, and that "fit" with your other coins. You don't want to keep a coin that makes your heart sink. Stay on this course, and at the end of the day, you'll have a matched collection with eye appeal. Enjoy the pursuit!

Similarly, these comments from Christine Karstedt, vice president of consignments for Stack's Bowers Galleries, may be of interest:

### The Enjoyment of Collecting Morgan Dollars
*by Christine Karstedt*

In the course of talking with friends and customers at the office, at our auctions, and at coin shows, I am often asked for my ideas on building a collection. The advice I give most often is this: collect coins for your personal enjoyment and ultimate sense of accomplishment. Do this, and everything else will fall neatly into place.

Be patient! Buy the reference books, study the series, relish the hunt. Develop an eye for quality. Collect with a purpose. Deal only with reputable people. If you follow these guidelines, you are bound to have years of personal satisfaction, and will likely assemble a beautiful and meaningful collection. When the time comes for you to sell, assuming the market is favorable and you've been careful when buying, the chances are excellent that you will realize a great financial reward. I have seen it happen many times.

# Buying Coins
## Ordering Coins by Mail

There are many ways to buy coins, and through the mail (or on the Internet with coins being sent to you by mail or other means) is one of the most important. In this way you have an opportunity to sample from the inventories of thousands of sellers across the nation, some of whom are long-time Morgan dollar specialists, and others who simply handle them casually, or as part of a more diverse business. If, in seeking a common Mint State coin such as an 1881-S, or one of the Carson City dollars from 1882 through 1884, you review advertisements in numismatic periodicals, or dealers' listings on the Internet, or review catalogs, you are apt to encounter many different opportunities.

Buying through the mail is probably the way that over a long period of years most numismatists have built their sets. Dealing with various sellers can be interesting, friendships can be formed, and receiving a package in the mail is always a delight. Also, it is fun to buy things one at a time—such as an 1878 7 Tail Feathers dollar from a dealer in Texas, an 1882-S from a seller in a coastal town in Maine, or a prooflike 1883-O from a vendor in the big-sky country of Montana, or wherever.

Although there are exceptions, most mail-order dealers offer a guarantee of satisfaction, although some deny this if a piece has been certified. Check first, and my advice would be to buy only from those who allow you to review the coin, as certification is one thing, and eye appeal, sharpness of strike, and quality of luster can be something else. Hopefully, you will be seeking quality.

## Beware of "Bargains"

Many mail-order dealers "sell to a price," and endeavor to offer what seem to be bargains. Even the leading numismatic periodicals are chock full of listings of "choice" Morgan dollars that do not come close to the ANA definition of *choice* (at least MS-63), and so on. In general, you get the quality you pay for. If you order a "gem" Morgan dollar at 60% of the market price, and later when you sell it find that it has been cleaned, or is barely MS-60, never mind MS-65, you have yourself to blame.

Bargain hunters and bottom feeders usually end up with subpar collections, only to discover the truth later, when it is too late. John Ruskin once said that the bitter taste of low quality lasts longer than the sweet taste of low price.

However, if a gem Morgan dollar is worth $1,000 in *Coin World* or *Numismatic News* listings, or in this book, and you are offered one for $500, you might be tempted. However, the chances are virtually certain it will not be certified by PCGS or NGC—and as a matter of fact, it might be one of the thousands of dangerous modern Chinese counterfeits that are on the market.

We all like to learn by doing, and when I was first gaining a foothold in the hobby I made my share of mistakes (and still make them occasionally). I once nearly bought a "Proof" double eagle of the rare 1883 date that was really a common 1883-S with the mintmark removed and the surface buffed to a high polish. In another instance I bought a "bargain" 1912-S nickel, and the glued-on mintmark fell off. And so it goes.

A good precept in the Morgan dollar series is to buy *only* pieces that have been certified and only those that are brilliant. Delicately toned coins can be very appealing as well, but for the uninitiated they are terra incognita, as artificially colored and toned coins abound, including in certified holders. Beyond that, of course, there are other variables—that is what this book is all about. However, this will save you from deep traps.

If you insist on buying "raw" coins, take them to a couple of other people who are familiar with Morgan dollars and who have gained numismatic expertise. Get some other opinions. If you have been derailed by a seller of "bargains," you will soon know.

Of course, there can be exceptions—but in today's age of established certification, there are not many.

To be sure, not all dealers like certified coins, and there are more than a few fine dealers who do, indeed, grade coins carefully—every bit as carefully as the leading certification services. However, it is an easy rule to start by buying certified coins.

## High Prices

In the annals of Morgan dollar collecting there are many instances in which specialists who have put together superb sets have "overpaid." However, if the *quality* and *rarity* are both present, then today's record price might well be tomorrow's real bargain.

However, for you, if you are just beginning your interest in Morgan dollars, such stretching to obtain great coins should wait until you have learned more.

## Buying in Stores

Time was when just about every medium-sized town or city in the United States had one or more shops offering coins, sometimes stamps as well, along with a selection of books, albums, folders, and accessories. During the coin market boom of the early 1960s such stores proliferated, and it was estimated that there were several thousand active dealerships. Numismatic publisher Chet Krause once figured that there were somewhere between 3,000 and 6,000 people involved, not all of whom had storefronts (since some dealt by setting up at conventions), but a good number did.

Then in time the number of shops diminished as the coin boom faded, expenses of operating a shop (salaries, insurance, security, rent, advertising, you name it) increased dramatically, and popular interest turned to other areas.

In the 1990s, sports cards, such as baseball cards, were all the rage, and in our small town (6,000 population) of Wolfeboro there were two card shops, and larger places were apt to have a half dozen or even more. Now, as you read these words, most of these card shops have closed their doors, victims of the diminishing of interest combined with new methods of selling—perhaps most dramatically the Internet, which burst into popularity in a large way a few years ago.

Still, there are many fine coin shops, offices, and stores in the larger cities. A glance at the directory issued by the Professional Numismatists Guild (PNG) reveals many possibilities in this regard.

The advantage of buying at a coin store, especially one in your town or region, is that if the proprietor or employees are inclined, you can "talk coins" at great length, observing a few "rules of engagement."

First, it is a good policy to buy something now and then. If you ask for a lot of advice and information, then when it comes to buying reference books, albums, a magnifying glass, and even some coins for your collection, the local store should be your first choice. The store is not in business for entertainment or any other aspect than making a profit, although at the same time the owner may immensely enjoy the world of numismatics. However, bills always remain to be paid, and to do this a proprietor has to issue a steady stream of sales slips, including a few to you.

There are busy times and not-so-busy times in the operation of any coin store, and after your initial visit to look around, if a spark of interest and friendship from the owner is seen, ask when a typical slow time is, and then return later. If the store is crowded on Saturday morning and empty on Tuesday afternoon, the latter would be a logical time to have an extended visit.

## Buying at Coin Shows

Scarcely a weekend goes by in the United States of America without a local, regional, or even national coin show taking place. The programs of shows vary widely, but from the standpoint of Morgan silver dollar acquisition, the format does not make a heck of a lot of difference.

Most shows are basic, and consist of a room or gallery in which a dozen or more, sometimes many more, dealers set up in a bourse (a popular coin term taken from the French *bourse*, or stock exchange). Typically, each has a couple of glass-topped cases, and within each case is an array of items for sale, usually offering some Morgan silver dollars in certified holders, mostly ANACS, NGC, ICG, and PCGS, but with the products of some other services as well.

Larger regional shows and national events, the latter including the impressive summer and the somewhat smaller spring conventions of the American Numismatic Association, have educational programs, displays by various modern mints of the world, cases of coins, tokens, medals, and paper money exhibited by members (though not often much in the way of Morgan dollars), and more. However, the focal point usually remains the bourse, often supplemented by one or more interesting auctions.

Coin shows are ideal for gathering information. Do your homework first, read through coin periodicals, ask friends, and jot down the names of some dealers you would like to meet. In a local show it is possible to literally meet them all, but in a large show with several hundred or more dealers, and with more activity, this is not always possible. In addition to people you hope to meet, at the show itself new possibilities will become evident as you see dealers with cases full of interesting things.

While techniques vary, as a dealer who has set up at shows for many years (my first ANA show was in Omaha in 1955), my preference is that someone state his or her favorite series and collecting objectives, even if a numismatic spark was ignited only a few days earlier. To me, it is always interesting to talk to a well-intentioned beginner who has a lot of intellectual curiosity. On the other hand, if you have been in the hobby for a long time and are now adding Morgan dollars to a list of other interests, by all means mention your past experiences.

The amount of time a dealer will have to devote to chatting with you will depend on the general press of business. If many are gathered around a bourse table at a given time, come back when things are not as busy. There are always slow times.

The willingness of a dealer to converse with you at a show or convention is an aspect of personality combined with the realities of a situation, just as it is in a coin shop. Some dealers simply like to "talk coins," and are a real delight to visit, and, of course, are a credit to the growth of the numismatic hobby. Other dealers, for their own reasons, project themselves as being interested in "big buyers," and concentrate on this aspect— giving time of day and more to someone who wants to write a check for, say, $10,000, but scarcely interested in discussing things with beginners. Also, even the most sociable dealer might be tired or exhausted after a long day at the bourse and may suggest that you come back at another time.

Dealers are people, too, and their sensitivities and sensibilities are no different from your own. However, for a dealer the opportunity to *conduct business* is wedged into a day or two or three, and this aspect must necessarily govern many actions. Still, there are enough dealers around who enjoy people and enjoy coin lore that you will have no lack of opportunity to chat and learn.

## BIDDING AND BUYING AT AUCTION, INCLUDING ONLINE

Auctions are another way to buy. In the United States there is a handful of firms that issue grand catalogs with Morgan silver dollars and many other coins for sale to the highest bidders.

Buying coins at auction is a bit different from buying them at a coin show where you can examine them individually, or ordering them directly by mail with a money-back guarantee. Auction sales are intended to be final, and the last thing an auctioneer wants is to have you or anyone else bid on, say, an MS-63 1886-O silver dollar, get it, and then send it back because it is not sharply struck.

The auctioneer wants the sale to be final, and the consignor expects that the auctioneer will attract bidders who are qualified to honor their commitments. This is not a time for "approvals." On the other hand, as a serious buyer of Morgan silver dollars, as I hope you will be as you read this book, you will indeed be interested in such aspects as sharpness of strike, quality of luster, and considerations beyond basic information such as "1886-O MS-63 (NGC)" or something similar. Such a description for an 1886-O might be satisfying enough to the majority of buyers, but possibly not to you. Accordingly, I offer several suggestions.

Important and expensive pieces are apt to be pictured in the catalog or illustrated on the web site of the auction house. Today, many if not most images of more valuable coins are taken electronically and posted on web sites, and if you have a computer, a better image can be sent to you by e-mail. For most Morgan dollars, assuming that the camera resolution is sufficient, you can quickly determine aspects of striking and, to a lesser extent, eye appeal. The last is a bit tricky, as photographs can be manipulated and, more often, different angles, intensities, and aspects of lighting can give a coin a different appearance. A skilled photographer with good lighting can turn a sow's-ear 1891-O dollar (usually unattractive) into a silk-purse dollar! However, in general a color photograph (but not black and white) is representative of the actual appearance of a coin you will receive.

Another possibility is to request mail inspection of the lots you are interested in. My recommendation is that you not waste your time or the time of the auctioneer by asking to see something inexpensive, such as a MS-63 1881-S, as such coins are common, and there are other places to buy them besides a particular auction sale. However, if you are buying a rarity and it is worth a substantial amount of money, asking to view it quickly is a great option. The usual arrangement is for the dealer to send it to you by Federal Express or other overnight means, and for you to look at it and send it back the same day, paying shipping and insurance charges both ways.

A third possibility, widely used by many advanced collectors, is to commission a trustworthy dealer to be your eyes at the auction and to represent you in person. By separate agreement with a dealer of your choice, you will agree to pay for what the dealer buys on your account. Then the dealer will examine the lots in person at the viewing session, determine in his or her own judgment what you would like to buy, or perhaps discuss the situation with you on the telephone, and then bid on your behalf. If, when you receive the coin after the sale, you are not happy with it, that is your problem, as your dealer agent, by examining lots in advance, is contractually bound to complete the purchase. Be aware of this, and if in doubt, don't bid. It is always much easier not to bid at all than to complicate life for yourself, your agent, and the auctioneer by bidding if you are not prepared to take the consequences.

Bidding at auctions can be an enjoyable experience. In person, an auction is a social as well as a numismatic event, and if the auctioneer has a good rapport with the audience, the experience can be very entertaining as well as informative and, of course, a good way to add to your collection.

In recent years the panorama has opened up dramatically through offerings on the Internet, particularly by the eBay service, but also at various dealer sites and in other ways. As can be readily learned from reading the message boards posted by various collectors and dealers, there is a tremendous number of traps among Internet offerings, particularly by sellers of coins who have few truly established numismatic credentials.

## USE CAUTION, ESPECIALLY ONLINE

My advice concerning Internet transactions is to buy Morgan dollars only from a rare coin dealer who is a member of the Professional Numismatists Guild (PNG) or, reflecting that not all dealers wish to belong to the PNG (and some fine dealers may not have sufficient financial worth to qualify), then a dealer whose credentials you have checked by talking with other dealers or friends who have had experience. Never, but *never*, no exceptions, buy a "bargain" Morgan dollar in an Internet auction, and I might go further by stating that it is probably worthwhile only to bid on Morgan dollars certified by one or another of the leading grading services (but make all the tests for quality and appearance before you bid). While certified coins can have their own problems and are not a deus ex machina device for building a great collection, in the beginning stages of your Morgan dollar investigations they can be a valuable safeguard.

Over the years many people have been stunned by buying casts, altered mintmarks, and the like. While it is illegal for someone to sell you a fake 1893-S dollar, the practicality of the matter is that if you buy such a piece on the Internet, the seller will probably say something like "Who, me? I'm not a rare coin dealer, I bought it in an estate. I didn't know it was fake!" Or, "That's your problem. Sue me." You can, of course, hire an attorney and bring suit, at a cost of a few thousand dollars at least, but this will at once sour you on numismatics, at least slightly, and result in an unpleasant transaction. It is much easier to simply avoid such possibilities. There are many established dealers conducting auction sales either on the Internet or by way of catalogs, who are reputable, stand behind what they offer, and are responsible in their activities.

## COIN CLUBS AND GROUPS

Some larger towns and cities, and most all regions, have coin clubs or numismatic societies with regular meetings, typically each month. Some also have coin shows complete with dealer bourses.

Across America there are several hundred such clubs, some active, some less so, but worth checking out if one is in your area. Nearly all clubs are affiliated with the American Numismatic Association (physical address: 818 North Cascade Avenue, Colorado Springs, CO 80903–3279; website: www.money.org), and you can obtain their addresses from the ANA.

While you are at it, you may want to sign up for ANA membership—a dynamic worldwide group with about 30,000 members, with traditions dating back to 1891.

## SEVERAL MUSEUMS OF NOTE

The ANA itself maintains a dandy museum (showcasing gems from the Harry W. Bass Jr. Collection, among other memorable displays) and numismatic library in Colorado Springs. The Smithsonian Institution in Washington, D.C., has a marvelous collection of rare coins. At present the main facility is closed to visitors, but on the ground floor of the Museum of American History there is a rarity-laden exhibit of coins and paper money, including some of America's greatest numismatic treasures. Certain of these trace their pedigrees to the Mint Cabinet, set up at the Philadelphia Mint in 1838 and supplemented regularly. The Mint Cabinet was moved to the Smithsonian in 1923. Beyond items on display, the Smithsonian staff often travel to major coin conventions to share items from their collection.

The American Numismatic Society, formed in New York City in 1858 by teenager Augustus B. Sage, holds forth in its new headquarters in a fine old building in the financial district of New York City at 140 William Street. Available for members and selected visitors are an excellent numismatic library (funded by the Harry W. Bass Jr. Foundation), a fine museum, and other facilities showcasing every aspect of numismatic scholarship, history, and appreciation.

Here and there around the United States there are other exhibits of interest and importance, including some with silver dollars. However, those just mentioned constitute the most important three.

# EXPLORING MORE DIE VARIETIES
## LET'S GET TECHNICAL (IF YOU WANT TO)

The numismatist who collects United States coins by design types, from 1793 to date, may just want one Morgan dollar to illustrate the motif. I presume that no such collectors have bought the present book to learn about their single coins!

Beyond that, most aspire to collect by dates and mints, sometimes including overdates, as described earlier. Accordingly, the preceding chapters will probably satisfy the majority of readers of this book. However, beyond that a wide world of specialized die varieties beckons, nearly 2,000 different die combinations of Morgan dollars. Some are obvious to the eye, but most require magnification to study and appreciate. These include repunching of the date numerals or mintmark, strange letters added to the reverse by the clashing of dies, or the doubling of Miss Liberty's ear or lips by shifting of the master die during the preparation of the working die.

As to whether this field is for you is a matter of preference. In other areas of collecting endeavor, some prefer simplicity, such as one copy of an interesting book. Others may want a first printing, or an edition with a typographical error. Some casual birdwatchers are content to see the first robin of spring, while others may spend a long time searching and get excited when they see a prothonotary warbler. In Colorado, some are satisfied to take the cog railway to the summit of Pikes Peak, elevation 14,100 feet. Others want to personally hike on foot the multiple Fourteeners, as they are called—the summits in Colorado reaching 14,000 feet or more.

In numismatics, John W. Adams spent many years trying to find as many minute die varieties as possible of cents dated 1794, while at the same time "collecting" their history and the biographies of former owners. Harry W. Bass Jr. would think nothing of buying multiples of common-date double eagles, so that in leisure he could spot small differences in dies, not at all valuable, but certainly interesting to him.

One thing about being a specialist is that there are many opportunities to find rare varieties that are not recognized by sellers or mentioned on certification-service holders. In the field of Morgan dollars from 1878 through 1921, just about anyone who has been at the game for a year or two has found a new die variety—perhaps not important in the scheme of life or how the world turns, but of interest to fellow enthusiasts. And, in the market among those who have similar interests, some varieties can be valuable.

# BEYOND THE BASICS: SPECIALIZED VARIETIES

## FIRST SIGNIFICANT DIE RESEARCH PUBLISHED

More than just a few collectors are apt to think that the pursuit of minor varieties is a phenomenon that arose after millions of silver dollars came into the numismatic market following the Treasury dispersals of 1962 through 1964. However, that is not so, and interest began decades earlier, indeed when Morgan dollars were still being minted.

In June 1898 in *The Numismatist*, the first in-depth article on Morgan dollar die varieties was published, under the title of "Die Varieties of Current United States Standard Dollars," by George W. Rice.[1] Little did Rice know that he would inaugurate a passion for die varieties that would in time grow to include many other articles and several extensive books.

Significantly, Rice in 1898 stated forthrightly, with no "perhaps" or "maybe," that in 1895 only Proofs had been struck. Rice's study of dollars 1878 to 1881:

> I have found U.S. standard dollars showing the use of two obverse and four reverse dies.
>
> I shall not attempt a lengthy description, noting only such features as can be easily remembered and recognized at a glance, leaving the interested reader to study out the many minute differences.
>
> **Obverse 1.** Bears the well-known large head, facing to left, with a wreath of cotton and grain; between the ears of grain at top a leaf reaches the pointed tip turned a little to left and nearly touching the base of letter I.
>
> **Obverse 2.** The leaf between ears of grain is appreciably shorter than on die 1, with tip more rounded and pointing to centre of base of letter I. A careful comparison will discover other differences, chiefly in the lines of the hair.
>
> **Reverse A.** The eagle grasps in his claw to right a bunch of three arrows. Observe that while the arrow heads are divergent, the feathered ends are parallel. The claw to left holds an olive branch of three leaves only. This reverse in combination with obverse 1, is the original design by Mr. Morgan, and having been accepted, the piece should take rank with U.S. dollars, even though none were subsequently struck for circulation. It exists only in Proof condition but in numbers sufficient to prevent its becoming exceedingly rare.
>
> **Reverse B.** Differs from A in that the olive branch is composed of three clusters of three leaves each. There are eight feathers in the spreading tail of the eagle. The arrow heads are slightly larger and the feathered ends of same a little narrower, but still parallel. I have placed this die second because in general treatment of wreath and eagle it more nearly resembles the original design than do the other dies.
>
> **Reverse C.** Closely copies die B, but the treatment of the entire design differs. It is all slightly contracted, the wreath more than other parts, with the leaves and berries differently arranged. The wing tips do not reach to the milling, and the A in AMERICA touches the edge of wing. The points of difference to be particularly noted are that there are but seven feathers drawn in the tail of the eagle and that the feathers on arrows are still arranged in parallel lines.

**Reverse D.** Shows the whole design again, re-engraved, slightly larger than any of the preceding dies. An attempt is made to give the feathered ends of arrows the appearance of being in line with the heads by making the upper feather wedge-shaped; considerably wider on the left than on the right. The die can be recognized at a glance by the shape of the feather. The centre leaf of the lower cluster is the longest; in dies B and C the upper one was longest.

The treatment of the design on this die shows it to be a copy of die C rather than of dies A and B.

I have found the above obverses and reverses combined as follows:

No. 1. Obverse 1 with reverse A.
No. 2. Obverse 1 with reverse B.
No. 3. Obverse 1 with reverse C.
No. 4. Obverse 1 with reverse D.
No. 5. Obverse 2 with reverse C.
No. 6. Obverse 2 with reverse D.

I shall conclude with a table of the issues of the mints as I have found them.

### PHILADELPHIA MINT

1878 No. 1. This mint and date only and all Proofs.
1878 No. 2. This mint and date only, both Proofs and for circulation.
1878 No. 3. I have failed to find from this mint, but believe it exists.
1878 No. 4.
1878 No. 5.
1878 No. 6.

In 1879 No. 6 was issued and without variation to date, though in 1895, Proofs only, numbering less than 1,000, were struck.

### SAN FRANCISCO MINT

1878 No. 3.
1879 No. 5.
1879 No. 6.
No. 6 only is found in all other years to date.

### CARSON CITY MINT

1878 No. 3.
1879 I have not seen.
1880 No. 5.
1881 and all subsequent coinage, No. 6 only.

### NEW ORLEANS MINT

I have found only No. 6, from 1879, the first year of coinage, to date.

## HOWARD R. NEWCOMB

Prominent among early numismatists who collected Morgan dollars by date and mint-mark was Howard R. Newcomb, of Detroit. Similar to Rice, he was especially attracted to the multiple varieties of the 1878 through 1880 era, as per this editorial comment in *The Numismatist,* March 1922:

The extent of the field of mintmarks can be partly realized when one considers the statement of Mr. Howard R. Newcomb, the well-known Detroit mintmark collector, that of the 1878, 1879, and 1880 dollars alone he has no less than 22 die and mint letter varieties.

In the meantime he spared no effort to track pieces he needed. Advertising in *The Numismatist*, December 1912, Newcomb stated that he desired to buy "perfection copies" of 1880-CC, 1884-CC, 1889-CC, 1886-S, 1887-S, 1888-S, and 1889-S, a reflection of the elusive nature of such pieces at the time.

In the same periodical in February 1913, an article by Newcomb on 1878 through 1880 dollars was printed, describing the varieties known to him and illustrating several. That summer the annual convention of the American Numismatic Association was conducted in Newcomb's hometown, August 23 to 27, at the Hotel Pontchartrain. Room rates ranged from $2.50 for a single with a sink and toilet to $3 for one with a tub bath or shower—if anything, reflective today, as you read this, that a basic silver dollar in 1913 had significant purchasing power, perhaps equal to $50 or so in the early 21st century. For this reason, few numismatists collected the denomination.

At the show Newcomb exhibited his dollars, garnering this review:

> The Carson City Mint is complete in Uncirculated condition. Of a branch mint, a piece that is considered by Mr. Newcomb to be of a great deal more rarity than the Carson City is a standard dollar of 1888 of the San Francisco Mint. The collection is complete with all the mints up through 1904.[2]

Newcomb continued his interest in silver dollars, although he and others referred to them as Bland dollars or standard dollars, never as Morgan dollars. *The Numismatist* in July 1925 printed this letter from Newcomb:

> There seems to be something peculiar about the standard silver dollar of 1903 issued from the New Orleans Mint. Although the government records indicate a coinage of 4,450,000 pieces, I failed to locate, in the last half dozen years, any specimens either in the hands of dealers or collectors, save one in my own collection and one in a prominent collection in Washington, D.C. They seem to be equally scarce even in circulation.
>
> Although silver dollars are not plentiful in circulation in these parts, I have enlisted the aid of the head cashiers in three of our larger stores to be on the lookout for this piece. It is customary in these stores when silver dollars are received not to give them out again in making change, but to deposit all of them. These men, for several years, have looked over thousands of silver dollars and not one has come to light. Two of our A.N.A. members, one in Los Angeles, the other in San Francisco, have also searched where the silver dollar is plentiful and they, too, have been unable to find any. The only explanation I can offer is that the government, during the late war, sold the entire mintage as bullion and the entire mintage rested in the government vault, undisturbed, until that time when so many millions of silver dollars were melted up.

The foregoing prompted this poignant observation by editor Frank Duffield in the same issue, significant as it indicates the general lack of numismatic interest in the series at the time:

Silver dollars are not collected extensively, but if they were, it is more than probable that other dates and mintmarks would be found to be far rarer than the recorded coinage would indicate.

## Later Studies

In 1963, Francis X. Klaes, a skilled photographer as well as a numismatist, published *Die Varieties of Morgan Silver Dollars*, essentially a pamphlet, but with superb descriptions of over 50 die varieties.

To the *Whitman Numismatic Journal* in November 1964, Neil Shafer contributed an article, "The Morgan Silver Dollars of 1878–1921: A Study of Major Die Varieties," citing as his sources writing by Walter Breen, articles in the *Numismatic Scrapbook Magazine*, and Howard R. Newcomb's article in *The Numismatist*, February 1913, this in addition to independent research:

> The main purpose of the present study is to list in chronological sequence those varieties found in the Philadelphia coinage of Morgan dollars in 1878. Also included will be hitherto unpublished facts concerning issues of 1878-S, 1878-CC, 1879-S and 1880-CC dollars as they relate to the 1878 Philadelphia coins. A clear picture of mint efforts to create a particular effect on the coin and to correct mechanical or artistic faults as they became known will be described in the background history and contemporary letters, the results of extensive research at the National Archives in Washington, D.C.

Shafer gave a fascinating review of the inception of the design in 1878, selections from Mint correspondence, and information regarding changes in the hub designs, among other information.

Today the basic source for information on known die varieties, significant and obscure, is the *Comprehensive Catalogue and Encyclopedia of Morgan and Peace Dollars*, by Leroy C. Van Allen and A. George Mallis. In the hobby today, listings are nearly universally referred to as "VAM numbers," for the surname initials of the authors.[3]

Seeking to narrow the field to more manageable proportions, Michael S. Fey, Ph.D. and Jeff Oxman created a compact book, pocket sized, of 137 pages, *The Top 100 Morgan Dollar Varieties: The VAM Keys*, now in its third edition (many photographs of die variety details in the present volume are from the Fey-Oxman work).

In the meantime, in 1976 Wayne Miller published *An Analysis of Morgan and Peace Dollars*, a basic guide for the collector interested in dates and mintmarks. However, he did include "a list of die varieties, all visible without magnification, which the author feels are of major significance."

Listed by Miller were 20 coins, including five different variations of the 1878 Doubled Tail Feathers (then called 7 over 8 Tail Feathers) and several Reverse of 1878 and Reverse of 1879 issues among dollars of 1878 through 1880. Beyond those, and overdates, and overmintmarks, his favorites included:

> **1882-O/S, VAMs 3, 4, 5, and 6.** What appears to be the center shaft of an "S" mintmark is clearly visible within the "O" mintmark. All varieties exhibit very small dots of metal, particularly upon the raised surfaces, due to rusted dies.
>
> **1888-O VAM 4,** Doubled Head variety with two complete sets of lips, chins and nose clearly visible. Very rare in grades above EF.

**1890-CC VAM 4,** the Tail Bar variety. Extra metal caused by a gouge in the die extends from the junction of the Eagle's tail feather and arrow feathers down to the wreath.

**1891-O VAM 4,** clashed die marks on the reverse reveal the "E" of LIB-ERTY below the Eagle's tail feathers on the left side. This phenomenon is also observable among 1884-P, 1886-O, and 1889-O dollars, but is most readily observable among 1891-O pieces.

**1896-O VAM 4,** with very small mintmark. This phenomenon is also observable among specimens of the 1899-O, 1900-O, 1902-O, and 1903-S. With the exception of the 1899-O, such "micro" mintmark dollars are very rare in grades above EF; even the 1899-O is very scarce in Uncirculated condition.

**1901 VAM 3,** the Shifted Eagle variety. Much of the Eagle is strongly doubled, particularly the tail feathers.

In 1982, Wayne Miller's *A Morgan Dollar and Peace Dollar Textbook* was published, an update and revision of his earlier work, and, similar to it, well done and very readable. I should also mention that in various editions of the VAM work the number scheme has changed slightly. For the latest information, the third (1992) or fourth (1997), essentially a reprint of the third, is recommended.

## Technicalities of Obverses and Reverses

While the reverse types listed earlier are of basic importance to anyone collecting varieties among basic dates and mintmarks, or following the Red Book listings, the Van Allen–Mallis text[4] gives details of four slightly different obverses plus several subvarieties of those obverses, and subvarieties of reverses.

With minor die differences among the "types" plus variations in the placement of the date and mintmark, the size of the mintmark, repunching of either or both the date and mintmark, and other differences, some slight, others obvious, there is almost no end to the possibilities for collecting. The 1997 VAM text lists nearly 2,000 different die combinations, or more than twice as many as listed in the first edition of that book (1971).

## Market Changes and Possibilities

Per the estimate of Van Allen and Mallis, there are 40 to 50 million Mint State Morgan dollars of the 1878 through 1904 years in existence today plus 10 to 15 million 1921 coins—there will never be a lack of coins to inspect! Only a small fraction of the available dollars have been certified.

Today, in the early 21st century, there is intense competition for basic Morgan dollar dates and mintmarks, common as well as rare, without regard to VAM varieties. This elevation in market values has had its effect, as Van Allen and Mallis noted:

> VAM collecting of silver dollar varieties by the Van Allen–Mallis numbering system increased dramatically after the initial versions of this book were published in 1971 and 1976. However, it reached a peak in the early 1980s and has decreased somewhat since then as the prices of coins increased tremendously making them less affordable.
>
> The investor dominates the silver dollar market much of the time, but becomes less of a factor during the market downturns. Collectors form a more stable base over the years.

Time was when 1,000-coin bags of common dates and mints of Morgan dollars were available at coin shows, and if things were quiet, dealers didn't mind having VAM specialists poke through a pile of sparkling dollars to pick out minor varieties of interest, thereby selling 10 or 20 common coins instead of just one. Those days are gone, probably forever, and at the largest shows today it is unlikely that even *one* original bag of Morgan dollars will be on display.

In an era of high prices, even for super-common dates and mintmarks of high-grade Morgan dollars, some dealers do not want to be "bothered" with VAM collectors asking to see coins, now mostly certified, and poring over them with magnifying glass in hand. Dealers often seek larger sales, and most could not care less about VAM varieties.

In the present era many of the higher-graded Morgan dollars, including common dates, are certified by NGC, ANACS, PCGS, or one or another of the other services. This raises the price of coins due to the cost of certification, and at the same time sharply reduces the number of coins a dealer can tote to a convention. The same number of pieces, once in a 1,000-coin cloth bag (weighing about 57 pounds) and capable of being put in a satchel, would fill a good-sized trunk!

These and other factors have changed the scene. VAM variety collecting is alive and well, but as a niche rather than a mainstream activity. Instead of aspiring to collect a vast panorama of varieties, many decide upon specialties, such as trying to find as many as possible of the well over 200 varieties of 1878 Philadelphia Mint dollars, or specializing in the many different overdates of the various mints in 1880, or endeavoring to acquire as many different as possible from the Fey-Oxman *Top 100 Morgan Dollar Varieties: The VAM Keys.*

What to do? How to begin? Probably the best thing is to acquire a copy of the VAM text and skim through it, to determine if the collecting of minutely different varieties is for you. Or, perhaps here and there you will become intrigued with a variety that is not a "top 100" or especially noticed elsewhere.

Your downside risk is nonexistent if you buy the VAM book, for the first 138 pages are crammed with basic information, historical data, mintage details, and more, too much to absorb all at once, but eminently useful if revisited from time to time. The techniques of collecting and studying die varieties are much the same across American numismatics, and the precepts the VAM text gives for Morgan dollars can be useful elsewhere. No doubt someone with "VAM knowledge" could glide easily into another specialty, such as copper coins of Connecticut, Capped Bust half dollars of 1807 through 1836, or Civil War tokens issued in Cincinnati.

# YEAR BY YEAR: AN ANALYSIS BY DATE AND MINTMARK

## HOW TO USE THE LISTINGS

In this chapter, each date and mintmark Morgan dollar issue from 1878 to 1921 is given a separate analysis, as are several major varieties, including tail-feather styles, overdates, and overmintmarks. The title photographs are of the obverses and reverses of actual coins of that variety (not composites of different coins). Most listings have information in the following categories.

## NARRATIVE INFORMATION

**Optimal Collecting Grade:** The author's opinion of a grade that offers a combination of high preservation and reasonable market price—a "lot of coin for the money."

**Circulation-Strike Mintage:** Quantity struck for circulation, as given in the *Annual Report of the Director of the Mint* and other Treasury Department sources. This figure does not include Proofs (made at the Philadelphia Mint each year and listed separately). When one Treasury figure covers several variety possibilities, the figure is noted as being estimated.

**Proof Mintage:** Mintage quantity given each year for Philadelphia Mint Proofs, from *Annual Reports.*

**Key to Collecting Circulation Strikes:** Synopsis of what to look for—general features of strike, appearance, and rarity, with emphasis on Mint State examples.

**Surface Quality:** Observations concerning the sharpness, or lack thereof, of the details seen on typical coins as a result of the striking process. Also, observations relating to the appearance and desirability of the mint frost or luster on the surface of a typical coin.

**Prooflike Coins:** Brief discussion of any prooflike circulation-strike coins in existence for that date and mintmark. Prooflike coins were struck from dies polished by the basining process. These can be a specialty on their own, and anyone interested in pursuing these in depth should study other information in print and consult other sources. Opinions can vary, often widely.

**Mintage and Distribution:** Delivery figures are sometimes given by month, representing the number of coins delivered by the coiner and registered on the records of a given mint. Such coins may or may not have been released into circulation. Many went into storage at the mints. Distribution notes mainly refer to how the issue was released, as into circulation near the time of coinage, or into storage, or a combination. Information is given concerning certain releases of bags and other quantities in later years.

**Die Varieties:** Varieties as listed by Leroy A. Van Allen and A. George Mallis in *Comprehensive Catalogue and Encyclopedia of Morgan and Peace Dollars* (the VAM-number source) and, in some instances, in other references, including *Walter Breen's Complete*

*Encyclopedia of U.S. and Colonial Coins* and Van Allen–Mallis's *Top 100 Morgan Dollar Varieties*. In nearly all instances the listings under Die Varieties represent major varieties that the author has found to be of interest. The opinions of others may differ. For details and many other varieties, consult the VAM text.

## PROOFS

**Mintage:** Commentary on the number of Proofs reported to have been struck.

**Key to Collecting Proofs:** Observations concerning Proofs' sharpness, contrast, and other characteristics, which can vary.

## CHART DATA

The Whitman Coin Guide (WCG™) consists of two charts: pricing and availability.

### PRICING

Suggested typical market prices for an average-quality specimen of the grade indicated. The values are intended to reflect what an informed buyer will pay to an established and reputable seller, at the time this book goes to press. Market values can and do vary over time, and among sellers and buyers at any given time. It is wise to check multiple sources before making purchases. When high-quality examples are the rule, not the exception (as with the 1881-S), the prices are easily enough used to find "nice" pieces. In other instances, such as for an 1891-O, an average-quality specimen may not be what you want, and a Morgan dollar specialist or auction house may justifiably ask a significantly higher price for a sharply struck coin with great eye appeal. In the marketplace, over-graded coins are often sold at bargain levels to entice the unwary. Great rarities, such as a sharply struck, truly beautiful specimen of a date and grade not often encountered, may deservedly bring a substantial premium over the typical price listed here, or may achieve record price at auction. Dealers who emphasize high-quality coins and/or good customer service may charge more than the typical prices listed.

Grades are per the Official ANA Grading Standards. Market prices beyond MS-65 and PF-65 are often speculative, and may change as more and more pieces become certified. For any given variety and grade, and at any given time, investor demand may have an influence and can cause wide fluctuations, both as investors enter a market en masse and as they leave it. On the other hand, demand by established collectors tends to be fairly stable and to grow over a period of time.

### AVAILABILITY

**Certified:** Certified-population data for Proof and circulation strikes have been compiled from reports by NGC and PCGS. Typically, certified populations constitute only a tiny percentage of existing pieces (field populations).

The reader should be aware of two facts about certification data. First, due to "grade-flation" (a trend in which coins are being graded to increasingly liberal standards), yesterday's MS-65 coins may be today's MS-66 coins. Second, a certified coin can be cracked out of its slab and recertified until its owner is satisfied with the result; thus, certification reports are related to the number of submission events, not necessarily to the number of certified coins in existence.

Be especially aware of price fluctuations and expansion of population-report data. Population figures only increase, never decrease. In other words, be careful.

**Field:** The author's estimate as to how many worn coins may survive worldwide. No accurate figures will ever be available, as distribution is so widespread and mostly outside numismatic circles.

**Certified DMPL:** Figures obtained from population-report data. Certified DMPL coins are *not* a subset of the general population of certified Mint State coins; they are a separate grouping.

# HOW TO READ THE GRIDS

Coin grade      Estimated retail price

| VG-8 | F-12 | VF-20 | EF-40 | AU-50 | MS-60 | MS-63 | MS-64 | MS-65 | MS-66 | MS-67 | PF-60 | PF-64 | PF-65 | PF-66 | PF-67 |
|------|------|-------|-------|-------|-------|-------|-------|-------|-------|-------|-------|-------|-------|-------|-------|
| $30 | $31 | $38 | $45 | $78 | $130 | $175 | $400 | $1,300 | $10,000 | $55,000 | $1,175 | $4,700 | $7,400 | $19,000 | $50,000 |

Coin grade          Number of times graded professionally by NGC and PCGS          Author's estimate of total number of Morgan dollars believed to exist in this grade

AVAILABILITY

| Population | MS-60 | MS-61 | MS-62 | MS-63 | MS-64 | MS-65 | MS-66 | MS-67 | MS-68+ |
|-----------|-------|-------|-------|-------|-------|-------|-------|-------|--------|
| Certified | 112 | 252 | 1,189 | 4,864 | 6,040 | 1,265 | 105 | 2 | 3 |
| Field | | 80,000–150,000 | | 50,000–75,000 | 25,000–35,000 | 3,000–4,500 | 200–300 | 8–12 | 1–5 |
| Certified DMPL | 10 | 24 | 82 | 122 | 121 | 20 | 0 | 0 | 0 |

| | PF-60 | PF-61 | PF-62 | PF-63 | PF-64 | PF-65 | PF-66 | PF-67 | PF-68+ |
|---|-------|-------|-------|-------|-------|-------|-------|-------|--------|
| Certified | 23 | 36 | 61 | 76 | 91 | 68 | 13 | 17 | 7 |
| Field | | 225–350 | | 140–190 | 120–160 | 100–140 | 60–90 | 25–35 | 12–18 |

# MORGAN SILVER DOLLARS, RARE COINS, AND LIFE IN 1878

## MONEY IN AMERICA: COINS IN CIRCULATION

Silver dollars were scarcely to be seen in circulation in the United States in early 1878. Such coins had not been minted since 1873, when the Liberty Seated design was discontinued. Even then, there were no dollars in the channels of commerce, as their silver or meltdown value was more than their face value, a situation that had been in effect since 1850. Virtually all Liberty Seated dollars were either exported or melted.

In 1878, silver dollars of the new Morgan design would become plentiful, thanks to the Bland-Allison Act. Coins in circulation consisted of the Indian Head cent, the nickel three-cent piece, the Shield design nickel five-cent piece, and Liberty Seated dimes, quarters, and half dollars. Trade dollars, made for foreign export, had no legal tender status in the United States and were supposed to be valued for the silver they contained, slightly over 90¢ worth. However, many were in the hands of the public as, indeed, at one time, until July 22, 1876, they had been legal tender for face value. Now, in 1878, they were considered a nuisance, and most banks took them in only at a deep discount, often for about 75¢ or so.

Now and again a two-cent piece would be encountered, these having been last minted for circulation in 1872. Silver trimes, a denomination abolished in 1873, were few and far between, as were silver half dimes, also last coined in 1873. Twenty-cent pieces were likewise elusive. Bank cashiers found all of these coins to be pesky, as there were never enough to be sorted into piles or compartmented. As to Liberty Seated dollars, none had circulated in America since 1850, and many adults had never seen one.

Gold coins had been hoarded by the American public, beginning in the final days of December, 1861, when the outcome of the Civil War continued to be uncertain. Starting in the spring of 1862, silver coins were hoarded as well. Filling the void created by the lack of coins were privately issued tokens and scrip notes, as well as federal Fractional Currency bills (denominations from 3¢ to 50¢) and several types of paper money. After the war ended, in April 1865, citizens continued to hold on to their silver and gold coins tightly, and it was not until years later, after about April 20, 1876, that silver coins reappeared in quantity in circulation. The Treasury Department turned loose a flood of such pieces, and once the public realized that dimes, quarters, and half dollars would become common, they spent the coins they had been hoarding for such a long time. By 1878 there was a glut of silver coins, dimes to half dollars, and for that reason the mintage of new coins of these denominations dropped precipitately beginning in 1879.

## THE MORGAN DOLLAR SCENARIO

In early 1878 quantities of Morgan dollars were released into circulation and met with an apathetic response. Years later, in 1930, Neil Carothers reviewed what happened:

> The coins were, in general, very badly received. In two regions they were accepted in large numbers. In the South they circulated because of an interesting social situation. As a class the recently emancipated slaves were illiterate. There were no gold coins in circulation, and the colored population refused to use greenbacks with their printed symbols. They gladly accepted the new silver coins, and from this situation came the custom of using silver dollars in the South. . . .
>
> In the West the aversion to paper money and the general desire to support silver led to the acceptance of the silver dollar. The North and East would have none of them.[1]

The new coins did not create any excitement in the numismatic community, and interested collectors either bought Proofs as part of sets or casually picked up pieces from banks.

## Other Events at the Philadelphia Mint

There was not a strong demand for new coins. Production of the Indian Head cent was a modest 5,797,500 pieces, plus perhaps 2,350 Proofs, a figure amounting to about a third of the 16,228,000 that would be struck the next year, 1879, but far more than the figure of only 852,500 for 1877. For the nickel three-cent piece, Shield nickel, and twenty-cent piece no pieces were struck for circulation, and output was limited strictly to Proofs for collectors.

Only 20 Proof gold coin sets were made. Although today such gold coins are the crème de la crème of the series, they were not appreciated in their own time.

Several new and interesting varieties of patterns were struck at the Mint, not only of silver dollars, but also for a new concept, the so-called Goloid Metric Dollar (sometimes capitalized in use, sometimes not), the last intended to have a metal content containing equal values of gold and silver.

## Meanwhile, on the American Scene in 1878

The aftermath of a business depression that began in 1873 saw about 10,500 businesses fail in the United States. Times continued to be difficult. An epidemic of yellow fever swept through the states on the Gulf Coast and also north to Tennessee, with an estimated 14,000 fatalities, including 4,500 in New Orleans.

In New Haven, Connecticut, on January 28, the nation's first commercial telephone exchange went into operation with 21 subscribers. In Providence, Rhode Island, Maximilian D. Berlitz, age 27, opened a school of language instruction, following nearly a decade of teaching at a seminary. He left Providence for a week and placed his students with a Frenchman who knew no English, and under this immersion system the students learned rapidly, setting the policy that Berlitz would employ afterward—instruction by speaking only in the language to be learned.

The Remington Arms Company improved its Remington typewriter, introduced in 1876, by adding a shift key to permit the use of upper- and lowercase letters on the same type bar. The partnership of Wyckoff, Seamans & Benedict purchased the typewriter business from Remington, established the separate Remington Typewriter Company, and years later in 1892 as a publicity stunt would pay $10,000 for the first specimen of the Columbian commemorative half dollar.

Two novels were particularly popular, *The Return of the Native*, by Thomas Hardy, and *The Europeans*, by Henry James. The *St. Louis Dispatch* began publication on December 12. It was soon acquired by Joseph Pulitzer, a Hungarian who had arrived in America in 1864, who used it to launch a newspaper empire. Among artists, Albert Bierstadt was active, and in this year created Sierra Nevada, one of many scenes of the American West. Bierstadt specialized in dramatic landscapes with effective use of natural light illuminating his subjects.

In Cincinnati, Proctor & Gamble introduced White Soap, which contained air bubbles and floated (in 1882 it was renamed Ivory and given the slogan "99-44/100% pure"). In New York, Louis Comfort Tiffany, a son of the famous jeweler, began to make art glass, in time lending his name to this genre. He experimented with various minerals and additives to give glass special tints and luster.

The steamer *J.M. White* was launched, taking its place as the most magnificent vessel ever utilized on the Mississippi River. Built at a cost of $300,000, the boat raced upstream from New Orleans to St. Louis in just three days, 23 hours, 9 minutes, setting a record. At the time, the river continued to be vital to inland commerce, but as years went on the railroads took much passenger and freight volume, and boats eventually fell to a minor position.

Rutherford B. Hayes for the first time invited local children to come to the lawn of the White House to participate in an Easter-egg "roll," which became an annual occasion.

In Petoskey, Michigan, the last large group of passenger pigeons was observed in the wild. After this time the population would decline precipitately, and years later, on September 1, 1914, the last known example would die at the Cincinnati Zoo. At an earlier time such birds were so numerous that flocks of them darkened the skies.

# 1878: 8 Tail Feathers

**Optimal Collecting Grade**
MS-64

**Circulation-Strike Mintage**
750,000 (estimated)[2]

**Proof Mintage**
500 (estimated)

Detail of 1878, 8 Tail Feathers.

**Key to Collecting Circulation Strikes:** The 1878 8 Tail Feathers dollar begins the series. This is the only year and mint of the style with 8 Tail Feathers and thus is highly important, although not rare. Although many were distributed in and soon after 1878, enough remained in Treasury holdings that today there is an ample supply of Mint State coins from which to choose. Most pieces are well struck and have excellent luster. All have the eagle with flat or shallow breast, per the early die standard, although the feathers on the eagle's breast can be well defined. Proofs are rare and are in special demand to illustrate this one-year reverse style.

**Surface Quality:** Typically quite well struck. The eagle's breast is shallow, not well rounded, this being characteristic of all reverses used in 1878. Usually with excellent luster, the frost being deep.

**Prooflike Coins:** Often one side is lustrous and the other is prooflike.

**Mintage and Distribution:** The 1878 8 Tail Feathers dollar, struck only for a limited time (March 12, 1878, and some weeks thereafter), is of unknown mintage, but about 750,000 is probably a good guess. Many were released into circulation in and closely after 1878. At the outset the Treasury thought the new dollars would be popular. By the late 1940s, they were considered to be scarce on the coin market, but in 1953 many bags were released from Treasury storage, filling demand. Through the 1950s and early 1960s many more bags were released, including many to Las Vegas casinos.

**Die Varieties:** Many varieties of 1878 8 TF dollars but only five of these (VAM-5, 9, 11, 15, and 17) have been singled out for mention in *The Top 100 Morgan Dollar Varieties.*

## 1878, 8 TAIL FEATHERS, PROOFS

**Mintage:** 500 is a popular estimate, although there is no official figure.

**Key to Collecting Proofs:** Minimal cameo contrast is the rule.[3] The demand for Proofs is especially strong, not as much from Proof specialists as from those who seek an example for a type set. Per usual for Proofs, low-grade examples usually lack eye appeal.

## Whitman Coin Guide (WCG™)

| VG-8 | F-12 | VF-20 | EF-40 | AU-50 | MS-60 | MS-63 | MS-64 | MS-65 | MS-66 | MS-67 | PF-60 | PF-64 | PF-65 | PF-66 | PF-67 |
|------|------|-------|-------|-------|-------|-------|-------|-------|-------|-------|-------|-------|-------|-------|-------|
| $37 | $40 | $45 | $50 | $75 | $135 | $230 | $375 | $1,250 | $9,000 | $55,000 | $1,400 | $4,300 | $7,300 | $12,000 | $40,000 |

**AVAILABILITY**

|  | MS-60 | MS-61 | MS-62 | MS-63 | MS-64 | MS-65 | MS-66 | MS-67 | MS-68+ |
|--|-------|-------|-------|-------|-------|-------|-------|-------|--------|
| Certified | 205 | 721 | 3,292 | 6,166 | 4,277 | 850 | 56 | 1 | 1 |
| Field | 30,000–50,000 | | | 25,000–40,000 | 5,000–10,000 | 1,250–2,000 | 200–300 | 10–20 | 1–5 |
| Cert. DMPL | 7 | 30 | 91 | 111 | 79 | 5 | 1 | 0 | 0 |
|  | PF-60 | PF-61 | PF-62 | PF-63 | PF-64 | PF-65 | PF-66 | PF-67 | PF-68+ |
| Certified | 9 | 19 | 41 | 42 | 60 | 30 | 16 | 4 | 0 |
| Field | 100–120 | | | 100–160 | 110–170 | 40–60 | 25–40 | 10–15 | 0 |

# 1878: DOUBLED (7 OVER 8) TAIL FEATHERS

**Optimal Collecting Grade**
MS-64

**Circulation-Strike Mintage**
500,000 (estimated)

One of many dies described as 1878 Doubled Tail Feathers. Traces of underfeathers are seen below the tips of the regular 7 Tail Feathers.

**Key to Collecting Circulation Strikes:** When it was decided to change the standard tail feather count from eight to seven, the reverse dies already on hand with eight tail feathers were adapted by impression of the master die for the seven tail feather motif. The impression did not obliterate certain tips of the first eight tail feathers, and today various dies show some of the earlier tail feathers still visible. As a handy rule of thumb, to command a market premium the number of vestigial tips visible under the seven tail feathers should be at least four, with the more the better, some having as many as seven showing. This used to be called 7 Over 8 Tail Feathers, a good description of the die-making process, but not reflective of the number of tail feathers that can be seen. Today, "Doubled Tail Feathers" is preferred.

**Surface Quality:** Usually seen with sharp strike on both sides. Check to be sure that the eagle's breast feathers are well defined. Certified examples of this reverse variety have been classified by the services as "weak" or "strong." ("Strong" refers to coins with four or more underfeather tips easily visible, not to the striking quality during the coining process.) Typically seen with satiny luster, although many are below average and some are dull, gray, and lifeless. Search for quality.

**Prooflike Coins:** Prooflike coins (one or both sides) are sometimes encountered, but not with deep mirror surfaces against frosty motifs.

VAM-33, 44

**Mintage and Distribution:** The 1878 Doubled Tail Feathers dollars were bagged and shipped from the Philadelphia Mint in early 1878. Many were circulated, but large quantities remained in storage, and later Treasury releases yielded many Mint State coins, including during the 1962 through 1964 era.

VAM-41

**Die Varieties:** VAM-41 shows the ends of seven feathers and also a doubling of the eagle's right leg and talon. *1878 Doubled Tail Feathers, "Tripled Blossoms," VAM-44:* The bottom edges of the blossoms and leaves in Liberty's headdress are tripled. The reverse is the same as VAM 33 with doubled legs and an extra five small tail feathers, this per the description in *The Top 100 Morgan Dollar Varieties,* which also notes that this may be the single most sought-after specialized variety in the series.

VAM-44

## Whitman Coin Guide (WCG™)

| VG-8 | F-12 | VF-20 | EF-40 | AU-50 | MS-60 | MS-63 | MS-64 | MS-65 | MS-66 | MS-67 |
|------|------|-------|-------|-------|-------|-------|-------|-------|-------|-------|
| $33 | $34 | $36 | $45 | $70 | $145 | $265 | $400 | $2,300 | $17,000 | $28,500 |

**AVAILABILITY**

| | MS-60 | MS-61 | MS-62 | MS-63 | MS-64 | MS-65 | MS-66 | MS-67 | MS-68+ |
|---|-------|-------|-------|-------|-------|-------|-------|-------|--------|
| Certified | 100 | 473 | 2,362 | 4,798 | 3,082 | 422 | 14 | 0 | 0 |
| Field | | 35,000–60,000 | | 20,000–35,000 | 7,500–15,000 | 500–1,000 | 20–100 | 0 | 1–5 |
| Cert. DMPL | 7 | 26 | 79 | 129 | 82 | 9 | 1 | 0 | 0 |

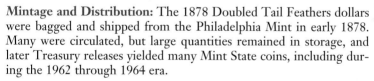

# 1878: 7 Tail Feathers, Reverse of 1878 (PAF)

Optimal
Collecting Grade
MS-64

Circulation-
Strike Mintage
7,850,000

Proof Mintage
250 (estimated)

Detail of 1878,
7 Tail Feathers.

**Key to Collecting Circulation Strikes:** The 7 Tail Feathers reverse occurs with the Reverse of 1878 with the eagle's breast flat and the arrow feathers parallel. These were struck in large quantity, being the design of choice after the brief 8 Tail Feathers coinage and the overstamping of many of those 8 Tail Feathers dies with this 7 Tail Feathers hub, creating the "Doubled Tail Feathers." Now, the present listing is for "pure" 7 Tail Feathers coins. These were made in large quantity and comprise most of the mintage of 1878.

**Surface Quality:** Most circulation strikes have excellent detail, but some show weakness on the eagle's talons and below. The eagle's breast is flat, rather than rounded. At first glance, a well-struck 1878 7 Tail Feathers may appear to be weak. However, close examination will reveal excellent breast feather detail on most. Usually seen with satiny luster, sometimes lifeless and rather dull on the obverse, while frosty on the reverse. Some are prooflike, but without sharp contrast between field and motifs.

**Prooflike Coins:** Prooflike coins are plentiful, but often with little contrast.

**Mintage and Distribution:** The mintage is estimated as 7,850,000, based on production from April 4 to June 28, 1878, assuming that no earlier dies were used on April 4 and later, and that after June 28 all dies were of the next style. This is not a strong premise, but may be approximate. The distribution of all 1878 dollars was extensive at the time, but many remained on hand through the time of the 1962 through 1964 Treasury release.

**Die Varieties:** Many varieties are listed by VAM and in *The Top 100 Morgan Dollar Varieties*. Collecting varieties all across the spectrum of the year 1878 is a popular pursuit with specialists.

## 1878, 7 TAIL FEATHERS (PAF), PROOFS

**Mintage:** 250 is a popular estimate, although there is no official figure. Van Allen and Mallis suggest that 200 Proofs were struck, all of the VAM-131 variety.

**Key to Collecting Proofs:** Striking is sometimes light above the ear. Medium to low cameo contrast. This variety will challenge you, not only to find one in the first place, but beyond that, to get one with good eye appeal. No wonder gems are apt to make auction bidders sit straight up in their chairs!

### Whitman Coin Guide (WCG™)

| VG-8 | F-12 | VF-20 | EF-40 | AU-50 | MS-60 | MS-63 | MS-64 | MS-65 | MS-66 | MS-67 | PF-60 | PF-64 | PF-65 | PF-66 | PF-67 |
|------|------|-------|-------|-------|-------|-------|-------|-------|-------|-------|-------|-------|-------|-------|-------|
| $28 | $29 | $33 | $40 | $45 | $70 | $110 | $250 | $1,050 | $5,500 | – | $2,750 | $5,600 | $12,500 | $24,000 | $60,000 |

#### AVAILABILITY

|  | MS-60 | MS-61 | MS-62 | MS-63 | MS-64 | MS-65 | MS-66 | MS-67 | MS-68+ |
|--|-------|-------|-------|-------|-------|-------|-------|-------|--------|
| Certified | 167 | 895 | 3,507 | 7,747 | 5,708 | 939 | 45 | 0 | 0 |
| Field | | 50,000–100,000 | | 45,000–60,000 | 15,000–25,000 | 1,000–1,800 | 90–130 | 0 | 0 |
| Cert. DMPL | 14 | 38 | 145 | 250 | 189 | 23 | 0 | 0 | 0 |
|  | PF-60 | PF-61 | PF-62 | PF-63 | PF-64 | PF-65 | PF-66 | PF-67 | PF-68+ |
| Certified | 6 | 7 | 18 | 45 | 31 | 20 | 9 | 2 | 0 |
| Field | | 60–80 | | 50–70 | 40–60 | 30–40 | 15–25 | 1–5 | 0 |

# 1878: 7 TAIL FEATHERS, REVERSE OF 1879 (SAF)

Optimal
Collecting Grade
MS-64

Circulation-
Strike Mintage
1,500,000
(estimated)

Proof Mintage
25 to 50 (estimated)

**Key to Collecting Circulation Strikes:** The two different basic reverse styles with 7 Tail Feathers, Reverse of 1878 (PAF) and Reverse of 1879 (SAF, as here), were not widely known. Nor are there any official mintage figures for either. Significant interest did not develop until the 1980s. Although not all Morgan dollar collectors are aware of the varieties, both are eminently worth owning. Even today, the price of the 1878 with Reverse of 1879, although considerably higher than that of the earlier style, does not reflect the true differential in rarity.

**Surface Quality:** Usually fairly well struck, but needle-sharp examples are elusive. Patience may be required to find a "keeper." Certification-service labels do not mention the quality of strike, and, accordingly, most buyers are not aware that there can be a difference! The breast of the eagle is rounded, characteristic of the Type 3 Reverse (Reverse of 1879). Excellent luster is seen on most, but there are exceptions, and cherrypicking is advised.

**Prooflike Coins:** Some are from prooflike dies, sometimes on one side only, and show good contrast between the fields and motifs, a cameo appearance.

**Mintage and Distribution:** Van Allen–Mallis note that 50 Proof Morgan dollars were delivered on November 8, 1878, and these would have been 1878 7 Tail Feathers with Reverse of 1879, assuming that the latest die had been used. However, the Mint often used old reverse dies for Proofs if they were serviceable. It is estimated that fewer than two dozen Proofs exist today, and this may be an optimistic figure. All are the VAM 215 variety. Concerning circulation strikes, the estimate is 1,500,000, assuming that most of those minted from June 28, 1878, to December 31, 1878, were with this reverse, but that some old reverses were still being employed.

**Die Varieties:** There are multiple varieties listed by VAM.

## 1878, 7 TAIL FEATHERS (SAF), PROOFS

**Mintage (net):** Unknown. VAM suggests 50, Michael Fuljenz suggests 25.[4] Breen comment: "300 struck between June 28 and 30, mostly melted."[5]

**Key to Collecting Proofs:** The strike is decent, and the coins have a degree of cameo contrast. This is the Holy Grail among early Proofs.

## Whitman Coin Guide (WCG™)

| VG-8 | F-12 | VF-20 | EF-40 | AU-50 | MS-60 | MS-63 | MS-64 | MS-65 | MS-66 | MS-67 | PF-60 | PF-64 | PF-65 | PF-66 | PF-67 |
|------|------|-------|-------|-------|-------|-------|-------|-------|-------|-------|-------|-------|-------|-------|-------|
| $28 | $29 | $35 | $40 | $50 | $85 | $175 | $490 | $2,050 | – | – | $16,500 | $115,000 | $180,000 | – | – |

**AVAILABILITY**

| | MS-60 | MS-61 | MS-62 | MS-63 | MS-64 | MS-65 | MS-66 | MS-67 | MS-68+ |
|---|-------|-------|-------|-------|-------|-------|-------|-------|--------|
| Certified | 119 | 477 | 1,763 | 3,123 | 2,291 | 482 | 19 | 0 | 0 |
| Field | | 8,000–12,000 | | 10,000–15,000 | 2,000–3,000 | 50–100 | 15–25 | 0 | 0 |
| Cert. DMPL | 4 | 13 | 36 | 74 | 31 | 6 | 0 | 0 | 0 |

| | PF-60 | PF-61 | PF-62 | PF-63 | PF-64 | PF-65 | PF-66 | PF-67 | PF-68+ |
|---|-------|-------|-------|-------|-------|-------|-------|-------|--------|
| Certified | 1 | 3 | 2 | 3 | 3 | 0 | 0 | 0 | 0 |
| Field | | 6–10 | | 5–9 | 5–10 | 1–2 | 0 | 0 | 0 |

# 1878-CC: ALL WITH REVERSE OF 1878 (PAF)

Optimal
Collecting Grade
MS-64

Circulation-
Strike Mintage
2,212,000

**Key to Collecting Circulation Strikes:** Only the Reverse of 1878 (with parallel top arrow feather) was used to produce 1878-CC dollars, and all have seven tail feathers. Most examples are in Mint State and are usually attractive.

**Surface Quality:** Striking quality varies. All have a flat breast on the eagle, according to the design, but most have sharply defined feathers. Some show parallel planchet lines, particularly on the cheek and jaw of Miss Liberty, where these features, on the original planchet, were not flattened out by the striking process. Some have lightness of detail in the lower part of the eagle and below. In 1982, Wayne Miller noted that this is "one of the most consistently well struck of all Morgan dollars."[6] The luster is very pleasing on the 1878-CC dollar, usually satiny.

**Prooflike Coins:** Some dies are prooflike, but these are in the distinct minority. However, in absolute terms enough exist that there is no difficulty finding one.

VAM-6

**Mintage and Distribution:** On April 17, 1878, the *Carson City Morning Appeal* included this commentary, including remarks on the dollar design not likely to prompt readers to acquire souvenirs:

VAM-11

> Dies at last. . . . Yesterday morning the new dies for the U.S. Mint arrived from Philadelphia. There were ten obverse, ten reverse and six collars. The dies were hardened yesterday and the big Ajax press will start up today. There are 632,325 blanks ready for the press, and when they get to work will turn out the dollars at the rate of 30,000 per day. . . . We have had our little say about the dollars coined in Philadelphia, and now the Coiner here is driven to following the footsteps, or rather the press whacks, of the concern on the Delaware. Great disgust was expressed at the general appearance of the dies.[7]

VAM-18

After the great Treasury release was halted in March 1964, the General Services Administration holding of 1878-CC dollars totaled 60,993, or 2.75% of the original mintage, per a later inventory. Even before 1962, bag quantities were traded in numismatic circles from an estimated (by me) 100,000 to 125,000 released from the Treasury from the late 1930s to 1962.

VAM-24

**Die Varieties:** Many die combinations exist for the 1878-CC from 30 die pairs, none of commanding importance to nonspecialists. *The Top 100 Morgan Dollar Varieties* singles out VAM-6, VAM-11, VAM-18, and VAM-24.

VAM-24

## Whitman Coin Guide (WCG™)

| VG-8 | F-12 | VF-20 | EF-40 | AU-50 | MS-60 | MS-63 | MS-64 | MS-65 | MS-66 | MS-67 |
|---|---|---|---|---|---|---|---|---|---|---|
| $80 | $90 | $100 | $125 | $140 | $250 | $330 | $550 | $1,700 | $5,400 | $30,000 |

### AVAILABILITY

| | MS-60 | MS-61 | MS-62 | MS-63 | MS-64 | MS-65 | MS-66 | MS-67 | MS-68+ |
|---|---|---|---|---|---|---|---|---|---|
| Certified | 346 | 1,406 | 5,791 | 12,104 | 10,284 | 2,735 | 405 | 14 | 0 |
| Field | 100,000–140,000 | | | 25,000–35,000 | 15,000–25,000 | 4,000–6,000 | 1,000–2,000 | 25–40 | 1–5 |
| Cert. DMPL | 6 | 25 | 107 | 278 | 232 | 64 | 3 | 0 | 0 |

# 1878-S: ALL WITH REVERSE OF 1878 (PAF)

Optimal
Collecting Grade
MS-65

Circulation-
Strike Mintage
9,774,000

**Key to Collecting Circulation Strikes:** The 1878-S dollar is plentiful in Mint State, with the typical example being MS-62 to MS-64 and with decent luster, more satiny than deeply frosty. The 1878-S comes only with the Reverse of 1878 (flat eagle's breast, seven tail feathers, parallel top arrow feather).

**Surface Quality:** Usually fairly well struck; however, some pieces show planchet striations on the face of Miss Liberty and show some weakness at the lower part of the eagle and below. As all are of the Type 2 Reverse (flat eagle's breast, parallel top arrow feather), at first glance the reverse may appear to be weakly struck. However, upon close examination most have well-defined feathers. Usually lustrous and very attractive, satiny or frosty (but not deeply frosty), is the rule.

**Prooflike Coins:** Some are struck from highly prooflike dies, many on just one side, although these are but a tiny fraction of the existing population.

**Mintage and Distribution:** Early coinage of the 1878-S dollars was not easy, for of the 10 pairs of dies sent from Philadelphia to the San Francisco Mint on April 8, three obverses and eight reverses were considered by the coiner to be unfit for use. I believe that 5,000,000 to 6,000,000 of these, and most of the original mintages of 1879-S, 1880-S, 1881-S, and 1882-S, were stored at the San Francisco Mint. Large quantities of these were released in subsequent years, mostly after 1913, and extensively in the 1950s, many going to Las Vegas, some held by banks and casinos as "cash reserves" with a secret appreciation potential.

**Die Varieties:** Dozens of die pairs, all of the Reverse of 1878 (PAF) style, were on hand at the San Francisco Mint by early summer, but it is not known how many were actually used that year, although the figures were at least 43 obverses and 38 reverses. Some reverses were kept and employed in 1879. The VAM text describes many varieties of minor doubling. Both Walter Breen and *The Top 100 Morgan Dollar Varieties* take note of the so-called Long Nock or Long Arrow Shaft variety, for which the left tip of the arrow is slightly longer than normal. Remarkably, virtually all known pieces show wear, this despite the use of at least five die pairs in the coinage.

## Whitman Coin Guide (WCG™)

| VG-8 | F-12 | VF-20 | EF-40 | AU-50 | MS-60 | MS-63 | MS-64 | MS-65 | MS-66 | MS-67 |
|------|------|-------|-------|-------|-------|-------|-------|-------|-------|-------|
| $28 | $29 | $35 | $40 | $45 | $60 | $78 | $115 | $270 | $750 | $8,750 |

**AVAILABILITY**

| | MS-60 | MS-61 | MS-62 | MS-63 | MS-64 | MS-65 | MS-66 | MS-67 | MS-68+ |
|---|-------|-------|-------|-------|-------|-------|-------|-------|--------|
| Certified | 250 | 1,346 | 7,388 | 22,595 | 25,818 | 7,475 | 1,077 | 51 | 1 |
| Field | | 350,000–600,000 | | 100,000–150,000 | 40,000–65,000 | 15,000–25,000 | 2,000–3,000 | 100–200 | 5–10 |
| Cert. DMPL | 3 | 19 | 79 | 178 | 178 | 43 | 5 | 0 | 0 |

# MORGAN SILVER DOLLARS, RARE COINS, AND LIFE IN 1879

## THE MORGAN DOLLAR SCENARIO

In 1879 the New Orleans Mint, inoperative since the early days of the Civil War, again struck coins, including silver dollars and high-denomination gold. While Morgan dollars were produced in quantity at the four mints, mintages of other silver denominations were small. The glut of silver coins in circulation continued.

## MINTS AND MINTAGES

This was the first full year since 1861 in which gold coins were readily available at banks. This also marked the first postwar year in which massive exports of large-denomination gold coins were made to foreign commercial centers.

In February 1879, Horatio C. Burchard became director of the Mint, successor to Dr. Henry R. Linderman (a numismatist who was in the fortunate position of being able to have rarities for his collection struck to order!). Burchard would continue the policy of the private making of patterns and other numismatic delicacies, and during his administration, which lasted until June 1885, many interesting things would be made, but not publicized.

At the Philadelphia Mint, the production of gold dollars was remarkably low in 1879, and just 3,000 were struck for circulation. There arose a great speculation in these small coins, and most were hoarded. Similarly, investors were agog with Proof trade dollars, not normally a popular denomination, and orders poured into the Mint, creating a blip in the coinage charts, rising for the year to a record 1,541 Proofs. The craze for gold dollars continued unabated for the next decade, but the passion for Proof trade dollars petered out after early 1880, by which time the astounding quantity of 1,987 1880-dated Proofs had been struck. In contrast, in the normal year of 1878 some 900 Proof trade dollars were made, and in 1881 the figure was 1,097.

## IN LEADVILLE, COLORADO

In this era, in the Rocky Mountains of Colorado, the town of Leadville, over 10,000 feet high, became the home to more than 30 silver mines, 10 smelters, and other activities resulting in about $15,000,000 a year in bullion being produced. By this time, Virginia City, Nevada, was fading in importance in the silver market. Throughout the West, large quantities of this precious metal continued to be refined, and the ready market provided by Uncle Sam under the 1878 Bland-Allison Act was a godsend. Morgan dollars were minted by the millions.

Leadville remained in the news for years afterward. One of the better-known stories of that mining camp involved Horace Tabor, a storekeeper who in 1880 grubstaked two prospectors with $65 worth of food. They struck pay dirt, and within a year Tabor became the owner of several important properties, including the Matchless Mine, which yielded a fortune. Tabor, in his fifties, became enamored of a local prostitute, Elizabeth "Baby Doe" McCourt, age 23; he divorced his wife and married his newfound love. Baby Doe became famous in the annals of Colorado and mining, and enjoyed a life of luxury for a time, living in a mansion and enjoying the social high life, including events at the richly appointed Tabor Opera House in Denver, financed by Horace.

## NICKELS AND DIMES

In Watertown, New York, the F.W. Woolworth Company had its inception when Frank Winfield Woolworth, age 27, was able to convince his employer to set up a counter featuring everything priced at 5¢. He then secured financing from one of his employers' backers for $400, with which he opened a store in Utica, again with all items priced at 5¢. Today, collectors of Shield-type nickels, the only kind in circulation, can only dream of Woolworth's intake! Actually, the number of incoming nickels fell below expectations, and in three months the store closed. However, the idea did not die, and the same backer financed Woolworth in the opening of a five-and-dime store in Lancaster, Pennsylvania, which threw open its doors on June 21 and indeed became a success, presumably with many Liberty Seated dimes mixed with the nickels!

Further stores were soon opened in Pennsylvania in Philadelphia, Harrisburg, and York, and in Newark, New Jersey, but played to lackluster response. However, other stores in Buffalo, New York, and in Erie and Scranton, Pennsylvania, and other locations, in low-income areas and neighborhoods proved to be dynamic successes, launching an empire that became an American icon.

Once, upon being queried at the great effort involved in selling items for 5¢ apiece, Woolworth stated, "Twenty nickels make a dollar, you know."[8]

## AUCTION NEWS

The year 1879 marked Edward Cogan's swan song on the rare coin auction stage, with his last sale featuring the Theodore Riley Collection, held on December 1 through 3, and among other things offering Mint State examples of the 1804 and 1823 cents.

In 1879 W. Elliot Woodward was considerably more active on the auction scene than he had been in 1878, and presented the numismatic community with five sales, including (among other properties) the collections of William Bowdoin, George W. Pratt, and John Robinson. The usual modus operandi of Woodward and other dealers was to buy coins and collections outright, then to auction them to realize a profit. It seems that relatively few sales consisted of outright consignments from sellers.

## MEANWHILE, ON THE AMERICAN SCENE IN 1879

On January 1, 1879, the resumption of specie payments—the giving out by banks of gold and silver coins at par in exchange for federal paper money—became law. In fact, by that time silver coins were already in circulation and had been since April 1876, and the exchange of gold coins at par became common in banking circles after December 17, 1878, all of this done in anticipation of January 1, 1879.

In New York City, William K. Vanderbilt, age 30, acquired Gilmore's Garden, built five years earlier, and renamed it Madison Square Garden. In time the facility became the venue for many events. The Metropolitan Life Insurance Company began offering small-face-value policies for wage earners and average citizens, launching mass insurance. The company expanded rapidly, hired 550 agents from England, and within three years increased its district offices from just 3 to 50.

On October 21, 1879, Thomas A. Edison demonstrated a successful electric light featuring a filament made from cotton thread impregnated with baked-on lampblack, enclosed in a vacuum. Although a number of other scientists had experimented with similar devices, Edison's, which burned for 45 hours, was the first to achieve success. At the time, much commercial illumination was done by coal gas and other gases, while homes were lighted with candles, kerosene lamps, whale oil lamps and other devices. Municipal lighting in some cities was accomplished with electric arc lamps, in which an arc passed between electrodes, a process quite well developed by 1879, but not suitable for home or office use.

The Pirates of Penzance opened on December 31 in New York City at the Fifth Avenue Theatre, and included melodies by Gilbert and Sullivan.

In New York City the architectural firm of McKim, Mead, and White was founded by Charles F. McKim (age 32), William Rutherford Mead (33), and Stanford White (26), and would go on to create many famous buildings, particularly in New York, but elsewhere as well. White became a pal and social (including low-life) sidekick of New York City sculptor Augustus Saint-Gaudens, who was later to achieve numismatic fame.

In Europe there were widespread failures in crops, creating a strong demand for American products, bringing prosperity to Midwestern agriculture and the railroads serving it, lifting the economy of an area that had seen great difficulties in recent years.

# 1879: ALL WITH REVERSE OF 1879 (SAF)

Optimal
Collecting Grade
MS-64

Circulation-
Strike Mintage
14,806,000

Proof Mintage
1,100

**Key to Collecting Circulation Strikes:** The 1879 dollar is very plentiful in all grades, as you might expect from the mintage figure. Mint State coins abound, but the quality of strike and luster can vary widely.

**Surface Quality:** Most examples are fairly well struck. Many have lightness of center details particularly noticeable above the ear of Miss Liberty, this being typical for nearly all of the series from this point forward. The extra metal needed to flow into the rounded breast of the eagle on the Type 3 (Reverse of 1879) dies took away from metal available to fill the high points on the obverse, resulting in some loss of detail. Usually seen lustrous, sometimes grainy if a particular die has been used for a long period of time.

**Prooflike Coins:** Prooflike coins exist, including some with high contrast. Many are one-sided prooflikes. Prooflike coins are scarce in comparison to frosty, lustrous examples.

**Mintage and Distribution:** Although dollars of this date have been plentiful from day one, indicating release near the time of coinage, many bags remained in storage. In Mint State supplies were plentiful in the 1950s and 1960s, often trading in quantity. However, few remained by the time of the Treasury releases of 1962 through 1964.

**Die Varieties:** Made for the coinage were 129 obverse dies and 86 reverse dies, although it is not known if all were used. In any event, reverse dies could be held over for use in a future year. There are many minor die variations, but none significant.

## 1879, PROOFS

**Mintage:** Mint record, 1,100. Breen comment: "250 coined in first quarter, 500 in second, total 750; of these 100 were melted in January 1880, leaving 650 net mintage."[9] I find the 650 figure to be unlikely in view that in proportion to the survival of other dates, there are too many certified coins; 1,100 or close to it seems to be more correct.

**Key to Collecting Proofs:** Most are of low contrast. Striking quality is average. Although the mintage is high, the challenge for quality is high as well.

## Whitman Coin Guide (WCG™)

| VG-8 | F-12 | VF-20 | EF-40 | AU-50 | MS-60 | MS-63 | MS-64 | MS-65 | MS-66 | MS-67 | PF-60 | PF-64 | PF-65 | PF-66 | PF-67 |
|---|---|---|---|---|---|---|---|---|---|---|---|---|---|---|---|
| $28 | $29 | $34 | $36 | $40 | $50 | $73 | $130 | $825 | $3,250 | $35,500 | $1,300 | $4,300 | $6,200 | $9,750 | $15,250 |

### AVAILABILITY

| | MS-60 | MS-61 | MS-62 | MS-63 | MS-64 | MS-65 | MS-66 | MS-67 | MS-68+ |
|---|---|---|---|---|---|---|---|---|---|
| Certified | 92 | 446 | 2,042 | 6,703 | 6,960 | 1,585 | 194 | 6 | 0 |
| Field | | 90,000–150,000 | | 40,000–60,000 | 18,000–25,000 | 2,500–3,500 | 200–300 | 15–25 | 0 |
| Cert. DMPL | 7 | 37 | 78 | 109 | 107 | 10 | 1 | 0 | 0 |
| | PF-60 | PF-61 | PF-62 | PF-63 | PF-64 | PF-65 | PF-66 | PF-67 | PF-68+ |
| Certified | 18 | 29 | 80 | 133 | 164 | 49 | 41 | 20 | 9 |
| Field | | 200–300 | | 200–300 | 225–350 | 100–150 | 75–125 | 50–75 | 5–15 |

# 1879-CC: ALL WITH REVERSE OF 1879 (SAF)

Optimal
Collecting Grade
MS-64

Circulation-
Strike Mintage
756,000

Detail of 1879-CC,
Large CC Over
Small CC.

Detail of 1879-CC,
Large CC.

**Key to Collecting Circulation Strikes:** Among basic date and mintmark issues, the 1879-CC is the first key or rare variety in the Morgan dollar series and is the second rarest (after 1889-CC) of all Carson City Morgans. Although thousands of Mint State coins exist, gems (MS-65 or better) are very difficult to find. There are two basic styles: the "perfect" or Large CC variety and the "Large CC Over Small CC," on which, at the Mint, there was an attempt to tool away the small CC, so that larger CC letters could be stamped in that area. The Large CC variety is the more available of the two but is also more popular than the Large CC Over Small CC.

**Surface Quality:** Most 1879-CC dollars are quite well struck on obverse and reverse. The 1879-CC is typically encountered with attractive luster, although some are frostier than others, and still others are dull and lifeless. Not much searching is needed to find a "nice" coin, as such pieces are the rule.

**Prooflike Coins:** Some are prooflike on one side or the other, this not being particularly unusual. The prooflike surface is often hazy or "gray," not deeply mirrorlike.

**Mintage and Distribution:** There were probably hundreds of thousands of 1879-CC dollars melted under the 1918 Pittman Act, but facts will never be known. In the early 20th century, quantities of these dollars were sent to the San Francisco Mint for storage, and others went to the Treasury Building in Washington, DC. At least several thousand were paid out by the latter depot in the early 1950s, one bag of 1,000 coins going via an intermediary to dealer Harry J. Forman. A bag from San Francisco went to someone in either Montana or Seattle.[10] After the great Treasury release was halted in March 1964, the General Services Administration (GSA) holding of 1879-CC dollars totaled 4,123, or 0.55% of the original mintage, per a later inventory.[11] The Redfield hoard, dispersed in the late 1970s, is said to have had 400 to 500 of the Large CC Over Small CC variety, these not coming from the GSA sales.

**Die Varieties:** Several varieties exist, but the Large CC and the Large CC Over Small CC are the only ones that have attracted much notice.

## Whitman Coin Guide (WCG™)

| VG-8 | F-12 | VF-20 | EF-40 | AU-50 | MS-60 | MS-63 | MS-64 | MS-65 | MS-66 | MS-67 |
|------|------|-------|-------|-------|-------|-------|-------|-------|-------|-------|
| $160 | $190 | $265 | $725 | $1,750 | $3,750 | $6,300 | $9,250 | $30,000 | $65,000 | $82,500 |

**AVAILABILITY**

| | MS-60 | MS-61 | MS-62 | MS-63 | MS-64 | MS-65 | MS-66 | MS-67 | MS-68+ |
|---|-------|-------|-------|-------|-------|-------|-------|-------|--------|
| Certified | 97 | 243 | 691 | 1,042 | 1,288 | 130 | 3 | 0 | 0 |
| Field | | 1,750–2,500 | | 1,300–1,600 | 1,200–1,500 | 150–200 | 2–4 | 0 | 0 |
| Cert. DMPL | 3 | 10 | 40 | 46 | 30 | 3 | 0 | 0 | 0 |

# 1879-O: All With Reverse of 1879 (SAF)

**Optimal Collecting Grade MS-64**

**Circulation-Strike Mintage 2,887,000**

**Key to Collecting Circulation Strikes:** The 1879-O dollar is plentiful in lower Mint State levels from 60 through 63. MS-64 coins are scarce, and in proportion to the demand for them, MS-65 pieces are rare. A good choice for value is an MS-63 or MS-64, but hand-picked for quality; that is, without too many bagmarks. Coins in AU grade, once called "slider Uncirculated," abound.

**Surface Quality:** Striking varies from sharp to average or below average, the last having weakness at the centers, in the hair strands above Miss Liberty's ear and the breast feathers of the eagle. Luster is typically frosty and attractive. Bagmarks are a huge problem.

**Prooflike Coins:** Some dies are prooflike, scarce as such, and DMPL are scarcer yet.

**Mintage and Distribution:** Through the 1950s the 1879-O dollar was considered scarce in Mint State, although AU pieces were plentiful. In 1957 thousands were released, and the market value plummeted. The 1962 Treasury release yielded multiple bags, but nothing like the quantities of other O Mint dollars turned loose at that time.

**Die Varieties:** 1879-O "O over Horizontal O" Mintmark, VAM-4. This variety is called O over Horizontal O by VAM, who say it may be a triple-punched (but not over horizontal) O, indicating that opinion is divided. Breen (*Encyclopedia*, 1988, Breen-5528) dismisses the O over Horizontal O and calls it a triple-punched O. *The Top 100 Morgan Dollar Varieties* calls it O over Horizontal O and makes no mention of tripling.

VAM-4

## Whitman Coin Guide (WCG™)

| VG-8 | F-12 | VF-20 | EF-40 | AU-50 | MS-60 | MS-63 | MS-64 | MS-65 | MS-66 | MS-67 |
|------|------|-------|-------|-------|-------|-------|-------|-------|-------|-------|
| $28 | $29 | $35 | $40 | $47 | $85 | $210 | $550 | $3,350 | $18,500 | $28,500 |

**AVAILABILITY**

| | MS-60 | MS-61 | MS-62 | MS-63 | MS-64 | MS-65 | MS-66 | MS-67 | MS-68+ |
|---|-------|-------|-------|-------|-------|-------|-------|-------|--------|
| Certified | 580 | 1,290 | 3,423 | 5,028 | 3,170 | 424 | 22 | 0 | 0 |
| Field | | 220,000–350,000 | | 15,000–25,000 | 5,000–8,000 | 450–700 | 30–50 | 0 | 0 |
| Cert. DMPL | 17 | 27 | 74 | 68 | 53 | 6 | 0 | 0 | 0 |

# 1879-S: Reverse of 1878 (PAF)

Optimal
Collecting Grade
MS-63

Circulation-
Strike Mintage
500,000 (estimated)

Detail of 1879-S
(PAF).

**Key to Collecting Circulation Strikes:** The 1879-S comes in two varieties; the Reverse of 1878, with flat eagle's breast and parallel top arrow feathers, is quite elusive, and the variety with Type 3 Reverse (Reverse of 1879), discussed in the next section of this book, is very common. The former, very rare variety was hardly known even to the most active dealers and collectors until recent decades. Amazingly, it was found that even well-worn pieces were very rare.

**Surface Quality:** Usually seen well struck. However, as with all Type 2 Reverse dollars, the eagle can appear to be weak, due to the flat breast. However, the individual feathers in the breast are usually well struck. Usually seen with attractive, frosty luster. Some have areas of die polish interrupting the frost.

**Prooflike Coins:** Semi-prooflike coins are seen with frequency in the context of the variety. Prooflike coins exist but are in the distinct minority. DMPL coins are very rare.

**Mintage and Distribution:** A handful of leftover reverses, shipped to San Francisco in 1878, created this coinage. No records exist as to mintage quantities, but 600,000 or so is my guess, simply because a half dozen or more die pairs were used. However, if even 100,000 were minted, most must have been melted under the Pittman Act, for not many exist today! Few ever went into circulation, and not many were in the Treasury releases of later years. The Redfield hoard (1976) is said to have contained 3,000 Mint State, but mostly bag-marked.[12] This is the only quantity rumored or reported to the author.[13]

**Die Varieties:** The 1879-S with Type 2 Reverse is often seen with minor retouching on the wing feathers of the eagle, a curiosity also seen on the 1878-S, but nowhere else in the series.

## Whitman Coin Guide (WCG™)

| VG-8 | F-12 | VF-20 | EF-40 | AU-50 | MS-60 | MS-63 | MS-64 | MS-65 | MS-66 | MS-67 |
|------|------|-------|-------|-------|-------|-------|-------|-------|-------|-------|
| $35 | $36 | $40 | $45 | $58 | $130 | $435 | $1,350 | $5,500 | $47,500 | $65,000 |

**AVAILABILITY**

| | MS-60 | MS-61 | MS-62 | MS-63 | MS-64 | MS-65 | MS-66 | MS-67 | MS-68+ |
|---|-------|-------|-------|-------|-------|-------|-------|-------|--------|
| Certified | 274 | 521 | 1,005 | 1,114 | 779 | 63 | 1 | 0 | 0 |
| Field | | 1,000-1,500 | | 900-1,200 | 700-800 | 60-100 | 1-3 | 0 | 1-5 |
| Cert. DMPL | 0 | 1 | 4 | 3 | 1 | 1 | 0 | 0 | 0 |

# 1879-S: REVERSE OF 1879 (SAF)

Optimal
Collecting Grade
MS-65

Circulation-
Strike Mintage
8,600,000
(estimated)

Detail of 1879-S
(SAF).

**Key to Collecting Circulation Strikes:** The 1879-S with Reverse of 1879 (SAF) is one of the most plentiful of all Morgan dollars in the early (1878–1904) date range. The majority of pieces are in Mint State and have excellent eye appeal.

**Surface Quality:** Usually very well struck on obverse and reverse. Typically very brilliant and very lustrous, the usual piece having come from a bag in the Treasury release of 1962 through 1964.

**Prooflike Coins:** Prooflike coins are common, sometimes on one side only. However, many two-sided prooflikes exist, including in higher grade.

**Mintage and Distribution:** Relatively few 1879-S dollars were paid out at the time of striking. Most remained stored within the granite walls of the San Francisco Mint. Later, huge quantities were paid out, including in 1942, when dozens if not hundreds of bags were taken from storage. The 1962 through 1964 Treasury release yielded many more, possibly over a million. Nearly all bags and quantities reported to the author contained 1879-S dollars of the Reverse of 1879 (SAF) variety.[14]

**Die Varieties:** Many die varieties exist, but none are dramatic enough to cause much attention.

## Whitman Coin Guide (WCG™)

| VG-8 | F-12 | VF-20 | EF-40 | AU-50 | MS-60 | MS-63 | MS-64 | MS-65 | MS-66 | MS-67 |
|------|------|-------|-------|-------|-------|-------|-------|-------|-------|-------|
| $28 | $29 | $34 | $37 | $41 | $50 | $63 | $82 | $165 | $370 | $800 |

### AVAILABILITY

| | MS-60 | MS-61 | MS-62 | MS-63 | MS-64 | MS-65 | MS-66 | MS-67 | MS-68+ |
|-----------|-------|-------|-------|-------|-------|-------|-------|-------|--------|
| Certified | 73 | 605 | 5,067 | 31,917 | 69,193 | 43,439 | 13,651 | 3,289 | 223 |
| Field | 600,000–1,000,000 | | | 200,000–300,000 | 160,000–240,000 | 120,000–150,000 | 20,000–30,000 | 5,500–6,500 | 200–300 |
| Cert. DMPL | 2 | 19 | 110 | 398 | 523 | 252 | 76 | 10 | 0 |

# MORGAN SILVER DOLLARS, RARE COINS, AND LIFE IN 1880

## THE MORGAN DOLLAR SCENARIO

By 1880 the Morgan-designed silver dollar had been coined by the millions, and examples were readily available at banks. In the American West, these heavy coins were staples in everyday commerce. Elsewhere, paper dollars literally filled the bill, and silver dollars were seldom seen.

Although it might seem logical that this new coin, reintroducing a denomination that had not been minted since 1873 nor seen in commerce since 1850, would be popular with collectors, this was not the case. Morgan dollars were nearly universally ignored, and little notice was given concerning them or their varieties.

So far as can be determined from contemporary catalogs and the sole independent coin collectors' magazine of the day, the *American Journal of Numismatics*, there was absolutely no interest in mintage figures, differences in tail feathers, or even CC, O, and S mintmarked coins. Those few collectors who desired such coins routinely obtained them as part of silver Proof sets from the Mint.

Although George T. Morgan had designed the new dollar, and his initial M was easy enough to see on the obverse neck truncation and on the reverse ribbon, the new coin was nearly universally called the Bland dollar, from Richard Bland, coauthor of the 1878 Bland-Allison Act.

This notice by Lancaster, Pennsylvania, dealer Charles Steigerwalt was published in his house organ, *The Coin Journal*, September 1880:

> In 1878 the demand for an increase of the circulating medium caused Congress to pass a law authorizing the re-issuing from the Mint of the standard dollar, and in consequence the Bland dollar with which our readers are familiar made its appearance from the Mint again in that year.
>
> Large numbers of this beautiful coin with its fine, classic head of Liberty have been issued since then and unless too large a quantity be coined and the coinage having to be suspended in consequence, collectors may look forward to a long continuance of this elegant piece.
>
> The collecting of the issues of U.S. silver has largely increased of late and we would recommend to any of our readers who have not done so already to commence at once as the finest pieces are being rapidly picked up and must necessarily increase in price before a very long time has elapsed. No collection presents a more attractive appearance than a line of fine silver ending in the latter years with the mirrorlike surface of the Mint Proof pieces.

## MEANWHILE, ON THE AMERICAN SCENE IN 1880

In an architect's rendition of the exterior and interior of a typical national bank of this era, the vault, where such items as bags of silver dollars would be stored, is on the first floor at the back on the right, behind the teller line and bookkeeping area. The "private" area was reserved for meetings, such as by the board of directors, or for use by the bank's chief operating officer who, in nearly all instances, was the cashier. To the left of the public area, stairs led to the second floor, which could have been used as professional offices or by the bank itself. In instances in which the upstairs was to be accessible at all hours, such as when used as a lodge meeting hall or private apartment, access would be provided by a separate door on the outside of the building. (*Banker's Almanac*, 1875)

The federal decennial census conducted in 1880 tallied the population of the United States at 50,155,783. Among these were over 100 people who revealed that they were millionaires. Los Angeles, a formerly sleepy pueblo in southern California, registered a population of 11,183 in the census, or about double the 5,728 people who had lived there a decade earlier.

Chinese immigrants were becoming a "problem" to certain Western interests, who resented the cheap labor that arrived during the building of railroads. The Chinese Exclusion Treaty was signed with China, giving the United States the authority to "regulate, limit or suspend" entry of laborers from that country. In the same year close to 550,000 English and nearly 440,000 Irish came to the United States to build new lives.

In New York City at Madison Square Theatre, the melodrama *Hazel Kirke* was particularly popular, eventually enjoying 486 performances there, setting a record. This was one of the standard stage plays of the era and succeeding decades, along with *East Lynne* and *Uncle Tom's Cabin*. Sarah Bernhardt made her American stage debut on November 8, at Booth's Theatre, also in New York City, subsequently appearing in a series of four plays. She later made two more American tours, the final one in 1915.

General Lew Wallace, who served in the Civil War, would become famous with his *Ben Hur, A Tale of the Christ*, a drama set in ancient Roman times, which was widely adapted for the stage by traveling shows, later for films, depicting the travails of unfortunate Christians under Roman emperors.

There were about 50,000 telephone subscribers in the United States. Municipal electric lighting increased in popularity, and arc lights were installed throughout the main commercial district of Wabash, Indiana, and along a mile of Broadway in New York City, the last becoming known as "the Great White Way."

For the first time, halftone photographs were used to illustrate newspapers, heralding the end to engravings, and inaugurating an era in which depictions of scenes and events would be less pleasing to the eye than they were for decades earlier. Change was slow in coming, and engravings remained the method of choice into the early 1890s. In this era, paper with high sulfur content was widely used for newspapers and books, creating publications that in the next century would become brittle and in some instances self-destruct. Accordingly, the pages of the *American Journal of Numismatics*, if read more than a few times, would fall apart.

In Rochester, New York, bank clerk George Eastman, age 26, perfected a process for making photographic dry plates. The sewing machine was all the rage for home use, and during the year the Singer Company sold 539,000 units. Various manufacturers supplied agents and stores in towns worldwide, and an intense competition developed. In time, just about every home had a sewing machine of one sort or another. Knitting machines were also popular, including certain models made by Dana Bickford, who is numismatically remembered for his 1874 pattern coin proposal for an international $10 gold piece. The Bickford Knitting Machine and its contemporaries permitted socks, scarves, and other items to be knitted on a small device that could be positioned on a table in the home.

President Ulysses S. Grant was not nominated by his party for the third term he desired, when James Abram Garfield, age 48, of Ohio, was chosen on the 36th ballot, ending a deadlock. In the November election Garfield beat his Democratic contender, Winfield Scott Hancock. Grant entered private life, but suffered from alcoholism and had problems with finances, the last being alleviated somewhat by the later publication of his biography. It was later said with some justification that Grant was a great general, but a poor president.

Exports of ice from America to tropical and other southern ports reached a high this year with 890,364 tons carried in 1,735 ships. The ice was packed in sawdust and other insulation and stored below decks, and on long voyages part of it would melt, but at the destinations the product was very valuable, selling for as much as $56 per ton.

In Minneapolis the milling company of Washburn and Crosby laid plans to market Gold Medal flour, after winning a gold medal in a competition. Samuel B. Thomas introduced Thomas brand English muffins in New York, and in the same city a distributor named Reynolds began selling "Philadelphia" brand cream cheese. By this time there were more than 95 A&P groceries in the East and Midwest (operated by the great Atlantic and Pacific Tea Company).

# 1880: ALL WITH REVERSE OF 1879 (SAF)

**Optimal Collecting Grade**
MS-64

**Circulation-Strike Mintage**
12,600,000

**Proof Mintage**
1,355

**Key to Collecting Circulation Strikes:** The 1880 dollars were made in enormous quantities and from many different dies, and strike quality varies from sharp to weak. However, there are so many available today that finding a choice one will be no problem. Many 1880 dollars show traces of overdating (see Die Varieties), but these require significant magnification to discern, and most collectors ignore them. More Proofs than usual are in very high grades, on the long side of Proof-65.

**Surface Quality:** Striking varies from sharp to average; many pieces show lightness in the hair strands over the ear of Miss Liberty. The luster is usually very good. Some coins struck from worn dies have metal flow and graininess and are to be avoided.

**Prooflike Coins:** Some are from prooflike dies, obverse or reverse, or both. DMPL coins were rare, until, per Wayne Miller, "a bag [1,000 pieces] of prooflike dollars appeared in 1971. . . . [Some] were gorgeous cameos. All had deep mirror surfaces, frosty devices, and minimal bagmarks. Many of [today's] gem cameo prooflike 1880 dollars . . . are probably from this bag."[15]

**Mintage and Distribution:** Dollars dated 1880 were very common by the early 1940s, when many more bags were paid out from storage in Philadelphia. In 1955, large quantities turned up in eastern banks, probably hundreds of thousands if not more in bank vaults in the 1950s, usually in lower Mint State. By the time of the Treasury release of 1962 through 1964, most were out of government hands.

**Die Varieties:** A number of dies prepared for use in 1879 were overpunched with the date 1880, showing traces of the earlier digits. All told, 91 obverses and 77 reverses were made, probably most of the obverses being new (not altered from 1879).

## 1880, PROOFS

**Mintage:** 1,355, a figure caused by the carry-along factor from those who were speculating in Proof Trade dollars this year. Today, many Proofs of this date have been cleaned.

**Key to Collecting Proofs:** Good strike. Usually with deep cameo contrast. The majority of coins have been cleaned (so, what else is new?). In case you wonder, this is why pristine, lightly toned, beautiful specimens from old-time collections trample price records into the dust.

## Whitman Coin Guide (WCG™)

| VG-8 | F-12 | VF-20 | EF-40 | AU-50 | MS-60 | MS-63 | MS-64 | MS-65 | MS-66 | MS-67 | PF-60 | PF-64 | PF-65 | PF-66 | PF-67 |
|------|------|-------|-------|-------|-------|-------|-------|-------|-------|-------|-------|-------|-------|-------|-------|
| $28 | $29 | $34 | $37 | $41 | $53 | $75 | $145 | $675 | $3,600 | – | $1,300 | $3,900 | $6,100 | $9,500 | $15,000 |

**AVAILABILITY**

| | MS-60 | MS-61 | MS-62 | MS-63 | MS-64 | MS-65 | MS-66 | MS-67 | MS-68+ |
|---|-------|-------|-------|-------|-------|-------|-------|-------|--------|
| Certified | 92 | 433 | 2,565 | 8,026 | 7,924 | 1,611 | 131 | 0 | 0 |
| Field | | 125,000–250,000 | | 60,000–100,000 | 20,000–30,000 | 2,000–3,000 | 150–250 | 0 | 0 |
| Cert. DMPL | 0 | 9 | 32 | 95 | 143 | 38 | 2 | 0 | 0 |
| | PF-60 | PF-61 | PF-62 | PF-63 | PF-64 | PF-65 | PF-66 | PF-67 | PF-68+ |
| Certified | 10 | 34 | 79 | 122 | 180 | 97 | 61 | 49 | 14 |
| Field | | 300–500 | | 200–300 | 300–400 | 125–175 | 120–150 | 100–150 | 30–40 |

# 1880-CC: Reverse of 1878 (PAF)

Optimal
Collecting Grade
MS-64

Circulation-
Strike Mintage
125,000 (estimated)

Detail of 1880-CC
(PAF).

**Key to Collecting Circulation Strikes:** The 1880-CC exists in two varieties: the Reverse of 1878 (with flat breast and parallel top arrow feather), as studied on this page, and the usually seen Reverse of 1879. The Reverse of 1878 is several times scarcer, but in the aggregate enough exist that the premium differential is not great. The 1880-CC dollars of both reverse types tend to be "baggy," with many contact marks. Finding a choice one will not be difficult, as enough examples exist in the marketplace.

**Surface Quality:** The strike is usually quite good. On the obverse there may be some slight weakness of hair strands near the ear. The eagle's breast is flat, per the reverse style, but the individual feathers are usually well defined. Typically with attractive frosty surfaces.

**Prooflike Coins:** Coins with significant prooflike surface are very rare. *Note:* Certification data are confused for the 1880-CC, as most have been certified without mention of the reverse style, and some have been certified as having overdate traces, while others with overdate traces omit this mention.

**Mintage and Distribution:** No dollars were coined from November 1, 1879, to May 1880. Each month the branch mints forwarded samples of silver and gold coins to Philadelphia for assaying, to assure that production was of the correct weight and fineness. In a shipment containing dollars from Carson City, minted in July 1880, one piece was found to be of insufficient fineness. The superintendent at Carson City was directed not to pay out any coins from that production run, and to send further samples for testing.

**Die Varieties:** Most if not all 1880-CC obverses were overdated, and some can be called 1880/79, with traces of the 79 showing within the last two digits. These varieties were first published widely in Coin World and elsewhere in the 1960s, which created a sensation, after which studies were done, including by Van Allen and Mallis, and various rarities sorted out. The variety with bold 79 digits under the 80 are VAM-4, 5, and 6.

## Whitman Coin Guide (WCG™)

| VG-8 | F-12 | VF-20 | EF-40 | AU-50 | MS-60 | MS-63 | MS-64 | MS-65 | MS-66 | MS-67 |
|---|---|---|---|---|---|---|---|---|---|---|
| $200 | $225 | $235 | $285 | $350 | $575 | $700 | $1,150 | $2,700 | $7,000 | $55,000 |

### AVAILABILITY

| | MS-60 | MS-61 | MS-62 | MS-63 | MS-64 | MS-65 | MS-66 | MS-67 | MS-68+ |
|---|---|---|---|---|---|---|---|---|---|
| Certified | 3 | 39 | 136 | 369 | 521 | 151 | 24 | 1 | 0 |
| Field | 20,000–35,000 | | | 15,000–20,000 | 6,000–10,000 | 3,000–5,000 | 200–300 | 20–30 | 0 |
| Cert. DMPL | 2 | 1 | 6 | 13 | 13 | 3 | 0 | 0 | 0 |

# 1880-CC: REVERSE OF 1879 (SAF)

**Optimal Collecting Grade**
MS-64

**Circulation-Strike Mintage**
466,000
(estimated)[16]

Detail of 1880-CC (SAF).

**Key to Collecting Circulation Strikes:** This variety, the Reverse of 1879 with slanted top arrow feather, is several times more plentiful (some would say many times more plentiful) than the Reverse of 1878 (parallel arrow feather). However, as many are extensively bag-marked, searching is needed to locate an example with good eye appeal. The 1880-CC is ever popular due to the magic of the CC mintmark.

**Surface Quality:** Strike varies from sharp in all areas to weak at the centers, examples of the last showing lack of definition in the hair strands near Miss Liberty's ear and on the breast feathers of the eagle. The luster on a typical 1880-CC is quite nice. Some pieces have plan-chet striations from the strip preparation process, these in the form of tiny parallel lines on the highest central points of the coin (which were the deepest areas of the dies, and thus not all characteristics of the original planchet were removed in the striking process).

**Prooflike Coins:** Many partially prooflike or semi-prooflike pieces exist and can be very attractive. Significantly mirrored prooflike coins are apt to be lightly struck at the centers. *Note:* Certification data are confused for the 1880-CC, as most have been certified without mention of the reverse style, and some have been certified as having overdate traces, while others with overdate traces omit this mention.

**Mintage and Distribution:** See notes under 1878-CC Reverse of 1878 (PAF).

**Die Varieties:** The VAM-5 and 6 varieties, High and Low 7 overdate varieties, are popular.

VAM-5 (8 / High 7)          VAM-6 (8 / Low 7)

## Whitman Coin Guide (WCG™)

| VG-8 | F-12 | VF-20 | EF-40 | AU-50 | MS-60 | MS-63 | MS-64 | MS-65 | MS-66 | MS-67 |
|------|------|-------|-------|-------|-------|-------|-------|-------|-------|-------|
| $150 | $185 | $210 | $275 | $325 | $445 | $490 | $600 | $1,250 | $2,050 | $22,500 |

**AVAILABILITY**

| | MS-60 | MS-61 | MS-62 | MS-63 | MS-64 | MS-65 | MS-66 | MS-67 | MS-68+ |
|---|-------|-------|-------|-------|-------|-------|-------|-------|--------|
| Certified | 59 | 348 | 1,607 | 4,427 | 6,724 | 3,377 | 1,183 | 40 | 0 |
| Field | 65,000–110,000 | | | 45,000–60,000 | 18,000–30,000 | 8,000–15,000 | 600–900 | 60–90 | 5–10 |
| Cert. DMPL | 2 | 16 | 57 | 139 | 233 | 53 | 3 | 0 | 0 |

# 1880-O: ALL WITH REVERSE OF 1879 (SAF)

Optimal
Collecting Grade
MS-64

Circulation-
Strike Mintage
5,305,000

**Key to Collecting Circulation Strikes:** All 1880-O dollars are from the reverse of 1879 with rounded eagle's breast and slanted top arrow feathers. A number of dies were overdated and show small traces of earlier digits. These have not created much attention in the marketplace, save for dyed-in-the-wool specialists. Certification reports are unreliable regarding overdates, as many coins were graded without checking for this feature. Since the 1970s and 1980s, the swing has been to certification for higher-grade Morgan dollars, and "sliders" are mostly called AU-55 or AU-58 now.

**Surface Quality:** Striking varies from strong to soft, but most are above average. Again, points to check are the hair above Miss Liberty's ear and the feathers on the eagle's breast. Cherry-picking is recommended. Luster varies from satiny to "greasy," but is generally satisfactory.

**Prooflike Coins:** Some dies are prooflike; such coins are usually quite attractive if relatively free from bagmarks. Those with DMPL surfaces are elusive.

**Mintage and Distribution:** Seemingly, many 1880-O dollars were placed into circulation, remained there for just a short time, and then were returned to storage, apparently at the New Orleans Mint itself. About 1946 some Uncirculated bags were released, making the issue plentiful, although before the 1880-O was not considered to be a rare date. Other bags emerged from hiding circa 1956 or 1957, and in the Treasury release in 1962 the issue was well represented. However, it was never plentiful in bag quantities on the numismatic market.

**Die Varieties:** For the 1880-O two different sizes and styles of mintmarks were used. The small mintmark, perfectly round in its outside outline, is thick and heavy, and has a relatively small interior space with the left and right sides not being parallel. The larger mintmark is also round in its exterior outline, but interior is narrow, sometimes with nearly parallel left and right interior surfaces. These mintmark sizes have not been widely collected. One variety, VAM-39, has a small o mintmark tilted measurably to the right.

Varieties with traces of the overdate include VAM-4 ("80/79") and VAM-5, 6, 6A, and 6B, all these being listed in *The Top 100 Morgan Dollar Varieties*, as are two "Hangnail" varieties, from a tiny die gouge, VAM-1A and 6B, both of which have overdate features. VAM-43 has slight doubling on Miss Liberty's ear and eyelid.

## Whitman Coin Guide (WCG™)

| VG-8 | F-12 | VF-20 | EF-40 | AU-50 | MS-60 | MS-63 | MS-64 | MS-65 | MS-66 | MS-67 |
|------|------|-------|-------|-------|-------|-------|-------|-------|-------|-------|
| $28 | $29 | $34 | $36 | $43 | $75 | $430 | $1,800 | $26,000 | $56,000 | $85,000 |

**AVAILABILITY**

| | MS-60 | MS-61 | MS-62 | MS-63 | MS-64 | MS-65 | MS-66 | MS-67 | MS-68+ |
|--|-------|-------|-------|-------|-------|-------|-------|-------|--------|
| Certified | 473 | 1,951 | 3,988 | 3,866 | 2,037 | 54 | 0 | 0 | 0 |
| Field | | 10,000–15,000 | | 6,000–9,000 | 2,500–4,000 | 80–150 | 0 | 0 | 0 |
| Cert. DMPL | 33 | 41 | 77 | 92 | 70 | 0 | 0 | 0 | 0 |

# 1880-S: ALL WITH REVERSE OF 1879 (SAF)

Optimal
Collecting Grade
MS-64

Circulation-
Strike Mintage
8,900,000

**Key to Collecting Circulation Strikes:** The 1880-S is a delightful Morgan dollar, usually combining excellent strike and luster with a plentiful supply of pieces in the marketplace. Indeed, among Morgan dollars of the early (1878–1904) years, the 1880-S is second only to the 1881-S in terms of availability. The majority of Mint State pieces in existence today were released during the dispersal of the Treasury hoard from 1962 through 1964.

**Surface Quality:** The 1880-S is usually seen quite well struck. Only a small percentage of pieces have weak striking and these can be easily enough avoided by the discriminating buyer. As is true of other Morgan dollar dates, certification services do not take striking into consideration. Most 1880-S dollars have deep, frosty luster of great beauty.

**Prooflike Coins:** Prooflike coins are not unusual.

**Mintage and Distribution:** Similar to several other San Francisco Mint issues of the era, much of the mintage of the 1880-S seems to have been stored in the mint, remaining there by at least 1913. Many were paid out over time, including in the 1950s. In *The Forecaster*, September 15, 1971, John Kamin estimated that about 1,600,000 more came out during the Treasury release, mostly in 1963.

**Die Varieties:** The 1880-S exists in many different die varieties. VAM-8, 9, 10, and 11, are overdated from 1879, but the features are not boldly defined. However, for dedicated VAM enthusiasts these are worth seeking. For the 1880-S, S mintmark punches of two different sizes were used. These are neither widely noticed nor collected except by VAM enthusiasts. VAM-35 has a large open mintmark tilted left.

## Whitman Coin Guide (WCG™)

| VG-8 | F-12 | VF-20 | EF-40 | AU-50 | MS-60 | MS-63 | MS-64 | MS-65 | MS-66 | MS-67 |
|------|------|-------|-------|-------|-------|-------|-------|-------|-------|-------|
| $28 | $29 | $34 | $37 | $41 | $50 | $65 | $85 | $175 | $375 | $900 |

**AVAILABILITY**

| | MS-60 | MS-61 | MS-62 | MS-63 | MS-64 | MS-65 | MS-66 | MS-67 | MS-68+ |
|------------|-------|-------|-------|---------|-----------------|-----------------|-------------|-----------|---------|
| Certified | 161 | 1,036 | 7,022 | 45,332 | 100,506 | 63,108 | 20,604 | 5,069 | 428 |
| Field | 700,000–1,100,000 | | | 300,000–400,000 | 250,000–325,000 | 150,000–225,000 | 25,000–35,000 | 4,000–6,000 | 400–600 |
| Cert. DMPL | 9 | 32 | 266 | 1,038 | 1,657 | 1,016 | 286 | 43 | 5 |

# Morgan Silver Dollars, Rare Coins, and Life in 1881

## The Morgan Dollar Scenario

The glut of dimes, quarters, and half dollars continued, and current mintages were small. Morgan dollars were spewed out by the millions, mandated by the provisions of the Bland-Allison Act of 1878. Huge quantities were piling up in the Mint and other vaults.

## Relating to Coinage

At the Mint, Chief Engraver Charles E. Barber created the Liberty Head portrait that would become famous on the 1883 nickel. In the meantime, in 1881 it was used on pattern cents, three-cent pieces, and five-cent pieces, an effort to standardize the designs of these minor coin denominations.

At the University of Pennsylvania, Joseph Wharton endowed the Wharton School of Finance and Commerce. Wharton, the owner of nickel mines at Lancaster Gap, Pennsylvania, was heavily involved in promotion and politics, and his name is closely interwoven with coinage, particularly in the production of copper-nickel and nickel alloys for use in minor denominations.

At the Philadelphia Mint only 640 quarter eagles were made for circulation. Although speculation and investment in gold dollars continued (see narrative under 1879), the quarter eagles escaped notice, and nearly all were routinely released into circulation. The circulation production of $3 gold pieces was also low, just 500, but these did not command much interest, either. Readers today might wonder how such treasures slipped by at the time. The answer is that collectors desiring $2.50 and $3 coins bought Proofs, and, in any event, the low mintage figures for circulation strikes were not widely known, there being no numismatic guides listing the same.

President Chester Alan Arthur, successor to the late James Garfield, commented: "The minting of silver dollars is unnecessary. We have coined 102 million of these dollars and only 34 million are in circulation."[17]

## Around the Hobby

The frenetic pace of auction sales held by leading catalogers touched a new record this year with 47 events on the calendar. What a smorgasbord of coins, tokens, medals, and paper money! New on the auction scene was Charles Steigerwalt, who had entered the rare coin trade in 1878. His first sale took place on February 28, 1881, and before the year ended he conducted four more events. H.G. Sampson and Harlan P. Smith were also fresh faces among auction catalogers this year. Lyman H. Low, who would achieve great prominence in later years, also issued his first catalog in 1881, on Christmas day, but copies are so rare today that few people have ever seen one.[18]

W. Eliot Woodward, in the rare coin auction field since 1860, offered a suite of sales highlighted in terms of quantity by the William Clogston offering, April 4–7, with 2,556 lots, with overflow sold in a separate catalog, April 8–9, with 1,310 lots. During this era Woodward and others continued to purchase collections intact from private owners and auction them for their own profit (hopefully), letting the chips fall where they might. Items that did not bring a satisfactory price were typically "bid in" and reoffered in a subsequent sale, sometimes the very next one.

Grading was erratic, and one person's "brilliant Proof" could be another's "polished Extremely Fine." Accordingly, relatively few purchases were made directly by mail. Instead, collectors at a distance typically placed their bids with trustworthy dealers or agents, who examined the lots in person and executed their bids. Among the dealers, Woodward's cataloging was considered to be better than most—or at least, fewer unfavorable things were said about him by his contemporaries. Indeed, Woodward remained above a lot (but not all) of the petty arguments that pervaded the profession during this particularly active decade in the auction sale business. When motivated he was not above firing a few printed salvos now and again, as with his protestations about private profiteering by Mint insiders,[19] or when he was annoyed or irked by one dealer or another (such as Ed. Frossard and the Chapman brothers).

## MEANWHILE, ON THE AMERICAN SCENE IN 1881

On July 2, 1881, President James Garfield was mortally wounded by disappointed office-seeker Charles J. Guiteau. Garfield was at the railroad station in Washington and was about to depart for New York City. Garfield held on to life bravely, but infection set in and he died on September 19 at age 49. He was succeeded by Vice President Chester Alan Arthur, age 50.

In this year Tennessee enacted the first of what were called "Jim Crow laws" against blacks, segregating them from whites, this provision allowing for "separate but equal" accommodations for black people, who were considered to be second-class citizens. The Supreme Court ruled that the federal income tax law of 1861 was unconstitutional. At the time, federal revenues were mainly obtained from tariffs and other taxes, but not by direct levies on incomes.

This era saw great growth in railroads, not only in the American West, where vast lengths of track were laid, but also throughout the East and Midwest. Dozens of different companies were formed, stock was sold, politicians were influenced, and many changes were effected. A favorite policy of railroads was to obtain subsidies or payments from towns that wanted service. Those that did not comply were left stranded. In some states, entire legislatures were influenced by railroad interests. Although there were many regulations, enforcement was erratic, and railroads often enjoyed monopolies, setting freight rates that were sometimes ruinous. On the stock exchange and in America in general, railroads dominated commercial activity and investment interest.

The Western Union Telegraph Company was formed by the consolidation of three firms, with arrangements by Jay Gould and William H. Vanderbilt. In time, Western Union gobbled up many smaller competitors. This was the rising age of monopolies, or "trusts," as they were popularly called.

Way out West, William H. Bonney, best known as the Billy the Kid, age 21, escaped jail where he was being held on a murder conviction. Finally, on July 15, Sheriff Patrick F. Garrett tracked him down at Fort Sumner in New Mexico Territory, and shot and killed him, by which time Billy the Kid had 21 notches on his pistol. His biography, *The True Life of Billy the Kid*, became a publishing sensation. On October 26 of the same year, at the OK Corral outside Tombstone in Arizona Territory, town marshal Virgil Earp, his two deputized brothers (Wyatt and Morgan), and Doc Holliday, an alcoholic gambler, broke up the gang headed by Ike Clanton. Such news events fueled popular interest in cowhands, Indians, outlaws, and the Wild West. Probably, these things contribute in a way to the mystique of Morgan dollars made in Carson City and San Francisco—from "Wild West silver."

On a 4,000-acre tract of land in Pullman, Illinois, near Chicago, the Pullman Palace Car Company began plans for a town built of brick, with housing for its workers calculated at a rate to earn 6% on investment. At the time, Pullman cars were the standard for first-class passenger travel in America, although various tycoons had private cars outfitted even more luxuriously. The term palace car was an old one and was earlier applied to certain horse-drawn vehicles. "Company towns" were all the rage, and leading manufacturers, mining companies, logging firms, and other enterprises often constructed communities complete with stores, schools, churches, and other centers of activity, all owned by the company. In a comic scenario not far from the truth, a worker exhibited a check for two cents, representing what was left of his monthly paycheck, after paying rent and what he owed at the company store.

During this era there were virtually no regulations for sanitary conditions and food processing and selling. Products such as butter, milk, and flour were often adulterated. In 1881 the states of Illinois, Michigan, New Jersey, and New York passed the first pure-food laws in the United States, leading in time to the passing of federal legislation in 1906 (effective January 1, 1907). Claims were often ridiculous and fraudulent regarding food and medicine, and just about anything could be sold under any label.

# 1881

Optimal
Collecting Grade
MS-64

Circulation-
Strike Mintage
9,163,000

Proof Mintage
984

Morgan's initial M
on neck truncation
(obverse).

Morgan's initial M
on ribbon bow
(reverse).

**Key to Collecting Circulation Strikes:** The 1881 dollar was struck in large quantities. The sharpness of striking varies widely on coins seen today, as does the quality of the luster. However, there is no shortage of "average" pieces in the marketplace. Sharply struck, lustrous coins with superb eye appeal are hard to find and mount a challenge for the serious collector.

**Surface Quality:** Most 1881 dollars are well struck on obverse and reverse, although below-average pieces are seen on occasion, these with light definition at the centers. The luster of the 1881 varies from grainy or "greasy" to lustrous and frosty.

**Prooflike Coins:** Some dies are with prooflike surface and are in the distinct minority.

**Mintage and Distribution:** The 1881 dollar was so common in the East in the 1950s that the coins were a nuisance to collectors who looked through bank bags. To these were added many Mint-sealed bags that were released circa 1955. By the time of the Treasury release in 1962 through 1964, this was not a date talked about when bags were discussed, but individual coins remained common.

**Die Varieties:** There are mostly minor varieties from 59 obverse and 47 reverse dies made, but the number used is not known.

## 1881, PROOFS

**Mintage:** 984. Two die pairs made, but only one known to have been used (with slight repunching). One reverse also used in 1882. Mintage by quarters: 700, 40, 0, 349; some melted.

**Key to Collecting Proofs:** Excellent strike and deep cameo contrast go together on most pieces.

## Whitman Coin Guide (WCG™)

| VG-8 | F-12 | VF-20 | EF-40 | AU-50 | MS-60 | MS-63 | MS-64 | MS-65 | MS-66 | MS-67 | PF-60 | PF-64 | PF-65 | PF-66 | PF-67 |
|------|------|-------|-------|-------|-------|-------|-------|-------|-------|-------|-------|-------|-------|-------|-------|
| $28 | $29 | $34 | $37 | $42 | $53 | $75 | $150 | $650 | $3,000 | $10,500 | $1,300 | $3,900 | $6,100 | $9,500 | $15,250 |

### AVAILABILITY

|  | MS-60 | MS-61 | MS-62 | MS-63 | MS-64 | MS-65 | MS-66 | MS-67 | MS-68+ |
|------|-------|-------|-------|-------|-------|-------|-------|-------|--------|
| Certified | 55 | 252 | 1,877 | 6,936 | 7,595 | 1,522 | 124 | 7 | 0 |
| Field |  | 80,000–150,000 |  | 50,000–75,000 | 25,000–35,000 | 3,000–4,500 | 200–300 | 8–12 | 1–5 |
| Cert. DMPL | 9 | 23 | 51 | 78 | 95 | 17 | 0 | 0 | 0 |
|  | PF-60 | PF-61 | PF-62 | PF-63 | PF-64 | PF-65 | PF-66 | PF-67 | PF-68+ |
| Certified | 20 | 33 | 58 | 96 | 126 | 40 | 39 | 17 | 7 |
| Field |  | 225–350 |  | 140–190 | 120–160 | 100–140 | 60–90 | 25–35 | 12–18 |

# 1881-CC

**Optimal Collecting Grade**
MS-65

**Circulation-Strike Mintage**
296,000

**Key to Collecting Circulation Strikes:** The 1881-CC dollar is easy to find in Mint State, often with deep luster and good strike. The low mintage of this issue and the popular Carson City mintmark contribute to the desirability. In worn grades this is one of the rarest dollars in the series!

**Surface Quality:** The strike is usually excellent on the 1881-CC, with good definition of the hair details and the eagle's breast feathers. Wayne Miller suggested that, "on the whole the 1881-CC is probably the highest quality Morgan dollar struck at the Carson City Mint."[20] The luster is typically deep and frosty, yielding a very attractive coin.

**Prooflike Coins:** Many 1881-CC have semi-prooflike surfaces and can be attractive if not heavily bagmarked.

**Mintage and Distribution:** No dollars were minted from April 1 to October 1, 1881, contributing to a low production for this year. Relatively few were released in the 1880s. Quantities were stored, including in the Treasury Building in Washington, DC. Many were paid out in the 1930s and at least a few bags more in 1954. After the great Treasury release was halted in March 1964, the General Services Administration holding of 1881-CC dollars totaled 147,485, or 49.82% of the original mintage, per a later inventory.[21]

**Die Varieties:** Although the Van Allen–Mallis text lists six different varieties from 25 pairs of dies sent to the mint, none are dramatically distinctive.

## Whitman Coin Guide (WCG™)

| VG-8 | F-12 | VF-20 | EF-40 | AU-50 | MS-60 | MS-63 | MS-64 | MS-65 | MS-66 | MS-67 |
|---|---|---|---|---|---|---|---|---|---|---|
| $350 | $385 | $400 | $425 | $435 | $450 | $510 | $565 | $900 | $1,275 | $4,250 |

**AVAILABILITY**

| | MS-60 | MS-61 | MS-62 | MS-63 | MS-64 | MS-65 | MS-66 | MS-67 | MS-68+ |
|---|---|---|---|---|---|---|---|---|---|
| Certified | 41 | 272 | 1,731 | 5,805 | 9,980 | 6,224 | 2,309 | 248 | 6 |
| Field | | 50,000–75,000 | | 60,000–85,000 | 30,000–45,000 | 15,000–25,000 | 3,500–5,000 | 250–400 | 10–15 |
| Cert. DMPL | 13 | 23 | 148 | 427 | 651 | 261 | 56 | 2 | 0 |

# 1881-O

Optimal
Collecting Grade
MS-64

Circulation-
Strike Mintage
5,708,000

**Key to Collecting Circulation Strikes:** The 1881-O is very common in About Uncirculated grade, once called "slider Uncirculated." Wayne Miller theorized that such coins were paid out into circulation in the greater New Orleans area, became redundant to commercial needs, and were brought back to the mint. To find a high-quality 1881-O will take some doing, but there are enough around that within a few months or so you should be successful.

**Surface Quality:** Strike is usually fairly sharp, but there are exceptions. Luster varies from frosty and attractive, these being in the distinct minority, to somewhat grainy and dull.

**Prooflike Coins:** Many 1881-O dollars have one or both dies with prooflike surface. However, bagmarks are endemic among these coins, and finding a truly choice example can be a real challenge.

**Mintage and Distribution:** Large numbers were released in and near the year of coinage; others remained stored. Quantities of 1881-O dollars filtered out of storage in the 1950s and possibly earlier, with the result that by time of the Treasury release of 1962 through 1964 this was not a rare issue. If there had been a question, it was answered by the distribution of many more bags.

**Die Varieties:** 55 obverses and 40 reverses were shipped to New Orleans. Varieties are minor.

## Whitman Coin Guide (WCG™)

| VG-8 | F-12 | VF-20 | EF-40 | AU-50 | MS-60 | MS-63 | MS-64 | MS-65 | MS-66 | MS-67 |
|------|------|-------|-------|-------|-------|-------|-------|-------|-------|-------|
| $28 | $29 | $34 | $37 | $41 | $50 | $73 | $175 | $1,350 | $14,500 | $26,500 |

**AVAILABILITY**

| | MS-60 | MS-61 | MS-62 | MS-63 | MS-64 | MS-65 | MS-66 | MS-67 | MS-68+ |
|---|-------|-------|-------|-------|-------|-------|-------|-------|--------|
| Certified | 223 | 1,077 | 4,201 | 11,393 | 7,061 | 993 | 20 | 0 | 0 |
| Field | | 75,000–150,000 | | 50,000–75,000 | 14,000–20,000 | 1,000–1,600 | 30–50 | 0 | 1–5 |
| Cert. DMPL | 32 | 92 | 340 | 640 | 486 | 16 | 0 | 0 | 0 |

# 1881-S

**Optimal
Collecting Grade
MS-65**

**Circulation-
Strike Mintage
12,760,000**

**Key to Collecting Circulation Strikes:** Among Morgan silver dollars minted in the 19th century, the 1881-S is the most available in Mint State. It is likely that at least half the original mintage remains in grades from MS-60 onward, which equals 6,000,000 or more coins. This is far and away the most available Mint State Morgan dollar of the 1878 through 1904 early year span. If you desire a single coin for a type set to illustrate the 1878 through 1921 Morgan dollar design, the 1881-S is an ideal candidate.

**Surface Quality:** Usually very sharply struck on all points, remarkable in view of the huge mintage figure of 12,760,000. In general, the San Francisco Mint earned high marks for quality, while the New Orleans Mint deserved a booby prize. Typically with satiny luster, often slightly prooflike.

**Prooflike Coins:** Many are from prooflike dies, often prooflike on just one side, such as having a frosty and lustrous obverse and a DMPL reverse—such coins being in limbo or Never-Never Land from the viewpoint of certification, as one number fits all.[22]

**Mintage and Distribution:** Of all San Francisco Mint Morgan dollars in the early range of the series, 1878 to 1904, the 1881-S has the highest mintage. Many were released in the 19th century, probably others were melted under the Pittman Act of 1918, but probably most remained stored in the San Francisco Mint. Many bags were released in 1938; tens of thousands were paid out in 1961, and millions more in the 1962 through 1964 Treasury release.

**Die Varieties:** To facilitate the large coinage, 85 obverse dies and a like number of reverse dies were combined, with more than 50 being listed by Van Allen and Mallis. None are of widespread interest, but there are enough repunchings and doubled mintmarks to make this date an interesting subspecialty.

## Whitman Coin Guide (WCG™)

| VG-8 | F-12 | VF-20 | EF-40 | AU-50 | MS-60 | MS-63 | MS-64 | MS-65 | MS-66 | MS-67 |
|------|------|-------|-------|-------|-------|-------|-------|-------|-------|-------|
| $28 | $29 | $34 | $37 | $41 | $50 | $65 | $82 | $165 | $370 | $825 |

**AVAILABILITY**

| | MS-60 | MS-61 | MS-62 | MS-63 | MS-64 | MS-65 | MS-66 | MS-67 | MS-68+ |
|---|-------|-------|-------|-------|-------|-------|-------|-------|--------|
| Certified | 335 | 2,264 | 16,662 | 92,646 | 175,284 | 95,580 | 27,620 | 5,522 | 298 |
| Field | 2,000,000–3,000,000 | | | 750,000–1,250,000 | 350,000–550,000 | 170,000–270,000 | 30,000–40,000 | 4,000–6,000 | 250–350 |
| Cert. DMPL | 8 | 34 | 120 | 528 | 897 | 538 | 165 | 13 | 3 |

# Morgan Silver Dollars, Rare Coins, and Life in 1882

## The Morgan Dollar Scenario

The *Annual Report of the Director of the Mint*, 1882, covering the fiscal year ending on June 30, told of storage and distribution of silver dollars during the past 12 months: in Philadelphia, 4,248,069 in mint, 8,053,808 distributed; in San Francisco, 25,114,407 in mint, 1,826,728 distributed; in Carson City: 1,260,901 in mint, 563,090 distributed; and in New Orleans: 4,742,295 in mint, 5,303,837 distributed.

President Chester Arthur had this to say about silver dollars of the day: "We now have 128 million of these 'jingers' and only 35 million are being used. We don't have room in the vault for them. The public doesn't want them. Why do we make them?"[23]

## Varieties Not Appreciated

The *American Journal of Numismatics*, July 1882, reflected the writer's disdain for die varieties of United States coins:

The increasing number of coin sales is very noticeable. We are in doubt whether this is to be regarded as an evidence of increased zeal on the part of collectors, and a greater interest in numismatics, or the reverse.

If we were to attempt to judge by the prices obtained for some of the rarest and choicest pieces, the task would be no easier, for while one dealer offers a cabinet full of "gems," and gets in return remarkably low prices, in another sale we find that pieces of little rarity and less real value, bring surprisingly large prices.

Occasionally we see on a catalogue some attraction like that recently offered by Mr. Frossard—the quarter-crown Gloriam Regni, of which but one was contained, so far as is known, in the collections of this country, and but two or three were known to exist abroad. In contrast, a dealer puts on the market a collection of U.S. coins, noticeable principally for those trivial differences in the dies which are inseparable from the method of cutting them, and finds his returns so little above the intrinsic value of the pieces when used in circulation, that one wonders how much will be left, after paying for labor, printing catalogues, commissions and postage, for the profit side of his venture.

While today, in the early 21st century, most auction interest is centered on date, mint, and die varieties of federal coins, in the 19th century such coins garnered far less print than did tokens and medals. It was not at all unusual in the 1880s for a scarce Hard Times token or Washington medal to merit several lines in an auction catalog, while a gem early silver coin, even from the 1790s, would be given just a few words! Generally, the greater the "story" a coin had, the more desirable it was to own. Building a set of date sequences of silver and gold series interested only a few people, and virtually no one cared about mintmark varieties, let alone small differences in die details. To discuss such at length in an auction catalog was apt to result in being bombarded with slings and arrows by a news editor.

## Old Silver Coins in Circulation in the 1880s

On July 1, 1882, there circulated about $50,000,000 in Liberty Seated dimes, quarters, and half dollars, plus a few silver three-cent pieces and half dimes. Some were new coins, minted in quantity from 1875 through 1878; millions were older pieces that had been hoarded by the public since 1862.

After the large-scale resumption of silver specie payments in 1876 and the release of quantities of coins by the government after April 20 of that year, citizens hoarding silver turned loose much of what they had. Although some Liberty Seated silver dollars may have been in circulation, most of the older dollars likely had been exported and/or melted.

In 1882, the Treasury itself was holding about $28,000,000 worth of mostly older silver coins, including much from a massive return from Latin America of an estimated $30,000,000 worth of old Liberty Seated coins, mostly quarters and half dollars, repatriated after 1876.

Historian Carothers wrote of the situation of the 1880s, a view of the entire decade:

> Millions of these coins were so badly worn that the public would not want them. They needed to be melted, but recoinage meant a definite loss. Congress did not consider the matter until 1882, when it gave an appropriation of $25,000—which permitted a small fraction of the amount to be recoined. Secretary McCullough in his annual report for 1884 made an urgent plea for a sum sufficient to cover the cost of a general recoinage, and in subsequent years many other requests were made. Congress did not face the situation until 1891.

For nearly a generation this great hoard lay in the Treasury. When applicants for new coins appeared at the Mint they were told to go to the Treasury office and buy from the idle stocks.[24]

Although in 1882 the quantity production of Liberty Seated dimes for circulation recommenced, quarters and half dollars remained in abundance and relatively few were coined. Yet, Morgan silver dollars, not needed in commerce, continued to be coined by the millions under the 1878 Bland-Allison Act.

## MEANWHILE, ON THE AMERICAN SCENE IN 1882

Clarence Dresser, a newspaper reporter for the *Chicago Daily News*, asked William H. Vanderbilt, chief principal of the New York Central Railroad, why the Chicago Limited train was being discontinued. "Don't you run it for the public benefit?" asked Dresser, to which Vanderbilt famously replied, "The public be damned!"

In the 1880s and 1890s, those who could afford to do so would often leave the heat of the city, this being before the era of air conditioning, and escape to the mountains or seashore. The Pemigewasset House in Plymouth, New Hampshire, was set in "the grandest mountain scenery in the continent." In 1881 the Pemigewasset National Bank set up its first office in this hotel, just in time to issue Series of 1875 currency, today highly prized by numismatists.

On September 4, 1882, in a special ceremony in New York City, Thomas A. Edison switched on electric lights in the offices of J.P. Morgan, marking the commercial distribution of electric power from the Edison Illuminating Company on Pearl Street in the same city, the financing of which was arranged by Morgan.

It was an era of mergers, acquisitions, and consolidations, and in this year John D. Rockefeller set up the Standard Oil Trust, which eventually controlled the majority of petroleum-refining capacity in America.

The Chinese Exclusion Act, passed in 1880, took effect in 1882, and provided that no Chinese laborers could enter for a period of 10 years. For many years, immigrants from China had come to America, particularly to California, where they worked in mining and railroad construction, usually at very low wages, causing resentment among whites who sought higher pay.

On April 3, Jesse James, famous bank robber, was shot and killed in Saint Joseph, Missouri, by one of his own gang members, who was attracted by a monetary reward offered for James's capture. The exploits and adventures of outlaws continued to fascinate the public, and news of his demise was widely published.

On March 24, Henry Wadsworth Longfellow died in Cambridge, Massachusetts. His poems, such as the epic and bittersweet "Evangeline" (1847), had become American classics. Not long afterward, another famous American poet, Ralph Waldo Emerson, died in Concord in the same state.

# 1882

**Optimal
Collecting Grade
MS-64**

**Circulation-
Strike Mintage
11,100,000**

**Proof Mintage
1,100**

**Key to Collecting Circulation Strikes:** The 1882 dollar is the next in the continuing series of high-mintage Philadelphia issues. The quality of pieces varies from sharply struck and very attractive to weakly struck and unprepossessing. Many coins are heavily bagmarked. Cherrypicking is advised to track down a piece that is just right, and enough are in the marketplace that you will be crowned with success with relatively little effort.

**Surface Quality:** Strike varies from excellent to weak. Cherrypicking is recommended. Again, certification services pay no attention, so you need to search on your own or employ a trustworthy dealer on your behalf. The luster ranges from frosty to somewhat dull, suggesting that time spent searching for quality can be advantageous. However, most coins, regardless of strike, are quite lustrous.

**Prooflike Coins:** Prooflike pieces exist and are in the distinct minority despite the high mintage for this date. Semi-prooflike or low-contrast prooflike coins are the rule.

**Mintage and Distribution:** The 1882 dollars were released in quantity in the East in early times, again in the 1950s, and last in the 1962 through 1964 era.

## 1882, PROOFS

**Mintage:** 1,100. Breen comment: "750 first quarter, 101 second, 100 third, 200 fourth, total 1,151; supposedly 50 melted; leaving 1,101."[25] Two obverse dies and two reverse dies were prepared.

**Key to Collecting Proofs:** Another good vintage year for Proofs—what with excellent strike and deep cameo contrast being the rule. Still, the majority have been cleaned—and those deep mirror fields make hairlines pop out at you.

**Die Varieties:** Many varieties from 58 obverse and 60 reverse dies made, but perhaps not all were used. No varieties are dramatic.

## Whitman Coin Guide (WCG™)

| VG-8 | F-12 | VF-20 | EF-40 | AU-50 | MS-60 | MS-63 | MS-64 | MS-65 | MS-66 | MS-67 | PF-60 | PF-64 | PF-65 | PF-66 | PF-67 |
|---|---|---|---|---|---|---|---|---|---|---|---|---|---|---|---|
| $28 | $29 | $34 | $37 | $41 | $50 | $70 | $100 | $475 | $1,850 | $22,000 | $1,300 | $3,900 | $6,100 | $9,500 | $15,250 |

**AVAILABILITY**

| | MS-60 | MS-61 | MS-62 | MS-63 | MS-64 | MS-65 | MS-66 | MS-67 | MS-68+ |
|---|---|---|---|---|---|---|---|---|---|
| Certified | 89 | 374 | 2,958 | 11,048 | 10,611 | 2,329 | 443 | 14 | 0 |
| Field | 125,000–225,000 | | | 70,000–100,000 | 25,000–40,000 | 4,000–6,000 | 600–900 | 30–50 | 0 |
| Cert. DMPL | 4 | 22 | 67 | 138 | 146 | 27 | 1 | 0 | 0 |
| | PF-60 | PF-61 | PF-62 | PF-63 | PF-64 | PF-65 | PF-66 | PF-67 | PF-68+ |
| Certified | 6 | 25 | 68 | 108 | 162 | 74 | 45 | 34 | 12 |
| Field | 200–300 | | | 150–250 | 200–220 | 110–150 | 70–90 | 50–70 | 20–30 |

# 1882-CC

Optimal
Collecting Grade
MS-65

Circulation-
Strike Mintage
1,133,000

**Key to Collecting Circulation Strikes:** The 1882-CC and the two successive Carson City issues, 1883-CC and 1884-CC, constitute the most widely available Carson City silver dollars. In 1964 the Treasury Department held back vast quantities of these issues, later distributing them to collectors and others. Today, beautiful pieces can be obtained for a reasonable price.

**Surface Quality:** Usually seen well struck. Typically seen with beautiful, deep, frosty luster.

**Prooflike Coins:** Prooflike pieces are encountered with some frequency, and some have deep mirror surfaces with sharp contrast, quite resembling Philadelphia Mint Proofs. Some coins are prooflike, even DMPL, in most areas of the field, except for satiny luster close to Miss Liberty's head and, on the reverse, surrounding the eagle's head.

**Mintage and Distribution:** At the turn of the 20th century large quantities were shipped from Carson City to the Treasury Building in Washington, DC. In August 1926, attendees of the ANA Convention who walked across the street from the headquarters hotel to the Treasury Building were delighted to be able to "exchange any old kind of a dollar there for an Uncirculated silver dollar of 1882-CC."[26] Over time many more were paid out, including in the early 1930s and in 1938 and the 1950s. Stephen D. Ruddel stated that about 50 bags were released from the Treasury Building in 1955, and many more bags were paid out at a later time, this being prior to 1964.[27] After the great Treasury release was halted in March 1964, the General Services Administration holding of 1882-CC dollars totaled 605,029, or 53.40% of the original mintage, per a later inventory.[28]

**Die Varieties:** No varieties from the 15 die pairs made for the coinage have captured the attention of others than dedicated VAM specialists.

## Whitman Coin Guide (WCG™)

| VG-8 | F-12 | VF-20 | EF-40 | AU-50 | MS-60 | MS-63 | MS-64 | MS-65 | MS-66 | MS-67 |
|------|------|-------|-------|-------|-------|-------|-------|-------|-------|-------|
| $90 | $100 | $110 | $125 | $145 | $185 | $220 | $265 | $460 | $1,100 | $7,500 |

### AVAILABILITY

|  | MS-60 | MS-61 | MS-62 | MS-63 | MS-64 | MS-65 | MS-66 | MS-67 | MS-68+ |
|--|-------|-------|-------|-------|-------|-------|-------|-------|--------|
| Certified | 95 | 636 | 3,409 | 10,798 | 14,772 | 7,324 | 1,784 | 106 | 1 |
| Field |  | 400,000–500,000 |  | 160,000–210,000 | 80,000–110,000 | 20,000–35,000 | 1,500–2,500 | 150–250 | 5–10 |
| Cert. DMPL | 7 | 39 | 308 | 803 | 1,094 | 442 | 64 | 1 | 0 |

# 1882-O

Optimal
Collecting Grade
MS-64

Circulation-
Strike Mintage
6,090,000

**Key to Collecting Circulation Strikes:** The 1882-O pieces seem to have been produced with relatively little care. As a handy rule, New Orleans pieces are more difficult to find with good strike and luster than are those from the other mints. If a palm were to be given for excellence in this regard, it would go to San Francisco, but Carson City pieces are usually well struck, and many Philadelphia pieces are as well.

**Surface Quality:** Strike varies from fairly decent to weak, but is usually above average. The luster is often dull and insipid, "greasy," or grainy. Finding a deeply frosty 1882-O can be a challenge.

**Prooflike Coins:** Strikings from prooflike dies are seen with some frequency and are most attractive in higher grades.

**Mintage and Distribution:** Although 1882-O was not a rare date and AU coins (sliders) were abundant on the rare coin market, few if any bags of Mint State coins gained notice until the 1950s, when a few came on the market, as in 1953 and 1957. However, most remained in storage until the great Treasury release of 1962 and early 1963, after which examples were very common.

**Die Varieties:** Many varieties were made from up to 33 die pairs. Most are repunched date or mintmark issues, not dramatic except perhaps for VAM-7, of which *The Top 100 Morgan Dollar Varieties* takes notice.

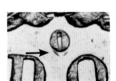

VAM-7

## Whitman Coin Guide (WCG™)

| VG-8 | F-12 | VF-20 | EF-40 | AU-50 | MS-60 | MS-63 | MS-64 | MS-65 | MS-66 | MS-67 |
|------|------|-------|-------|-------|-------|-------|-------|-------|-------|-------|
| $28 | $29 | $34 | $37 | $42 | $52 | $75 | $125 | $1,200 | $7,900 | $14,500 |

### AVAILABILITY

| | MS-60 | MS-61 | MS-62 | MS-63 | MS-64 | MS-65 | MS-66 | MS-67 | MS-68+ |
|---|-------|-------|-------|-------|-------|-------|-------|-------|--------|
| Certified | 162 | 675 | 3,759 | 11,931 | 10,171 | 1,157 | 32 | 5 | 1 |
| Field | 250,000-400,000 | | | 50,000-75,000 | 25,000-35,000 | 2,000-3,000 | 50-75 | 4-8 | 1-2 |
| Cert. DMPL | 10 | 58 | 169 | 294 | 240 | 26 | 1 | 0 | 0 |

# 1882-O/S

**Optimal Collecting Grade**
MS-64

**Circulation-Strike Mintage**
Small part of mintage for 1882-O

**Key to Collecting Circulation Strikes:** The 1882-O/S is a worthwhile addition to your collection, with a reasonable grade goal being MS-63 or MS-64, not because of price, but because pieces at higher levels are virtually impossible to find. Beyond that, be sure to buy one with the overmintmark distinct under a good 4x glass. On some the under-S is weak, and these should be avoided. Traces of die rust are normal and not a negative factor.

**Surface Quality:** Striking varies from sharp to weak. On all known examples there is graininess in some areas, due to tiny raised dots from light rust pits in the dies.

**Prooflike Coins:** In 1982, Wayne Miller reported that he had "seen two or three [prooflike] pieces; none evidenced any die pitting."[29] A few DMPL coins have been certified in low Mint State grades.

**Mintage and Distribution:** Little is known of the specific mintage and distribution of this overmintmark, as it was not closely studied until recent decades. Examples have been found mixed with quantities of regular 1882-O dollars as a tiny percentage of those in certain bags.

**Die Varieties:** 1882-O/S: VAM-3 (O/S Flush), VAM-4 (O/S Recessed), and VAM-5 (O/S Broken). VAM-3 in most die states may be the best bet, but even these can be weak.

VAM-3          VAM-4          VAM-5

## Whitman Coin Guide (WCG™)

| VG-8 | F-12 | VF-20 | EF-40 | AU-50 | MS-60 | MS-63 | MS-64 | MS-65 | MS-66 | MS-67 |
|------|------|-------|-------|-------|-------|-------|-------|-------|-------|-------|
| $35 | $38 | $45 | $60 | $110 | $235 | $850 | $2,500 | $40,000 | – | – |

**AVAILABILITY**

| | MS-60 | MS-61 | MS-62 | MS-63 | MS-64 | MS-65 | MS-66 | MS-67 | MS-68+ |
|--|-------|-------|-------|-------|-------|-------|-------|-------|--------|
| Certified | 174 | 538 | 943 | 615 | 436 | 7 | 0 | 0 | 0 |
| Field | | 3,000–5,000 | | 800–1,500 | 500–1,000 | 8–12 | 0 | 0 | 0 |
| Cert. DMPL | 0 | 0 | 0 | 0 | 0 | 0 | 0 | 0 | 0 |

# 1882-S

Optimal
Collecting Grade
MS-65

Circulation-
Strike Mintage
9,250,000

**Key to Collecting Circulation Strikes:** The 1882-S exists in large quantities in Mint State, so examples can be obtained easily. Most are fairly attractive. Many 1882-S dollars are heavily bagmarked, these fitting into the grade categories from MS-60 to MS-62. Many 1882-S dollars are prooflike, but just a small percentage of Mint State coins are in existence. However, in absolute terms there are enough to supply the demand.

**Surface Quality:** Striking ranges from sharp to somewhat weak, with most being above average The luster is typically deeply frosty and very attractive, similar to 1881-S.

**Prooflike Coins:** Prooflike pieces exist with some frequency, some of which are prooflike on just one side. Generally, the contrast between the mirrored fields and the devices is not great.

**Mintage and Distribution:** Although many 1882-S dollars were paid out in the 19th century, it is likely that millions remained in storage in the San Francisco Mint and that some were tucked away in the Treasury Building in Washington, DC. At the 1926 ANA Convention held in Washington, collectors were delighted to buy Uncirculated coins for face value at the cash window there. During the 1962 through 1964 Treasury release it is estimated that over 1,000,000 more were disbursed, adding to an already generous supply.

**Die Varieties:** Although many die varieties exist from 55 pairs sent to San Francisco, none are particularly widely collected except by specialists. VAM-20 has the S mintmark tilted significantly to the left and is worthy of notice.

## Whitman Coin Guide (WCG™)

| VG-8 | F-12 | VF-20 | EF-40 | AU-50 | MS-60 | MS-63 | MS-64 | MS-65 | MS-66 | MS-67 |
|------|------|-------|-------|-------|-------|-------|-------|-------|-------|-------|
| $28 | $29 | $34 | $37 | $41 | $50 | $65 | $82 | $165 | $370 | $875 |

**AVAILABILITY**

| | MS-60 | MS-61 | MS-62 | MS-63 | MS-64 | MS-65 | MS-66 | MS-67 | MS-68+ |
|---|-------|-------|-------|-------|-------|-------|-------|-------|--------|
| Certified | 85 | 452 | 4,300 | 26,598 | 55,733 | 34,006 | 10,566 | 2,396 | 129 |
| Field | 400,000-700,000 | | | 200,000-300,000 | 150,000-220,000 | 100,000-130,000 | 15,000-25,000 | 1,500-2,500 | 125-200 |
| Cert. DMPL | 0 | 4 | 37 | 154 | 240 | 105 | 17 | 0 | 0 |

# MORGAN SILVER DOLLARS, RARE COINS, AND LIFE IN 1883

## THE MORGAN DOLLAR SCENARIO

The *American Journal of Numismatics*, published since 1866, continued to be the only independent magazine in the sphere of coin collecting in the United States. Although many fine articles, news notes, and accounts of auctions were printed, there was little editorial interest in Morgan silver dollars, which continued to be called "Bland dollars."

*Dye's Coin Encyclopædia* was published in Philadelphia, and was an immense volume of 1,152 pages containing many interesting, but not necessarily coordinated or logically arranged, articles on various aspects of ancient, world, and American coinage. Although market values were listed for many older coins, there was little about Morgan silver dollars, except that Proofs from 1878 to 1881 were worth $1.25 to $1.75 each.

In this era there were no regularly issued price or valuation guides for rare coins, and most information had to be gleaned from the prices realized at auction sales. Morgan dollars were rarely offered singly, but appeared as part of Proof sets for various years. Mintmarks continued to be ignored.

Regarding Morgan silver dollars, among selected John W. Haseltine sales of the year, his auction of January 18 included an 1880-O dollar, "the O very small," Uncirculated, which sold for face value; and an 1880-S dollar, "the S very small," in the same grade, which brought $1.05. Haseltine's sale of June 27 to 29 (the S.S. Crosby Collection) included two Proof 1878 8 Tail Feathers dollars at $1.20 apiece.

Haseltine's auction of November 15 and 16 (Chandler and Boisdore collections) included this as Lot 476: "1878 Bland or standard dollar. Uncirculated. Semi-proof surface. Slightly haymarked."[30] The coin brought face value of $1. From Haseltine's offerings and those of his contemporaries it can be seen that there was little economic advantage for dealers to handle Bland dollars in this era.

The 1883 *Annual Report of the Director of the Mint* included this review of silver dollars by Director Horatio C. Burchard, who expressed his displeasure with the situation:

> Since the passage of the act, in 1878, requiring the monthly purchase of not less than two million dollars worth of silver bullion, and its coinage into silver dollars, $154,370,899 had been coined prior to October 1883. That this, with the $81,000,000 worth of fractional silver coin in the country, a total of $235,000,000, is in excess of the requirements of the country for silver circulation is apparent from the large amount of these coins in the vaults of the Treasury not represented by outstanding certificates and not required to be held for their payment, namely, over 39,000,000 silver dollars, and nearly $27,000,000 of fractional silver coin, a total of $66,000,000.
>
> My views in this regard to the policy of further continuing the coinage of silver dollars were expressed in my report two years ago, and remain unchanged. While believing that the equal coinage of both metals by all nations is desirable in order to give greater stability to the values of commodities and credits, yet, in view of our inability to continue the increase of our silver circulation at the present rate without ultimately expelling a large portion of the present stock of gold, as well as of the waning hope for the co-operation of leading commercial nations in securing the general use of silver and its unlimited coinage as money, and of the present abundant paper and increasing gold circulation in this country, I suggest the question again for the consideration of legislators, whether the law directing the monthly coinage of not less than two million dollars' worth of silver bullion into standard dollars should not be modified or repealed.

Silver dollars continued to pile up at the mints. Many of those reported as "distributed" simply went into other vaults, such as in banks. For the fiscal year ending June 30, 1883:

**Philadelphia Mint:** 4,354,571 on hand. Distributed during the year, 11,494,617
**San Francisco Mint:** 30,841,960 on hand. Distributed, 1,622,447
**Carson City Mint:** 1,914,522 on hand. Distributed, 466,379
**New Orleans Mint:** 6,193,537 on hand. Distributed, 6,588,758

## MEANWHILE, ON THE AMERICAN SCENE IN 1883

By 1883 the Standard Oil Trust employed 100,000 people and controlled the output of 20,000 wells. Electrical transmission lines were expanding, and more and more cities and buildings used this type of illumination. By this time street lighting by arc lights had become common.

On March 24, 1883, the first telephone connection was made between New York and Chicago. In New York City only 2% of the homes were connected to water systems. Some tenement houses had primitive plumbing facilities, but most private houses had privies in the backyards. Time zones were adopted by United States railroads, designated, for example, as Eastern Standard Time, also with Central, Rocky Mountain, and Pacific zones. Under this system, still in use today, Eastern Standard Time was three hours ahead of Pacific Standard Time.

On November 3, 1883, the U.S. Supreme Court ruled that American Indians were aliens by birth. Minorities in America, including recent immigrants, Indians, and blacks, had few rights and virtually nothing in the way of public benefits. Companies, including trusts, dominated labor practices, and workers essentially remained as peons. Instead of going to high school, many children went to work in mines and textile mills.

On May 24 the Brooklyn Bridge was opened to connect the island of Manhattan with the borough of Brooklyn. Measuring 5,985 feet long and costing $1,500,000, the structure was the largest suspension bridge of its era. It had been anticipated for years, and when it opened, following a gala celebration, commerce between the two districts of New York City expanded many times, as previously most connections had been made by boat.

The typewriter was gaining in popularity, and more than 3,000 of the Remington make were sold, an increase from 2,350 in 1882. Mark Twain's *Life on the Mississippi,* the first book composed on a typewriter, was published. Robert Louis Stevenson's *Treasure Island* also reached print and included the character Long John Silver with his song refrain, "Fifteen men on a dead man's chest—Yo-ho-ho and a bottle of rum!" Joseph Pulitzer, owner of the *St. Louis Post-Dispatch,* purchased the *New York World* from Jay Gould, the latter newspaper having 15,000 circulation. Pulitzer turned the *World* into a sensational paper, and raised the circulation to 345,000.

Jumbo the elephant, a drawing card at the Royal Zoological Gardens in London, had been bought for $10,000 by P.T. Barnum, who brought him to America in 1882, billing him as the largest elephant in the world, and introducing a new adjective, *jumbo,* to our language. For the next several years, until he was hit and killed by a freight train in Ontario in September 1885, Jumbo was prominent on the American scene.

## ELSEWHERE IN NUMISMATICS

In this year a silver coinage for Hawaii was struck at the San Francisco Mint, of the denominations of 10 cents, 25 cents, 50 cents, and one dollar, totaling a face value of $1,000,000. Featured on the obverse was a portrait of King Kalakaua. The issue was largely sponsored by Claus Spreckels, San Francisco sugar magnate, who controlled large districts in Hawaii.

Large quantities of double eagles continued to be exported to foreign banks and commercial centers. However, in 1883 the coinage of this denomination consisted mainly of examples struck in San Francisco, where 1,189,000 were made, and at Carson City (59,962). In Philadelphia, only Proofs were made, for collectors, and only to the extent of 92 pieces, creating a rarity.

The 1883 Liberty Head nickel without CENTS was the focal point of the hobby this year, not so much with old-time collectors as with newcomers. During the entire decade, collecting of many different things, including stamps, fossils, autographs, and more, would reach exciting levels never before seen. America had a fairly healthy economy and was not at war, and many citizens turned their attention to enjoying hobbies, music, amateur theatricals, and reading.

# 1883

Optimal
Collecting Grade
MS-65

Circulation-
Strike Mintage
12,290,000

Proof Mintage
1,039

**Key to Collecting Circulation Strikes:** Among Morgan dollars of the 1880s, the 1883 Philadelphia Mint issue is among the most available. Produced in quantity, such pieces were often struck in haste, and some care needs to be exercised to find attractive pieces. Regardless of striking quality—sharp or weak—most pieces have satiny mint luster.

**Surface Quality:** The majority of 1883 Morgan dollars range from average strikes to sharp, but some weakly impressed examples exist here and there. Cherrypicking is recommended, as always. The 1883 is usually lustrous and frosty, although some pieces can be slightly dull.

**Prooflike Coins:** Many are from prooflike dies, one side or the other, or both. Some DMPL coins exist with excellent cameo contrast and are rare, but no doubt the market for such is diminished by the availability of Proof strikings.

**Mintage and Distribution:** The 1883 was released into circulation from the era of striking onward, creating a "common date" from the beginning. Many bags were paid out in the 1950s and 1960s. The Continental-Illinois Bank hoard, distributed later, had 12 to 15 bags.

## 1883, PROOFS

**Mintage:** 1,039. Breen comment: "Mintage: First quarter 650, second 195, third 50, fourth 175, total 1,070, of which 1039 were delivered with the Proof sets, leaving 31 which were all melted at year's end."[31]

**Key to Collecting Proofs:** Usually well struck. Good cameo contrast between the design and the mirrored fields, but not as dramatic as on the Proofs of recent years. Finding a nice one may require some searching. If you can afford higher grades, the best way to start is to inspect pieces that have been certified as Proof-64 or finer, then go from there to determine quality. If I were buying, I would rather have a lightly toned and very appealing Proof-64, certified, than a Proof-66, certified, that has blotches or is too dark.

**Die Varieties:** There are no die varieties that have commanded wide attention, but the specialist in Van Allen–Mallis varieties has well over a dozen possibilities from which to choose.

## Whitman Coin Guide (WCG™)

| VG-8 | F-12 | VF-20 | EF-40 | AU-50 | MS-60 | MS-63 | MS-64 | MS-65 | MS-66 | MS-67 | PF-60 | PF-64 | PF-65 | PF-66 | PF-67 |
|------|------|-------|-------|-------|-------|-------|-------|-------|-------|-------|-------|-------|-------|-------|-------|
| $28 | $29 | $34 | $37 | $41 | $50 | $70 | $100 | $220 | $500 | $2,250 | $1,300 | $3,900 | $6,100 | $9,750 | $15,500 |

**AVAILABILITY**

| | MS-60 | MS-61 | MS-62 | MS-63 | MS-64 | MS-65 | MS-66 | MS-67 | MS-68+ |
|---|---|---|---|---|---|---|---|---|---|
| Certified | 37 | 266 | 1,904 | 9,881 | 16,571 | 7,618 | 1,633 | 192 | 6 |
| Field | 150,000–250,000 | | | 100,000–150,000 | 50,000–90,000 | 25,000–40,000 | 3,000–5,000 | 200–300 | 10–15 |
| Cert. DMPL | 8 | 28 | 141 | 319 | 379 | 121 | 15 | 0 | 0 |
| | PF-60 | PF-61 | PF-62 | PF-63 | PF-64 | PF-65 | PF-66 | PF-67 | PF-68+ |
| Certified | 13 | 20 | 78 | 118 | 129 | 73 | 35 | 17 | 2 |
| Field | 225–350 | | | 190–230 | 180–220 | 120–150 | 50–75 | 30–50 | 4–7 |

# 1883-CC

Optimal
Collecting Grade
MS-65

Circulation-
Strike Mintage
1,204,000

**Key to Collecting Circulation Strikes:** The 1883-CC joins the 1882-CC and 1884-CC as one of a trio of very plentiful Carson City dollars in Mint State. There is a great pride of possession for such a piece as nearly all are well struck and very attractive, this in combination with a reasonable market price.

**Surface Quality:** The 1883-CC is typically seen well struck. Usually seen with deep, frosty luster, bright and attractive.

**Prooflike Coins:** Some dies are prooflike, often deeply mirrored and with cameo or frosted devices, quite like a Philadelphia Mint Proof except for certain aspects of the edge treatment and, of course, the telltale mintmark. Some have DMPL fields, but with auras of satiny frost close to the outline of Miss Liberty's portrait and the edges of the eagle.

**Mintage and Distribution:** Most of the mintage was shipped to the Treasury Building in Washington, DC, after the mint ceased operations in 1899. Afterward, bags were paid out on occasion, including in 1938 and 1939. Others were available in quantity in the early 1950s, but the market value of a bag was not sufficient to encourage trade. In 1955 about 50 bags came out and mostly went into numismatic hands. After the great Treasury release was halted in March 1964, the General Services Administration holding of 1883-CC dollars totaled 755,518, or 62.75% of the original mintage, per a later inventory.[32]

**Die Varieties:** Minor varieties exist from up to 10 die pairs used.

## Whitman Coin Guide (WCG™)

| VG-8 | F-12 | VF-20 | EF-40 | AU-50 | MS-60 | MS-63 | MS-64 | MS-65 | MS-66 | MS-67 |
|------|------|-------|-------|-------|-------|-------|-------|-------|-------|-------|
| $90 | $100 | $110 | $125 | $145 | $185 | $220 | $240 | $470 | $850 | $3,750 |

### AVAILABILITY

| | MS-60 | MS-61 | MS-62 | MS-63 | MS-64 | MS-65 | MS-66 | MS-67 | MS-68+ |
|---|-------|-------|-------|-------|-------|-------|-------|-------|--------|
| Certified | 113 | 608 | 3,727 | 12,563 | 19,759 | 11,284 | 2,792 | 247 | 3 |
| Field | 400,000–500,000 | | | 200,000–250,000 | 90,000–120,000 | 30,000–40,000 | 5,000–8,000 | 250–400 | 10–15 |
| Cert. DMPL | 12 | 58 | 361 | 1,315 | 1,845 | 916 | 146 | 7 | 0 |

# 1883-O

Optimal
Collecting Grade
MS-65

Circulation-
Strike Mintage
8,725,000

**Key to Collecting Circulation Strikes:** Produced in quantity, the typical 1883-O coin seen today is apt to have unsatisfactory luster and a typical strike. Cherrypicking is definitely recommended, this making all the difference between your high-quality collection and the ordinary quality of most others. For the collector of certified coins, New Orleans dollars are a breeze: look at the label and write a check.

**Surface Quality:** Striking varies all over the place for the 1883-O, with some quite flat at the centers, and others needle sharp, the latter being in the distinct minority. Careful selection is advised. The 1883-O is common in Mint State, and thus there are many opportunities to view candidates for your collection. The luster ranges from medium frosty to somewhat dull and grainy. Some were made from worn-out dies past retirement age, and these have granularity and metal flow lines. Cherrypicking is again advised, this in combination with seeking a sharp strike.

**Prooflike Coins:** Prooflike coins are plentiful, but the majority show poor contrast between the fields and the devices, or are heavily bagmarked, or both. A DMPL coin with cameo contrast is a joy to behold.

**Branch Mint Proofs:** A numismatic tradition exists, dating back well over a century, that 12 full Proofs were struck of the 1883-O Morgan dollar. And, they may have been, although the differentiation between a cameo DMPL and a "branch mint Proof" would be difficult to explain. Proofs have been certified on at least two instances.

**Mintage and Distribution:** Although AU examples of 1883-O dollars were aplenty in the early 20th century, no information has been located about Treasury releases of Mint State bags. However, this never was a rare issue. Bags were released in the 1930s, many came out of hiding in 1952, and others were paid out until about 1957, after which time no new finds were reported in the numismatic community. Then, in November 1962 and for a short time afterward, many bags were released from a Philadelphia Mint vault sealed in 1929, exhausting the supply. It is believed that the bulk of about 10,000,000 coins from that vault were 1883-O, 1884-O, and 1885-O.

**Die Varieties:** Many die varieties exist from among 40 obverse and 36 reverse dies sent to New Orleans for this year's coinage.[33] Perhaps the most significant is VAM-4, with the mintmark sharply doubled, the traces of an earlier mintmark appearing below the final, heavy mintmark. Some of VAM-1 are from a rotated reverse die, usually 35° to 75°.

## Whitman Coin Guide (WCG™)

| VG-8 | F-12 | VF-20 | EF-40 | AU-50 | MS-60 | MS-63 | MS-64 | MS-65 | MS-66 | MS-67 |
|------|------|-------|-------|-------|-------|-------|-------|-------|-------|-------|
| $28 | $29 | $34 | $37 | $41 | $50 | $65 | $82 | $165 | $425 | $4,000 |

**AVAILABILITY**

| | MS-60 | MS-61 | MS-62 | MS-63 | MS-64 | MS-65 | MS-66 | MS-67 | MS-68+ |
|------|-------|-------|-------|-------|-------|-------|-------|-------|--------|
| Certified | 378 | 2,252 | 19,168 | 80,826 | 75,680 | 16,306 | 1,636 | 63 | 0 |
| Field | 1,250,000–2,000,000 | | | 400,000–700,000 | 200,000–300,000 | 30,000–50,000 | 3,000–5,000 | 100–200 | 10–15 |
| Cert. DMPL | 26 | 92 | 389 | 893 | 769 | 154 | 15 | 0 | 0 |

# 1883-S

**Optimal
Collecting Grade
MS-64**

**Circulation-
Strike Mintage
6,250,000**

**Key to Collecting Circulation Strikes:** Following the run of numismatically available San Francisco coins from 1878 through 1882, now with the 1883-S we encounter a key issue. In contrast with the earlier dates, the 1883-S is very difficult to find, especially at higher Mint State levels. Among 1883-S dollars, bagmarks are a significant problem. These must have been stored and handled roughly.

**Surface Quality:** The 1883-S usually is seen with above average to quite sharp strike, quite attractive. The luster ranges from medium frosty to deep and is generally pleasing to the eye.

**Prooflike Coins:** Some dies are prooflike, but not necessarily deeply mirrored. Among 1883-S dollars in Mint State, these are encountered with regularity, that is, when Mint State pieces themselves are found—for all 1883-S dollars are elusive at that grade level. DMPL coins are exceedingly rare.

**Mintage and Distribution:** The distribution of the 1883-S began in large quantity soon after the mintage, with the result that examples in all grades were available to numismatists generations ago. However, by the 1940s the issue was viewed as scarce. In the 1950s some bags were released, but probably just a few. At least part of a bag found its way to Nevada investor LaVere Redfield. I am not aware of any quantities in the 1962 through 1964 Treasury release.

**Die Varieties:** The VAM text lists seven different die varieties, none of which has achieved wide popularity.

## Whitman Coin Guide (WCG™)

| VG-8 | F-12 | VF-20 | EF-40 | AU-50 | MS-60 | MS-63 | MS-64 | MS-65 | MS-66 | MS-67 |
|------|------|-------|-------|-------|-------|-------|-------|-------|-------|-------|
| $29 | $30 | $36 | $50 | $140 | $650 | $2,250 | $4,400 | $32,500 | $85,000 | $175,000 |

**AVAILABILITY**

|  | MS-60 | MS-61 | MS-62 | MS-63 | MS-64 | MS-65 | MS-66 | MS-67 | MS-68+ |
|--|-------|-------|-------|-------|-------|-------|-------|-------|--------|
| Certified | 224 | 715 | 1,325 | 1,249 | 623 | 27 | 4 | 2 | 0 |
| Field | 10,000–20,000[a] | | | 2,000–3,000 | 1,000–1,250 | 50–75 | 5–8 | 4–6 | 0 |
| Cert. DMPL | 0 | 1 | 2 | 0 | 2 | 0 | 0 | 0 | 0 |

a Mostly of low quality.

# MORGAN SILVER DOLLARS, RARE COINS, AND LIFE IN 1884

## THE MORGAN DOLLAR SCENARIO

In 1884 President Chester Alan Arthur remarked concerning silver dollars: "Well, we got a mess of these things now. We made 185 million and only 40 million are out."[34] Indeed, silver dollars had been minted in immense quantities since 1878. Vaults and other storage spaces were stuffed with the unwanted coins.

## NUMISMATIC TIDBITS

The silver trade dollar of 420 grains weight, intended for the export trade to China and minted in quantity from 1873 until early 1878, and in Proof format after that time (recall the speculation in Proofs of 1879 and early 1880), was for all practical purposes discontinued in 1884, except that somehow 10 coins were struck in silver with the 1884 date and a handful in copper.

While 683,500 double eagles were struck at the San Francisco Mint and 81,139 at Carson City, at Philadelphia only Proofs were made in 1884, and just to the extent of 71 pieces. Even that number is probably significantly in excess of the number of numismatists actually collecting $20 coins by date sequence, and no doubt a few dozen were melted. The fact that just 48 Proof $5 coins and only 45 Proof $10 pieces were struck may more nearly reflect the demand by collectors. Few people were interested in and could afford to buy high-denomination gold. In 1885, $5 was about the norm for a worker's weekly pay in a textile factory, and although such employees had difficulty enough in meeting basic needs, the illustration reflects the value of money at the time. America was stratified socially, and, for one, T. Harrison Garrett, in Baltimore, had a seemingly unlimited amount of funds and each year bought full gold Proof sets, in a year in which no more than 48 such sets found buyers.

Gold dollars continued to be popular with speculators, and in addition there was a strong demand from jewelers. Accordingly, of the 5,230 struck with "Uncirculated" or frosty finish, probably most were snapped up. Today, nowhere near that many exist, due to damage (use in jewelry), melting, and other attrition, but choice coins are still readily available.

At Coney Island, New York, in 1884, the first roller coaster opened, erected by Lemarcus A. Thompson, who would soon become famous in the amusement-business world. During the 1880s Coney Island was developed by Austin Corbin and his associates. Corbin, a native of Newport, New Hampshire, is numismatically important as the founder of the First National Bank of Davenport.[35] This particular institution, charter no. 15, was the very first National Bank in America to open its doors, not by intention but by mistake. Authorities in Washington, DC, had instructed banks under the new charter system to start business on a given Monday, but someone misunderstood the directions. Apparently the notice arrived on Saturday, and the bank threw open its doors on that very day, beating everyone else by 48 hours!

## ONE MAN'S OPINION

The *American Journal of Numismatics*, April 1884, included a paper presented by collector G.P. Thruston at an 1883 meeting of the American Numismatic and Archaeological Society. The theme was a familiar one: collectors should not waste their time collecting varieties, but should concentrate only on major types. Again, commentaries such as this discouraged potential collectors of varieties and mintmarks. (On the other hand, it is unlikely that many 1884 readers would have shared Thruston's enthusiasm for holed coins.) Excerpts:

> The intense interest taken in completing sets or series of our own coinage, has seemed to me something of a mystery, partly due perhaps to local contagion, partly to the high market prices paid for a few rarities, and only partly due to the intrinsic merit of the subject. Each year of coinage is sought for with eagerness, over-nice shades of condition are instituted, new varieties

are named, slight differences are magnified, an additional star—a cracked die—a mere difference of date—an irregular profile perhaps, all tending in some measure at least to place an over-estimate upon the value of a series, as compared with the true historic value of such issues.

The history of our American coinage must be, of course, of paramount importance to us—its colonials, its first national issues, its fine early dollars and its various denominations; but after securing, for instance, the well-defined varieties of halves and quarters, of dimes and half dimes, to strive after and pay excessive prices for merely rare dates, when the same general types and varieties can be easily obtained, should surely not be encouraged.

I would venture the suggestion that the value of Uncirculated and Proof sets of recent coinage is also over-estimated by the average American collector. Some evidence of circulation is often the best proof of genuineness. A slight defacement should not necessarily depreciate. Our collections are not entitled to the same standard of perfection as engravings and statuary, excepting perhaps as to medals or coins valued chiefly as works of art. The neat hole punched in my fine half dollar of 1794 does not really lessen its value, or disturb my equanimity. The handsome representation of Liberty, the clear-cut date and the well preserved reverse are there; all that is historic is still there.

## MEANWHILE, ON THE AMERICAN SCENE IN 1884

Grover Cleveland was the winner in the election of November 1884, coming from behind and benefiting from a faux pas in his opponent's campaign.

In Dayton, Ohio, John Henry Patterson, age 40, formed the National Cash Register Company by buying the patents owned by a small firm. Patterson would set up a veritable one-company trust in the cash register trade, buying out competitors and bashing those who would not yield to his demagoguery. Associated with Patterson at one time was Thomas Watson, who later formed International Business Machines (IBM).

In Kentucky, Hillerich and Bradsby introduced the Louisville Slugger baseball bat, at the request of Peter "The Gladiator" Browning, on the Louisville Eclipse team. Made of seasoned ash, the new bat proved to be more effective and longer lasting than those earlier used by Browning, which endured for just about three hits per game.

Montgomery Ward produced a mail-order catalog with 240 pages describing 10,000 items, offered with the guarantee that merchandise not satisfactory could be returned, and that the company would pay transportation both ways.

Ottmar Mergenthaler patented the linotype, a mechanical typesetting machine that, through an ingenious mechanism, created metal slugs, each containing a line of text, the width of a newspaper print column, ready to be set into a form or made into a stereotype plate.[36] Louis Edison Waterman invented the first practical (somewhat) fountain pen, which had to be filled with an eyedropper.

Mark Twain's *Adventures of Huckleberry Finn* was popular, solidifying his fame as one of the most widely read authors in America.

Augustus Saint-Gaudens's Shaw Memorial was completed for the Boston Common and was placed near the Massachusetts State House. On December 6, 1884, 36 years after the work began, the Washington Monument was finally finished. The dedication was conducted on February 22, 1885, with an address given by John Sherman (later of 1890 Sherman Silver Purchase Act fame).[37]

All the rage in the home were hand-cranked tabletop reed organs, which used small wooden "cobs" or strips of paper on which musical arrangements were encoded. Advertisers made extravagant claims, some suggesting that these little devices could fill a music hall with sound! A leading brand was the Gem Roller Organ made by the Ithaca Calendar Clock Co., not far from Cornell, "high above Cayuga's waters."

# 1884

**Optimal Collecting Grade**
MS-65

**Circulation-Strike Mintage**
14,070,000

**Proof Mintage**
875

**Key to Collecting Circulation Strikes:** The 1884 Philadelphia Mint dollar is readily available in Mint State and has been for many years, even before the Treasury releases of the early 1960s. Quality varies all over the place, from sharp and lustrous to rather insipid. Today, while the 1884 remains plentiful in terms of single coins, quantities are seldom encountered.

**Surface Quality:** The striking varies but is usually average or above average. The luster varies from deeply frosty (and desirable as such) to rather grainy and insipid.

**Prooflike Coins:** Some prooflike pieces exist and are in the distinct minority.

**Mintage and Distribution:** Although Treasury Department figures for monthly production of the 1884 have not been seen for the months from January to June, 1884, the numbers afterward are these: July, 1,000,000; August, 1,200,000; September, 1,200,000; October, 1,300,000; November, 1,350,000; and December, 1,280,165. This would indicate a rate of over a million dollars per month to create an ultimate total of 14,070,000. Circulation strikes of the high-mintage 1884 dollar have been common from day one. Apparently, many were turned loose in the channels of commerce in the 1880s, while millions others remained stored in 1,000-coin cloth bags. This reserve was tapped on occasion in the 1950s, when there were calls by banks for Morgan dollars for use as holiday gifts and souvenirs.

## 1884, PROOFS

**Mintage:** 875, all from a single pair of dies. First struck on January 3, 1884, per a Mint record book.

**Key to Collecting Proofs:** Good strike and deep cameo contrast.

**Die Varieties:** At least 60 die pairs were employed to coin 1884-dated Morgan dollars at the Philadelphia Mint. By 1992, Van Allen and Mallis identified 12 varieties with features such as having a dash under the 8 (VAM 2, 6, 7, and 11, such dashes thought to have been placed in the working die to aid the positioning of the four-digit date logotype), "Very Far Date" (VAM-9, with first digit of date especially far to the left of the neck of Miss Liberty), and a couple of varieties with slight doubling (VAM-10 with doubled 188, stars, and facial features; VAM-12 with some reverse letters doubled).

## Whitman Coin Guide (WCG™)

| VG-8 | F-12 | VF-20 | EF-40 | AU-50 | MS-60 | MS-63 | MS-64 | MS-65 | MS-66 | MS-67 | PF-60 | PF-64 | PF-65 | PF-66 | PF-67 |
|------|------|-------|-------|-------|-------|-------|-------|-------|-------|-------|-------|-------|-------|-------|-------|
| $28 | $29 | $34 | $37 | $41 | $50 | $70 | $100 | $290 | $775 | $4,700 | $1,300 | $3,900 | $6,100 | $9,750 | $15,500 |

**AVAILABILITY**

| | MS-60 | MS-61 | MS-62 | MS-63 | MS-64 | MS-65 | MS-66 | MS-67 | MS-68+ |
|---|-------|-------|-------|-------|-------|-------|-------|-------|--------|
| Certified | 34 | 252 | 1,741 | 8,354 | 11,444 | 3,851 | 659 | 72 | 4 |
| Field | 150,000-250,000 | | | 75,000-125,000 | 40,000-65,000 | 10,000-15,000 | 1,250-1,750 | 200-300 | 20-25 |
| Cert. DMPL | 3 | 16 | 66 | 115 | 157 | 47 | 5 | 0 | 0 |

| | PF-60 | PF-61 | PF-62 | PF-63 | PF-64 | PF-65 | PF-66 | PF-67 | PF-68+ |
|---|-------|-------|-------|-------|-------|-------|-------|-------|--------|
| Certified | 9 | 17 | 47 | 76 | 98 | 49 | 28 | 6 | 2 |
| Field | 125-200 | | | 100-150 | 125-160 | 75-125 | 40-60 | 15-20 | 5-8 |

# 1884-CC

Optimal
Collecting Grade
MS-65

Circulation-
Strike Mintage
1,136,000

**Key to Collecting Circulation Strikes:** Again with the 1884-CC we have a Carson City Mint variety that exists in numismatic abundance. After the coins were struck, virtually all were inadvertently saved for generations of numismatists yet unborn, to come to light in 1964 and to be distributed into the market (see below). Today, while worn 1884-CC dollars are understandably rare, Mint State coins abound. Accordingly, the market price is very reasonable, and pieces are within the reach of all.

**Surface Quality:** The strike is typically average to above average, even sharp, but some pieces are weak at the centers. Cherrypicking is advised but will not be a great effort. The luster of some is deeply frosty and attractive, but on others is "indifferent," to quote Wayne Miller.[38]

**Prooflike Coins:** Some are from prooflike dies, including DMPL pieces, and are seen with some frequency in view of the numbers in the Treasury hoard. Cameo contrast is the rule, not the exception, with 1884-CC.

**Mintage and Distribution:** In 1884 in Carson City, 1,136,000 Morgan dollars were coined. Early in the 20th century, tons of undistributed coins were shipped to the Treasury Building in Washington, where, in 1,000-coin bags weighing 56 pounds each, they were tossed into storage. Occasionally, some would be paid out to answer the call for dollars, including an estimated 50 bags in 1955.[39] However, most remained intact. After the great Treasury release was halted in March 1964, the General Services Administration holding of 1884-CC dollars totaled 962,638, or 84.73% of the original mintage, per a later inventory.[40]

**Die Varieties:** Multiple die pairs were used to create 1884-CC dollars, and 11 combinations are listed by VAM. However, no variety is significant enough to create wide attention.

## Whitman Coin Guide (WCG™)

| VG-8 | F-12 | VF-20 | EF-40 | AU-50 | MS-60 | MS-63 | MS-64 | MS-65 | MS-66 | MS-67 |
|------|------|-------|-------|-------|-------|-------|-------|-------|-------|-------|
| $110 | $115 | $120 | $135 | $145 | $190 | $225 | $250 | $450 | $825 | $5,100 |

### AVAILABILITY

| | MS-60 | MS-61 | MS-62 | MS-63 | MS-64 | MS-65 | MS-66 | MS-67 | MS-68+ |
|---|-------|-------|-------|-------|-------|-------|-------|-------|--------|
| Certified | 134 | 863 | 4,974 | 15,547 | 21,803 | 10,815 | 2,351 | 172 | 3 |
| Field | 400,000–500,000 | | | 250,000–300,000 | 70,000–90,000 | 25,000–40,000 | 5,000–8,000 | 400–700 | 50–100 |
| Cert. DMPL | 12 | 53 | 330 | 1,145 | 1,965 | 774 | 167 | 6 | 0 |

# 1884-O

**Optimal Collecting Grade**
MS-65

**Circulation-Strike Mintage**
9,730,000

**Key to Collecting Circulation Strikes:** The 1884-O was minted in quantity, and examples are readily available today in all Mint State grades from MS-60 to 65 and beyond. Wayne Miller considered the 1884-O to be the most common Mint State Morgan dollar except for 1921, if all Mint State levels are considered.[41]

**Surface Quality:** Striking ranges from poor (no hair detail above Miss Liberty's ear, little definition of breast feathers on the eagle) to very sharp, but is typically average or a bit above. Cherrypicking is advised. The luster ranges from grainy or insipid to frosty, but generally will not win any awards.

**Prooflike Coins:** There are many prooflike coins in existence, one-sided as well as two-sided examples. However, most show little contrast and are the antithesis of cameo, and most are heavily bagmarked.

**Mintage and Distribution:** Logically, the work of turning out 9,730,000 coins was spread over the year. Although many were paid out and used in circulation in the 19th century, as evidenced by the plentitude of worn pieces in existence today, and although many were melted under the provisions of the 1918 Pittman Act, large quantities remained in storage. In 1933 and 1934, and again in 1938, multiple bags were turned loose by the Treasury Department. In November 1962 and for a short time afterward many bags were released from a Philadelphia Mint vault sealed in 1929, exhausting the supply. It is believed that the bulk of about 10,000,000 coins from that vault were 1883-O, 1884-O, and 1885-O.

**Die Varieties:** About three dozen different die varieties are known from as many as 40 die pairs used, none of which is dramatic enough to be listed in the Red Book, although the specialist can find many of interest. On most the O mintmark is elliptical and heavy, although small, with a narrow vertical opening at the center. However, VAM-2 has a round O mintmark, with a narrow slit. VAM-6 with repunched mintmark is the only listing in *The Top 100 Morgan Dollar Varieties.* Breen (*Encyclopedia,* 1988) gives Breen-5577 ("oval" O) and Breen-5578 (round O), noting the latter forms a minority among known 1884-O dollars.

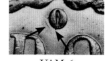

VAM-6

In 1884 the change was made from an elliptical O mintmark, in use since 1879, to the new round O, continued in use through 1904.

## Whitman Coin Guide (WCG™)

| VG-8 | F-12 | VF-20 | EF-40 | AU-50 | MS-60 | MS-63 | MS-64 | MS-65 | MS-66 | MS-67 |
|------|------|-------|-------|-------|-------|-------|-------|-------|-------|-------|
| $28 | $29 | $34 | $37 | $41 | $48 | $60 | $82 | $160 | $425 | $3,250 |

**AVAILABILITY**

| | MS-60 | MS-61 | MS-62 | MS-63 | MS-64 | MS-65 | MS-66 | MS-67 | MS-68+ |
|---|-------|-------|-------|-------|-------|-------|-------|-------|--------|
| Certified | 328 | 1,862 | 24,561 | 126,092 | 135,875 | 29,906 | 2,978 | 164 | 2 |
| Field | 1,500,000–2,500,000 | | | 700,000–1,100,00 | 300,000–425,000 | 75,000–125,000 | 4,000–7,000 | 200–300 | 40–50 |
| Cert. DMPL | 25 | 85 | 356 | 1,063 | 1,234 | 337 | 59 | 1 | 1 |

# 1884-S

**Optimal Collecting Grade MS-60**

**Circulation-Strike Mintage 3,200,000**

**Key to Collecting Circulation Strikes:** Large quantities of 1884-S dollars were released into circulation in the 19th century. Accordingly, worn examples are fairly plentiful today and are available for a nominal price. Mint State coins are elusive at any and all levels and are keys in the series. Not much attention was paid to the 1884-S in Mint State until after the coin boom of the late 1930s (ignited by the commemorative craze). Afterward, the coin took its place as one of the more difficult S Mint varieties to acquire.

**Surface Quality:** The striking is usually average. However, some have light striking at the center of the reverse. The luster on the 1884-S is generally of a satiny nature, often dull, not deeply frosty, although some of the latter exist.

**Prooflike Coins:** A few prooflike pieces are known (Wayne Miller in 1982 estimated a half dozen) with "indifferent lustre and little contrast."[42] DMPL coins are unknown, a Holy Grail in the Morgan series, although how the "Proof" described by Thomas L. Elder as Lot 225 in his J.B. Wilson Sale, October 1908, would rate today must be left to the imagination.

**Mintage and Distribution:** Striking of 1884-S dollars seems to have been paced throughout the year, and figures (available from July onward) show that 3,200,000 were struck. Distribution was mainly to the channels of commerce in the 19th century, plus whatever pieces may have been melted under the Pittman Act in 1918. Some coins remained in Treasury control, and multiple bags were distributed from San Francisco Mint storage in 1926, attracting little notice at the time, and passing into circulation. Some others were paid out at the cash window at the Treasury building in Washington in the 1930s, taking care of the demand at the time. In the 1950s some bags were paid out at San Francisco, but few remained in numismatic hands, as collector interest was not widespread. Where they went is anyone's guess, but Nevada casinos are a possibility.

**Die Varieties:** The Van Allen–Mallis text lists seven different die varieties, none of which are widely collected beyond specialists. At least 20 pairs of dies were used in the coinage. Some small amounts of lower Mint State grade 1884-S dollars remained in numismatic circles here and there, such as per the Dan Morafka offer in 1964 of a roll of 20 pieces for $450. In that year the Morgan dollar market was up for grabs, rumors proliferated, and no one knew whether a million 1884-S dollars had been paid out in the Treasury release since 1962, or just a handful had. The latter is probably close to the truth, as I am not aware of any significant quantities.

In the years after 1964, as the framework of the Morgan dollar was built, it was realized that the 1884-S dollar was basically rare in Mint State in relation to the demand, and those that did exist were in lower grades.

## Whitman Coin Guide (WCG™)

| VG-8 | F-12 | VF-20 | EF-40 | AU-50 | MS-60 | MS-63 | MS-64 | MS-65 | MS-66 | MS-67 |
|------|------|-------|-------|-------|-------|-------|-------|-------|-------|-------|
| $29 | $31 | $40 | $65 | $290 | $7,200 | $35,000 | $115,000 | $235,000 | $350,000 | $500,000 |

**AVAILABILITY**

| | MS-60 | MS-61 | MS-62 | MS-63 | MS-64 | MS-65 | MS-66 | MS-67 | MS-68+ |
|--|-------|-------|-------|-------|-------|-------|-------|-------|--------|
| Certified | 77 | 233 | 209 | 82 | 22 | 3 | 1 | 1 | 1 |
| Field | | 1,000–2,000 | | 350–600 | 60–125 | 10–15 | 2–4 | 1–2 | 1–2 |
| Cert. DMPL | 0 | 1 | 0 | 0 | 0 | 0 | 0 | 0 | 0 |

# Morgan Silver Dollars, Rare Coins, and Life in 1885

## The Morgan Dollar Scenario

In 1885 the Carson City Mint struck silver dollars and high-denomination gold coins, then ceased minting operations. Afterward, it was used as an assay office and storage facility. Finally, in 1889, the coining presses were put back into operation.

The *Annual Report of the Director of the Mint*, for the fiscal year ended June 30, 1885, told of the silver dollar problem (excerpts):

> The mints of the United States were never designed to be repositories either of large stocks of bullion or of coin. This is indicated by the small capacity and number of their original vaults. The best of these in the Mint at Philadelphia are very primitive in design and in safety appliances. Indeed, all of the institutions, as far as I am informed, with the exception of the Mint at San Francisco, are supplied with vaults the security of which mainly depends upon the integrity and efficiency of guards and patrols by night, and upon the presence of officers and employees by day.

> But, as a matter of fact, still further dependence is placed on the legal preservation of public order and the efficiency of local police. Confidence in such personal, as distinguished from structural, means of security seems happily to have suffered no relax from serious disturbances of public order. Yet it may well be asked should even this long immunity from popular violence be accepted as a guaranty against the possibility of any future occurrence of the kind in large cities like New York, Philadelphia, and New Orleans? Or should indeed such immunity in the past serve as a justification on the part of the government for not exhausting all practicable structural means for the safe custody in the mints not only of their regular store, but also of coin, for which the Treasury and Sub-treasuries at present offer but a scant asylum?

> The demand upon the mints for facilities for the storage and safe custody of bullion and coin becomes more and more urgent as their available capacity becomes taxed through the accumulation, especially of coin, of which the Treasury and Sub-treasuries of the United States are unable to relieve these institutions, through similar exigencies on their own part, or through considerations of expense attending every movement of specie.

> The lack of ample security at the mints under the necessity of makeshifts to provide even a tolerably safe storage, becomes a source of great anxiety to the officers in charge, the requirements of whose original trusts are seen to be greatly exceeded by the additional responsibility as custodians of vast sums of public moneys. When, too, it is remembered that the vaults provisionally arranged to meet the present emergency for the storage of coin are far from what they should be as such repositories, the accountability of the officers in the mints becomes one which in strict justice should not be imposed. Some of the provisional vaults, which I have personally examined, in the most active mint in the country [at Philadelphia], are scarcely more than closets or ordinary cellars opening into workshops, thoroughfares, and dark recesses, and depending more on neighboring traffic for security than on any security of their own.[43]

The same report told of mintage and distribution of new dollars during the preceding 12 months:

> **Philadelphia Mint:** 10,834,807 coins on hand. Distributed 11,336,977
> **San Francisco Mint:** 32,029,467 on hand. Distributed: 3,516,033
> **Carson City Mint:** 3,170,308 on hand. Distributed 326,976
> **New Orleans Mint:** 16,221,999 on hand. Distributed 5,193,639

In April 1885 the *American Journal of Numismatics* commented:

> It is a fact worth noticing in connection with the continued coinage of the silver dollar beyond all possible need, that as one of the consequences the country now has various different kinds

of circulation, viz: gold, silver, national greenbacks, the first issue of bills of the National Banks with green backs, the second, or brown backs, gold certificates, silver certificates, postal currency various issues, postal notes, and in some sections the old bank notes are not yet all redeemed; many of these issues are directly traceable to the persistent coinage of silver beyond all reason.

Although no one knew it at the time, the storage of silver dollars would have a sweeping effect on numismatics of a future generation, when millions of long-hidden, sparkling, mint-fresh coins would become available for face value. This treasure trove would profoundly affect in a positive way the rare coin market of the second half of the 20th century and onward.

## MEANWHILE, ON THE AMERICAN SCENE IN 1885

Ulysses S. Grant died on July 23, 1885. He had been elected president in 1868 and reelected in 1872, but failed in his third-term bid in 1876. His remains lay in state in New York City Hall for several days. His final resting place was constructed in New York City on Riverside Drive, giving rise to the humorous popular question, "Who is buried in Grant's Tomb?"

The Westinghouse Electrical & Manufacturing Company was founded by George West-inghouse, who acquired rights to certain electrical apparatus including a transformer, induction motor, and alternator. The firm soon became prominent in the large-scale distribution of electrical current. Westinghouse, primarily centered near Pittsburgh, Pennsylvania, would grow to become one of America's largest companies.

In Mannheim, Germany, Karl Friedrich Benz, age 41, successfully operated a gasoline-driven motor vehicle, which attained a speed of nine miles an hour, this being a one-cylinder device with three wheels and chain drive. During this era others experimented with automobiles as well, although in America they would not become commercially viable until more than a decade hence.

In California, the Leland Stanford, Jr., University (today Stanford University) was established by railroad millionaire Leland Stanford Sr., age 61, in memory of his son, Leland Jr., who died in 1884 at age 15. The University would open its doors in 1891. Also in 1885, Bryn Mawr College for women opened near Philadelphia, and the Georgia Institute of Technology was founded in Atlanta. In Chicago the Home Insurance Building at LaSalle and Monroe streets opened, a 10-story structure, the world's first skyscraper, with a framework mainly of steel supporting other elements.

The postal rate for first-class letters was doubled from one cent to two cents. Popular works of fiction included *King Solomon's Mines*, by British author H. Rider Haggard, and *The Rise of Silas Lapham*, by American William Dean Howells. Generally, a novel or other work of fiction that achieved popularity in England enjoyed worthwhile sales in the United States as well.

At Cove Neck, Long Island, New York, Sagamore Hill, a 22-room mansion costing $16,695, was completed for Theodore Roosevelt, age 26, a widower, who was spending time on a ranch in Dakota Territory. Roosevelt was a lover of the outdoors. In the same year the National Audubon Society was formed. In Salem, Massachusetts, Parker Brothers was founded by George Swinerton Parker, age 18, who had created a game, "Banking," in which players endeavored to accumulate wealth. No one would dream that a half century later the same firm would achieve record sales with another financial game, "Monopoly."

Lobsters were a popular edible, and in this year the catch reached a record 130 million pounds. In Maryland, nearly 50 million bushels of oysters were harvested. Oysters were especially popular, and many towns and cities had eating establishments called oyster houses and oyster saloons. In Lowell, Massachusetts, Dr. Augustin Thompson introduced Moxie Nerve Food, a cure-all that was also a stimulating beverage. Later, carbonation was added. In the early 20th century health claims were dropped, and Moxie was promoted as the beverage of choice for Americans seeking refreshment. The product went on to sell greatly, particularly in the northeastern United States, where during the early 20th century it is said to have outsold Coca-Cola.

# 1885

**Optimal Collecting Grade**
MS-65

**Circulation-Strike Mintage**
17,787,000

**Proof Mintage**
930

**Key to Collecting Circulation Strikes:** The 1885 Philadelphia Mint Morgan dollar has been common for a long time, far before the Treasury releases of the early 1960s. Made in quantity, these pieces are seen today in varying degrees of eye appeal. Apart from the need to be selective as to quality, this will be an easy date to find.

**Surface Quality:** The striking is usually above average, but some hunting may be needed to find a particularly sharp piece. The luster is usually frosty, although many grainy pieces exist.

**Prooflike Coins:** Some dies are prooflike and are most attractive in the higher grades.

**Mintage and Distribution:** Delivery figures by month: January, 985,000; February, 900,000; March, 1,300,000; April, 1,400,000; May, 1,400,000; June, 1,400,000; July, 1,800,000; August, 1,800,000; September, 1,700,000; October, 1,700,000; November, 1,700,000; December, 1,700,000. This date seems to have been distributed steadily over a long period of time. In 1954, quantities of bags were distributed for the holiday demand, and in the 1962 through 1964 Treasury release the rest were paid out, by which time probably only a few hundred thousand remained.

## 1885, PROOFS

**Mintage:** 930. 2 obverse dies, 1 reverse die prepared. Delivery figures by month: January, 200; February, 0; March, 200; April–May, 0; June, 150; July–August, 0; September, 50; October– November, 0; December, 330.

**Key to Collecting Circulation Strikes:** Proofs are usually well struck. Medium cameo contrast. More than just a few of this date have been dipped so many times that the mirror surfaces are dull gray. Such coins are not for you.

**Die Varieties:** At least 89 obverse and 88 reverse dies were used. In 1982 the VAM text described 20 combinations. None have dramatically different characteristics.

## Whitman Coin Guide (WCG™)

| VG-8 | F-12 | VF-20 | EF-40 | AU-50 | MS-60 | MS-63 | MS-64 | MS-65 | MS-66 | MS-67 | PF-60 | PF-64 | PF-65 | PF-66 | PF-67 |
|------|------|-------|-------|-------|-------|-------|-------|-------|-------|-------|-------|-------|-------|-------|-------|
| $28 | $29 | $34 | $37 | $41 | $50 | $63 | $85 | $165 | $400 | $1,350 | $1,300 | $3,900 | $6,250 | $9,750 | $16,500 |

**AVAILABILITY**

|  | MS-60 | MS-61 | MS-62 | MS-63 | MS-64 | MS-65 | MS-66 | MS-67 | MS-68+ |
|--|-------|-------|-------|-------|-------|-------|-------|-------|--------|
| Certified | 108 | 725 | 7,080 | 36,151 | 52,148 | 17,653 | 3,025 | 278 | 6 |
| Field | 400,000–700,000 | | | 265,000–450,000 | 150,000–225,000 | 40,000–60,000 | 5,000–8,000 | 250–400 | 10–15 |
| Cert. DMPL | 1 | 38 | 240 | 816 | 1,088 | 501 | 123 | 5 | 0 |
|  | PF-60 | PF-61 | PF-62 | PF-63 | PF-64 | PF-65 | PF-66 | PF-67 | PF-68+ |
| Certified | 7 | 24 | 59 | 95 | 120 | 43 | 36 | 5 | 4 |
| Field | 200–300 | | | 150–224 | 150–250 | 80–120 | 65–75 | 10–12 | 7–10 |

# 1885-CC

Optimal
Collecting Grade
MS-64

Circulation-
Strike Mintage
228,000

**Key to Collecting Circulation Strikes:** The 1885-CC exists by the hundreds of thousands of pieces, as more than half of the original mintage survived and was distributed in the late 20th century. Most examples are brilliant, lustrous, and attractive to the eye. Ironically, the 1885-CC is the rarest of all Morgan dollars in circulated grades, eclipsing the 1889-CC, 1893-S, and all other contenders (not counting the Proof-only 1895); but there are so many Mint State coins around that worn pieces are generally unappreciated.[44]

**Surface Quality:** Striking ranges from somewhat weak to very sharp, but most are above average. Most are well struck with brilliant, frosty luster.

**Prooflike Coins:** Some are struck from prooflike dies. DMPL coins with good cameo contrast exist and are highly sought.

**Mintage and Distribution:** Delivery figures by month: January, 100,000; February, 100,000; March–July, 0; August, 28,000; September–December, 0. Nearly all of the 1885-CC dollars were bagged and stored, not paid out, thereby creating a numismatic rarity. In later years bags were distributed from the Treasury Building in Washington, DC, after which they remained available on the numismatic market. Many bags were paid out in the 1950s in particular. After the great Treasury release was halted in March 1964, the General Services Administration holding of 1885-CC dollars totaled 148,285, or 65.03% of the original mintage, per a later inventory.[45]

**Die Varieties:** Although 10 die pairs were made for this coinage, only four combinations have been described by VAM, none dramatic.

## Whitman Coin Guide (WCG™)

| VG-8 | F-12 | VF-20 | EF-40 | AU-50 | MS-60 | MS-63 | MS-64 | MS-65 | MS-66 | MS-67 |
|------|------|-------|-------|-------|-------|-------|-------|-------|-------|-------|
| $450 | $465 | $475 | $500 | $525 | $550 | $600 | $725 | $950 | $2,200 | $8,000 |

**AVAILABILITY**

| | MS-60 | MS-61 | MS-62 | MS-63 | MS-64 | MS-65 | MS-66 | MS-67 | MS-68+ |
|--|-------|-------|-------|-------|-------|-------|-------|-------|--------|
| Certified | 64 | 379 | 2,109 | 6,514 | 10,113 | 5,567 | 1,719 | 112 | 6 |
| Field | 80,000–110,000 | | | 50,000–75,000 | 25,000–40,000 | 10,000–15,000 | 1,400–1,800 | 70–100 | 10–15 |
| Cert. DMPL | 11 | 55 | 243 | 520 | 621 | 278 | 56 | 2 | 0 |

# 1885-O

**Optimal
Collecting Grade**
MS-65

**Circulation-
Strike Mintage**
9,815,000

**Key to Collecting Circulation Strikes:** The 1885-O dollars were among the bonanza delights of the 1962 through 1964 Treasury releases, after which bags were common, all filled with bright, sparkling coins—but not necessarily well struck or with deep luster. Today, cherrypicking is the order of the day, but with so many coins from which to choose, the exercise will not take much time. Be advised that at coin shows not all dealers want fussy buyers poking around piles of Morgan dollars to find choice ones or, worse (in their view), obscure VAM varieties. One leading dealer was all heated up at a convention after having several Morgan dollar "weenies" (as he called them) in succession stop at his table and ask to look for die varieties. They didn't buy anything, not because they did not want to, but because the dealer never gave them a chance.

**Surface Quality:** The strike can range from flat at the centers to fairly sharp, the same general rule being applicable to other New Orleans pieces of the era. Luster ranges from frosty to grainy or dull. Cherrypicking is advised.

**Prooflike Coins:** Some are seen with prooflike dies, but usually not with great contrast against the devices.

**Mintage and Distribution:** Delivery figures by month: May, 900,000; June, 925,000; July, 100,000; August, 600,000; September, 800,000; October, 800,000; November, 800,000; December, 800,000. Many 1885-O dollars were paid out in the early years, and as a result these were common in circulation. Mint bags from storage were paid out in later years as well. In November 1962 and for a short time afterward many bags were released from a Philadelphia Mint vault sealed in 1929, exhausting the supply. It is believed that the bulk of about 10,000,000 coins from that vault were 1883-O, 1884-O, and 1885-O.

**Die Varieties:** Ten die pairs were used. There are no "must have" varieties, although VAM-9 may be the most interesting.

## Whitman Coin Guide (WCG™)

| VG-8 | F-12 | VF-20 | EF-40 | AU-50 | MS-60 | MS-63 | MS-64 | MS-65 | MS-66 | MS-67 |
|------|------|-------|-------|-------|-------|-------|-------|-------|-------|-------|
| $28 | $29 | $34 | $37 | $41 | $48 | $60 | $80 | $160 | $370 | $1,500 |

**AVAILABILITY**

| | MS-60 | MS-61 | MS-62 | MS-63 | MS-64 | MS-65 | MS-66 | MS-67 | MS-68+ |
|---|-------|-------|-------|-------|-------|-------|-------|-------|--------|
| Certified | 149 | 1,149 | 17,944 | 105,750 | 138,579 | 42,708 | 6,393 | 682 | 9 |
| Field | 1,250,000–2,000,000 | | | 400,000–700,000 | 350,000–500,000 | 75,000–125,000 | 9,000–12,000 | 700–1,000 | 20–30 |
| Cert. DMPL | 24 | 52 | 280 | 891 | 1,019 | 348 | 55 | 2 | 0 |

# 1885-S

Optimal
Collecting Grade
MS-64

Circulation-
Strike Mintage
1,497,000

**Key to Collecting Circulation Strikes:** The 1885-S dollar fits into the medium-scarce category, neither common nor rare. There are enough around that for a reasonable price you can easily own an MS-63 or MS-64, but not so easy for an MS-65. Many are softly struck, more like a typical New Orleans dollar than one from San Francisco, so you will need to spend some time searching.

**Surface Quality:** Most have some flatness at the center of the obverse and the center of the reverse, in contrast to most earlier-dated San Francisco coins, which are well struck. Some excellent strikes exist of 1885-S, but searching is needed to find them. Most are with attractive luster.

**Prooflike Coins:** Some are from prooflike dies, sometimes on one side only. DMPLs exist and are very rare.

**Mintage and Distribution:** Delivery figures by month: January, 500,000; February, 500,000; March, 200,000; April, 100,000; May, 100,000; June, 50,000; July, 0; August, 47,000; September–December, 0. Quantities of 1885-S were stored for years at the San Francisco Mint. Occasionally, a few bags would fall into the hands of dealers, this being the case in the 1950s, while in the meantime others would be shipped to Nevada and enter circulation via the gaming tables. Further bags were paid out during the Treasury release of 1962 through 1964, but not many in comparison to the deluge of New Orleans coins.

**Die Varieties:** No dramatic die varieties exist for this year. Among 20 pairs of dies used, VAM-6 is interesting in that it shows a sharply repunched S, the final S mintmark being larger and to the right of the outline of an earlier S.

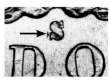

VAM-6

## Whitman Coin Guide (WCG™)

| VG-8 | F-12 | VF-20 | EF-40 | AU-50 | MS-60 | MS-63 | MS-64 | MS-65 | MS-66 | MS-67 |
|------|------|-------|-------|-------|-------|-------|-------|-------|-------|-------|
| $29 | $31 | $45 | $60 | $120 | $220 | $315 | $675 | $1,800 | $7,000 | $50,000 |

### AVAILABILITY

| | MS-60 | MS-61 | MS-62 | MS-63 | MS-64 | MS-65 | MS-66 | MS-67 | MS-68+ |
|--|-------|-------|-------|-------|-------|-------|-------|-------|--------|
| Certified | 152 | 740 | 2,393 | 4,175 | 3,484 | 683 | 43 | 2 | 0 |
| Field | | 25,000–40,000 | | 10,000–15,000 | 5,000–8,500 | 1,250–1,750 | 80–120 | 7–10 | 0 |
| Cert. DMPL | 0 | 1 | 0 | 3 | 6 | 1 | 0 | 0 | 0 |

# Morgan Silver Dollars, Rare Coins, and Life in 1886

## The Morgan Dollar Scenario

Huge quantities of unneeded Morgan silver dollars continued to spew forth from the Philadelphia, New Orleans, and San Francisco mints (the Carson City Mint having ceased coinage in 1885). The 1886 *Annual Report of the Director of the Mint* noted that the relocation of the Philadelphia Mint's steam plant would make possible "the proper location of vaults for the storage of coin and bullion in the centre of the building, instead of along the outer walls as at present." Even so, the burgeoning supply of dollars forced the use of storage outside the Mint, and at the Mint itself, guards were posted with Gatling guns in case of trouble. Of course, from a numismatic viewpoint today the veritable mountain of silver dollars was wonderful. Not so, however, with the Director of the Mint in 1886, who reported:

> The Department is again called upon to meet an emergency similar in kind to that described at the beginning of the last fiscal year. From the emergency at that time relief was found in the provision of two empty vaults connected with the vacant apartments in the United States Post-Office building in that city. These vaults were fitted for the reception of silver dollars and made ready for occupation about December 1, 1885. At the instance of the Department they were supplied with time-locks and metallic lattice for the storage of silver dollars in excess of what could be kept at the Mint, and the delivery of which to the Treasury or sub-treasury might not be called for.
>
> The anomalous course has thus been forced upon the Mint service of retaining the immediate custody, under the personal responsibility of the Superintendent of the Mint at Philadelphia, of the bulk of the output to that institution, instead of delivering the same according to custom to the United States Treasury. The anomaly is all the greater that the storage of this treasure is not upon the premises of the Mint itself, but in a separate building with separate environments, thus requiring a special watch for its safety.
>
> Up to the 30th of October, 1886, a date subsequent to that of this report and while it was in press, the amount of silver dollars thus stored in the Post-Office building was $20,250,000. This is the sum of the daily output of the mint for less than a year, the vaults of the Mint proper, including a number of provisional vaults without special safety appliances, having been filled to repletion and in a manner very objectionable, from the fact that sufficient space for gangways has not been available for examination and count.
>
> On the same date I forwarded you a communication from the Superintendent of the Mint at Philadelphia stating that the vaults in the Post-Office building will be completely filled at the end of 20 days, when they will contain some $21,500,000, and that no further space will be available for storage of silver dollars in the Mint building except by recourse to the very objectionable expedient of piling solid vault No. 6. This vault contains 1,733,000 pieces, which, from the circumstance that it is without safety appliances and that it is upon the outer walls of the building, are all that can be stored therein, with the usual requirement of gangway spaces necessary for purposes of examination and count.
>
> Even if this vault be filled to its cubical capacity, storage can be found for the output of less than two months' work. The emergency is thus forced upon the attention of the Department either to provide space, with suitable safety appliances and guard, for the storage at Philadelphia of the further output of the Mint, or else to provide for its transfer from time to time, at short intervals, to the custody of the United States Treasury.
>
> The vaults in the United States Post Office building still remain in the custody of the Superintendent of the Mint at Philadelphia, owing to the impracticability of their transfer to the custody of the United States Treasury while open to the reception of the daily output of the Mint. When these vaults, however, be finally filled, I have to recommend that the custody of the same be transferred to the United States Treasury.

Owing to the bulky character of the silver treasure, for the storage of which temporary and unsuitable expedients have had to be adopted at the Mint at Philadelphia, I took occasion in my last annual report to point out as the greatest danger to which this treasure is exposed whatever danger there be from popular disorder. In order to be prepared for any contingency of the kind, however remote, I undertook to secure, through the cooperation of the War Department, a suitable defensive armament for the Mint at Philadelphia. The armory was early in the year newly equipped with Gatling guns mounted on tripods and with repeating rifles, &c. An armorer has been detailed from the roll of the Mint and a portion of his time given to the proper care of these arms.

The 1886 *Annual Report* went on to state that during the fiscal year ending June 30, the Philadelphia Mint had 27,974,020 silver dollars on hand and had distributed a further 3,323,972. At San Francisco there were 19,229,530 silver dollars, and only 2,865,009 had been paid out during the year. The New Orleans Mint had 3,279,237 silver dollars on hand and had distributed 5,092,762.

The vaults of the Carson City Mint were completely empty, following the distribution of 80,236 coins. Not stated was the fact that most of these coins, indeed representing the bulk of the mintage of CC dollars of 1882, 1883, and 1884, and many of other dates as well, had simply been transferred to other Treasury Department vaults—to remain in unintended safekeeping, to emerge in the 1960s to delight a future generation of numismatists.

President Grover Cleveland had this to say:

Last year we spent 23 million dollars plus labor and storage for silver dollars that no one wants. Now we have 247 million of them. This gamble on a silver price increase is a bust. In the beginning, when we bought the silver, the dollar content was 94.5 cents. On the 31st day of July, 1886, silver dropped to its lowest price. Now these things are only worth 78 cents.[46]

## Meanwhile, on the American Scene in 1886

On May 1 in Chicago, policemen fired into a crowd of striking workers, precipitating the Haymarket massacre, killing four people and wounding many others. On May 4, the Knights of Labor staged a peaceful rally to protest the murder, but someone detonated a bomb that mortally wounded seven policemen. The police fired into the crowd and caused many more casualties. This marked the first major labor demonstration conflict in America. More strikes were held during 1886 than in any previous year, and the American Federation of Labor was formed by Samuel Gompers.

The Postal Telegraph Company was organized and achieved success, breaking into the monopoly held by Western Union. The *New York Tribune* became the first newspaper to install a Mergenthaler linotype machine. Frederick Eugene Ives developed a new process for halftone engraving, using small dots of varying sizes.

Robert Louis Stevenson's *The Strange Case of Dr. Jekyll and Mr. Hyde* and *Kidnapped* became popular, as did *Little Lord Fauntleroy*, by Frances Hodgson Burnett.

The enterprise that would become Sears, Roebuck & Company began business in North Redwood, Minnesota, when Richard W. Sears, 23, bought a consignment of gold-filled watches, stated retail value $25 each, that had been refused by a local jeweler. Sears used the telegraph to offer these attractive watches for just $14 each, enabling him to offer a good product cheaper than local jewelers could. Sears cleared $5,000 in six months, and resigned from the railroad to set up business in Minneapolis.

In Atlanta on May 8, Coca-Cola was first sold at Jacob's Pharmacy by pharmacist John S. Pemberton, who had formulated a headache and hangover remedy that included cocaine (not regulated by law at the time), an extract from cola nuts, and fruit syrup. The concoction had been advertised since March 29, billed as an "esteemed brain tonic and intellectual beverage."

In New York City, the Statue of Liberty, formally designated Liberty Enlightening the World, was dedicated by President Grover Cleveland.

# 1886

Optimal
Collecting Grade
MS-65

Circulation-
Strike Mintage
19,963,000

Proof Mintage
886

**Key to Collecting Circulation Strikes:** Dollars of 1886 are very common, but often dies were used like the Energizer Bunny—they just kept going and going, and going some more. As a result, more than a few surviving Mint States coins are grainy and show metal flow lines. Cherrypicking is recommended. Worn 1886 dollars are common, and without doubt huge numbers of them went into refinery furnaces during the run-up of silver bullion prices in the 1980s, as few numismatists wanted them.

**Surface Quality:** The strike varies, but most are fairly sharp. As a rule of thumb the luster on the 1886 is rather dull, often grainy, as dies seem to have been used for a long time. Cherrypicking is needed to find one with deep mint frost.

**Prooflike Coins:** Prooflike coins are occasionally seen, usually with low contrast. DMPL coins with cameo contrast are very elusive.

**Mintage and Distribution:** Delivery figures by month: January, 1,700,000; February, 1,700,000; March, 1,700,000; April, 1,700,000; May, 1,700,000; June, 1,563,000; July, 1,600,000; August, 1,800,000; September, 1,900,000; October, 1,800,000; November, 1,400,000; December, 1,400,000. Dollars dated 1886 were paid out over a long period of years and therefore have been common in numismatic circles. Large quantities of bags were distributed in 1951 and 1952, and, probably, several thousand bags in 1954—after which time they were super-common. The remaining bags left Treasury vaults during the 1962 through 1964 release.

## 1886, PROOFS

**Mintage:** 886. Delivery figures by month: January–February, 0; March, 360; April–May, 0; June, 165; July–August, 0; September, 100; October–November, 0; December, 261. Two obverse die varieties are known, one with 1 (1886) repunched, the other showing traces of repunching of 18 and 6; the last variety has just 179 edge reeds, instead of the usual 188 to 190.

**Key to Collecting Proofs:** Strike is usually decent. Contrast medium to low. Nice 1886 Proof dollars exist, but they are harder to find than certain other dates mentioned thus far.

**Die Varieties:** There are no dramatic die varieties known from the 63 obverse and 60 reverse dies made for the coinage, though some doubled dates may be of interest.

## Whitman Coin Guide (WCG™)

| VG-8 | F-12 | VF-20 | EF-40 | AU-50 | MS-60 | MS-63 | MS-64 | MS-65 | MS-66 | MS-67 | PF-60 | PF-64 | PF-65 | PF-66 | PF-67 |
|------|------|-------|-------|-------|-------|-------|-------|-------|-------|-------|-------|-------|-------|-------|-------|
| $28 | $29 | $34 | $37 | $41 | $48 | $60 | $82 | $160 | $400 | $1,050 | $1,300 | $3,900 | $6,100 | $9,750 | $15,500 |

### AVAILABILITY

| | MS-60 | MS-61 | MS-62 | MS-63 | MS-64 | MS-65 | MS-66 | MS-67 | MS-68+ |
|---|-------|-------|-------|-------|-------|-------|-------|-------|--------|
| Certified | 166 | 1,204 | 10,925 | 60,338 | 86,793 | 34,063 | 7,300 | 1,099 | 22 |
| Field | 1,400,000–1,800,000 | | | 300,000–500,000 | 200,000–300,000 | 75,000–100,000 | 10,000–15,000 | 1,250–1,750 | 35–50 |
| Cert. DMPL | 8 | 38 | 112 | 452 | 467 | 192 | 39 | 1 | 0 |

| | PF-60 | PF-61 | PF-62 | PF-63 | PF-64 | PF-65 | PF-66 | PF-67 | PF-68+ |
|---|-------|-------|-------|-------|-------|-------|-------|-------|--------|
| Certified | 9 | 30 | 71 | 80 | 104 | 68 | 35 | 11 | 0 |
| Field | 250–350 | | | 140–180 | 130–160 | 80–120 | 50–75 | 25–40 | 1–2 |

# 1886-O

Optimal
Collecting Grade
MS-63 or MS-64

Circulation-
Strike Mintage
10,710,000

**Key to Collecting Circulation Strikes:** The 1886-O dollars are very common in worn grades today and exceedingly rare in choice to gem Mint State. Most all were released in the 19th century or melted in 1918, and few were ever saved for numismatic purposes.

**Surface Quality:** Striking varies from flat at the centers to fairly sharp, with most being quite decent. Cherrypicking is advised, to the extent that it can be done among Mint State coins, which are not often encountered. The luster on the 1886-O ranges from flat, grainy, and lifeless to fairly frosty, the last being in the distinct minority. Again, careful buying is advised, but this must be done over a period of time, as one certainly does not have the opportunity to view a significant number of 1886-O dollars side by side.

**Prooflike Coins:** Rare with prooflike surface on one side or the other. DMPL coins exist and are exceedingly rare and desirable if in high grades with good eye appeal.

**Mintage and Distribution:** Delivery figures by month: January, 900,000; February, 900,000; March, 900,000; April, 900,000; May, 900,000; June, 900,000; July, 600,000; August, 900,000; September, 910,000; October, 900,000; November, 1,000,000; December, 1,000,000. No hoards are known. A few bags are believed to have been paid out in the 1950s, keeping this coin out of the rarity class at the time.

**Die Varieties:** Among varieties, VAM-1A is significant. *1886-O "Raised E on Reverse," VAM-1A:* Raised E prominent below the eagle's tail feathers, above the upper left of the ribbon bow.

VAM-1A

## Whitman Coin Guide (WCG™)

| VG-8 | F-12 | VF-20 | EF-40 | AU-50 | MS-60 | MS-63 | MS-64 | MS-65 | MS-66 | MS-67 |
|------|------|-------|-------|-------|-------|-------|-------|-------|-------|-------|
| $28 | $29 | $37 | $45 | $80 | $750 | $3,350 | $9,250 | $185,000 | $480,000 | – |

### AVAILABILITY

|  | MS-60 | MS-61 | MS-62 | MS-63 | MS-64 | MS-65 | MS-66 | MS-67 | MS-68+ |
|--|-------|-------|-------|-------|-------|-------|-------|-------|--------|
| Certified | 334 | 790 | 1,102 | 818 | 289 | 2 | 1 | 0 | 0 |
| Field |  | 3,500–5,000 |  | 1,250–1,750 | 250–300 | 3–5 | 1 | 0 | 0 |
| Cert. DMPL | 4 | 3 | 6 | 4 | 4 | 0 | 0 | 1 | 0 |

# 1886-S

**Optimal Collecting Grade**
MS-64

**Circulation-Strike Mintage**
750,000

**Key to Collecting Circulation Strikes:** My comments for 1886-S are not much different from 1885-S: nearly all coins have excellent eye appeal, but some searching is needed to find a sharp strike. I suggest that MS-63 and MS-64 are grades that are eminently affordable to most advanced numismatists, and MS-65 coins are, of course, even more worthwhile. However, for most grades the 1886-S is rarer than the 1885-S.

**Surface Quality:** Above average strike is the rule for 1886-S, although very sharp strikes require some searching to find. The luster on the 1886-S is typically of high quality. This issue is reminiscent of certain San Francisco dollars earlier in the decade, when sharp strike and quality were the rule, not the exception.

**Prooflike Coins:** Prooflike coins are seen with some frequency, perhaps 20% or more coins having some prooflike characteristics. DMPL coins are seen occasionally.

**Mintage and Distribution:** Delivery figures by month: January–September, 0; October, 300,000; November, 300,000; December, 150,000. In 1886 it is likely that few 1886-S dollars were paid out. By the second decade of the 20th century the variety was considered to be one of the great rarities in the series, exceeded only by the "impossible" 1889-S. Both issues were mostly stored in the San Francisco Mint. Beginning about 1942, and continuing until the 1950s, the San Francisco Mint had quantities available for the asking, and many went to the Nevada casinos, but there was no numismatic market. In time, most hoard coins were circulated in the casinos, and many may have been melted under the Pittman Act in 1918. A few bags came out in Montana in 1956. By the time of the Treasury release of 1962 through 1964, quantities on hand were very small.

**Die Varieties:** Minor varieties exist, mostly involving slight repunching.

## Whitman Coin Guide (WCG™)

| VG-8 | F-12 | VF-20 | EF-40 | AU-50 | MS-60 | MS-63 | MS-64 | MS-65 | MS-66 | MS-67 |
|------|------|-------|-------|-------|-------|-------|-------|-------|-------|-------|
| $50 | $65 | $78 | $95 | $150 | $310 | $480 | $800 | $2,900 | $8,500 | $30,000 |

### AVAILABILITY

| | MS-60 | MS-61 | MS-62 | MS-63 | MS-64 | MS-65 | MS-66 | MS-67 | MS-68+ |
|---|-------|-------|-------|-------|-------|-------|-------|-------|--------|
| Certified | 116 | 493 | 1,649 | 2,526 | 1,872 | 361 | 43 | 6 | 0 |
| Field | 17,500–22,500 | | | 6,000–9,000 | 3,000–5,000 | 1,000–1,500 | 90–125 | 10–15 | 0 |
| Cert. DMPL | 2 | 6 | 20 | 36 | 30 | 2 | 0 | 0 | 0 |

# MORGAN SILVER DOLLARS, RARE COINS, AND LIFE IN 1887

## THE MORGAN DOLLAR SCENARIO

At the Philadelphia Mint, where all dies were manufactured, several 1886-dated silver dollar obverses were overdated 1887 and subsequently used for coinage at the Philadelphia and New Orleans mints.

The Carson City Mint, emptied of all silver dollars by June 30, 1886 (see 1886 narrative), remained closed for coinage, and its presses were idle. However, during the fiscal year ended June 30, 1887, 25 bags of San Francisco Mint dollars, 1,000 coins per bag, had been shipped to Carson City. As of June 30, 15,179 had been paid out, probably a window on the actual need for silver dollars in circulation at the time in Nevada, and 9,821 remained on hand.

At the other mints, vaults continued to be stuffed with Morgan dollars, necessitating in some instances the use of other facilities for the overflow (see 1886 narrative). Now at the Philadelphia Post Office there were 21,750 cloth bags of silver dollars containing 1,000 coins each. At this and all other facilities there were no sealed vaults the contents of which could be audited, then put under lock. Instead, according to the *Annual Report*, for each year, "It is estimated that at the annual settlement and other counts the weighing of the bullion and coin requires no less than eight handlings." The present reader can easily see how stored silver dollars acquired so many bagmarks over a long period of years.

From the following it is seen that the Morgan dollar coinage, while pleasing to western mining interests and politicians of that district, also produced significant revenue for the United States government in an era before personal income taxes, in fiscal year 1887 yielding over $7 million in profit:

> There were manufactured during the [fiscal] year, by three mints, 33,266,831 silver dollars. The amount of silver used in this coinage was 28,588,682.89 standard ounces, the cost of which was $25,343,272.39. In addition to this employment there was wasted by the operative officers 15,337.87 standard ounces, costing $13,473.13, and sold in sweeps 35,548.50 standard ounces, costing $31,994.86, making the total amount of silver used in the silver dollar coinage 28,639,569.26 standard ounces, costing $25,388,740.51. The seignorage [profit] on silver dollars coined during the year was $7,923,558.61.

## THE MORGAN DESIGN

The *American Journal of Numismatics*, April 1887, included this unsigned commentary, possibly from an English contributor, perhaps obliquely referring to the portrait and eagle on the current dollar:[47]

> American coins, compared to those of other nations, appear to the writer to be unquestionably the most uninteresting series in the world. No portraits of past presidents; no historical memories awakened; nothing but rows of coins almost exactly alike, save an interminable row of different dates.
>
> The (no doubt) well-meaning, but everlasting eagle (manipulating a claw full of spears with indifferent success), and the equally interminable female portrait (whom no one seems to know, but who, like Queen Victoria, retains her youthful features on the coins, as the ages roll by, in a wondrous manner), are certainly discouraging to a collector.

Such comments, seemingly in a never-ending parade in print, no doubt deterred many from collecting the current American series, including silver dollars.

## MEANWHILE, ON THE AMERICAN SCENE IN 1887

The Interstate Commerce Act was passed by Congress on February 1, and required that railroads set equitable rates for customers. There had been wide abuses in this field earlier, with railroads enjoying a monopoly position in transportation in many American cities, soliciting payments and subsidies for service and connections, and leaving stranded certain towns that did not want to comply. Similarly, railroads often set rates at will for coal, grain, and other commodities. Despite the legislation of 1887, problems would continue for many years and, in fact, would be the pivotal theme of Frank Norris's 1901 novel, *The Octopus*. In the greater Los Angeles district, the railroad building, mergers, and other activities reached a high pace amid much publicity, bringing thousands of new people into the area. The western movement would gain momentum in coming years as the warm climate of the Golden State, extensive employment opportunities, and other advantages were publicized in print, including, beginning in the early 20th century, many brochures and postcards.

The Comptometer multicolumn mechanical calculating machine was introduced by the Felt & Tarrant Manufacturing Company, Chicago. Later, related devices would be made and marketed by Burroughs, Marchant, Victor, and others, all operating on ingenious trains of interconnected gears, levers, keys, and display numerals.

William Randolph Hearst, age 23, who published the *San Francisco Evening Examiner* (which he had inherited from his father), chartered a train to travel to the scene of a fire that had destroyed the Del Monte Hotel in Monterey, built by railroad magnate Charles Crocker. This contributed to Hearst's ambition to cover breaking events and sensationalize them, giving rise to a publishing empire largely built on hype. This was a standard way to build circulation, and Joseph Pulitzer of the *New York World*, another publication, also enjoyed sensational coverage. Later, both Hearst and Pulitzer would become more relaxed and professional, in the meantime having built fortunes.

In England the first adventure of Sherlock Holmes was published, *A Study in Scarlet*, by Dr. Arthur Conan Doyle, age 28, whose influx of medical patients into his office was below expectations, giving him time to engage in writing—fortunately for generations of future readers. The bittersweet saga related in *Study* was set in America, which would furnish the scenario for a later popular book by Doyle, *The Valley of Fear*. Augustus Saint-Gaudens was achieving fame at his studio in New York City, and in 1887 two of his sculptures, *Amor Caritas* and *Seated Lincoln*, achieved notice.

In West Orange, New Jersey, Thomas Edison built the first phonograph driven by a motor. Sound was recorded on rotating wax cylinders mounted on a steel mandrel. Edison believed that this device had a bright future for office dictation use, but that popular or home use would not be important. In the next decade Edison would produce many dictating machines, which indeed found good employment, and also licensed these devices for playing music in what were called phonograph parlors, through machines that accepted a cent in a coin slot.

On Mackinac Island, Michigan, the Grand Hotel opened with 262 rooms and a 900-foot veranda, giving a fine panorama of vessels passing through the Straits of Mackinac connecting lakes Michigan and Huron. This became a favorite watering spot for citizens of Chicago and other Midwestern cities. In the meantime, in the East, Saratoga Springs in Upstate New York, the White Mountains in New Hampshire, and the Blue Ridge Mountains were magnets for summer visitors seeking to escape the heat of Philadelphia, New York, Boston, and other cities in an era in which air conditioning was not available. Similarly, seaside resorts along the New England coast and New Jersey enjoyed good business, typically connected to metropolises by railroads running on frequent schedules.

# 1887/6

**Optimal Collecting Grade MS-64**

**Circulation-Strike Mintage 350,000**[48]

Traces of an under-6 define the 1887, 7 Over 6 overdate, distinctive only on early die states as shown here.

**Key to Collecting Circulation Strikes:** There is a significant demand for the overdate 1887/6, VAM-2, and examples are elusive in all grades. While grade-for-grade the 1887/6 is rare in comparison to the regular 1887, enough MS-64 and MS-65 coins exist that the connoisseur can locate an example. This variety is not everyone's numismatic cup of tea, and as the overdate is not easily seen without magnification, some have chosen not to include it in their collections. The prices of examples have been like a "roller coaster ride," as popularity and availability have both varied over the years.[49]

**Surface Quality:** Average. Usually with deep mint frost.

**Prooflike Coins:** Prooflike coins are occasionally seen, usually with low contrast. Some DMPL coins have been certified and are rare.

**Mintage and Distribution:** In 1887 there were 55 obverse dies used to strike Morgan dollars. As only one die is known to have been overdated, it might not be stretching too far to suggest that, on average, the mintage of 1887/6 was 1/55 of the 20,290,000 total for the year.

**Die Varieties:** 1887/6 VAM-2. Overdate feature prominent only on early and medium states, after which it fades (and specimens are not desirable).

## Whitman Coin Guide (WCG™)

| VG-8 | F-12 | VF-20 | EF-40 | AU-50 | MS-60 | MS-63 | MS-64 | MS-65 | MS-66 | MS-67 |
|------|------|-------|-------|-------|-------|-------|-------|-------|-------|-------|
| $38 | $40 | $48 | $75 | $160 | $340 | $500 | $825 | $2,250 | $13,500 | – |

### AVAILABILITY

| | MS-60 | MS-61 | MS-62 | MS-63 | MS-64 | MS-65 | MS-66 | MS-67 | MS-68+ |
|---|-------|-------|-------|-------|-------|-------|-------|-------|--------|
| Certified | 37 | 85 | 294 | 433 | 349 | 138 | 9 | 0 | 0 |
| Field | | 20,000–30,000 | | 3,000–5,000 | 1,000–2,000 | 200–300 | 10–15 | 0 | 0 |
| Cert. DMPL | 0 | 0 | 1 | 2 | 7 | 3 | 0 | 0 | 0 |

# 1887

**Optimal Collecting Grade**
MS-65

**Circulation-Strike Mintage**
19,940,000[50]

**Proof Mintage**
710

**Key to Collecting Circulation Strikes:** The 1887 is as common as can be. Today, examples remain plentiful, but as most are weakly struck in one area or another, or have poor luster, or are afflicted with both negatives, being fussy is the order of the day when buying one. Proofs are rarities in proportion to their mintage.

**Surface Quality:** Striking varies from flat at the centers, as usual, to fairly decent. Cherry-picking is advised. The 1887 is a plentiful date, so many opportunities will exist. The luster is typically dull and somewhat "greasy," at a low level of quality. Cherrypicking is needed to find a deeply lustrous example. Apparently, this large-mintage issue was produced in haste.

**Prooflike Coins:** Many prooflike coins exist, as do many DMPLs, but relatively few have cameo contrast.

**Mintage and Distribution:** Delivery figures by month: January, 2,020,000; February, 1,950,000; March, 2,020,000; April, 2,000,000; May, 1,900,000; June, 1,500,000; July, 0; August, 1,500,000; September, 1,700,000; October, 2,000,000; November, 2,000,000; December, 1,700,000. Bags from this huge mintage were paid out over a long period of time, with especially large quantities appearing from the 1950s onward. Today, this is the most common of all early Morgan dollar dates, the bane of many coin shop owners presented with "an old and valuable silver dollar that has been in the family for years."

**Die Varieties:** Although at least 55 obverse and 54 reverse dies were made for intended use for this coinage (including one overdated die, 1887/6, described earlier), none besides the overdate are of particular interest except to the super-dedicated VAM enthusiast.

## 1887, PROOFS

**Mintage:** 710. Delivery figures by month: January–February, 0; March, 380; April–May, 0; June, 90; July–August, 0; September, 40; October–November, 0; December, 200.

**Key to Collecting Proofs:** Usually a decent strike. Medium to low contrast. Diminished mintage quantities of this and other dates of this era add to the challenge of finding high-quality pieces. Incidentally, the majority of the Proof-66, Proof-67, and Proof-68 or finer pieces represent coins certified in recent years. Earlier, many would have been called Proof-65. Skeptical? Just dig out some old population reports for, say, 1990, and see how many Proofs of any date are listed in such high grades.

### Whitman Coin Guide (WCG™)

| VG-8 | F-12 | VF-20 | EF-40 | AU-50 | MS-60 | MS-63 | MS-64 | MS-65 | MS-66 | MS-67 | PF-60 | PF-64 | PF-65 | PF-66 | PF-67 |
|------|------|-------|-------|-------|-------|-------|-------|-------|-------|-------|-------|-------|-------|-------|-------|
| $28 | $29 | $34 | $37 | $41 | $48 | $60 | $82 | $165 | $400 | $1,650 | $1,300 | $3,900 | $6,100 | $9,750 | $16,500 |

**AVAILABILITY**

| | MS-60 | MS-61 | MS-62 | MS-63 | MS-64 | MS-65 | MS-66 | MS-67 | MS-68+ |
|---|-------|-------|-------|-------|-------|-------|-------|-------|--------|
| Certified | 160 | 1,140 | 14,644 | 89,582 | 126,323 | 39,138 | 4,900 | 369 | 4 |
| Field | 1,000,000–1,500,000 | | | 500,000–800,000 | 300,000–450,000 | 80,000–110,000 | 6,000–10,000 | 500–800 | 50–75 |
| Cert. DMPL | 5 | 18 | 138 | 557 | 794 | 295 | 44 | 0 | 0 |
| | PF-60 | PF-61 | PF-62 | PF-63 | PF-64 | PF-65 | PF-66 | PF-67 | PF-68+ |
| Certified | 9 | 24 | 66 | 88 | 109 | 67 | 40 | 7 | 2 |
| Field | 200–300 | | | 150–175 | 125–175 | 100–150 | 40–60 | 15–25 | 3–5 |

# 1887/6-O

Optimal
Collecting Grade
MS-60

Circulation-
Strike Mintage
200,000
(estimated)[51]

Traces of
an under-6
define the 1887-O,
7 Over 6 overdate,
distinctive only on
early die states as
shown here.

**Key to Collecting Circulation Strikes:** The 1887/6-O overdate, VAM-3, is very scarce in all grades. The 1887/6-O can be a cherrypicker's delight, for although in recent years the certification services have been alert to the existence of 1887/6-O, there are many "raw" pieces that have never been studied for this feature. All known Mint State coins are in lower grades, seemingly indicating potential for finding some higher ones by carefully studying "regular" 1887-O dollars, some of which are gems (numerically, not necessarily from aspects of strike or luster).

**Surface Quality:** Lightly struck at the center, and some are very lightly struck. Luster ranges from dull to average, not deeply frosty.

**Prooflike Coins:** No prooflike examples have been seen or reported.

**Mintage and Distribution:** Struck from a single die pair and at the New Orleans Mint mixed with production from other presses. Examples were included in some Treasury releases, but no details are known.

**Die Varieties:** 1887/6-O VAM-3. Overdate feature prominent only on early and medium states, after which it fades (and specimens are not desirable).

VAM-3

## Whitman Coin Guide (WCG™)

| VG-8 | F-12 | VF-20 | EF-40 | AU-50 | MS-60 | MS-63 | MS-64 | MS-65 | MS-66 | MS-67 |
|------|------|-------|-------|-------|-------|-------|-------|-------|-------|-------|
| $38 | $40 | $48 | $75 | $175 | $450 | $1,900 | $4,800 | $27,000 | $55,000 | – |

**AVAILABILITY**

| | MS-60 | MS-61 | MS-62 | MS-63 | MS-64 | MS-65 | MS-66 | MS-67 | MS-68+ |
|---|-------|-------|-------|-------|-------|-------|-------|-------|--------|
| Certified | 81 | 123 | 243 | 244 | 93 | 1 | 0 | 0 | 0 |
| Field | 1,500-2,500 | | | 700-1,200 | 200-300 | 0 | 0 | 0 | 0 |

# 1887-O

Optimal
Collecting Grade
MS-64

Circulation-
Strike Mintage
11,350,000

**Key to Collecting Circulation Strikes:** Although the 1887-O is hardly in the common-date category, enough exist that a nice MS-63 coin can be found with little effort. However, among these only a fraction have a combination of sharp strike and attractive luster—yielding a great opportunity for cherrypicking. When you find one, the cost will not be any more than others are paying for pieces with poor eye appeal. Check any and all examples for the overdate feature (see previous listing).

**Surface Quality:** The striking of the 1887-O is usually average or below average, sometimes quite poor. Sharp pieces do exist but searching is needed to find them. At the New Orleans Mint during this era many dies were spaced too far apart, perhaps facilitating the coining process, but resulting in pieces that hardly deserve numismatic prizes. The luster on the 1887-O ranges from grainy and dull to frosty, but is usually subpar. You, as an informed buyer, can find a nice one—with some effort.

**Prooflike Coins:** Prooflike dies were used extensively, and pieces with a degree of prooflike surface, sometimes deep and accentuated with cameo devices, are elusive, but not great rarities. However, most are lightly struck at the center.

**Mintage and Distribution:** Delivery figures by month: January, 900,000; February, 1,000,000; March, 1,000,000; April, 1,000,000; May, 1,000,000; June, 1,000,000; July, 600,000; August, 1,050,000; September, 1,000,000; October, 1,000,000; November, 1,000,000; December, 1,000,000. Some small part of these were of the 1887/6-O variety, probably from a single die pair in a single press run. The 1887-O was sufficiently well distributed in the 19th century that worn coins are plentiful today, although probably more than a few were destroyed during the great run-up in silver bullion prices that peaked in January 1980. Bags were released over a long period of years, including 1938, 1953, and 1957, per interviews I have conducted, and no doubt on other occasions as well. Examples from Treasury releases of 1962 through 1964 constitute the majority of pieces available in Mint State today. Bags were released as late as March 1964.

**Die Varieties:** Most die varieties as described by Van Allen and Mallis consist of date repunchings of a minor nature. However, VAM-2 has the date numerals tripled, quite interesting, described by them as "one of the largest shifts of date doubling known." The two earlier dates are not prominent, but under a magnifying glass they can be seen easily enough. VAM-22, listed in *The Top 100 Morgan Dollar Varieties*, has slight doubling on the obverse, and die rust is seen below the eagle's tail.

VAM-2

VAM-22

## Whitman Coin Guide (WCG™)

| VG-8 | F-12 | VF-20 | EF-40 | AU-50 | MS-60 | MS-63 | MS-64 | MS-65 | MS-66 | MS-67 |
|------|------|-------|-------|-------|-------|-------|-------|-------|-------|-------|
| $29 | $31 | $37 | $42 | $55 | $70 | $115 | $350 | $2,100 | $45,000 | – |

**AVAILABILITY**

| | MS-60 | MS-61 | MS-62 | MS-63 | MS-64 | MS-65 | MS-66 | MS-67 | MS-68+ |
|---|-------|-------|-------|-------|-------|-------|-------|-------|--------|
| Certified | 203 | 777 | 2,953 | 7,168 | 4,076 | 373 | 12 | 0 | 0 |
| Field | | 40,000–60,000 | | 22,500–30,000 | 8,000–12,000 | 1,000–2,000 | 20–30 | 0 | 0 |
| Cert. DMPL | 8 | 32 | 82 | 128 | 146 | 9 | 1 | 0 | 0 |

# 1887-S

Optimal
Collecting Grade
MS-64

Circulation-
Strike Mintage
1,771,000

**Key to Collecting Circulation Strikes:** The 1887-S dollar is a delight to own, as a coin selected with care will be well struck and very attractive. This date and mint is somewhat scarce in the series, but hardly a "stopper." A grade such as MS-63 offers a lot of coin for the money.

**Surface Quality:** Usually seen well struck; with few exceptions a no-problem issue. However, some are light at the centers, most noticeably on the eagle's breast. Usually seen with attractive frosty luster.

**Prooflike Coins:** Prooflike coins are occasionally encountered. Nicks and marks can be a problem due to storage and repeated handling in bags. Several hundred were in the Redfield hoard dispersed after 1976.[52]

**Mintage and Distribution:** Delivery figures by month: January–May, 0; June, 16,000; July, 0; August, 420,000; September, 400,000; October, 450,000; November, 400,000; December, 85,000. Many coins went into storage at the San Francisco Mint, the procedure used for others of this era. From the early 1940s through the 1950s large quantities were paid out, but most did not land in numismatic hands.

**Die Varieties:** Among the minor die varieties, VAM-2, with the S mint-mark sharply doubled and with the upper right serif of an earlier mint-mark boldly visible within the top opening of the final S, has merited listing in *The Top 100 Morgan Dollar Varieties*. A strong glass is needed to appreciate it.

VAM-2

Treasure-hunt possibility? Maybe! All dies for the 1887 coinage were prepared at the Philadelphia Mint. At least one overdated obverse die, 1887/6, was used by each of the Philadelphia and New Orleans mints. Might an 1887/6-S exist somewhere out there? Less than half of the die combinations have been described by Van Allen and Mallis, so, indeed, there is a potential.

## Whitman Coin Guide (WCG™)

| VG-8 | F-12 | VF-20 | EF-40 | AU-50 | MS-60 | MS-63 | MS-64 | MS-65 | MS-66 | MS-67 |
|------|------|-------|-------|-------|-------|-------|-------|-------|-------|-------|
| $30 | $32 | $40 | $48 | $60 | $125 | $240 | $650 | $2,300 | $8,250 | $32,500 |

**AVAILABILITY**

| | MS-60 | MS-61 | MS-62 | MS-63 | MS-64 | MS-65 | MS-66 | MS-67 | MS-68+ |
|---|-------|-------|-------|-------|-------|-------|-------|-------|--------|
| Certified | 207 | 942 | 2,666 | 3,945 | 2,567 | 464 | 29 | 1 | 0 |
| Field | | 35,000–50,000 | | 10,000–15,000 | 4,000–6,000 | 750–1,250 | 35–50 | 4–7 | 4–7 |
| Cert. DMPL | 2 | 9 | 23 | 32 | 28 | 1 | 0 | 0 | 0 |

# MORGAN SILVER DOLLARS, RARE COINS, AND LIFE IN 1888

## THE MORGAN DOLLAR SCENARIO

On October 17 and 18, 1888, S. Hudson Chapman and his younger brother Henry held their sale No. 25, featuring the Ferguson Haines Collection. Ferguson Haines, who lived on the Atlantic coast in Biddeford, Maine, was a combination collector and dealer. Over a long period of time, he sold or consigned groups of coins to various dealers who obligingly placed his name on the catalog cover. No doubt when, in 1874, he purchased intact the collection of bankrupt James L. Hill of Madison, Wisconsin, the coins were fed into a series of sales. However, in *Numisma*, November 1883, this notice was printed: "Mr. Ferguson Haines, of Biddeford, Maine, is going out of the coin business, but will continue as a collector." Notwithstanding the foregoing, Haines could not resist dealing and was listed in this trade as late as 1892.

Although numismatic plums in the Ferguson catalog included a New England shilling and a rare 1838-O half dollar, among other items, the offering of silver dollars is worth noting here. Often the supposition of one generation becomes the fact of another, and so it may have been with a certain 1883-O Morgan dollar in the sale, described as "Very rare. Only 12 Proofs struck." The piece fetched $3.00. A few lots later, a coin described as a Proof 1884 was bid up to $3.50. Whether these would be called prooflike (or even DMPL) today, or whether they were especially struck as Proofs for presentation may be forever unlearned, unless some contemporary accounts of ceremonies are located.

Certain regular Philadelphia Mint Proofs, a complete date run, except for 1878, including these coins (and prices realized):

| | | | | | |
|------|--------|------|--------|------|--------|
| 1879 | $1.15  | 1882 | $1.30  | 1885 | $1.15  |
| 1880 | $1.20  | 1883 | $1.30  | 1886 | $1.20  |
| 1881 | $1.40  | 1884 | $1.15  |      |        |

Morgan silver dollars attracted little notice, and although the Chapman descriptions mentioned a couple of mintmarks, by and large, there was no interest in Carson City, New Orleans, or San Francisco issues of any silver or gold denomination. Collecting was by date, and coins from Proof sets filled the bill nicely. The Mint Cabinet on view in Philadelphia followed precisely the same procedure and routinely added Proofs, but ignored pieces with CC, O, or S mintmarks.

## OTHER ASPECTS OF COIN COLLECTING

In December 1875, J.W. Scott had launched a house organ, *The Coin Collector's Journal*, with highly esteemed numismatist Édouard Frossard as editor. However, Frossard soon departed Scott in order to conduct his own business, and David U. Proskey was named to fill the editor's chair. The latter was of very uncertain reputation. In *Numisma*, January 1881, Ed. Frossard referred to his successor as having a "big India rubber conscience." In his auction catalog of July 1882, W. Elliot Woodward was more direct, calling Proskey a liar. Now, in January 1888, the *Journal* breathed its last, having run through 13 volumes and 157 issues.[53]

In a boating accident on Chesapeake Bay the unseen hand of death struck down numismatic connoisseur T. Harrison Garrett, who had been collecting coins since the 1860s and who had assembled the largest and finest cabinet in private hands in America. At the peak of his enthusiasm and career, he left behind him a widow and three sons, one of whom, John Work Garrett, would cut his own swath in numismatic history.

A four-page leaflet dated September-October 1888 was published by George F. Heath, M.D., of Monroe, Michigan, under the title of *The American Numismatist*. The good doctor was probably unaware that Charles E. Leal of Paterson, New Jersey, had issued a similarly named magazine earlier. Someone must have informed Heath, for "American" was dropped immediately, and all future issues were known as *The Numismatist*.[54]

Every once in a while in the coin collecting hobby a periodical is blessed with an editor of wide intellectual interests, curiosity, and intelligence. Heath was such a person, and the succeeding issues published by him, until his death in 1908, are filled with interesting metaphors, allusions, and poetic phraseology, as this in the very first number:

> Of one thing all may rest assured, this paper has come to see its year out and though small and unpretentious, will, like the Irishman's flea, "get there just the same," and when least expected. And so without further ado we launch our frail bark on the journalistic seas, and with clear skies and a flowing sail go out on our mission.

Of course, a generation of later readers, including those of the present text, might scratch their heads (no pun intended) to determine the meaning of the "Irishman's flea," a reference that must have been familiar to Heath's readers back in 1888. Perhaps Heath will excuse the present writer for suggesting that another of his comments in the first issue might well apply today to those interested in Morgan silver dollars: "There is nothing you can collect that will represent so much, if properly selected, or will cost so little, if properly bought, as a variety of fifty, one or two hundred coins."

The number of coin collectors there were or are in America has long been a topic of discussion. In 1888 Heath estimated 20,000. Today the number is in the many millions, including, perhaps, 200,000 or so with serious coin-buying budgets. Who knows?

## Meanwhile, on the American Scene in 1888

Electricity was becoming more popular and in wider use, and by this time most major cities had electric street lighting. On February 2, 1888, in Richmond, Virginia, the first electric trolley car went into service on 12 miles of track. This sparked a revolution in urban transportation, and in the early 1890s several hundred cities would have electric rail cars, often connecting with other towns and cities. By the early 20th century the interurban railway system linked the majority of cities and towns on the Atlantic seaboard, and many in the Midwest and the far West. Such lines would be a dynamic part of America until the waning years of the second decade of the 20th century, when the rising popularity of the automobile put most out of business.

Nicola Tesla developed an alternating-current motor more powerful and efficient than the direct-current motors then in use. In St. Louis, William Seward Burroughs devised a key-actuated adding machine, then set about with partners to form the American Arithmometer Company. During the coming decade such devices would be improved, and by the turn of the 20th century they were common in banks, stores, and elsewhere.

In March what became known as the Blizzard of 1888 dropped nearly two feet of snow on much of the northeastern United States. Drifts exceeded 10 feet and the wind in some areas reached 50 to 60 miles an hour. Many towns and cities were effectively shut down for several days or more, railroad transportation stopped, and it became impossible for people and animals to remain outdoors safely. At least 400 people died. In time, this would be remembered as the greatest of all American blizzards.

In Washington the *National Geographic Magazine* published its first issue in October, becoming the quarterly publication of the National Geographic Society.

In Rochester, New York, George Eastman introduced the Kodak camera, the trade word being devised simply for being short and memorable. "You push the button, we do the rest," became the slogan of Kodak. Owners of these devices took pictures and sent them to Rochester to be developed and reloaded. Soon, hundreds of already established photographers and daguerreotypists around America would take on the developing of amateur film as well, launching a popular nationwide pastime and hobby.

# 1888

**Optimal Collecting Grade**
MS-65

**Circulation-Strike Mintage**
19,183,100

**Proof Mintage**
833

**Key to Collecting Circulation Strikes:** The 1888 rates as a common date in the Morgan series, although the quality of individual specimens can vary dramatically. Extended die use caused granularity and metal flow lines on some. On the other hand, more than just a few 1888 dollars are attractive and prooflike.

**Surface Quality:** The strike varies from poor to decent. Truly sharp pieces are in the distinct minority and require cherrypicking to find. Luster ranges from grainy to good. Again, careful buying is recommended, but is not as difficult as with, for example, the Philadelphia Mint dollars of 1886 and 1887.

**Prooflike Coins:** Prooflike coins are often seen, usually with low contrast.

**Mintage and Distribution:** Delivery figures by month: January, 1,700,000; February, 1,700,000; March, 1,560,000; April, 1,434,000; May, 1,600,000; June, 1,620,000; July, 600,000; August, 1,534,000; September, 2,000,000; October, 2,000,000; November, 1,850,000; December, 1,585,000. Although circulation strikes of the 1888 were available in worn grades, from early distributions, this was not considered to be a truly common date in Mint State until the 1950s, when long-stored bags were liberated. However, at the time these coins were generally ignored, and those who encountered quantities in banks (as I did) let them remain there. During the Treasury release of 1962 through 1964, millions more came out, even as late as March 1964.

**Die Varieties:** Varieties mainly involve date repunching on the obverse, although several reverses show slightly repunched features, these from 64 obverse and 54 reverse dies prepared.

## 1888, PROOFS

**Mintage:** 833. At least two obverse dies were used, one with slight repunching of the date. Delivery figures by month: March, 432; September, 100; December, 300; unknown month, 1.[55]

**Key to Collecting Proofs:** Lightly struck at the centers. Low contrast. About this time the Mint became sloppy in the making of Proofs, and not long afterward dealer Harlan P. Smith filed a formal complaint. Still, Proofs of the era beginning about now are not on a visual par with those earlier in the decade. Be picky, picky, picky, and *perhaps* you will find a nice one!

## Whitman Coin Guide (WCG™)

| VG-8 | F-12 | VF-20 | EF-40 | AU-50 | MS-60 | MS-63 | MS-64 | MS-65 | MS-66 | MS-67 | PF-60 | PF-64 | PF-65 | PF-66 | PF-67 |
|---|---|---|---|---|---|---|---|---|---|---|---|---|---|---|---|
| $28 | $29 | $34 | $37 | $41 | $48 | $65 | $85 | $205 | $550 | $12,500 | $1,300 | $3,900 | $6,100 | $10,250 | $17,000 |

### AVAILABILITY

| | MS-60 | MS-61 | MS-62 | MS-63 | MS-64 | MS-65 | MS-66 | MS-67 | MS-68+ |
|---|---|---|---|---|---|---|---|---|---|
| Certified | 84 | 553 | 4,728 | 25,222 | 30,772 | 8,747 | 1,548 | 86 | 1 |
| Field | 250,000–400,000 | | | 120,000–160,000 | 75,000–125,000 | 45,000–65,000 | 2,000–3,000 | 150–250 | 15–20 |
| Cert. DMPL | 3 | 14 | 76 | 164 | 201 | 73 | 14 | 4 | 0 |
| | PF-60 | PF-61 | PF-62 | PF-63 | PF-64 | PF-65 | PF-66 | PF-67 | PF-68+ |
| Certified | 7 | 27 | 63 | 68 | 87 | 33 | 20 | 3 | 0 |
| Field | 250–350 | | | 160–200 | 130–170 | 60–90 | 25–35 | 10–12 | 0 |

# 1888-O

Optimal
Collecting Grade
MS-64

Circulation-
Strike Mintage
12,150,000

**Key to Collecting Circulation Strikes:** The 1888-O is plentiful in Mint State, mostly from Treasury hoard dispersals, but most are at lower Mint State levels, and striking and luster are often far below par. However, with some searching it is possible to find an attractive example.

**Surface Quality:** The strike varies all over the place, from flat to sharp, but most show weakness at the center obverse and center reverse, really subpar. Dedicated cherrypicking is needed to find a sharp coin. The luster varies from grainy and rather dull to frosty and attractive.

**Prooflike Coins:** Prooflike coins are easily enough found.

**Mintage and Distribution:** Delivery figures by month: January, 1,000,000; February, 1,000,000; March, 1,200,000; April, 1,200,000; May, 1,100,000; June, 750,000; July, 600,000; August, 1,000,000; September, 1,200,000; October, 1,000,000; November, 1,000,000; December, 1,100,000. Although many 1888-O dollars were released in the 19th century, others went into storage. In 1946 a few bags were turned loose, and in the 1950s many bags were paid out, including some from the Treasury Building in Washington, DC. In 1957 quantities were obtained by dealer Harry J. Forman. During the 1962 through 1964 Treasury release, at least 100,000 came out of the long-sealed vault at the Philadelphia Mint that also yielded the fabulous 1903-O dollars. Facts are elusive, and some have suggested millions were released.

**Die Varieties:** Most 1888-O dollars have a medium-sized, round O mintmark with a fairly large open center. Fewer have a medium-sized elliptical O with a narrow vertical slit in the center. *The Top 100 Morgan Dollar Varieties* suggests that the elliptical O is worth multiples of the price of the regular round O; the variety would seem to be ripe for cherrypicking. VAM-1B, called the "Scarface" variety in *The Top 100 Morgan Dollar Varieties,* has a prominent die crack across Miss Liberty's face, called "the most dramatic die break in the Morgan dollar series. Rare in all grades." VAM-9 is known with the reverse rotated from 30° clockwise to 175° counterclockwise, the result of the die being loose in its chuck. The 1888-O Hot Lips variety is a collectors' favorite, showing doubled features on Miss Liberty's face, particularly at and near her mouth *(Guide Book of U.S. Coins).* "It is the strongest double obverse of the Morgan dollar series and commands a large premium," note Van Allen and Mallis. Further, "It is usually weakly struck and is unknown in Uncirculated grades. Scarce in AU" *(The Top 100 Morgan Dollar Varieties).*

*1888-O "E on Reverse," VAM-1A, Clashed Die Reverse:* Shows a raised partial E, a clashmark from the incuse of LIBERTY on the obverse. Most examples of this variety also show a prominent die crack on the obverse from the rim through R (of PLURIBUS).

## Whitman Coin Guide (WCG™)

| VG-8 | F-12 | VF-20 | EF-40 | AU-50 | MS-60 | MS-63 | MS-64 | MS-65 | MS-66 | MS-67 |
|------|------|-------|-------|-------|-------|-------|-------|-------|-------|-------|
| $28 | $29 | $34 | $37 | $41 | $48 | $67 | $100 | $550 | $2,250 | $11,500 |

**AVAILABILITY**

| | MS-60 | MS-61 | MS-62 | MS-63 | MS-64 | MS-65 | MS-66 | MS-67 | MS-68+ |
|---|-------|-------|-------|-------|-------|-------|-------|-------|--------|
| Certified | 62 | 424 | 3,100 | 13,701 | 15,353 | 2,984 | 233 | 1 | 0 |
| Field | 80,000–150,000 | | | 50,000–75,000 | 35,000–60,000 | 6,000–9,000 | 200–300 | 1–2 | 1–5 |
| Cert. DMPL | 6 | 22 | 94 | 297 | 354 | 83 | 7 | 0 | 0 |

# 1888-S

**Optimal Collecting Grade**
MS-64

**Circulation-Strike Mintage**
657,000

**Key to Collecting Circulation Strikes:** The 1888-S is scarce in Mint State in the context of Morgan dollars, but enough exist that there is no difficulty tracking down an example in MS-63 or MS-64. While many if not most San Francisco Morgan dollars are sharply struck, the 1888-S is an exception.

**Surface Quality:** The strike varies from poor to sharp, with sharp pieces being in the minority. Careful cherrypicking is recommended. The luster of the 1888-S is usually attractive, although there are some exceptions.

**Prooflike Coins:** Prooflike coins, one-sided as well as two-sided, were plentiful a couple decades ago, but are widely scattered now. These can be very attractive. The Redfield hoard yielded some marvelous DMPL examples.

**Mintage and Distribution:** Delivery figures by month: January–March, 0; April, 160,000; May, 150,000; June, 239,000; July, 28,000; August, 10,000; September, 70,000; October–December, 0. The 1888-S was distributed in a manner similar to 1887-S. Examples were scarce on the numismatic market in early times, but in 1942 large quantities were released from storage in the San Francisco Mint. From then onward, they were a drag on the market, and as they kept coming out, many if not most were sent to Nevada casinos and elsewhere, to be used in commerce. After the 1950s, quantities became scarce, and in time the issue became valuable. Relatively few were left by the time of the 1962 through 1964 Treasury release. The Redfield hoard is said to have had 5,000 to 10,000 coins, including thousands of prooflike examples.

**Die Varieties:** VAM-2 and 6 show repunching of the S mintmark, mainly as a filling of the interior openings.

## Whitman Coin Guide (WCG™)

| VG-8 | F-12 | VF-20 | EF-40 | AU-50 | MS-60 | MS-63 | MS-64 | MS-65 | MS-66 | MS-67 |
|------|------|-------|-------|-------|-------|-------|-------|-------|-------|-------|
| $100 | $150 | $165 | $185 | $205 | $290 | $440 | $875 | $2,650 | $10,500 | $28,500 |

### AVAILABILITY

| | MS-60 | MS-61 | MS-62 | MS-63 | MS-64 | MS-65 | MS-66 | MS-67 | MS-68+ |
|---|-------|-------|-------|-------|-------|-------|-------|-------|--------|
| Certified | 122 | 520 | 1,757 | 2,908 | 2,258 | 353 | 29 | 3 | 0 |
| Field | 25,000–40,000 | | | 8,000–14,000 | 5,000–8,000 | 500–800 | 50–80 | 7–12 | 0 |
| Cert. DMPL | 3 | 12 | 48 | 110 | 59 | 5 | 1 | 0 | 0 |

# Morgan Silver Dollars, Rare Coins, and Life in 1889

## The Morgan Dollar Scenario

The overflowing storage space for millions of silver dollars continued to be a headache, but perhaps relief was in sight; per the *Annual Report of the Director of the Mint*, 1889:

> During the last fiscal year there have been material improvements in the way of additional accommodations for the storage of coin at the Mint at Philadelphia. The last of the small brick vaults in the basement for the use of the cashier was lined with steel and furnished with modern doors and improved locks. There was constructed beneath the central court-yard of the Mint a steel-lined, burglar-proof vault with a storage capacity of 85,000,000 silver dollars.
>
> There was also constructed a large steel vault in the central area of the Mint on a level with the main floor of the building, said to be the only one of its style in the United States, divided into compartments for the daily use of the melter and refiner, the coiner, and the superintendent, for the immediate safe-keeping of the large silver bars received on purchases.

Elsewhere in the same report, this was noted: "During the year, 42,000,000 silver dollars were transferred from the mint at Philadelphia, and 8,000,000 from the mint at New Orleans, to the Treasury of the United States at Washington, for storage."

## Morgan Dollars in Numismatics

On the auction scene, the Chapman brothers' sale No. 29, held June 17 and 18, 1889, included an 1831 Proof set, a Higley copper with broad axe motif, and other rarities, along with a nice selection of Morgan silver dollars. The last is notable in that it included branch mint coins showcased as such, never mind that their market value was nominal. What the Chapmans called "Proof" may well have been equivalent to today's DMPL circulation-strike designation.

## Here and There in the Coin Hobby

In October 1889, Director of the Mint James P. Kimball was succeeded in the post by Edward O. Leech, who would serve until May 1893.

In this year, nickel three-cent pieces, gold dollars, and three-dollar gold coins were struck for the last time. Gold dollars had been a popular speculation since 1879, and now the opportunity to buy new issues on the ground floor ended. No doubt this dampened the enthusiasm of certain investors. In any event, the market was showing signs of easing from the frenetic retail and auction pace of a few years earlier.

The sixth issue of Dr. George F. Heath's magazine, *The Numismatist*, dated November-December 1889, included an essay titled "Numismatics," which included these thoughts:

> The science of coins and medals is as old as antiquity itself. There is probably no other branch of collecting so ancient and honorable, or that has received the attention of the students of all ages, as that of coin collecting.
>
> When the first collection was made can never be known, but that the ancients indulged in this delightful study and pastime, there is no doubt; but it was during the Middle Ages, when the mists of darkness that had hung over the world for so long a period, began to give way before the lights of advancing civilization in long-darkened Europe, that the collecting and treasuring of these "types of active and extinct civilization" was vigorously prosecuted, opening up as they did to the student of history the true records of the past, "more historic than written history." . . .
>
> The authentic history revealed by these coins is compared with the legendary history and finally the whole fabric is woven and built up to make the whole structure grand and true. This I know is fanciful, but the world has passed through a similar epoch, and why may it not again?
>
> Who knows but that the coin bearing the inscription, "United States of America, In God We Trust," passing current today, may tell as strange a story 2,300 years hence as that coin in your cabinet of Macedon bearing the name of Philip or Alexander tells us today.

If there are "sermons in stones," etc., what eloquence and learning must be stored up in these bits of metal? If they could only talk, what strange stories would they tell?

## MEANWHILE, ON THE AMERICAN SCENE IN 1889

On November 2, 1889, North Dakota was admitted as the 39th state of the Union and South Dakota as the 40th. Not long thereafter, November 8, Montana became the 41st state, and on November 11 Washington became the 42nd.

On April 22, white homesteaders were set to race across a line to stake out land in the Oklahoma Territory, formerly the home of Native Americans. However, "sooners," as they were called, jumped the gun and established early claims, setting off many disputes. Overnight, towns like Oklahoma City and Guthrie sprung up. This and other factors contributed to an immense land and development boom in the prairie states, not only Oklahoma but Kansas, Illinois, Nebraska, and surrounding areas. Municipalities selling bonds as well as commercial enterprises seeking to raise money offered interest rates typically of 7 to 8%, sometimes reaching 10%, to Eastern investors, who jumped on the bandwagon to gain several interest points above what could be obtained in east-coast financial markets. National banks jumped into the scene and invested much of their capital. However, in the very early 1890s the bubble collapsed, causing much financial hardship.

The I.M. Singer Company marketed its first electrically driven sewing machine, adding a new dimension to a vast market. By this time many if not most American homes had sewing devices, stores of various manufacturers were in every city and medium-sized town, and exhibits proliferated at state fairs and exhibitions.

On November 14, 1889, newspaper writer Nellie Bly (Elizabeth Cochrane) left Hoboken, New Jersey, at 9:30 in the morning in an effort to circle the world in 80 days, to emulate or even eclipse the record of the fictional hero of Jules Verne's 1873 novel. Nellie turned in a fine performance and returned just 72 days later.

In Rochester, Minnesota, what became the Mayo Clinic was established with a staff including Drs. William Worrall Mayo and sons William James and Charles Horace. Soon, the clinic would draw patrons from all over the United States and beyond.

On July 8, 1889, the *Wall Street Journal* began publication, evolving from a financial news summary distributed by Dow Jones & Company.

At Hartford, Connecticut, the first coin-operated telephone was installed. Soon, such devices would become common in railroad depots, hotels, restaurants, and elsewhere in an era in which home service had yet to achieve a wide reach. In the early 1890s it was not at all unusual for a medium-sized town to have just one or two dozen telephones, all in public locations.

In England, Robert Hope-Jones, age 30, devised an electrical apparatus for operating the pipe organ, controlling the stops through cables from a remote keyboard console. Hope-Jones later moved to America and popularized what he called the Unit Orchestra, whose investors included Mark Twain (Samuel L. Clemens). The Unit Orchestra later evolved into the famous Wurlitzer theater organ made in North Tonawanda, New York.

In Paris the Universal Exhibition opened, centered about the Eiffel Tower, which soared 984 feet, or nearly twice the height of the Washington Monument. In New York City the first significant skyscraper was opened at 50 Broadway and stood 13 stories tall. This type of structure was built on a steel frame that supported floors, outside walls, and other elements of construction. In the same year the Otis Company installed the first electric elevator, in the Demerest Building on Fifth Avenue, New York City.

On May 31 an earthworks dam on the Conemaugh River burst above Johnstown, Pennsylvania, sending a wall of water through the town and causing horrific destruction. It was estimated that 2,000 or more people were drowned or burned to death (the latter when a large floating mass of driftwood backed up by a stone railway bridge caught fire).

On March 4, 1889, William Henry Harrison was inaugurated as president of the United States, succeeding Grover Cleveland.

# 1889

Optimal
Collecting Grade
MS-65

Circulation-
Strike Mintage
21,726,000

Proof Mintage
811

**Key to Collecting Circulation Strikes:** The mintage figure of 21,726,000 for the 1889 dollar sweeps away any other total in the early (1878–1904) Morgan series. Most 1889 dollars in any grade are indifferently struck and have miserable luster, sort of grayish, dull, and numismatically forgettable. As grading services make no mention of sharpness of strike or quality of luster, you have the opportunity, at least in theory, to land a gem for a "regular" price.

**Surface Quality:** Strike ranges from poor to sharp, mostly average or below average. The luster on the 1886 is often dull and insipid. Finding a deeply frosty coin in combination with a sharp strike can be a first-class challenge!

**Prooflike Coins:** Some prooflike coins exist but are not common.

**Mintage and Distribution:** Delivery figures by month: January, 2,000,000; February, 1,710,000; March, 2,000,000; April, 1,878,000; May, 2,064,000; June, 2,164,000; July, 800,000; August, 1,900,000; September, 1,860,000; October, 2,000,000; November, 2,000,000; December, 1,350,000. If Mint records are correct, that 57 obverse dies were made for this coinage, then the average per die was an incredible 381,158. Perhaps a typographical error crept in.

The mintage this year set a record for any date and mint that would stand until 1921. Many circulated in the 19th century, many were melted under the 1918 Pittman Act, and many others were dribbled into circulation in the 20th century. By 1950, Mint State pieces were scarce, but this was undone by massive releases of bags beginning circa 1954. Enough remained that many more bags were distributed as part of the 1962 through 1964 Treasury release.

**Die Varieties:** Although 57 obverse dies and 50 reverses were used for this coinage, no particularly memorable die varieties exist.

## 1889, PROOFS
**Mintage:** 811.

**Key to Collecting Proofs:** Average strike, usually flat at the centers. Medium to low cameo contrast. As you might expect, lack of sharpness is hardly ever mentioned in price lists or catalogs—but you can look at the pictures and tell.

## Whitman Coin Guide (WCG™)

| VG-8 | F-12 | VF-20 | EF-40 | AU-50 | MS-60 | MS-63 | MS-64 | MS-65 | MS-66 | MS-67 | PF-60 | PF-64 | PF-65 | PF-66 | PF-67 |
|------|------|-------|-------|-------|-------|-------|-------|-------|-------|-------|-------|-------|-------|-------|-------|
| $28 | $29 | $34 | $37 | $41 | $48 | $65 | $85 | $345 | $1,250 | $11,500 | $1,300 | $3,900 | $6,100 | $9,750 | $15,500 |

**AVAILABILITY**

| | MS-60 | MS-61 | MS-62 | MS-63 | MS-64 | MS-65 | MS-66 | MS-67 | MS-68+ |
|--|-------|-------|-------|-------|-------|-------|-------|-------|--------|
| Certified | 159 | 926 | 7,511 | 26,045 | 22,410 | 3,571 | 394 | 4 | 1 |
| Field | 300,000–500,000 | | | 100,000–150,000 | 30,000–50,000 | 7,500–12,500 | 500–750 | 7–11 | 5–10 |
| Cert. DMPL | 6 | 23 | 59 | 147 | 141 | 45 | 4 | 0 | 0 |

| | PF-60 | PF-61 | PF-62 | PF-63 | PF-64 | PF-65 | PF-66 | PF-67 | PF-68+ |
|--|-------|-------|-------|-------|-------|-------|-------|-------|--------|
| Certified | 9 | 27 | 43 | 74 | 86 | 35 | 29 | 6 | 2 |
| Field | 250–500 | | | 150–200 | 125–175 | 60–90 | 40–60 | 15–20 | 5–8 |

# 1889-CC

**Key to Collecting Circulation Strikes:** The 1889-CC dollar is one of the great keys in the Morgan series, and among Carson City issues it is far and away the most elusive. In comparison to the demand for them, examples are rare in all grades. However, for those who can afford one, attractive MS-63, 64, and 65 coins appear on the market with regularity, and gorgeous DMPL specimens are sometimes offered.

**Surface Quality:** Usually an average strike at best, often below average. The luster varies from rather shallow and satin-like to frosty, but usually not deeply frosty.

**Prooflike Coins:** Many 1889-CC dollars are semi-prooflike, more than 25% of the survivors it would seem. Some DMPL pieces exist and have cameo contrast.

**Mintage and Distribution:** Delivery figures by month: January–September, 0; October, 100,000; November, 100,000; December, 150,000. Of the 350,000 1889-CC dollars made, many thousands were paid out in the 19th century, yielding a supply of circulated pieces for numismatists today. Scattered single coins and small groups (no hints of bags) were paid out from the Treasury Building in Washington, DC, in 1933 and 1934, such disbursements continuing over a long period of years. From pre-1964 holdings stored out West, several bags of Mint State coins were held in Nevada and were described to me years ago. I had a chance to buy a bag, from Ben Stack, but did not. Where they are now, I do not know. However, as Mint State pieces are few and far between on the market today, some of these groups must still be tightly held, if, indeed, reports of them are true. After a while one tends to be a skeptic. On the other hand, in numismatics there is no end of surprises, and every few years an "impossible" hoard or large group of something or other comes on the market to surprise and delight all of us.

**Die Varieties:** Although several die varieties have been identified from 10 obverse dies sent to Carson City for the 1889 coinage, and 7 reverses, they are not significant.

## Whitman Coin Guide (WCG™)

| VG-8 | F-12 | VF-20 | EF-40 | AU-50 | MS-60 | MS-63 | MS-64 | MS-65 | MS-66 | MS-67 |
|------|------|-------|-------|-------|-------|-------|-------|-------|-------|-------|
| $600 | $900 | $1,175 | $2,500 | $5,750 | $22,000 | $40,000 | $65,000 | $325,000 | – | – |

**AVAILABILITY**

|  | MS-60 | MS-61 | MS-62 | MS-63 | MS-64 | MS-65 | MS-66 | MS-67 | MS-68+ |
|--|-------|-------|-------|-------|-------|-------|-------|-------|--------|
| Certified | 42 | 129 | 189 | 128 | 71 | 6 | 0 | 1 | 1 |
| Field | | 5,000–7,500 | | 500–1,000 | 150–250 | 10–20 | 0 | 0 | 0 |
| Cert. DMPL | 14 | 40 | 78 | 75 | 27 | 0 | 0 | 0 | 0 |

# 1889-O

Optimal
Collecting Grade
MS-64

Circulation-
Strike Mintage
11,875,000

**Key to Collecting Circulation Strikes:** The 1889-O was struck in prodigious quantities, many of which were released into circulation in the 19th century and others of which were part of later Treasury holdings. Today Mint State coins are very common, but sharply struck gems with beautiful luster are rare. Gems exist and can be found.

**Surface Quality:** Usually lightly struck at the centers and not very satisfactory. Aggressive searching is needed to find a sharp one. Luster ranges from dull to somewhat frosty.

**Prooflike Coins:** Prooflike coins are seen with frequency, often having cameo contrast.

**Mintage and Distribution:** Delivery figures by month: January, 1,100,000; February, 1,000,000; March, 1,000,000; April, 1,100,000; May, 1,100,000; June, 1,100,000; July, 500,000; August, 975,000; September, 1,000,000; October, 1,000,000; November, 1,000,000; December, 1,000,000. Truly Mint State–quality examples of 1889-O were scarce in the several decades after they were minted, although lightly worn coins (sliders) were in abundance. However, in 1938, and possibly even before then, Mint State bags were paid out from the Treasury Building in Washington, DC. Coins of this mint lacked the "numismatic magic" of their CC cousins, and little interest was expressed in them. Other bags were released now and again. During of the Treasury release of 1962 through 1964, only a few bags seem to have reached dealers, and most coins were poorly struck.

VAM-1A

**Die Varieties:** It is the rule that for each year of Morgan dollar a single style of four-digit logotype punch was used. Dies from all mints have the numerals spaced in the same proportion and the digits aligned the same vertically. However, 1889 is an exception, and on some dies the 88 digit pair is more closely spaced than the 89 digits (e.g., VAM-10), and vice versa on others (e.g., VAM-7 and others among Philadelphia coins; seemingly all branch mint coins).

VAM-1A

Two varieties of O mintmarks were used this year, an elliptical O with a small, vertical, slit opening in the center, and the much more plentiful round O with wide opening at the center. Although many die varieties exist among 1889-O dollars, only a few are significant. VAM-6 displays date repunching, most prominent on the first two numerals. Several varieties exist with rotated reverse dies.

VAM-1A

*1889-O "Raised E on Reverse," VAM-1A:* This variety shows a raised letter E between the eagle's tail and the upper left of the ribbon, similar to a variety of 1886-O, but from a different reverse die. Such pieces are very scarce, "by far the rarest of the major 'E' clash dollars."[56]

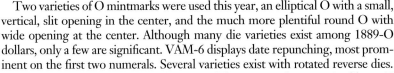

VAM-1A

## Whitman Coin Guide (WCG™)

| VG-8 | F-12 | VF-20 | EF-40 | AU-50 | MS-60 | MS-63 | MS-64 | MS-65 | MS-66 | MS-67 |
|------|------|-------|-------|-------|-------|-------|-------|-------|-------|-------|
| $28 | $29 | $34 | $37 | $45 | $135 | $400 | $850 | $5,800 | $17,000 | – |

**AVAILABILITY**

| | MS-60 | MS-61 | MS-62 | MS-63 | MS-64 | MS-65 | MS-66 | MS-67 | MS-68+ |
|---|-------|-------|-------|-------|-------|-------|-------|-------|--------|
| Certified | 92 | 485 | 1,779 | 3,161 | 2,307 | 188 | 15 | 0 | 0 |
| Field | | 25,000–40,000 | | 10,000–15,000 | 4,000–7,500 | 250–400 | 20–30 | 0 | 0 |
| Cert. DMPL | 2 | 8 | 31 | 52 | 29 | 3 | 1 | 0 | 0 |

# 1889-S

Optimal
Collecting Grade
MS-64

Circulation-
Strike Mintage
700,000

**Key to Collecting Circulation Strikes:** There are not many Morgan dollars with a total mintage of less than a million, and this is one of them. Examples are desirable in all grades, but enough exist in Mint State that serious collectors can be satisfied easily.

**Surface Quality:** Usually seen fairly well struck. Typically encountered with excellent luster.

**Prooflike Coins:** Many have prooflike surfaces. DMPL specimens usually have good contrast.

**Mintage and Distribution:** Delivery figures by month: January–October, 0; November, 200,000; December, 500,000. In 1889 most of these dollars seem to have been moved only within the walls of the San Francisco Mint, into a storage vault. In 1937 a few bags were paid out, then many bags in the 1940s, after which the 1889-S was regarded as common. In the 1950s, bags could be obtained for face value at the Mint, but there was not a strong demand for them. Probably, many were sent to casinos. All told, perhaps 50,000 to 100,000 were preserved by collectors and investors.

**Die Varieties:** From the five die pairs made for this coinage, there are no varieties exciting enough to write home about, but the specialist will find several to be of at least passing interest. VAM-2 has the S mintmark tilted notably to the left. VAM-4 and VAM-7 have slightly doubled mintmarks.

## Whitman Coin Guide (WCG™)

| VG-8 | F-12 | VF-20 | EF-40 | AU-50 | MS-60 | MS-63 | MS-64 | MS-65 | MS-66 | MS-67 |
|---|---|---|---|---|---|---|---|---|---|---|
| $45 | $55 | $60 | $70 | $105 | $210 | $375 | $625 | $1,700 | $5,000 | $23,000 |

**AVAILABILITY**

| | MS-60 | MS-61 | MS-62 | MS-63 | MS-64 | MS-65 | MS-66 | MS-67 | MS-68+ |
|---|---|---|---|---|---|---|---|---|---|
| Certified | 125 | 580 | 1,954 | 3,797 | 3,327 | 794 | 89 | 1 | 0 |
| Field | | 25,000–40,000 | | 7,000–11,000 | 6,000–9,000 | 1,500–2,250 | 200–300 | 1–2 | 0 |
| Cert. DMPL | 3 | 7 | 23 | 33 | 32 | 5 | 2 | 0 | 0 |

# MORGAN SILVER DOLLARS, RARE COINS, AND LIFE IN 1890

## THE MORGAN DOLLAR SCENARIO

On July 14, 1890, the Sherman Silver Purchase Act was signed by President Benjamin Harrison, and replaced the Bland-Allison Act of 1878. The new legislation provided for the purchase of 54,000,000 ounces of silver annually, this being an estimate of the amount available from domestic mines, continuing an undisguised price support. For a few weeks the international price of silver rose on the news, but by September it went into a protracted decline, due mainly to increased production from foreign mining interests.

The silver was to be purchased by a new issue of federal currency, Coin Notes, redeemable in the holder's choice of gold or silver coins. The initial bills, known as the Series of 1890, bear reverses of unusual engraving intricacy and are highly prized by numismatists today. In 1891 the reverse designs were simplified. Many who received Coin Notes redeemed them in gold coins, depleting government supplies and, in combination with poor business conditions, contributing to the Panic of 1893.

As a reflection of a yearly scenario, coins dated 1889 reserved for the February 1890 meeting of the Assay Commission included the following dollars: 1889 (14,589); 1889-CC (175); 1889-O (5,938); and 1889-S (846). From this immense quantity of dollars, members of the commission, composed of a mixture of government officials and private citizens, selected a few samples to be analyzed for metal content and weight.

In 1890 the *Annual Report of the Director of the Mint*, gave the cost of producing an average gold or silver coin at the mints: Philadelphia, $0.0215; San Francisco, $0.0404; New Orleans, $0.0183; and Carson City, $0.0816.

While at San Francisco and Philadelphia other denominations were coined, down to dimes, therefore muddying the waters of analysis, at New Orleans the only production was of silver dollars, and the cost of 1.8 cents each was cheaper in any event than coinage elsewhere. Perhaps the casual, indeed sloppy, workmanship (as reflected by the generally poor strikes of O-Mint dollars) was more economical!

## DOLLARS AT AUCTION

Over a period of several days from January 20 to 24, 1890, the estate collection of Philadelphia pharmacist Robert Coulton Davis crossed the auction block in a catalog prepared by the New York Coin & Stamp Co. Although there were still no popularly issued guides for those seeking mintmark varieties, a few numismatists had aspired to save branch mint coins, Davis among them.

Morgan dollars in the sale included the following (prices realized in parentheses):

1878, 8 Tail Feathers, Proof ($1.50)
1878, 7 Tail Feathers, sharp and perfect Proof ($1.25)
1879 sharp and perfect Proof ($1)
1879-O sharp and perfect Proof. It is said that only 12 of these Proof dollars were coined ($6)
1879-CC Proof surface, Uncirculated ($1.25)
1879-S Proof surface, Uncirculated ($1.25)
1880 sharp and perfect Proof ($1)
1880-O sharp, brilliant Uncirculated ($1.25)
1880-S Proof surface; Uncirculated ($1.25)

1881 sharp and perfect Proof ($1.25)
1881-CC sharp, brilliant Uncirculated ($2.40)
1881-O sharp, brilliant Uncirculated ($1.90)
1881-S sharp, brilliant Uncirculated ($1.25)
1882 sharp and perfect Proof ($1.10)
1883 sharp and perfect Proof ($1.10)
1884 sharp and perfect Proof ($1)
1885 sharp and perfect Proof ($1)
1885-O Proof surface; Uncirculated ($1.25)
1885-CC sharp, brilliant Uncirculated ($3.40)
1886 sharp and perfect Proof ($1.05)

The comment about 12 Proofs having been struck of the 1879-O was conjectural. Certain of the Proofs sold for face value, seemingly a profitless transaction except for dealers who were executing commissions from customers and charging them nominal fees, usually 5%.

The Davis Collection had many mouth-watering rarities, including an 1876-CC twenty-cent piece (which in time would become famous), the 1838-O half dollar (already possessing renown among mintmark specialists), and Proof gold coins of the "rare year" 1875.

In *Numisma*, datelined the same month, Ed. Frossard gave a review of the event:

> One of the largest and finest collections of American coins and medals that has been formed in the United States was that of the late Dr. R.C. Davis, of Philadelphia. This collection once comprised nearly the entire series of the national coinage in gold, silver and copper, besides the most complete collection of pattern and experimental pieces in existence. Even in its somewhat mutilated form, with the entire collection of patterns and several of the rare cents and other coins missing, this collection yet presented a brilliant array of beautiful and desirable coins.

The Morgan silver dollar was the subject of a first-page article in the March 1890 issue of *The Numismatist*. The text noted in part, "The face of Liberty on the present [Morgan] dollar is the likeness of Miss Annie Williams, a Philadelphia school teacher, and the design will be retained as an ideal of purely American features."

## MEANWHILE, ON THE AMERICAN SCENE IN 1890

The number of immigrants entering America in the previous decade totaled 5,246,613. The decennial federal census placed the population of the United States at 62,662,250. For the study of 1890 census results Herman Hollerith developed a system of punching holes in sheets of paper to record data, somewhat similar to that used earlier on the Jacquard loom, music rolls for reed organs, and other devices that stored information. It was revealed that only about 3% of young American men and women aged 18 through 21 attended college. Typical education of the era was provided by grammar school and a year or two of high school. In the United States the top 1% of the population earned more money than all in the poorest 50%.

On January 25, 1890, at 3:41 in the afternoon, Nellie Bly completed her trip around the world, taking 72 days, 6 hours, 11 minutes, and 14 seconds, much to the delight of her sponsor, the *New York World*. Railroad trackage in the United States amounted to about 125,000 miles, connecting virtually every town and city of importance. Safety regulations and requirements were often few and far between, and during the year about 10,000 Americans were killed in various railroad accidents and another 80,000 received serious injuries. Bicycles were extremely popular, with pneumatic rubber tires and safety features contributing to their widespread use. During the coming decade many clubs and organizations would be formed by cyclists, who often went for day-long excursions. An extensive manufacturing industry arose to supply the demand.

On February 9, some 11 million acres of land in South Dakota, formerly belonging to the Sioux Indians, were opened to homesteaders. On December 29 what became known as the Battle of Wounded Knee, the last major resistance by Indians to the American government, saw nearly 500 armed troops of the U.S. Seventh Cavalry kill about 300 (out of a contingent of 350) Sioux men, women, and children. The Indians had been essentially defenseless.

On July 2, 1890, Congress passed the Sherman Anti-Trust Act in an effort to stem companies' combining to monopolize aspects of American trade and commerce. However, the legislation had little actual effect, and it was not until the 20th century that trust-busting, as it was called, achieved reforms. In 1890 Yosemite National Park was created under an act of Congress, as was Sequoia National Park.

In the first week of July 1890, Wyoming was added as a state to the Union, and on July 16 Idaho joined the roster. Following the wild boom times of the 1880s, many homesteaders as well as commercial interests ran into difficulties in the prairie states. In Kansas, banks foreclosed on about one third of all farm mortgages. Citizens in the district became a political force, reacting against abuses laid to banks and other financiers, commercial interests, and railroads.

# 1890

**Optimal
Collecting Grade**
MS-64

**Circulation-
Strike Mintage**
16,802,000

**Proof Mintage**
590

**Key to Collecting Circulation Strikes:** The 1890 dollar is a very common coin in Mint State, and circulated pieces are likewise plentiful. Nearly all are lightly or even poorly struck and with dull, unattractive luster. Some show graininess and metal flow. If you want a nice one, buy a Proof! As is so often the case with "common dates," most exist in lower Mint State levels, and for MS-65 and higher grades the supply drops off logarithmically.

**Surface Quality:** Striking varies from weak to not so weak, but is not often seen sharp. The typical 1890 is average or below average, with flatness over the ear. As a rule of thumb, the luster on the 1890 is rather dull, often grainy, as dies seem to have been used for a long time.

**Prooflike Coins:** Some are prooflike, and are also usually of low contrast. However, some DMPLs exist with cameo contrast and are worth a premium over the others.

**Mintage and Distribution:** Delivery figures by month: January, 1,350,000; February, 1,700,000; March, 1,800,000; April, 1,800,000; May, 1,200,000; June, 1,200,000; July, 600,000; August, 152,000 1,000,000+; September, 1,300,000; October, 1,500,000; November, 1,600,000; December, 1,600,000. 1890 dollars were released fairly continuously over a long period of years, defining this as a common date. Large quantities were paid out in 1941 and 1942 and again in the mid-1950s, but many bags remained, and the final ones were disbursed during the Treasury releases of 1962 through 1964. Some of these were coated with grease.

## 1890, PROOFS

**Mintage:** 590, the lowest figure for any Proof Morgan dollar after 1878 and before 1921. Delivery figures by month: January–February, 0; March, 265; April–November, 0; December, 125.

**Key to Collecting Proofs:** Above average strike for some, flat centers for others. Medium to low contrast. Better quality workmanship than in 1889, if only slightly.

**Die Varieties:** Varieties specifically identified among the 48 obverses and 49 reverses of this coinage mainly consist of date doubling. VAM-7 and 14 each have the Slanted Date, with the digit 1 significantly closer to the dentils than is the 0. All are from the four-digit logotype.

## Whitman Coin Guide (WCG™)

| VG-8 | F-12 | VF-20 | EF-40 | AU-50 | MS-60 | MS-63 | MS-64 | MS-65 | MS-66 | MS-67 | PF-60 | PF-64 | PF-65 | PF-66 | PF-67 |
|------|------|-------|-------|-------|-------|-------|-------|-------|-------|-------|-------|-------|-------|-------|-------|
| $28 | $29 | $34 | $37 | $40 | $48 | $75 | $150 | $1,950 | $12,500 | – | $1,300 | $3,900 | $6,100 | $9,750 | $15,500 |

AVAILABILITY

|  | MS-60 | MS-61 | MS-62 | MS-63 | MS-64 | MS-65 | MS-66 | MS-67 | MS-68+ |
|--|-------|-------|-------|-------|-------|-------|-------|-------|--------|
| Certified | 160 | 833 | 4,518 | 11,669 | 7,286 | 674 | 6 | 0 | 0 |
| Field | | 250,000–400,000 | | 50,000–80,000 | 12,500–17,500 | 700–1,000 | 5–10 | 0 | 1–5 |
| Cert. DMPL | 8 | 23 | 91 | 146 | 125 | 8 | 0 | 0 | 0 |

|  | PF-60 | PF-61 | PF-62 | PF-63 | PF-64 | PF-65 | PF-66 | PF-67 | PF-68+ |
|--|-------|-------|-------|-------|-------|-------|-------|-------|--------|
| Certified | 4 | 16 | 35 | 66 | 82 | 36 | 35 | 26 | 2 |
| Field | | 200–300 | | 110–130 | 100–130 | 60–90 | 50–70 | 40–60 | 11–12 |

# 1890-CC

**Optimal
Collecting Grade
MS-64**

**Circulation-
Strike Mintage
2,309,041**

**Key to Collecting Circulation Strikes:** The mintage figure for the 1890-CC dollar, far and away the largest in the Carson City series, does not translate to pieces' being common in Mint State today. Most probably, quantities were placed into circulation in the 19th century, and perhaps many bags were melted under the provisions of the 1918 Pittman Act. By the time the supply on hand in the Treasury Building was checked, in 1964, there were fewer than 4,000 pieces in sight. Today, many if not most 1890-CC dollars are decently struck, and most have attractive luster. However, more than just a few are very "baggy." Certification quantities fall off a cliff past MS-64.

**Surface Quality:** Striking varies from weak at the centers to fairly sharp, the last being the general rule. Usually seen with attractive mint luster.

**Prooflike Coins:** Prooflike coins are seen with frequency, but even a few bagmarks can make such pieces unattractive. Prooflikes are often lightly struck above the ear.

**Mintage and Distribution:** Delivery figures by month: January, 150,000; February, 188,000; March, 200,000; April, 200,000; May, 150,000; June, 200,000; July, 200,000; August, 200,000; September, 200,000; October, 200,000; November, 176,000; December, 245,041 Quantities of 1890-CC dollars were shipped to San Francisco and to the Treasury Building in Washington, DC, after the Carson City Mint ended operations. In the early 1930s at least a few bags were paid out in Washington. In 1941 and 1942 additional bags were paid out at the same location, followed in 1942 and 1943 by many bags in San Francisco. From the latter a few thousand coins are believed to have gone to dealers and collectors, and the others into circulation. In the 1950s bags were released in Washington to dealers with "connections," furnishing a decent supply. By 1956 and 1957 bags were becoming scarce. After the great Treasury release was halted in March 1964, the General Services Administration holding of 1890-CC dollars totaled 3,949, or 0.17% of the original mintage, per a later inventory.[57]

**Die Varieties:** Regarding the more than a half-dozen attributed varieties known from 15 or more die pairs prepared, the best known of the year is VAM-4, the Tail Bar, which displays from the bottom arrow feather to the olive branch below, the result of a die gouge.

VAM-4

## Whitman Coin Guide (WCG™)

| VG-8 | F-12 | VF-20 | EF-40 | AU-50 | MS-60 | MS-63 | MS-64 | MS-65 | MS-66 | MS-67 |
|------|------|-------|-------|-------|-------|-------|-------|-------|-------|-------|
| $90 | $95 | $105 | $130 | $200 | $430 | $775 | $1,500 | $5,000 | $23,000 | – |

**AVAILABILITY**

| | MS-60 | MS-61 | MS-62 | MS-63 | MS-64 | MS-65 | MS-66 | MS-67 | MS-68+ |
|---|-------|-------|-------|-------|-------|-------|-------|-------|--------|
| Certified | 237 | 988 | 3,279 | 4,601 | 2,989 | 354 | 11 | 0 | 0 |
| Field | | 20,000–30,000 | | 10,000–15,000 | 5,000–8,000 | 600–900 | 20–30 | 1–5 | 1–5 |
| Cert. DMPL | 31 | 83 | 281 | 426 | 330 | 27 | 0 | 0 | 0 |

# 1890-O

Optimal
Collecting Grade
MS-64

Circulation-
Strike Mintage
10,701,000

**Key to Collecting Circulation Strikes:** The 1890-O is plentiful enough in Mint State, "raw" and also in "slabs," but the majority are lightly struck in one area or another. Some were struck from dies that should have been put out to pasture or sent to the glue factory, and flow lines and granularity tell the tale today. However, enough sharp pieces exist that getting one will be no problem. MS-65 coins are much more elusive than are MS-64s.

**Surface Quality:** The typical 1890-O shows areas of light striking in the center. A few sharp pieces exist but require searching. As always, certification services do not make a distinction, thereby giving you an advantage. The luster is usually attractive and rich on the 1890-O.

**Prooflike Coins:** Some dies are prooflike and can be attractive in higher grades. However, among prooflike coins, striking is often soft. Some selected DMPL coins are gorgeous to behold.

**Mintage and Distribution:** Delivery figures by month: January, 1,000,000; February, 1,000,000; March, 1,000,000; April, 1,000,000; May, 750,000; June, 700,000; July, 700,000; August, 740,000; September, 850,000; October, 1,000,000; November, 1,000,000; December, 961,000. While many were paid out in earlier times, including in 1953 and 1954, an estimated 500,000 or more, possibly many more, were stored in the Philadelphia Mint and were included in the releases of 1962 through 1964.

**Die Varieties:** There are numerous varieties involving repunched dates, mintmark placement, etc. VAM-10 has two diagonal ridges extending from the dentils right of the date, one ridge piercing the last number of the date, the result of die gouges. VAM-2 can be found with the reverse die misaligned 20° to 60° from normal.

## Whitman Coin Guide (WCG™)

| VG-8 | F-12 | VF-20 | EF-40 | AU-50 | MS-60 | MS-63 | MS-64 | MS-65 | MS-66 | MS-67 |
|------|------|-------|-------|-------|-------|-------|-------|-------|-------|-------|
| $29 | $31 | $34 | $37 | $50 | $75 | $105 | $275 | $1,850 | $9,500 | – |

### AVAILABILITY

| | MS-60 | MS-61 | MS-62 | MS-63 | MS-64 | MS-65 | MS-66 | MS-67 | MS-68+ |
|---|-------|-------|-------|-------|-------|-------|-------|-------|--------|
| Certified | 90 | 472 | 2,641 | 6,902 | 5,862 | 625 | 23 | 0 | 0 |
| Field | | 100,000-150,000 | | 40,000-60,000 | 15,000-25,000 | 1,200-1,600 | 60-100 | 0 | 5-10 |
| Cert. DMPL | 5 | 12 | 62 | 183 | 249 | 25 | 1 | 0 | 0 |

# 1890-S

**Optimal
Collecting Grade**
MS-64

**Circulation-
Strike Mintage**
8,230,373

**Key to Collecting Circulation Strikes:** With the 1890-S, the San Francisco Mint again turned out coins that for the most part are well struck, lustrous, and very attractive, this at a time when workmanship at New Orleans was often downright sloppy. While the 1890-S is by no means a common date, choice and gem examples are well within the reach of most readers of this book.

**Surface Quality:** Usually seen well struck. Exceptions should not be purchased. Usually encountered with attractive luster. The VAM text mentions that cloudy spots are sometimes seen on the surface, these due to dampness after striking.

**Prooflike Coins:** Quite a few prooflike coins exist, but not many have the combination of deep mirror quality (DMPL) plus freedom from bagmarks.

**Mintage and Distribution:** Delivery figures by month: January, 500,000; February, 600,000; March, 600,000; April, 600,000; May, 800,000; June, 800,000; July, 800,000; August, 760,000; September, 700,000; October, 660,000; November, 667,373; December, 743,000. Many 1890-S dollars were released in the era they were minted, and many others went into storage at the San Francisco Mint. Probably, many were melted under the Pittman Act in 1918. Bags were paid out over a period of years, including large quantities in the 1940s and 1950s. As the 1890-S has a large mintage figure, the issue was viewed as common and attracted scant numismatic interest. The Redfield hoard (1976) is said to have contained 20 to 40 bags.

**Die Varieties:** Among varieties from 29 or more obverse and 46 reverse dies made for this coinage, VAM-12 has a notably repunched date, particularly at the tops of 90. VAM-17 has the mintmark sharply tilted to the left.

## Whitman Coin Guide (WCG™)

| VG-8 | F-12 | VF-20 | EF-40 | AU-50 | MS-60 | MS-63 | MS-64 | MS-65 | MS-66 | MS-67 |
|------|------|-------|-------|-------|-------|-------|-------|-------|-------|-------|
| $28 | $29 | $34 | $37 | $45 | $70 | $105 | $250 | $1,000 | $3,250 | $7,500 |

**AVAILABILITY**

| | MS-60 | MS-61 | MS-62 | MS-63 | MS-64 | MS-65 | MS-66 | MS-67 | MS-68+ |
|---|-------|-------|-------|-------|-------|-------|-------|-------|--------|
| Certified | 187 | 943 | 2,849 | 5,807 | 4,845 | 980 | 173 | 7 | 0 |
| Field | 50,000–75,000 | | | 25,000–40,000 | 15,000–25,000 | 2,000–3,000 | 300–500 | 12–18 | 1–5 |
| Cert. DMPL | 2 | 12 | 51 | 68 | 57 | 14 | 0 | 0 | 0 |

# Morgan Silver Dollars, Rare Coins, and Life in 1891

## The Morgan Dollar Scenario

The act of March 3, 1891, the Trade Dollar Recoinage Act, directed the secretary of the Treasury, "as soon as practicable, [to] coin into standard silver dollars the trade dollar bullion and trade dollars now in the Treasury, the expense thereof to be charged to the silver profit fund." Trade dollars, first minted in 1873, intended for export in the China trade but having full legal tender status domestically, were a great success, and mintages were substantial. On July 22, 1876, the trade dollar was demonetized, after which the coins were valued only at their silver content, or less than a dollar. By 1891, such coins were rarely seen.

By November 1, 1891, the coinage of Morgan dollars from silver taken from melted-down trade dollars totaled 3,260,100. Interestingly, the 1891-O dollars struck at the New Orleans Mint used bullion remaining from the Bland-Allison Act of 1878, as well as metal from the Sherman Silver Purchase Act of 1890, and metal from the new trade dollar melting act. However, the coins themselves were never marked as to the origin of the silver, and today they cannot be differentiated.

## Morgan Dollar Design to be Replaced?

During the year, the Mint had given thought to replacing the time-worn (numismatists today would say time-honored) Liberty Seated design used on smaller denominations and had sent a circular to selected artists inviting their suggestions, plus replacing the Morgan dollar: "It has been decided to invite designs for the obverse and reverse of the silver dollar, and for the obverse only of the half dollar, quarter dollar, and dime."

Of course, the Morgan dollar design was not all that old, having been in use for just a few years over a decade, but it and Morgan were not liked by Chief Engraver Charles E. Barber, and he was probably part of the effort to replace it.

However, outside help was not used, and the obverses of the dime, quarter, and half dollar were redone in pattern form by Barber. The reverses of the quarter and half dollar were also changed by Barber, while the dime reverse was unchanged from earlier years. Patterns were not made available to collectors, but examples were placed in the Mint Cabinet. The new coins went into circulation the following year, 1892.

The Morgan silver dollar remained untouched, having weathered the latest assault.

## ANA Formed

In March 1891, Dr. George F. Heath, editor of *The Numismatist* (and also mayor of his hometown, Monroe, Michigan), mused in print:

> What's the matter with having an American Numismatic Association? Would it be possible? Would it be practicable? All in favor of such a scheme, send in your names. If a sufficient number are received, we can think of organizing on some inexpensive basis.

In coming months the idea would take root and, eventually, flower. "Make it easy" to get in the ANA, and make it "so interesting" that members will "find it hard to get out," Heath suggested in another issue.

In the meantime, in August 1891, Heath commented concerning the population of numismatists:

> There are said to be over 20,000 collectors of coins in this country. While we believe this to be much too high an estimate, we will, in the absence of proof to the contrary, accept it. Taking these figures for what they are worth, it is probable that less than 5% collect scientifically or intelligently; about 40% are still in the "medieval" age, and the balance just emerging from the "barbaric" state.

How many collectors were there? Facts are elusive. Heath's number of those who collect "scientifically or intelligently" amounted to an estimated 1,000. In the same year the Mint produced 650 silver Proof sets, seemingly indicating that about this many people desired such items. Of course, of those who did collect, probably most saved coins from circulation, or collected tokens and medals, or were interested in foreign coins, or whatever. Perhaps Heath's guess at 1,000 advanced collectors was about right.

For two days, October 7 and 8, a group of interested men convened at the Commercial Hotel at the corner of Lake and Dearborn Streets, Chicago. Dr. Heath had arrived early, on the 1st, to complete arrangements.

"Two days were spent in a pleasant and harmonious convention; a constitution and bylaws were adopted, that, while not perfect, we believe will serve the Association well. Thirty-one members were present in person, or represented by proxy," Heath reported in *The Numismatist* in December, adding this metaphorical comment:

> We were in at the launching and saw the good ship Numisma go out with flowing sails and a clear sky on her 12 months voyage. Sixty souls comprise her officers and crew. Monthly stops will be made and passengers received. Numismatists! This Ark has been fitted out with special reference to your comfort and convenience. Make haste and come aboard, an awful shower is coming up.
>
> At the inaugural meeting of the ANA, W.G. Jerrems, Jr., was elected president; Joseph Hooper, vice president; Charles T. Tatman, secretary, and David Harlowe, secretary. Among other officers, S. Hudson Chapman was named as librarian and curator and Ed. Frossard took the post of "counterfeit detector," the last to serve as arbiter of coins of disputed authenticity.

## Meanwhile, on the American Scene in 1891

On September 18, 1891, 900,000 acres in Oklahoma Territory, formerly owned by the Sauk, Fox, and Potawatomi Indians, were opened by the government to white settlers who desired to homestead, and about 15,000 people crossed the prairie land to stake claims.

In Cripple Creek, Colorado, a new gold rush began after Robert Womack discovered precious metal at a place called Poverty Gulch on the western slope of Pikes Peak. The district was named from a small stream in which a cow had become crippled while crossing. By 1900 Cripple Creek would be called the richest gold district on earth and have over 50,000 citizens, dozens of mining companies, and well over 100 saloons.

Financial conditions remained difficult in Kansas and other prairie states, many bond issuers and loan writers defaulted, companies shut their doors, and thousands of homesteaders gave up their efforts and headed back to the East. However, most citizens remained. Financial and agricultural conditions would remain difficult during the next several years. If the government would buy silver in unlimited quantities, conditions would improve, many politicians thought. The "free silver" movement gained momentum in coming years.

Asa G. Candler bought rights to Coca-Cola (see 1886) for $2,300. In time, advertising slogans such as "wonderful nerve and brain tonic and remarkable therapeutic agent" gave way to promotion of Coca-Cola as a tasty and enjoyable beverage.

In this year the American Express Company introduced its "travelers cheques," sold through banks and others who received commissions with a charge of 1% being paid by the purchaser. The idea copied that introduced in England by Thomas Cook & Son in 1874. Soon, American Express Travelers Cheques were a mainstay with tourists and foreign travelers who were protected from loss by theft.

In New York City on May 5, Carnegie Hall was opened to the public, with a concert in which Peter Ilych Tchaikovsky was one of the conductors. Andrew Carnegie furnished $2 million to erect the structure, which soon became an American landmark and focal point for musical talent.

# 1891

Optimal
Collecting Grade
MS-64

Circulation-
Strike Mintage
8,693,556

Proof Mintage
650

**Key to Collecting Circulation Strikes:** The 1890 is a high-mintage dollar usually seen in low quality. Of course, if you have been a "constant reader" of this book to the present point, you know that this translates into O-P-P-O-R-T-U-N-I-T-Y for you.

**Surface Quality:** The strike is usually average or below, not often sharp. Careful selection is suggested. The luster is often insipid and grainy, not at all attractive. Deeply lustrous, sharply struck pieces require cherrypicking to find.

**Prooflike Coins:** Prooflike coins are sometimes seen, sometimes lightly struck. Gorgeous DMPL coins exist and are memorable, but the availability of somewhat similar-appearing Proofs probably dampens the market somewhat.

**Mintage and Distribution:** Delivery figures by month: January, 1,600,000; February, 1,200,000; March, 1,200,000; April, 1,000,000; May, 1,250,000; June, 900,000; July, 350,000; August, 500,000; September, 200,000; October, 250,000; November, 243,556; December, 0. Many 1,000-coin bags were put into storage. In 1954 and 1955, quantities were released, followed by many more—so many that by 1960 such coins were the most common date to be found in Philadelphia banks, a nuisance to those seeking other varieties.

## 1891, PROOFS

**Mintage:** 650. Delivery figures by month: January–February, 0; March, 240; April–May, 0; June, 110; July–August, 0; September, 100; October, 0; November, 200; December, 0.

**Key to Collecting Proofs:** Striking can be weak at the centers. Medium cameo contrast. Low mintage, the possibility of a weak strike, and so many cleaned and dipped coins on the market add up to a challenge. However, many have been certified at Proof-65 or higher.

**Die Varieties:** Varieties are mainly positional, although VAM-2 shows slight doubling on the obverse.

## Whitman Coin Guide (WCG™)

| VG-8 | F-12 | VF-20 | EF-40 | AU-50 | MS-60 | MS-63 | MS-64 | MS-65 | MS-66 | MS-67 | PF-60 | PF-64 | PF-65 | PF-66 | PF-67 |
|---|---|---|---|---|---|---|---|---|---|---|---|---|---|---|---|
| $29 | $31 | $35 | $38 | $45 | $65 | $175 | $800 | $6,500 | $13,750 | $52,500 | $1,300 | $3,900 | $6,100 | $9,750 | $15,500 |

### AVAILABILITY

| | MS-60 | MS-61 | MS-62 | MS-63 | MS-64 | MS-65 | MS-66 | MS-67 | MS-68+ |
|---|---|---|---|---|---|---|---|---|---|
| Certified | 147 | 787 | 3,055 | 4,753 | 2,710 | 232 | 4 | 1 | 0 |
| Field | | 150,000–250,000 | | 25,000–40,000 | 6,000–9,000 | 250–400 | 4–6 | 1–2 | 1–2 |
| Cert. DMPL | 4 | 13 | 29 | 36 | 24 | 1 | 0 | 0 | 0 |
| | PF-60 | PF-61 | PF-62 | PF-63 | PF-64 | PF-65 | PF-66 | PF-67 | PF-68+ |
| Certified | 5 | 19 | 42 | 56 | 87 | 35 | 54 | 16 | 2 |
| Field | | 200–300 | | 150–200 | 120–140 | 70–90 | 70–90 | 30–35 | 3–5 |

# 1891-CC

**Optimal Collecting Grade**
MS-64

**Circulation-Strike Mintage**
1,618,000

**Key to Collecting Circulation Strikes:** The 1891-CC is a "must have" coin because it is from Carson City and is usually available in Uncirculated grade. However, although the mintage figure is generous for a CC dollar, today the coin is not in the "common" class. Still, enough are around, especially MS-63 and MS-64, that you can find a choice one. Virtually all are lustrous and have superb eye appeal, but not all are sharply struck. Do some looking around before you write a check.

**Surface Quality:** The striking varies from poor to sharp, but is usually average or finer. Cherrypicking is advised, but in this case it will not involve a great deal of effort. The luster is typically deeply frosty and beautiful.

**Prooflike Coins:** Partially and fully prooflike coins exist, but usually have low contrast in relation to the design features, and, accordingly, the demand for them is not great.

**Mintage and Distribution:** Delivery figures by month: January, 200,000; February, 150,000; March, 190,000; April, 76,000; May, 86,000; June, 186,000; July, 120,000; August, 120,000; September, 120,000; October, 120,000; November, 120,000; December, 130,000. Many 1891-CC dollars were released into circulation in the early years, yielding a generous population of worn coins today. Bags probably were melted under the 1918 Pittman Act. Other bags were paid in the 1940s and 1950s, resulting in a good supply for numismatists. However, by the time of the 1962 through 1964 Treasury release, most were gone. After 1964 the General Services Administration holding of 1891-CC dollars totaled 5,687, or 0.35% of the original mintage, per a later inventory.[58]

**Die Varieties:** Although 24 obverse dies and 23 reverse dies were sent to Carson City, only a handful of varieties have been listed by VAM. One, VAM-3, the so-called Spitting Eagle, has a die gouge at the eagle's beak, fancifully resembling saliva. Any promoter wanting to sell one of these for a stretchy price had better hide a copy of *The Top 100 Morgan Dollar Varieties* from potential customers, for on page 95 it says: "Heavily promoted the VAM-3 is not only 'not rare,' but is actually the most common of all the 1891-CC varieties!"

VAM-3

## Whitman Coin Guide (WCG™)

| VG-8 | F-12 | VF-20 | EF-40 | AU-50 | MS-60 | MS-63 | MS-64 | MS-65 | MS-66 | MS-67 |
|------|------|-------|-------|-------|-------|-------|-------|-------|-------|-------|
| $90 | $95 | $105 | $130 | $210 | $375 | $675 | $1,150 | $4,400 | $12,500 | $33,000 |

### AVAILABILITY

| | MS-60 | MS-61 | MS-62 | MS-63 | MS-64 | MS-65 | MS-66 | MS-67 | MS-68+ |
|---|-------|-------|-------|-------|-------|-------|-------|-------|--------|
| Certified | 398 | 1,294 | 3,582 | 5,909 | 4,164 | 626 | 34 | 2 | 0 |
| Field | 50,000–70,000 | | | 20,000–30,000 | 10,000–15,000 | 1,250–1,750 | 60–100 | 3–5 | 1–5 |
| Cert. DMPL | 18 | 36 | 133 | 192 | 67 | 2 | 0 | 0 | 0 |

# 1891-O

**Optimal Collecting Grade MS-64**

**Circulation-Strike Mintage 7,954,529**

**Key to Collecting Circulation Strikes:** The 1891-O dollar is famous as an example of poor to casual striking sharpness, although some sharp ones can be found. In view of the paucity of MS-65 coins and the high prices (justifiably, if the striking is nice), I recommend seeking coins at the MS-63 and MS-64 levels. The 1891-O had a bad reputation years ago for being less than lovely, but the advent of slabbing has helped. In any event, just buy one—don't even think of buying a duplicate!

**Surface Quality:** Usually seen weak at the center. Some were made from tired dies and show granularity and flow lines. Some are also weakly struck at the date. A few sharp strikes do exist. Luster usually ranges from satiny to grainy or dull, not deep and frosty.

**Prooflike Coins:** Quite a few prooflike and partially prooflike coins exist, many of which are well struck (an exception to the general rule for 1891-O). DMPL coins exist, some well struck, others not.

**Mintage and Distribution:** The 1891-O silver dollars are unique in the series in that, during the year, coins were made from silver obtained under three different pieces of legislation: the 1878 Bland-Allison Act, the 1890 Sherman Silver Purchase Act, and the 1891 Trade Dollar Recoinage Act. No specific coin can be attributed to a specific act, but the situation is interesting to contemplate. Delivery figures by month: January, 1,000,000; February, 500,000 + 500,000; March, 414,082 + 500,000; April, 600,000; May, 5,831 + 400,000; June, 200,000 + 500,000; July, 500,000; August, 560,000; September, 400,000; October, 500,000; November, 950,000; December, 424,616. Totals: 1,919,913 under the 1878 Bland-Allison Act, 2,500,000 under the 1890 Sherman Silver Purchase Act, 3,534,616 under the 1891 Trade Dollar Recoinage Act, the last eventually resulting in the destruction of 3,471,488 trade dollars. In later years, bags were paid out on occasion, with the result that this was never a rare date in numismatic circles. In 1946 and 1947 many were released, after which time the few dealer specialists in the Morgan series were well stocked. Afterward, the 1891-O moved to the list of scarce coins, only to become common once again, following large releases circa 1955 and 1956, these coming from the Treasury Building in Washington, DC. More came out from Philadelphia in the 1962 through 1964 release, with Harry J. Forman, for one, handling many bags at the time. However, the 1891-O release was far smaller than for the New Orleans Mint years of the early 1880s.

**Die Varieties:** This year 30 obverse dies and 29 reverses were sent from Philadelphia to New Orleans and, presumably, most were used, although relatively few varieties have been described in print. VAM-1 exists with the reverse die rotated 50° to 120° from the normal alignment.

## Whitman Coin Guide (WCG™)

| VG-8 | F-12 | VF-20 | EF-40 | AU-50 | MS-60 | MS-63 | MS-64 | MS-65 | MS-66 | MS-67 |
|------|------|-------|-------|-------|-------|-------|-------|-------|-------|-------|
| $29 | $31 | $37 | $40 | $50 | $155 | $340 | $825 | $7,500 | – | – |

**AVAILABILITY**

| | MS-60 | MS-61 | MS-62 | MS-63 | MS-64 | MS-65 | MS-66 | MS-67 | MS-68+ |
|---|-------|-------|-------|-------|-------|-------|-------|-------|--------|
| Certified | 110 | 519 | 1,847 | 3,431 | 2,284 | 152 | 2 | 0 | 0 |
| Field | 40,000–60,000 | | | 10,000–15,000 | 4,000–6,000 | 300–500 | 5–10 | 0 | 1–5 |
| Cert. DMPL | 1 | 5 | 8 | 14 | 9 | 2 | 0 | 0 | 0 |

# 1891-S

Optimal
Collecting Grade
MS-64

Circulation-
Strike Mintage
5,296,000

**Key to Collecting Circulation Strikes:** The 1891-S is usually seen well struck, lustrous, and with a generous measure of eye appeal—a Morgan dollar as a Morgan dollar should be. Many beautiful MS-63 and MS-64 coins are on the market, and there are enough in higher grades for those who can afford them, although the prices are reasonable across the board.

**Surface Quality:** Usually seen well struck. A no-problem issue, with few exceptions. Usually seen lustrous, but some are spotted due to moisture on the surfaces after striking.

**Prooflike Coins:** Prooflike coins are sometimes encountered and are attractive. Contrast varies and, as always, bagmarks can be a problem.

**Mintage and Distribution:** Delivery figures by month: January, 785,000; February, 685,000; March, 700,000; April, 1,000,000; May, 850,000; June, 1,000,000; July, 6,000; August–September, 0; October, 70,000; November, 100,000; December, 100,000. Most of the 1891-S dollars seem to have gone into storage at the San Francisco Mint. It is likely that some were melted under the 1918 Pittman Act, but no records were kept. One bag of these "old" dollars was paid out to a San Francisco bank in 1919. Many other bags were released for use in circulation or for gaming tables in Nevada (but garnered no reportorial interest). In 1941 and 1942, especially large quantities were released, filling the numismatic pipeline, after which this was considered to be a common variety, this status remaining until at least the early 1950s. After that time, dispersals were fewer, and the 1891-S was not common in bag quantities. However, the Redfield hoard (1976) is said to have had about five bags, most coins being well struck but heavily bagmarked.

**Die Varieties:** No dramatic die varieties exist, although there are certain positional differences from the coinage that took place from 27 pairs of dies shipped to San Francisco this year.

## Whitman Coin Guide (WCG™)

| VG-8 | F-12 | VF-20 | EF-40 | AU-50 | MS-60 | MS-63 | MS-64 | MS-65 | MS-66 | MS-67 |
|---|---|---|---|---|---|---|---|---|---|---|
| $28 | $30 | $35 | $38 | $45 | $65 | $135 | $285 | $1,450 | $4,600 | $12,000 |

AVAILABILITY

| | MS-60 | MS-61 | MS-62 | MS-63 | MS-64 | MS-65 | MS-66 | MS-67 | MS-68+ |
|---|---|---|---|---|---|---|---|---|---|
| Certified | 126 | 535 | 1,949 | 3,976 | 3,116 | 618 | 74 | 9 | 0 |
| Field | | 25,000–40,000 | | 12,000–15,000 | 7,500–10,000 | 1,250–1,750 | 100–200 | 12–18 | 1–5 |
| Cert. DMPL | 3 | 20 | 71 | 120 | 64 | 10 | 0 | 0 | 0 |

# Morgan Silver Dollars, Rare Coins, and Life in 1892

## The Morgan Dollar Scenario

Whereas, in the 1860s, the Comstock Lode of Nevada had been the epicenter of silver bullion production in the United States, by 1892 the scenario had changed dramatically, and Colorado was by far the most important. On July 1, 1892, the Treasury Department owned 357,171,273 silver dollars. A further 7,466,596 were in national banks (as of July 12, 1892), and 49,350,866 were in general circulation and in other banks for a total of 413,988,935 silver dollars.

Presumably, the 49,350,866 in circulation represented the real demand for such coins. If the mints had struck Morgan dollars only in 1878 and 1879, and none in years after that, there would have been enough in existence to satisfy the needs of commerce.

## New Coin Designs and the Columbian Exposition

In 1892 new dime, quarter, and half dollar designs were released, the work of Charles E. Barber. There was virtually no public interest in the motifs, no lament for the demise of the long-lived Liberty Seated motif, and no critical analysis by newspaper reports of the new design.

Editor Heath of *The Numismatist* dismissed Barber's efforts: "To the numismatist or lover of the beautiful in design and art, they will be but another disappointment, hardly noticeable now because expected, and we are getting so used to them."

Nor were the Barber coins of much interest to the general public, as strange as this may seem to numismatists reading this today. One reason may be that national attention was focused on the forthcoming commemorative half dollars to be issued in connection with the World's Columbian Exposition, which did receive extraordinary amounts of press coverage.

On October 12, 1892, the Exposition was dedicated in Chicago in a ceremony, although the exhibits were not yet fully in place. The layout comprised 686 acres with many buildings and exhibit areas, nearly all made of inexpensive materials and designed to last for just a short time. Issued in connection with it were commemorative half dollars, bearing on the obverse a depiction of Christopher Columbus, and on the reverse two hemispheres and a ship.

Great hoopla prevailed, and it was anticipated that at their sales price of $1 each, or twice face value, they would be a fine investment, soon becoming worth $2 apiece, some said. Others thought the whole idea to be a farce. All of this made for merriment in the popular papers, as did the paying of $10,000 for the first-struck coin as a publicity stunt by the makers of the Remington typewriter.

The 1892 commemorative half dollar was followed by an 1893-dated version the next year. These saw wide sale both at the Exposition and elsewhere at $1 each, but so many were produced that large quantities remained unsold and were put into circulation at face value, disappointing many who had bought them at a premium.

## Among the Dealers

The January 1892 issue of *The Numismatist* included a biography of Lyman Haynes Low, noting that the well-known dealer, born in 1844, had become interested in coins as a youth in 1856. In 1878 he became deeply involved in the hobby, and in 1883:

> He manifested his devotion to the study of numismatics by making the purchase and sale of coins his exclusive business. His knowledge of this important branch of historical research is generally and deservedly recognized, few of our American collectors having larger experience or putting it to better service. He has twice crossed the ocean, and visited principal cities of Europe, and enjoys the personal acquaintance of prominent numismatists abroad.

While in an earlier era W. Elliot Woodward had been called the "lion of the day" by the *American Journal of Numismatics* and was highly respected for his knowledge and ethics, in

1892 the mantle could have been well placed upon Low. While others had integrity and the Chapmans led the field in the quality of their catalogs, Low also devoted much time to writing and scholarship, unlike his contemporaries. Today we still benefit from his studies on Hard Times tokens, his editing (in 1894) of the Betts book on early American medals, and his editorship of the *American Journal of Numismatics*. Not long hence, in *The Numismatist*, December 1894, Low would be named as "the best known numismatist in this country."

Another dealer, Édouard Frossard, age 54, was profiled in the March issue of *The Numismatist*. Born in Switzerland, he came to the United States when he was 20 years old. In 1872 he began collecting old copper cents and also dealing in coins in a limited way. By 1892 he was "recognized as one of the principal dealers and numismatic authorities in the state," the state being New York. He had cataloged over 100 sales, had written a monograph on copper half cents and cents, and had published the magazine *Numisma* beginning in 1877.

Apparently, *high speed* in cataloging was desirable in the era, at least to some dealers (the thoughts of consignors not being given), for the biography went on to say that Frossard considered himself to be "the most rapid expert cataloguer in the United States," and in defense of this claim stated that he cataloged the Montanye Collection, comprising 1,200 lots, sold by H.G. Sampson, "within 48 hours from the moment he sat down to write the description of the first number, to the finish." At a later time another dealer, Thomas L. Elder, would boast that he could catalog a thousand lots a day. The obvious aspect left unsaid: What about the quality of the cataloging work?

Then as now, some collectors and dealers preferred to complain, rather than make the best of and enjoy what many have called the world's finest hobby. Apparently the tireless, selfless Dr. Heath was not performing his editorial duties to the satisfaction of certain readers of *The Numismatist*, prompting this item:

> It would be impossible to please all of our readers. We regret that we cannot.
>
> Exceptions there have ever been since the morning stars sang together. There is a record of a snake being in Eden, and later of fallen angels. Some stars do not shine, some waters are bitter, some birds do not sing, and some roses give no perfume. Exceptions are everywhere.
>
> There are some persons who would grumble going to glory in a palace car; some will sit on the edge of a cloud, resplendent in all the magnificent effulgence reflected from the great white throne, and blame St. Peter for passing them into a place, that in their opinion, is not what it has been cracked up to be.
>
> If any of our readers have got into the wrong pew and don't enjoy our sermonettes, they can leave the hymn and book in the pew, and pass off quietly. The ushers at the door will refund the money.

## MEANWHILE, ON THE AMERICAN SCENE IN 1892

In the presidential election in November, Republican William Harrison failed in his bid for reelection, and Democratic Grover Cleveland was elected, taking his second term in the White House, but not continuous with the first.

The McKinley Tariff Act resulted in diminished exports of agricultural products, contributing to the continuing economic problems of the Midwest. Hard times spread to other areas of the country, including silver-producing states that were already under duress. A general chill pervaded American business, soon culminating in the depression of 1893.

On January 1, 1892, Ellis Island was opened as an immigration depot. In ensuing years, until 1954, 20 million people passed through its gates. On October 18, 1892, long distance telephone service was instituted between New York and Chicago. Augustus Saint-Gaudens created the memorable sculpture, Diana, to be used atop the new Madison Square Garden in New York City.

# 1892

Optimal
Collecting Grade
MS-64

Circulation-
Strike Mintage
1,036,000

Proof Mintage
1,245

**Key to Collecting Circulation Strikes:** The 1892 Morgan dollar is scarce in Mint State. Most are in lower grade ranges, MS-60 to 62, and poorly struck. Really choice MS-64 and gem MS-65 or finer coins are very hard to find. Proofs exist in proportion to the mintage figure. Among surviving Proofs, many are choice or gem quality.

**Surface Quality:** Varies from weak to sharp, but usually average to below average. Some hunting is recommended to find a sharp one. Luster varies from dull and poor to lustrous and "flashy."

**Prooflike Coins:** Semi-prooflike coins are seen on occasion, but gems are very elusive and sharply struck DMPLs are rarer yet.

**Mintage and Distribution:** Delivery figures by month: January–May, 0; June, 58,000; July, 68,000; August, 110,000; September, 200,000; October, 200,000; November, 200,000; December, 200,000. Apparently, only a few 1892 silver dollars were released into circulation in the 19th century, and the date could not be found in banks or circulation, prompting interested collectors to acquire Proofs instead. As Proofs were readily available in relation to the number of active Morgan dollar specialists, almost nothing appeared in print about the elusive nature of circulation strikes. In the late 1950s and early 1960s many bags were paid out, by which time the 1892 was considered to be a key date. This status changed quickly, and the supply soon outpaced the demand. By time of the Treasury release of 1962 through 1964, most were gone.

## 1892, PROOFS

**Mintage:** 1,245, a high figure explained by the introduction of the new Barber Proof dime, quarter, and half dollar included as part of the silver Proof set. Delivery figures by month: January–February, 0; March, 620; April–May, 0; June, 375; July–August, 0; September, 100; October–November, 0; December, 150. All are from a single die pair.

**Key to Collecting Proofs:** Striking sometimes below average.

**Die Varieties:** Nine pairs of dies are recorded for the 1892 coinage. No particularly memorable variations were made, and none are listed in *The Top 100 Morgan Dollar Varieties*.

## Whitman Coin Guide (WCG™)

| VG-8 | F-12 | VF-20 | EF-40 | AU-50 | MS-60 | MS-63 | MS-64 | MS-65 | MS-66 | MS-67 | PF-60 | PF-64 | PF-65 | PF-66 | PF-67 |
|---|---|---|---|---|---|---|---|---|---|---|---|---|---|---|---|
| $30 | $32 | $43 | $53 | $90 | $175 | $450 | $975 | $4,150 | $37,500 | – | $1,300 | $3,900 | $6,100 | $9,750 | $15,500 |

### AVAILABILITY

| | MS-60 | MS-61 | MS-62 | MS-63 | MS-64 | MS-65 | MS-66 | MS-67 | MS-68+ |
|---|---|---|---|---|---|---|---|---|---|
| Certified | 101 | 437 | 1,361 | 2,740 | 2,089 | 317 | 4 | 0 | 0 |
| Field | | 50,000–80,000 | | 15,000–25,000 | 3,000–5,000 | 600–900 | 3–5 | 0 | 1–5 |
| Cert. DMPL | 4 | 7 | 17 | 24 | 32 | 6 | 0 | 0 | 0 |
| | PF-60 | PF-61 | PF-62 | PF-63 | PF-64 | PF-65 | PF-66 | PF-67 | PF-68+ |
| Certified | 21 | 36 | 67 | 123 | 169 | 71 | 50 | 29 | 8 |
| Field | | 350–500 | | 200–300 | 150–225 | 125–175 | 80–110 | 55–75 | 10–15 |

# 1892-CC

**Optimal Collecting Grade**
MS-64

**Circulation-Strike Mintage**
1,352,000

**Key to Collecting Circulation Strikes:** Although the 1892-CC has a generous mintage figure for a Carson City dollar, survivors from the Treasury hoard were in the tens of thousands, not in the hundreds of thousands, and all but one coin were gone by the time of the General Services Administration sales. Most 1892-CC dollars are well struck and attractive, although there are some exceptions to be avoided. Year in and year out this coin has been in great demand. MS-63 and MS-64 offer excellent acquisition possibilities, or even higher grades if your budget permits.

**Surface Quality:** Striking varies from weak to sharp, with most being above average. Usually lustrous and attractive.

**Prooflike Coins:** Prooflike coins exist but are in the minority. Most of these have excellently mirrored surfaces. DMPLs are seen occasionally and are beautiful if not overly bagmarked.

**Mintage and Distribution:** Delivery figures by month: January, 106,000; February, 110,000; March, 110,000; April, 110,000; May, 110,000; June, 116,000; July, 110,000; August, 40,000; September, 126,000; October, 120,000; November, 140,000; December, 154,000. Stocks of 1892-CC dollars were kept in vaults in Carson City and were later moved to the San Francisco Mint for the most part, although some bags went to the Treasury Building in Washington, DC. At San Francisco many bags were paid out over a long period of years, including in 1926 and 1927, accelerating in the late 1940s and early 1950s. Most of these went into circulation. Meanwhile, bags were paid out from the Treasury Building, with Stephen D. Ruddel estimating that in the single year of 1955 about 50 were released. Quite a few of these went into numismatic hands, to the extent that as late as 1982, Wayne Miller could state in his *Morgan and Peace Dollar Textbook* that large quantities were available. However, Treasury vaults had been emptied by 1964. The series of GSA sales commencing in October 1972 did not include any silver dollars of 1889-CC, 1892-CC, or 1893-CC.

**Die Varieties:** No dramatic varieties exist from 10 die pairs made. VAM listings are positional. For these and other Carson City issues, the CC mintmark was punched in separately, with two impressions of a C punch. Thus, there are variations in spacing, with the 1892-CC VAM-5 having the letters farther apart than usually seen.

## Whitman Coin Guide (WCG™)

| VG-8 | F-12 | VF-20 | EF-40 | AU-50 | MS-60 | MS-63 | MS-64 | MS-65 | MS-66 | MS-67 |
|------|------|-------|-------|-------|-------|-------|-------|-------|-------|-------|
| $175 | $200 | $285 | $450 | $690 | $1,350 | $1,800 | $2,500 | $7,900 | $25,000 | $60,000 |

### AVAILABILITY

| | MS-60 | MS-61 | MS-62 | MS-63 | MS-64 | MS-65 | MS-66 | MS-67 | MS-68+ |
|---|-------|-------|-------|-------|-------|-------|-------|-------|--------|
| Certified | 226 | 883 | 2,409 | 3,120 | 2,438 | 485 | 34 | 3 | 0 |
| Field | | 20,000–30,000 | | 8,000–12,000 | 4,000–6,000 | 1,000–1,500 | 40–65 | 5–8 | 0 |
| Cert. DMPL | 13 | 31 | 82 | 60 | 44 | 3 | 0 | 0 | 0 |

# 1892-O

Optimal
Collecting Grade
MS-64

Circulation-
Strike Mintage
2,744,000

**Key to Collecting Circulation Strikes:** Somewhat similar to the scenario for 1891-O, the 1892-O is usually seen poorly struck and with subpar eye appeal. However, in 1977 a bag of 1,000 coins was examined and "contained a considerable number of fully struck gem pieces."[59] From this marvelous find may come most of the gems now in collections. Enough 1892-O dollars exist that there are many purchase opportunities for grades such as MS-63 and MS-64, but careful examination is highly recommended.

**Surface Quality:** "This is probably the most consistently flat struck date of the entire Morgan series," the VAM text notes, going on to state, "A small number of full strikes exist, however." In terms of shallow definition this is a dandy rival for the 1891-O. Wayne Miller (1982) joined the thumbs-down chorus. Accordingly, cherrypicking is strongly recommended. Luster is often grainy and unattractive.

**Prooflike Coins:** Prooflike coins are seldom encountered, and when they are, quality is often lacking. All have some flatness of strike.

**Mintage and Distribution:** Delivery figures by month: January, 120,000; February, 105,000; March, 140,000; April, 310,000; May, 300,000; June, 149,000; July, 150,000; August, 300,000; September, 300,000; October, 300,000; November, 270,000; December, 300,000. Quantities were released into circulation in the early years, giving the 1892-O the status of being a common date. However, it was not until bags were released in the 1950s from the Treasury Building in Washington, DC, that Mint State coins became plentiful. Then the supply tightened, and in the numismatic marketplace these became premium coins. At the time, scarcely anyone cared whether a Morgan dollar of any date was well struck or poorly struck. Then during the 1962 through 1964 Treasury release a deluge issued forth from a vault containing New Orleans coins, put under seal in 1929. However, the 1892-O was not among those found in great quantity.

**Die Varieties:** Varieties are mostly positional. VAM-10 has the O mintmark tilted noticeably to the right. *The Top 100 Morgan Dollar Varieties* takes note of VAM-7, Doubled Ear, from a very slightly doubled die.

VAM-7

## Whitman Coin Guide (WCG™)

| VG-8 | F-12 | VF-20 | EF-40 | AU-50 | MS-60 | MS-63 | MS-64 | MS-65 | MS-66 | MS-67 |
|------|------|-------|-------|-------|-------|-------|-------|-------|-------|-------|
| $30 | $32 | $40 | $48 | $70 | $190 | $345 | $1,050 | $5,500 | $42,500 | $67,500 |

### AVAILABILITY

| | MS-60 | MS-61 | MS-62 | MS-63 | MS-64 | MS-65 | MS-66 | MS-67 | MS-68+ |
|--|-------|-------|-------|-------|-------|-------|-------|-------|--------|
| Certified | 97 | 367 | 1,671 | 3,807 | 3,124 | 230 | 9 | 1 | 0 |
| Field | 30,000–50,000 | | | 15,000–25,000 | 5,000–7,500 | 400–600 | 12–16 | 1–2 | 1–5 |
| Cert. DMPL | 0 | 1 | 0 | 6 | 2 | 3 | 0 | 0 | 0 |

# 1892-S

**Optimal
Collecting Grade**
AU-50

**Circulation-
Strike Mintage**
1,200,000

**Key to Collecting Circulation Strikes:** Years ago, worn 1892-S dollars were common in dealers' stocks, and little attention was paid to them. Then, after the 1962 through 1964 Treasury releases were analyzed, and no cascade of Mint State 1892-S dollars had been found, a great demand arose for circulated pieces to supply the date and mint. The few Uncirculated coins that did exist mounted to ever-higher market levels, while more than just a few AU pieces were sold as being in Mint State (casting a pall on the market for this rarity). Today, most collectors will opt for an inexpensive VF or an affordable EF, the 1892-S often being one of the few Morgan dollars in a set that is not Mint State.

**Surface Quality:** Usually above average and quite good. Typically seen with satiny luster or somewhat prooflike.

**Prooflike Coins:** Among high-grade 1892-S dollars, many are somewhat prooflike (not at all DMPL), perhaps half of the population.

**Mintage and Distribution:** Delivery figures by month: January, 100,000; February, 100,000; March, 100,000; April, 100,000; May, 100,000; June, 100,000; July, 100,000; August, 100,000; September, 100,000; October, 100,000; November, 100,000; December, 100,000, the last concluding a unique record of consistent monthly coinage for an entire year. Many 1892-S dollars were placed into circulation in the late 19th and early 20th centuries. Others were stored in the San Francisco Mint. At least one bag was paid out in 1925 and 1926, but little numismatic notice was taken of the coins.

I am not aware of any bags of Mint State 1892-S dollars released after the 1930s, although now and again a few pieces would be found mixed with other coins. For a long time the 1892-S, although rare in Mint State, was not greatly desired. In 1982, Wayne Miller noted that a half dozen or so Uncirculated coins had come to light in recent years, and that "probably fewer than 200 specimens exist in choice BU [MS-63] or better condition."

Miller also noted that "most" investment advisory letters stated that the 1892-S dollar "is one of the few key date Morgans which is not instantly saleable in choice BU condition." In 1992, Maurice Rosen suggested that the lack of demand was probably because many AU coins were offered as "Uncirculated," although true Uncirculated coins were rare. Philosophies change, and today a gem would, indeed, find a ready market.

**Die Varieties:** Varieties include VAM-2 (date slightly doubled) and VAM-7 (92 of date doubled), as well as various mintmark positions and orientations. For a long time this variety existed in small but sufficient quantities to satisfy collector demand.

## Whitman Coin Guide (WCG™)

| VG-8 | F-12 | VF-20 | EF-40 | AU-50 | MS-60 | MS-63 | MS-64 | MS-65 | MS-66 | MS-67 |
|---|---|---|---|---|---|---|---|---|---|---|
| $40 | $50 | $140 | $325 | $1,650 | $36,000 | $64,000 | $115,000 | $190,000 | $260,000 | $335,000 |

**AVAILABILITY**

| | MS-60 | MS-61 | MS-62 | MS-63 | MS-64 | MS-65 | MS-66 | MS-67 | MS-68+ |
|---|---|---|---|---|---|---|---|---|---|
| Certified | 7 | 16 | 33 | 12 | 14 | 6 | 4 | 10 | 1 |
| Field | | 100–200 | | 100–150 | 40–60 | 10–15 | 5–8 | 8–10 | 1–2 |
| Cert. DMPL | 0 | 0 | 0 | 0 | 0 | 0 | 0 | 0 | 0 |

# Morgan Silver Dollars, Rare Coins, and Life in 1893

## The Morgan Dollar Scenario

The *Annual Report of the Director of the Mint*, 1894, told of the repeal in 1893 of the most recent piece of silver-purchase legislation:

> On November 1, 1893 the silver purchasing clause of the Act of July 14, 1890 was repealed, so since then the purchase of silver has been restricted to the silver contained in gold deposits, the amount received in payment of charges of silver deposits, surplus silver bullion returned by the operative officers of the coinage mints on the annual settlement of their accounts at the close of each fiscal year, and uncurrent and mutilated domestic silver coin purchased for the subsidiary silver coinage under the provisions of Section 3526, Revised Statutes of the United States.

This was seemingly bad news for the Morgan silver dollar series—but for the next several years, mintage figures would diminish sharply, creating several numismatic rarities.

In June 1893 *The Numismatist* commented on the storage of Morgan dollars in just one of the many Treasury and mint vaults:

> It is said that it would require 250 freight cars to carry away the $93,000,000 of silver dollars stored up in a single vault of the U.S. Treasury. It is consequently no wonder that the counting, conducted by 60 experts, occupies from two to three months and costs $6,000.

## "Half a Square Mile" of Silver Dollars!

In July, *Harper's Weekly* published an article that detailed the situation:

> It is known vaguely that the federal government is buying every month 4,500,000 ounces of silver, and that this represents about the product of the silver mines of the United States. It is not known what an enormous bulk of silver the laws of Congress have compelled the government to purchase and keep.
>
> The government has been buying silver ever since 1878, when the law known as the Bland law went into effect. Until August 13, 1890, the Treasury purchased every month $2 million worth of bullion to be coined into standard dollars. It might have expended $4 million in that way, and the country ought to be thankful, perhaps, that the different Secretaries restrained themselves from going to the utmost limit of the statute. Nevertheless, the government purchased under the law of 1878, 308,199,261.71 ounces, at a cost of $323,635,576.19. . . .
>
> There are in circulation about $380,000,000 in silver, most of which is in silver certificates, the metal back of these notes being stored in the Treasury. Stated roughly, 300,000,000 standard silver dollars would cover a space of nearly one-half a square mile.
>
> Since August 13, 1890, the government has been buying 4,500,000 ounces of silver a month. On the silver purchased under the act of 1878 the government made a profit of about $70,000,000 by stamping a lie on every 375 grains of fine silver. On the silver purchased under the act of 1890 the government has lost about $40,000,000 by the depreciation of its stock of bullion on hand.
>
> The amount purchased under the act of 1890, most of which is stored in the vaults of the Treasury, was about 157,000,000 ounces on the 1st of July. The government owns, therefore, about 4,000 tons of silver, for which it is obliged to find storage room. Moreover, it must go on buying and storing more than 140 tons of silver a month, and is issuing against the metal paper money, which it is redeeming in gold and receiving for its dues, but which is not regarded as money or a valid representative of money in any other country in the world except Mexico and the South American republics, with whom we trade through London, and who, inconsistently perhaps, demand payment of our debts to them for hides, coffee, and other articles that we import in gold exchange.

But we are now concerning ourselves with the load of silver bullion which the government is storing. It is difficult to foresee what will be done with this amount of material. Even if the Sherman law is repealed, there it is, and if the government undertakes to sell it, the silver market will go even lower than it did the other day, when the silver miners of Colorado threatened to close their mines because India was about to stop the free coinage of silver. In other words, the silver miners insist that the government shall buy and maintain the price of their product, although the Treasury vaults now hold 4,900 tons of it which it cannot sell, on which it has lost millions of the money of the taxpayers, and which is threatening the credit of the government. If the silver miners have the right to demand this, why is it absurd for the farmers to demand that the government store their crops and loan them money on them?[60]

## A SCANDAL IN NEW ORLEANS

As if the Treasury did not have enough problems, in 1893 there was a big contretemps way down yonder in New Orleans, within the walls of the Mint. Tens of thousands of dollars in currency had vanished. According to the cashier's report, on Saturday afternoon, June 24, he had closed the vault and departed from the premises. A fire broke out afterward, and was discovered on Monday morning. All of the paper money in safekeeping had been destroyed.

The cashier was arrested and charged with stealing $25,000, suit was brought against Superintendent Andrew W. Smyth, and accusations flew everywhere. The president of the United States fired the superintendent, assayer, melter and refiner, and the coiner—the greatest termination, for alleged cause, of top management any mint had ever seen. On July 22, 1893, a new crew assumed these posts. However, a court found the cashier to be innocent.

## MINTMARKS (INCLUDING DOLLARS) TO THE FORE!

Columbian half dollars and Isabella quarters notwithstanding, probably *the* numismatic event of 1893 was the publication of Augustus G. Heaton's *Mint Marks*. Up to this time there had been little collector interest in branch-mint coinage. Heaton's readers now learned "causes of attractiveness," as he put it, of various coins produced with mintmarks. These "causes" are interesting to read today.

## MEANWHILE, ON THE AMERICAN SCENE IN 1893

The main event of the year was the World's Columbian Exposition in Chicago, open from May 1 to October 30. On opening day, President Cleveland pushed a button to throw a switch connecting electricity to what seemed like millions of light bulbs, plus machinery and fountains.

Also at the fair, Florenz Ziegfeld began his career as an impresario by staging several popular attractions. Among the visitors to the Columbian Exposition was Milton S. Hershey, a caramel manufacturer of Lancaster, Pennsylvania. While there he saw some chocolate-making devices shown by a German company and ordered one for his factory. History would soon be made, and in 1894 he would incorporate the Hershey Chocolate Company.[61] By the end of 1893, more than 21 million people had visited the fair.

In March, Grover Cleveland was inaugurated, becoming the first president to serve two non-continuous terms.

In 1893 the economic situation remained unfortunate as European investors, disillusioned with their returns, withdrew funds. Foreclosures continued on agricultural lands as well as in businesses, and several important railroads went into receivership. On May 5 there was a dramatic drop in prices of common stocks, and on June 27 there was a panic. Eventually, more than 500 banks would close and more than 15,000 companies would fail.

During this period there was a great controversy concerning gold and silver coins as well as "greenbacks" and other paper money. While the issues were complex, in general many people in the prairie and western states of America favored unlimited coinage of silver in particular, and extensive issues of currency, as a solution to their economic malaise. People in larger cities, particularly in the East, favored coins with significant intrinsic values, such as double eagles, which contained nearly full face value's worth of precious metal.

# 1893

**Optimal Collecting Grade**
MS-64

**Circulation-Strike Mintage**
378,000

**Proof Mintage**
792

**Key to Collecting Circulation Strikes:** In Mint State, the dollars of 1893 are elusive in comparison to the demand for them. MS-63 and MS-64 are worthwhile grades for value. Although many coins are lightly struck, there are quite a few sharp ones. Worn examples are scarce in their own right and offer an economical alternative for anyone not wanting to buy a Mint State coin.

**Surface Quality:** Usually above average on circulation strikes. Proof strikings of the 1893 are usually lightly struck at the centers, "and are the most poorly struck Morgan Proofs," per Van Allen and Mallis. Usually frosty and attractive.

**Prooflike Coins:** Prooflike coins are elusive and have little contrast.

**Mintage and Distribution:** Delivery figures by month: January, 200,000; February, 150,000; March, 0; April, 28,000. Coinage of circulation strikes was then suspended. Not much is known about early releases of 1893 Morgan dollars, except that the low mintage attracted numismatic interest. Worn coins were plentiful in bank holdings and in circulation. Some bags were liberated in the early 1950s, by which time the date was numismatically scarce. A few bags came out in 1962 through 1964, but the issue remained scarce.

## 1893, PROOFS

**Mintage:** 792. Delivery figures by month: January–February, 0; March, 320; April–May, 0; June, 145; July–August, 0; September, 100; October–November, 0; December, 227.

**Key to Collecting Proofs:** Indifferent striking as a result of poor workmanship—the dies were spaced too far apart. Good cameo contrast. Again a challenge, a sporting occasion.

**Die Varieties:** There are no die varieties of compelling importance from the seven pairs of dies on hand for use in this coinage.

## Whitman Coin Guide (WCG™)

| VG-8 | F-12 | VF-20 | EF-40 | AU-50 | MS-60 | MS-63 | MS-64 | MS-65 | MS-66 | MS-67 | PF-60 | PF-64 | PF-65 | PF-66 | PF-67 |
|---|---|---|---|---|---|---|---|---|---|---|---|---|---|---|---|
| $185 | $190 | $195 | $250 | $385 | $700 | $1,025 | $2,000 | $6,500 | $52,000 | – | $1,500 | $3,900 | $6,100 | $9,750 | $15,500 |

**AVAILABILITY**

| | MS-60 | MS-61 | MS-62 | MS-63 | MS-64 | MS-65 | MS-66 | MS-67 | MS-68+ |
|---|---|---|---|---|---|---|---|---|---|
| Certified | 79 | 365 | 1,135 | 1,788 | 1,816 | 278 | 6 | 0 | 0 |
| Field | 15,000–25,000 | | | 10,000–15,000 | 4,000–6,000 | 400–600 | 10–15 | 0 | 1–5 |
| Cert. DMPL | 1 | 3 | 1 | 0 | 0 | 0 | 0 | 0 | 0 |
| | PF-60 | PF-61 | PF-62 | PF-63 | PF-64 | PF-65 | PF-66 | PF-67 | PF-68+ |
| Certified | 12 | 31 | 62 | 64 | 81 | 41 | 29 | 24 | 10 |
| Field | 250–350 | | | 125–160 | 90–120 | 70–100 | 50–75 | 30–50 | 15–20 |

# 1893-CC

**Optimal Collecting Grade**
MS-63

**Circulation-Strike Mintage**
677,000

**Key to Collecting Circulation Strikes:** The 1893-CC is, sadly, the last of the Carson City dollars—ending a romantic numismatic era. Today, surviving pieces are much loved, much desired by numismatists. Mint State 1893-CC dollars are well known for being extensively bagmarked, some actually appearing quite abused. Accordingly, the majority of Mint State pieces are in lower MS grades. A piece MS-63 or finer, with minimum bagmarks, is a numismatic find and is very special. Discount poor strikes and "baggy" coins, and you'll find that remaining pieces in the marketplace are few and far between. A really choice 1893-CC in any grade from MS-63 upward will be a find. Many attractive circulated coins exist and for many buyers will neatly fill the 1893-CC space.

**Surface Quality:** Average or below average, sometimes the lightness on the reverse not only being at on the eagle's breast (as expected) but also on the extremities of the wings. Luster is often satiny and attractive, although there are exceptions. Excessive bagmarks often negate any appeal luster might have.

**Prooflike Coins:** Prooflike pieces are elusive and are usually lightly struck at the centers.

**Mintage and Distribution:** Delivery figures by month: January, 130,000; February, 150,000; March, 140,000; April, 120,000; May, 137,000; June–December, 0. The coinage of silver dollars was suspended at the Carson City Mint on May 23, sounding the death knell for the most plentiful denomination, by far, among CC issues. In ensuing years, many bags and single coins of various dates (no accounting was kept) were paid out. On July 1, 1899, the status of Carson City as a mint was officially ended, although no coins had been struck since 1893. As of that time there were 5,008,552 Carson City dollars stored there. By July 1, 1900, there were no dollars in the Carson City building. The remaining coins were shipped to vaults in the San Francisco Mint and the Treasury Building in Washington, DC. From these depots, bags were paid out in the normal course of business as early as 1920, continuing over the next three decades, at which time little numismatic notice was taken of them. In the 1950s more bags were released, with Harry J. Forman handling at least 10 toward the end of the decade. The well ran dry, and the General Services Administration had only one 1893-CC dollar in its inventory after 1964. The Redfield hoard (1976) contained a few thousand, many of which were scraped by a counting machine used to inventory the pieces.

**Die Varieties:** Positional varieties exist for the date logotype and mintmark letters, none of which is spectacular, these from 10 obverse dies sent to Carson City plus 5 reverse dies, the last to add to usable dies still on hand.

## Whitman Coin Guide (WCG™)

| VG-8 | F-12 | VF-20 | EF-40 | AU-50 | MS-60 | MS-63 | MS-64 | MS-65 | MS-66 | MS-67 |
|------|------|-------|-------|-------|-------|-------|-------|-------|-------|-------|
| $230 | $315 | $600 | $1,250 | $2,050 | $3,850 | $5,850 | $10,000 | $70,000 | – | – |

**AVAILABILITY**

| | MS-60 | MS-61 | MS-62 | MS-63 | MS-64 | MS-65 | MS-66 | MS-67 | MS-68+ |
|---|-------|-------|-------|-------|-------|-------|-------|-------|--------|
| Certified | 274 | 756 | 1,479 | 1,472 | 710 | 16 | 1 | 0 | 0 |
| Field | 10,000–20,000 | | | 2,500–4,000 | 800–1,200 | 20–30 | 0 | 0 | 0 |
| Cert. DMPL | 0 | 1 | 7 | 4 | 2 | 1 | 0 | 0 | 0 |

# 1893-O

Optimal
Collecting Grade
MS-63

Circulation-
Strike Mintage
300,000

**Key to Collecting Circulation Strikes:** If you like a challenge, the 1893-O presents one. Many are peppered with bagmarks. Mint State coins are very elusive in both an absolute and a relative (to the demand) sense. Choice MS-64 coins are rare and MS-65 coins are of sufficient fame that an auction house might showcase one in a news release. Worn 1893-O dollars are fairly scarce, as the low mintage might suggest (the smallest figure of any New Orleans Mint dollar of type), and are a worthwhile buy for anyone not wanting to pay for a Mint State coin.

**Surface Quality:** Striking is usually below average, but sometimes sharp on the reverse and, on the same coin, light at the center of the obverse. Searching is required to locate an overall sharp example. Luster is often, dare I say, *lackluster?* However, there are exceptions to be found.

**Prooflike Coins:** Prooflike coins are seldom encountered, and when they are, quality is often lacking.

**Mintage and Distribution:** Delivery figures by month: January, 300,000; February–December, 0. Not much can be written about the distribution of 1893-O dollars, as little is known. Many were distributed in the early days, accounting for the worn pieces in existence now. From about 1948 to 1955 several thousand or more coins were paid out from the Treasury Building in Washington, DC, seemingly in singles and groups, as no record has been found of a full bag. The Treasury release of 1962 through 1964 included scattered coins, but, again, no account has been found of even a single bag.

**Die Varieties:** There are several positional varieties for the 1893-O, none spectacular. Ten obverse dies were sent to New Orleans this year, but enough reverses were on hand that no more were needed.

## Whitman Coin Guide (WCG™)

| VG-8 | F-12 | VF-20 | EF-40 | AU-50 | MS-60 | MS-63 | MS-64 | MS-65 | MS-66 | MS-67 |
|------|------|-------|-------|-------|-------|-------|-------|-------|-------|-------|
| $175 | $200 | $315 | $525 | $785 | $2,350 | $6,350 | $16,000 | $200,000 | – | – |

### AVAILABILITY

|  | MS-60 | MS-61 | MS-62 | MS-63 | MS-64 | MS-65 | MS-66 | MS-67 | MS-68+ |
|--|-------|-------|-------|-------|-------|-------|-------|-------|--------|
| Certified | 104 | 305 | 567 | 446 | 112 | 8 | 1 | 0 | 0 |
| Field | | 2,000–3,000 | | 800–1,200 | 175–250 | 15–25 | 1–5 | 0 | 0 |
| Cert. DMPL | 0 | 1 | 9 | 5 | 1 | 3 | 0 | 0 | 0 |

# 1893-S

Detail of 1893-S.

**Optimal Collecting Grade**
VF-20

**Circulation-Strike Mintage**
77,000

**Key to Collecting Circulation Strikes:** The 1893-S is the object of great desire in the Morgan dollar series. No single issue has greater popularity across the board. The majority of known pieces, into the thousands, are in the single grade category of Very Fine. Not G or VG, not EF or AU, but VF. Most such pieces circulated in the American West, and for an appropriate but apparently restricted time, to bring them to this grade. Mint State coins exist. However, among the great Treasury release coins of 1962 through 1964, no bag or even small group was found, although many stray pieces were identified, nearly all in the aforementioned VF grade. Many fake 1893-S dollars exist. Absolutely and positively do not buy any "1893-S" dollar that has not been certified by a leading service, and avoid like the plague offerings of uncertified coins "from an old estate" or "from my grandfather's collection" offered on the Internet. While few will be able to afford a Mint State 1893-S, enough attractive VF coins exist that out there somewhere is one just right for you.

**Surface Quality:** Usually seen well struck, and even worn pieces are apt to have good detail. The luster is usually deep and rich on Mint State specimens, when they can be found. Proof-likes are in the minority.

**Prooflike Coins:** About half of the known Mint State coins have a degree of prooflike character.

**Mintage and Distribution:** Delivery figures by month: January, 100,000; February–December, 0. Tens of thousands of 1893-S dollars went into circulation. However, those of 1893-S are almost all VF. A strong clue is provided by the experience of dollar specialist E.S. Thresher, who in *The Numismatist*, July 1925, said that despite years of looking, he had not found an 1893-S. I can envision a scenario in which, sometime after 1925, tens of thousands were turned loose in circulation in the Rocky Mountain states, routinely used, and not numismatically noticed. This would neatly explain the VF concentration. Apart from 20 Mint State coins said to have been found in a bag in Great Falls, Montana, and reported by Wayne Miller, I do not know of any group of high-grade coins found in the 1950s or later. However, Walter Breen reported that Harry Warner, once active in the bulk sale of silver dollars, had handled a full bag. If so, then we may all be surprised and delighted someday if these appear (for the present the availability estimates in this book do not consider these).

**Die Varieties:** There is just one die pair known, distinguished by having a very tiny raised diagonal die line on the crossbar of the T (LIBERTY), diagnostic.

## Whitman Coin Guide (WCG™)

| VG-8 | F-12 | VF-20 | EF-40 | AU-50 | MS-60 | MS-63 | MS-64 | MS-65 | MS-66 | MS-67 |
|------|------|-------|-------|-------|-------|-------|-------|-------|-------|-------|
| $2,500 | $3,800 | $5,100 | $8,100 | $18,500 | $97,500 | $185,000 | $320,000 | $600,000 | $700,000 | $1,000,000 |

**AVAILABILITY**

| | MS-60 | MS-61 | MS-62 | MS-63 | MS-64 | MS-65 | MS-66 | MS-67 | MS-68+ |
|---|-------|-------|-------|-------|-------|-------|-------|-------|--------|
| Certified | 3 | 12 | 12 | 12 | 13 | 7 | 1 | 1 | 0 |
| Field | | 25-35 | | 16-20 | 13-15 | 7-10 | 0-1 | 2 | 0 |
| Cert. DMPL | 0 | 0 | 0 | 0 | 0 | 0 | 0 | 0 | 0 |

# MORGAN SILVER DOLLARS, RARE COINS, AND LIFE IN 1894

## THE MORGAN DOLLAR SCENARIO

By June 1894 there was considerable interest in mintmarked coins, due in part to Augustus G. Heaton's *Mint Marks*. Among the earlier specialists in coins with mint letters was W.M. Friesner, of Los Angeles, whose coins were auctioned by Ed. Frossard. Included in the sale were mintmarked Morgan dollars as well as Philadelphia Mint Proofs.

The Friesner sale lacked many mintmarked issues of the early Morgan dollar series, probably as they were not available on the general market. In the 1880s most newly struck coins were bagged and tossed into storage vaults. This exact situation is reflected in this excerpt from a letter from Augustus G. Heaton in the December 1894 issue of *The Numismatist*, after some previously rare dollars, and one of the higher price-getters in the Friesner sale, came to light:

> Regarding 1880-S silver dollars, these show the opportunities bankers sometimes have for gaining desirable coins, especially in the dollar series, as such pieces are apt to remain for years in bank or mint vaults until a chance demand brings them into circulation. But large quantities often undergo several transfers without the bags being opened, while collectors are hunting in vain for desirable specimens.
>
> If numismatists could delve into Treasury and bank reserves there would at times be great discoveries, not only in mintmarks but in Philadelphia coinage, and the prices of some dates would have the bottom knocked out. This has occurred and will again, by the grace of our banker collectors, but the under-bags earliest put in the vault are seldom reached, and export and recoinage add to the doubt that gives coin hunting a fascinating uncertainty.

Friesner probably followed the advice given in Heaton's *Mint Marks*, and ordered coins directly from the mints. There is no other way to explain how his 1892 and 1893 Morgan dollars were complete.

Frossard's listings are further significant in that some coins are noted as having "slight discoloration," or what we would call toning today. Toning can *enhance* a specimen's value, but in the 1890s collectors liked their coins "brilliant," even if this meant polishing them! Thus, many coins owned by collectors then—such as Proofs—are today in grades of about PF-60. Had they not been cleaned or polished, any and all Proof Morgan dollars from the 19th century would be gems today!

## BAGMARKS ON DOLLARS

During this period, stored Morgan dollars continued to be handled regularly, often several times a year during inspections and audits. Each time, more nicks and other abrasions were added to the coins, producing what are called bagmarks. No doubt this machine, described in *The Numismatist*, December 1894, inflicted even more marks on the coins run through its teeth, which were said to resemble a circular saw!

> The feat of counting 2,000 silver dollars per minute is now being performed at the Mint by a little machine invented by Sebastian Heines, the chief carpenter of the institution, and by its aid the work of counting the coin and weighing the silver bars can, it is thought, be completed soon.
>
> The slow process of counting by hand led Mr. Heines to experiment, with the result, after the expenditure of much thought and time, of turning out a very successful machine. Mr. Morgan, of Mint Director Preston's office, was greatly interested in the experiment, and, upon witnessing the final successful test of the invention, he granted permission for its use in counting the great mass of silver dollars. The machine when worked to its limit easily disposes of two bags of coins, containing $2,000, in a minute.
>
> The machine consists of a hopper, into which the coins are dropped. A cogwheel, the teeth of which resemble those of a circular saw, carries the coins to the tubes, and from there they

are forced out upon a little table, containing 20 grooves, each holding just 50 coins. A turn of the crank counts 1,000 coins, which are immediately put into a bag, and a second 1,000 follows before the expiration of the minute.

One might imagine that each pass-through could reduce a coin's grade by a point!

## A VIEW OF THE COIN MARKET

The March 1894 issue of *The Numismatist* included the editor's view of market activity:

> There is no possible doubt but the depressed condition of the times has its effect on the coin market. Coin buying like any other collecting is a luxury, and such luxuries usually come from the surplus over and above the living and ordinary expenses of the purchaser. The result of the stringent times is consequently the dropping to a great extent of luxuries from the list, and numismatics, philately, anthropology, and all the archaeologies and collectings where cash enters as a modicum of exchange have to suffer. One collector usually puts $500 annually into coins writes that he has made less than one fourth that investment in the past year, and we doubt not but that this proportion of falling off will follow with most collectors.
>
> And yet the dealers say the season has been quite a fair one; that there has not been an appreciable dropping off in trade. This is probably due to two causes: (first) The largely increased number of buyers of late. (second) The fact that many of our monied collectors see in these close times many opportunities to invest their surplus cash in standard coins at such prices as will ultimately bring them large returns in their investment.

This reflected what became a truism: Often in future times of distress in the economy in general and the stock market in particular, rare coin sales suffered less than many other areas did, and in some eras rare coins would experience boom times while other indexes were falling.

The frequency of auctions in 1894 was much reduced from the halcyon times of a decade earlier. Although quality is a matter of taste, likely most would agree with John W. Adams's opinion that in this post-Woodward year the better sales were conducted by Ed. Frossard and the Chapman brothers.

## MEANWHILE, ON THE AMERICAN SCENE IN 1894

Amid continuing uncertain economic conditions, although the depression of 1893 was beginning to wane, many laborers were restive, and during the year about 750,000 went out on strike. Notably, in June 1894 there was a great walkout in Illinois at the Pullman Railroad Car Manufacturing Works. In sympathy, an estimated 40,000 railway employees went on strike in the West. In early July the United States government sent troops to protect the mails and insure peace in interstate commerce, while strikers refused to allow trains to proceed. Much damage occurred, particularly in Chicago, where many buildings remaining from the Columbian Exposition were torched and railroad station yards were destroyed. This great demonstration by labor projected strikes into sharp political focus, and afterward the rights of laborers were more carefully considered than before, by those seeking office in state and national elections.

In June, Congress voted Labor Day as a legal holiday, designating the first Monday in September. In time, the popularity of this late-summer respite spread to just about everyone.

Texas was primarily known for its cattle, but things were beginning to change. In Corsicana a well drilled for water suddenly began spouting gooey black stuff, and within a few years hundreds of thousands of barrels per year came from this particular district.

*Billboard* magazine began with eight pages issued on a monthly basis, later going to a weekly frequency. This soon became the standard periodical for traveling shows and carnivals, in time rendering obsolete the long-established *New York Clipper*. Traveling theater companies, stage entertainers, orators, and amusement operators did a lively business. Just about any town worthy of notice had its own opera house, usually of two or more stories, with merchants on the ground floor and a high-ceilinged auditorium above.

# 1894

Optimal
Collecting Grade
MS-64

Circulation-
Strike Mintage
110,000

Proof Mintage
972

**Key to Collecting Circulation Strikes:** The 1894 is the first true key date in the Philadelphia Mint lineup of Morgan dollars. This year the mintage dropped to just 110,000, or less than a third of 1893, itself a low figure, indeed the smallest circulation-strike figure in the series except for the 1893-S. Examples are elusive in all grades, from well-worn on up. Mint State coins are mostly in lower ranges, through MS-62, then falling off in availability through MS-63, more so for MS-64, and emerging as a rarity in MS-65. Proofs are readily available, and an amazing number are gems. A nice Proof furnishes an alternative for an impossible-to-find, or nearly impossible, gem Mint State coin. Circulated examples are rare as well.

**Surface Quality:** Usually above average in striking sharpness. Proofs are usually well struck and very attractive, sometimes white and "creamy," rather than deeply lustrous and flashy.

**Prooflike Coins:** A few prooflike coins exist, including a handful of DMPLs, and are rare and desirable in high grades.

**Mintage and Distribution:** Delivery figures by month: January–July, 0; August, 48,000; September, 12,000; October, 50,000; November–December, 0. Few 1894 dollars were released in the late 19th and early 20th centuries. Several bags were paid out in the 1950s and early 1960s. A bag of dollars turned up in Montana circa 1961, but by that time the price of the 1894 had risen, and this quantity did not disturb the structure. In the early 1960s a bag of mixed 1893 and 1894 dollars surfaced in San Francisco. The 1894 does not seem to have been part of the 1962 through 1964 Treasury release, save for a few scattered coins.

## 1894, PROOFS

**Mintage:** 972. Delivery figures by month: January–February, 0; March, 252; April–May, 0; June, 179; July–August, 0; September, 200; October–November, 0; December, 341.

**Key to Collecting Proofs:** Usually well struck. Good cameo contrast. These offer a good value.

**Die Varieties:** Although seven obverse and five reverse dies were made up for this coinage, it is not certain that all were used. Only two die combinations are described by VAM. Beware 1894-O dollars with tooled-away mintmarks posing as rarer 1894 Philadelphia issues.

## Whitman Coin Guide (WCG™)

| VG-8 | F-12 | VF-20 | EF-40 | AU-50 | MS-60 | MS-63 | MS-64 | MS-65 | MS-66 | MS-67 | PF-60 | PF-64 | PF-65 | PF-66 | PF-67 |
|---|---|---|---|---|---|---|---|---|---|---|---|---|---|---|---|
| $1,000 | $1,175 | $1,250 | $1,450 | $1,650 | $3,350 | $4,900 | $9,500 | $40,000 | $60,000 | – | $2,850 | $5,000 | $7,000 | $10,750 | $17,000 |

**AVAILABILITY**

| | MS-60 | MS-61 | MS-62 | MS-63 | MS-64 | MS-65 | MS-66 | MS-67 | MS-68+ |
|---|---|---|---|---|---|---|---|---|---|
| Certified | 105 | 393 | 585 | 524 | 345 | 25 | 4 | 0 | 0 |
| Field | | 2,500–3,500 | | 1,000–2,000 | 400–600 | 30–50 | 5–8 | 0 | 0 |
| Cert. DMPL | 0 | 1 | 1 | 1 | 2 | 0 | 0 | 0 | 0 |

| | PF-60 | PF-61 | PF-62 | PF-63 | PF-64 | PF-65 | PF-66 | PF-67 | PF-68+ |
|---|---|---|---|---|---|---|---|---|---|
| Certified | 27 | 23 | 71 | 98 | 123 | 73 | 49 | 28 | 11 |
| Field | | 300–400 | | 200–300 | 180–220 | 130–160 | 70–90 | 60–80 | 25–35 |

# 1894-O

**Optimal Collecting Grade**
MS-64

**Circulation-Strike Mintage**
1,723,000

**Key to Collecting Circulation Strikes:** Mint State examples of the 1894-O dollar are often wretched in appearance. Is there hope? Yes, there is, but a great deal of searching will be needed to find an example that is decent or above average (but not sharp) in striking details and with attractive luster—a cherrypicker's challenge and delight. Probably the best way is to view coins certified as MS-63 and MS-64, with patience, and see what happens. The luster is often nice on higher-grade pieces, if that's a help. Or, you can give up and buy a worn specimen, saving both time and money.

**Surface Quality:** The strike is usually below average. Diligent searching is needed to ferret out a piece with excellent detail. Luster is typically satiny and attractive on higher-grade pieces (which are elusive), dull on lower-grade ones.

**Prooflike Coins:** Prooflike coins are elusive, and when encountered are apt to be of low contrast, bagmarked, and unattractive.

**Mintage and Distribution:** Delivery figures by month: January–June, 0; July, 263,000; August, 400,000; September, 360,000; October, 300,000; November, 250,000; December, 150,000. Although few accounts exist of Treasury payouts of 1894-O dollars, the variety was not in great demand, possibly because of the poor appearance of most pieces, and thus market levels were low through the 1940s. In the early 1950s several bags surfaced, giving dealers an adequate supply. More were part of the Treasury release of 1962 through 1964, but interest remained apathetic.

**Die Varieties:** Although 10 obverse and 7 reverse dies were furnished for this coinage, not that many combinations have been identified by numismatists. None are "keepers," except as a representative of the date and mint.

## Whitman Coin Guide (WCG™)

| VG-8 | F-12 | VF-20 | EF-40 | AU-50 | MS-60 | MS-63 | MS-64 | MS-65 | MS-66 | MS-67 |
|------|------|-------|-------|-------|-------|-------|--------|--------|-------|-------|
| $48 | $53 | $58 | $95 | $225 | $650 | $3,750 | $10,000 | $54,000 | – | – |

**AVAILABILITY**

| | MS-60 | MS-61 | MS-62 | MS-63 | MS-64 | MS-65 | MS-66 | MS-67 | MS-68+ |
|--------------|-------|-------|-------|-------|---------|-------|-------|-------|--------|
| Certified | 178 | 408 | 448 | 481 | 525 | 16 | 0 | 0 | 0 |
| Field | | 2,500–4,000 | | 1,250–1,750 | 600–900 | 15–25 | 0 | 0 | 1–5 |
| Cert. DMPL | 0 | 2 | 2 | 0 | 0 | 0 | 0 | 0 | 0 |

# 1894-S

Optimal
Collecting Grade
MS-64

Circulation-
Strike Mintage
1,260,000

**Key to Collecting Circulation Strikes:** The 1894-S dollar is a numismatic delight. Most are well struck, lustrous, and pleasing to the eye. In MS-63 and MS-64 grades, examples will fit well into a high-quality collection. MS-65 coins are difficult to find and justifiably more expensive.

**Surface Quality:** The 1894-S is usually seen well struck, the only date and mint of this year for which this can be said. Typically with excellent luster. Some have distracting die-polishing lines in the field, consisting of minute raised lines that to the uninitiated can make a coin appear as if it has been cleaned.

**Prooflike Coins:** Prooflike pieces are scarce, but the VAM notes that they are more available than the other prooflike issues of the year span 1893 to 1895.

**Mintage and Distribution:** Delivery figures by month: January–June, 0; July, 160,000; August, 300,000; September, 300,000; October, 250,000; November, 150,000; December, 100,000. Bags of 1894-S dollars were paid out in the 1950s, the source being the usual: vaults at the San Francisco Mint. Several bags came out in Deer Lodge, Montana, one of which was not "pure" and had just 980 coins, the balance being twenty 1893-S dollars! Bags of 1894-S dollars continued to be available at face value in the 1950s, but demand was low. By the time of the 1962 through 1964 Treasury bonanza, it seems that all bags were gone.

**Die Varieties:** Although 18 obverses and 13 reverses were furnished for the 1894-S coinage, it is likely that not all were used, for less than half that number of combinations can be identified today. Varieties are not significant and are mainly with regard to minor differences in date or mintmark position.

## Whitman Coin Guide (WCG™)

| VG-8 | F-12 | VF-20 | EF-40 | AU-50 | MS-60 | MS-63 | MS-64 | MS-65 | MS-66 | MS-67 |
|------|------|-------|-------|-------|-------|-------|-------|-------|-------|-------|
| $55 | $63 | $95 | $155 | $415 | $675 | $1,175 | $1,850 | $5,800 | $15,000 | $27,500 |

**AVAILABILITY**

|  | MS-60 | MS-61 | MS-62 | MS-63 | MS-64 | MS-65 | MS-66 | MS-67 | MS-68+ |
|--|-------|-------|-------|-------|-------|-------|-------|-------|--------|
| Certified | 133 | 474 | 1,143 | 1,563 | 1,209 | 175 | 18 | 3 | 0 |
| Field |  | 10,000–15,000 |  | 5,000–8,000 | 2,000–3,000 | 200–300 | 20–30 | 5–8 | 0 |
| Cert. DMPL | 1 | 3 | 8 | 11 | 3 | 0 | 0 | 0 | 0 |

# MORGAN SILVER DOLLARS, RARE COINS, AND LIFE IN 1895

## THE MORGAN DOLLAR SCENARIO

In Philadelphia in 1895 no silver dollars were minted for general circulation, and production was limited to just 880 Proofs for collectors. The *Annual Report of the Director of the Mint* stated that 12,000 circulation strikes were made, but later research by Henry T. Hettger would reveal that this was an accounting-entry error, and that the pieces were of earlier date.

The production of dollars at the other two operating mints, New Orleans and San Francisco, was low for the era, creating varieties that a later generation would recognize as rare, especially in higher grades.

Storage of Morgan dollars continued to be a first-class headache for the Treasury Department. In storage at the Carson City Mint as of July 1, 1895, were 5,168,394 such coins; while at Philadelphia in the Mint were 50,221,267; the New Orleans Mint held 9,610,000; and at the San Francisco Mint 36,749,500 had piled up.

Augustus G. Heaton, of *Mint Marks* fame, visited the Treasury Building next to the White House in Washington, and was led on a tour by United States Treasurer Daniel N. Morgan, and allowed to peer into various storage areas. In Vault 1, measuring 89 feet long by 51 feet wide by 12 feet high, were 103,308,000 silver dollars! Vault 2 was packed with 48,000,000 more dollars. Also in storage were fractional silver coins, gold coins, and wrapped bundles of paper money—the numismatic equivalent of heaven. However, it was the silver dollars that dominated. Neither Heaton nor anyone else realized that these dollars, and others yet to be minted, would profoundly affect the numismatic hobby in America several generations later, yielding a treasure trove for all. At that same later time, Liberty Seated and Barber dimes, quarters, and half dollars of the 1880s and 1890s, never saved in bulk, would all become scarce, and many quite rare.

## COMMENTS ON THE DOLLAR DESIGN

In the May 1895 issue of *The Numismatist* two articles focused on the need to revise the existing coinage designs, with the largest silver coin of the realm, the silver dollar, being particularly in the limelight. The National Sculpture Society, acting with the American Numismatic and Archaeological Society, was endeavoring to upgrade the coinage. It was stated that an exhibition was held at the Academy of Fine Arts in New York City, and that prizes of $300 and $200 were given for the first- and second-best ideas for a new silver dollar. However, "there is no chance worth mentioning that the Treasury will accept any of the designs," it was noted, quoting an article from the *Washington Evening Star*. "Unfortunately, artists generally are wretched coin designers. They will not realize that a piece of money is not a thing to paint a picture upon, and the models they offer are mostly the wildest freaks."
Further:

> Designs offered by artists show that they imagine that any eagle will do for the purpose. This is a big mistake. The eagle required is the heraldic eagle, showing the bird as it is represented in the coat of arms of the United States. . . . Attempts to vary it on the coins have been notably unsuccessful. Eagles have been nailed upon the wall at the Mint in Philadelphia to serve as models in various attitudes, but the designs thus produced have been mercilessly ridiculed. The flying eagle on the nickel cent was removed because some people insisted that it was a buzzard.[62]

The second article on coinage art, or the lack thereof, was titled "Uncle Sam's Ugly Dollar," and included this:

> All the sculptors and artists in the United States have severely criticized the existing coinage. The designs of European coins, they declare, are infinitely superior. The French coins are probably the most artistic of any, although the St. George and the Dragon of the British sovereign

is undoubtedly a very handsome and artistic design. The first impression which the head of Liberty of the silver dollar gives, so say the sculptors, is that of weakness and indecision. This is not befitting a powerful, progressive nation like the United States. Sculptors also criticize the pose of the eagle.

## Some Prominent Dealers

Augustus G. Heaton, who continued to be one of the more prolific writers of the time, contributed an installment of "A Tour Among the Coin Dealers" to *The Numismatist* in January.[63]

"As the great majority of American collectors either live at a distance from the large commercial centers where dealers are found or travel so little as to know but one or two of the trade personally, we offer our quite extended and widespread observations in coin hunting to the readers of *The Numismatist*," Heaton noted.

Located on Union Square in a large room on the second floor of an imposing building was the New York Stamp & Coin Company, managed by David Proskey, who was described as "still a young man but one of the best numismatic judges of coins in the trade, and very just in valuation." Proskey, financed by H.P. Smith, employed a clerk or two to help handle a large stock of coins and stamps as well as minerals, curiosities, and other artifacts. By this time Proskey, earlier criticized for his ethics by certain of his contemporaries, seems to have grown wiser along with growing older—for in this era little negative was said about him.

Not far away in New York City on 14th Street was to be found Ed. Frossard, who was described as "rather a large middle-aged man of smooth shaven, pleasant face." His dealership was not particularly impressive and consisted simply of a desk and small safe in the office of an insurance company; however, he "has generally some choice pieces to show and often more or less of some collection entrusted to him to be cataloged and sold. He issues at intervals a sheet entitled *Numisma* that has a wide correspondence regarding coins, curios, and objects of historic interest."

## Meanwhile, on the American Scene in 1895

The Free Silver movement continued to gather momentum on the political scene, as more people felt that the government should purchase unlimited amounts of this metal, thereby bringing great prosperity to certain areas of the Midwest and West that had seen unfortunate times since the fallen value of metal that began in a significant way in the mid-1870s.

In Atlanta the Cotton States Exposition was held and attracted 800,000 visitors. Among the items on view were the Liberty Bell, brought by rail from Philadelphia; exhibitions by "Buffalo Bill Cody"; and many of commercial displays. Concerts were conducted by John Philip Sousa and Victor Herbert.

The Supreme Court, in the antitrust action of *U.S. v. E.C. Knight Company*, involving the sugar trust, dismissed the case, stating that controlling manufacturing processes had only an incidental effect on interstate commerce. Seemingly freed from the threat of government intervention, trusts became more powerful than ever. In another decision, the Supreme Court ruled that personal income taxes were illegal.

On Thanksgiving, 1895, the first automobile race in the United States took place along a 53-mile course connecting Chicago and Milwaukee. The *Chicago Times-Herald* put up a $2,000 prize for the winner; 80 automobiles entered, but only six were able to get running. The average time for those completing the race was 5.25 miles an hour. James Franklin Duryea was the winner. Meanwhile, in Europe, races were held regularly and several different brands of automobile were popular.

In 1895 Kodak introduced a pocket version of its camera. Amateur photography became one of America's most popular hobbies. In America and in France, motion pictures were projected to small, admission-paying audiences for the first time. Virtually overnight, a dynamic industry was launched. Among changes in the social scene, the American Bowling Congress was founded in 1895, and the Gillette razor was invented.

# 1895

Optimal
Collecting Grade
PF-65

Circulation-
Strike Mintage
None

Proof Mintage
880

## 1895, PROOFS

**Mintage:** 880. Delivery figures by month: January–February, 0; March, 290; April, 0; May, 180; June–August, 0; September, 90; October–November, 0; December, 320.

**Key to Collecting Proofs:** In 1895, at the Philadelphia Mint, there was no coinage of silver dollars for circulation. Striking was limited to Proofs, of which only 880 were made. Early in 1896, when samples of the previous year's precious metal coinage were submitted to the Assay Commission for review, the dollar was represented by a single Proof. Today, most of the Proofs remain and are cherished by numismatists. With the low production figure, the 1895 is far and away the rarest date in the series. The ownership of an attractive Proof is a fine thing to contemplate. Proof 1895 dollars are well struck.

As to their appearance, the contrast between the devices and the mirrored fields is medium, sort of satiny on the high spots, not deep cameo. As might be expected, the majority of these and other Proof Morgan dollars have been dipped or cleaned, although quite a few have remained in grades of Proof-65 or finer. Excellent strike, good contrast is the rule. There have been resubmissions galore to grading services, and one of these years I would not be surprised to find the population report totals will exceed the mintage figure.

**Die Varieties:** By the 1980s the American Numismatic Association Certification Service had identified five different obverse dies used to strike the Proof coinage for this year, a remarkable number.

## Whitman Coin Guide (WCG™)

| VG-8 | F-12 | VF-20 | EF-40 | AU-50 | MS-60 | MS-63 | MS-64 | MS-65 | MS-66 | MS-67 | PF-60 | PF-64 | PF-65 | PF-66 | PF-67 |
|------|------|-------|-------|-------|-------|-------|-------|-------|-------|-------|-------|-------|-------|-------|-------|
|      |      |       |       |       |       |       |       |       |       |       | $45,000 | $55,000 | $77,500 | $81,000 | $95,000 |

### AVAILABILITY

|          | PF-60 | PF-61 | PF-62 | PF-63 | PF-64 | PF-65 | PF-66 | PF-67 | PF-68+ |
|----------|-------|-------|-------|-------|-------|-------|-------|-------|--------|
| Certified | 25 | 51 | 109 | 109 | 107 | 48 | 38 | 16 | 4 |
| Field | | 250–350 | | 150–225 | 150–250 | 70–90 | 70–90 | 45–50 | 18–20 |

# 1895-O

**Optimal
Collecting Grade**
AU-50

**Circulation-
Strike Mintage**
450,000

**Key to Collecting Circulation Strikes:** The 1895-O is often seen in circulated grades, and among higher-level pieces, AU examples are encountered with frequency. There are scads of high EF and AU coins around, indicating that many 1895-O dollars must have been in circulation for only a short time, "Mint State" coins do exist, including some that should be designated AU. To obtain a decent one, look at the MS-63 grade, at least, and be prepared to spend a lot of money. No matter the grade, most are casually if not lightly struck and have dull, insipid luster. The 1895-O emerged as the single circulation-strike variety that is not known to have been a part of any Treasury releases via bags.

**Surface Quality:** Striking is usually below average to average, not often sharp. Cherrypicking is encouraged, not easy to do with 1895-O as Mint State pieces are quite elusive. High-grade pieces usually show attractive, satiny luster.

**Prooflike Coins:** Among Mint State coins, many are prooflike or partially so, with decent contrast.

**Mintage and Distribution:** Delivery figures by month: January, 200,000; February, 100,000; March, 0; April, 100,000; May, 50,000; June–December, 0. Probably 100,000 or more were placed into circulation in or near the year of mintage. Some went into storage. I have heard suggestions that from several dozen to a couple hundred Mint State coins came out of the Treasury Building in the early 1950s, but how they would grade today is anybody's guess. Uncirculated coins of years ago are often classified as AU today. I have found no account or even a rumor of any being a part of the 1962 through 1964 Treasury release.

**Die Varieties:** Several die varieties are known from five pairs of dies. None shows dramatic differences.

## Whitman Coin Guide (WCG™)

| VG-8 | F-12 | VF-20 | EF-40 | AU-50 | MS-60 | MS-63 | MS-64 | MS-65 | MS-66 | MS-67 |
|------|------|-------|-------|-------|-------|-------|-------|-------|-------|-------|
| $285 | $320 | $400 | $575 | $1,300 | $14,500 | $50,000 | $80,000 | $165,000 | $390,000 | $700,000 |

**AVAILABILITY**

|  | MS-60 | MS-61 | MS-62 | MS-63 | MS-64 | MS-65 | MS-66 | MS-67 | MS-68+ |
|--|-------|-------|-------|-------|-------|-------|-------|-------|--------|
| Certified | 44 | 81 | 69 | 32 | 23 | 6 | 2 | 1 | 0 |
| Field | | 125–175 | | 75–125 | 30–45 | 7–11 | 2–3 | 1–2 | 0 |
| Cert. DMPL | 2 | 4 | 3 | 0 | 0 | 0 | 0 | 0 | 0 |

# 1895-S

**Optimal
Collecting Grade
MS-63**

**Circulation-
Strike Mintage
400,000**

**Key to Collecting Circulation Strikes:** Mint State 1895-S dollars are well known for being extensively bagmarked, some actually appearing quite abused. Accordingly, the majority of Mint State pieces are in lower MS grades. A piece MS-63 or finer, with minimum bagmarks, is a numismatic find and is very special. Circulated specimens are elusive, as the mintage might indicate, but an attractive example can be a reasonable financial as well as aesthetic alternative to a baggy MS-60.

**Surface Quality:** The strike is typically excellent. Rich luster is seen on high-grade specimens.

**Prooflike Coins:** Prooflike coins exist and are desirable if in high grades, but the contrast is not strong.

**Mintage and Distribution:** Delivery figures by month: January, 0; February, 100,000; March, 100,000; April, 100,000; May, 100,000; June–December, 0. While some 1895-S dollars were paid out in the early years, the issue remained elusive for a long time. In 1942 the San Francisco Mint turned loose a few bags. Into the early 1950s, more bags were paid out, but in the absence of a significant market for quantities, most went into circulation.

**Die Varieties:** Among the 10 obverse and 6 reverse dies created for this coinage are the following varieties. *1895-S "S Over Horizontal S," VAM-4:* Per Van Allen and Mallis, "original S shows as a triangular raised metal [area] to the left outside of the upright S and has a diagonal line through the top and bottom loops of S." However, the feature is not particularly easy to discern. *1895-S Dramatically Repunched S, VAM-3:* With the earlier mintmark punched too high and too close to the left ribbon. The final mintmark was punched in a centered position, but much of the earlier mintmark is still seen.

VAM-4

## Whitman Coin Guide (WCG™)

| VG-8 | F-12 | VF-20 | EF-40 | AU-50 | MS-60 | MS-63 | MS-64 | MS-65 | MS-66 | MS-67 |
|---|---|---|---|---|---|---|---|---|---|---|
| $440 | $550 | $825 | $1,100 | $1,700 | $3,750 | $5,500 | $7,500 | $23,500 | $95,000 | – |

**AVAILABILITY**

| | MS-60 | MS-61 | MS-62 | MS-63 | MS-64 | MS-65 | MS-66 | MS-67 | MS-68+ |
|---|---|---|---|---|---|---|---|---|---|
| Certified | 43 | 188 | 343 | 512 | 582 | 41 | 6 | 0 | 0 |
| Field | | 2,500–4,000 | | 800–1,200 | 600–900 | 40–60 | 7–10 | 0 | 0 |
| Cert. DMPL | 1 | 2 | 9 | 12 | 27 | 0 | 2 | 1 | 0 |

# Morgan Silver Dollars, Rare Coins, and Life in 1896
## The Morgan Dollar Scenario

### ANNA WILLIAMS

The May 1896 issue of *The Numismatist* informed readers that Anna W. Williams, who had posed for George T. Morgan for the silver dollar of 1878, was about to be married. It was related that when George T. Morgan came to America in 1876, an early task at the Phila-delphia Mint was to redesign the silver dollar:

> After many months of labor the young engraver completed the design for the reverse side of the coin upon which he represented the American eagle. His attention was then turned to the other side, and his original inclination was to place on it a fanciful head representing the God-dess of Liberty. But the ambitious designer was too much of a realist to be satisfied with a mere product of fancy. Finally he determined the head should be the representation of some American girl and forthwith searched for his beauteous maid.
>
> Mr. Morgan was so enthusiastic that he declared Miss Williams' profile was the most nearly perfect he had seen in England or America. His design for the silver dollar was accepted by Congress, so the silver coins have been pouring from the mints all these years adorned with the stately face of a Quaker City maiden.
>
> It was a long search, although pleasant. He told his friends of his desires, and one of them spoke of the really classic beauty of Miss Anna Williams. The designer was introduced to the girl. Mr. Morgan was at once impressed by her beautiful face and studied it carefully. Then he told her what he desired, and she promptly refused to permit herself to be the subject of the design. Her friends, however, induced her to pose before an artist. After five sittings the design was completed.
>
> Miss Williams is a decidedly modest young woman. She resides on Spring Garden Street, not far from the school in which for years she has been employed as an instructor in philoso-phy and methods in the kindergarten department. She is slightly below the average height, is rather plump, and is fair. She carries her figure with a stateliness rarely seen, and the pose of the head is exactly as seen on the silver dollar. The features of Miss Williams are reproduced as faithfully as in a good photograph.

## The "Cross of Gold" Speech

The political campaign pitted William J. Bryan, the "silver-tongued orator of the Platte," who advocated the free and unlimited coinage of silver, against Ohio Governor William McKinley, a Republican whose backing included Eastern industrialists. The capstone of the campaign, Bryan's stirring "Cross of Gold" speech, delivered to the Democratic National Convention on July 8, is one of the most famous in election history.

Here is part of what Bryan said:

> You come to us and tell us that the great cities are in favor of the gold standard. We reply that the great cities rest upon our broad and fertile prairies. Burn down your cities and leave our farms, and your cities will spring up again as if by magic; but destroy our farms and the grass will grow in streets in every city in the country.
>
> Having behind us the producing masses of this nation and the world, supported by the commercial interests, the laboring interests, the toilers everywhere, we will answer their demand for a gold standard by saying unto them: You shall not press down upon the brow of labor this crown of thorns; you shall not crucify mankind on a cross of gold.

Although it created a sensation at the time, votes from the South, prairie states, and mining states in the Rocky Mountains were not sufficient to overcome those dropped in ballot boxes in the cities on the coast and in industrial regions. In November, McKinley was the winner with a 600,000 margin in the popular vote, and with 274 electoral votes to Bryan's 175.

This campaign spawned dozens of different medals and tokens, most of a satirical nature, with some (called "Bryan dollars" today) consisting of large discs of silver, illustrating how large a dollar would be if it were made of full intrinsic value of the metal. Despite the hundreds of millions of ounces of silver that had been purchased by the Treasury Department since the early days of the Bland-Allison Act in 1878, the value of the precious metal continued to decline, and in 1896 a silver dollar contained only 52¢ worth of metal.

## MEANWHILE, ON THE AMERICAN SCENE IN 1896

In a decision on May 18, 1896, the Supreme Court in the case of *Plessy v. Ferguson* ruled that states could provide black citizens with "separate but equal" public facilities, including education, transportation, and accommodations. The only dissenter, Justice John Harlan, stated that the "Constitution is colorblind," but he was decades ahead of his contemporaries on the bench. Throughout nearly all of the South, blacks were forced to sit in special sections of railroad cars, to utilize the balconies but not the orchestra sections of theaters, and to stay away from restrooms, fountains, schools, hospitals, and recreational facilities designated for white people. Prejudices were also widespread against immigrants, particularly the Irish and Italians, and many social functions were off-limits to Jews.

On August 16 a gold strike was made in the Klondike district of Canada, on the Yukon River not far from the border of Alaska. This initiated the latest in a series of "rushes" for precious metal. It took about 10 months for the news to precipitate widespread action in the United States, and in 1897 and 1898 an estimated 20,000 to 30,000 treasure hunters went to the district. On April 25, 1896, the prosperous and solidly established city of Cripple Creek had a disastrous fire that leveled most of its business district, which was soon rebuilt.

In the southeast part of Florida at a site known as Fort Dallas, which had just three residences in 1894, the town of Miami was incorporated in 1895, and by 1896 was growing by small leaps and bounds, soon to become large jumps. The fortunes of Miami received a further boost when Henry Flagler opened the Royal Palm Hotel, an elegant winter resort, joining several others he had constructed along the Atlantic coast in Florida, easily reached by the tracks of his Florida East Coast Railway.

On April 20 at Koster and Bial's Music Hall in New York City, Thomas Edison's Vitascope projection device was used to throw pictures on a large screen before a paying audience. A sensation ensued, newspaper coverage was intense, and within a few years motion picture parlors were opened all across America, typically showing short scenes with action, such as acrobats, railroad trains, and slapstick comedy, with nothing in the way of a plot. On the musical scene such numbers as "Sweet Rosie O'Grady," "A Hot Time in the Old Town Tonight," and "When the Saints Go Marching In" were popular.

In Pittsburgh, H.J. Heinz devised the trademark "57 varieties" as a memorable slogan, inspired by an advertisement he saw for a firm offering 21 styles of shoes. Boxes of Cracker Jack were first sold this year, made in Chicago and consisting of candy-coated popcorn mixed with peanuts—a product that today is essentially unchanged. Tootsie Rolls were launched in New York City, named for Clara (nicknamed Tootsie), the six-year-old daughter of confectioner Leo Hirshfield. At his Saint Louis brewery, the largest in America, Adolph Busch introduced Michelob beer, which was billed as a premium brand and sold only on draft until years later in 1961.

Lagging Europe, American entrepreneurs made slow but satisfactory progress developing the automobile. In 1896 the Duryea Motor Company (Springfield, Massachusetts) made the first car for public sale. In Detroit, Henry Ford experimented with his motorized Quadracycle steered by a tiller, and in Massachusetts Francis and Freling Stanley devised the famous Stanley Steamer, a car that developed remarkable power and was ideal for hill climbs and other rugged events. In the meantime, bicycling was widely popular, clubs were active in most towns and cities, and annual sales amounted to about $60 million. Popular photography also commanded the attention of countless Americans.

# 1896

Optimal
Collecting Grade
MS-65

Circulation-
Strike Mintage
9,976,000

Proof Mintage
762

**Key to Collecting Circulation Strikes:** The 1896 is the first Philadelphia Mint dollar of the 1890s to be common in Mint State. Examples abound, including choice MS-63 and 64 pieces as well as gem MS-65 or finer. Luster varies but is usually above average. Regardless of your budget, here lies the possibility for a nice Mint State coin in your collection.

**Surface Quality:** The strike is typically above average. The luster ranges from satiny to frosty. Some cherrypicking is advised to find one with deep luster.

**Prooflike Coins:** Prooflike pieces are seen with some occasion but are usually not with deep contrast.

**Mintage and Distribution:** Delivery figures by month: January, 0; February, 900,000; March, 900,000; April, 900,000; May, 900,000; June, 900,000; July, 162,000; August, 1,300,000; September, 1,300,000; October, 1,200,000; November, 514,000; December, 1,000,000. Although there seems to have been a supply of 1896 dollars in circulation since day one, in the 1950s vast quantities were let loose into Eastern banking circles, creating a nuisance for collectors searching through bags in quest of scarce dates. More were paid out from Treasury vaults in coming years, through the early 1960s.

**Die Varieties:** Produced in quantity, the 1896 was minted from nearly 20 known die pairs. No varieties have strongly captured the fancy of numismatists, and probably the most dramatic of the lot is VAM-5, with slight doubling on the first and last digits.

## 1896, PROOFS

**Mintage:** 762. Delivery figures by month: January–February, 0; March, 287; April–May, 0; June, 125; July–August, 0; September, 100; October–November, 0; December, 250.

**Key to Collecting Proofs:** Good strike. Deep cameo contrast. Some nice ones are around. Whew! Those nasty years of weak striking, beginning in 1888, are over!

## Whitman Coin Guide (WCG™)

| VG-8 | F-12 | VF-20 | EF-40 | AU-50 | MS-60 | MS-63 | MS-64 | MS-65 | MS-66 | MS-67 | PF-60 | PF-64 | PF-65 | PF-66 | PF-67 |
|------|------|-------|-------|-------|-------|-------|-------|-------|-------|-------|-------|-------|-------|-------|-------|
| $28 | $29 | $34 | $37 | $41 | $48 | $65 | $120 | $250 | $475 | $6,750 | $1,300 | $3,900 | $6,100 | $9,750 | $15,500 |

### AVAILABILITY

| | MS-60 | MS-61 | MS-62 | MS-63 | MS-64 | MS-65 | MS-66 | MS-67 | MS-68+ |
|---|-------|-------|-------|-------|-------|-------|-------|-------|--------|
| Certified | 123 | 741 | 5,824 | 21,773 | 26,670 | 7,655 | 1,310 | 84 | 0 |
| Field | 500,000–800,000 | | | 70,000–100,000 | 40,000–70,000 | 12,000–16,000 | 2,000–3,500 | 60–90 | 5–10 |
| Cert. DMPL | 8 | 32 | 114 | 308 | 427 | 183 | 12 | 1 | 0 |
| | PF-60 | PF-61 | PF-62 | PF-63 | PF-64 | PF-65 | PF-66 | PF-67 | PF-68+ |
| Certified | 7 | 16 | 41 | 70 | 117 | 61 | 35 | 28 | 14 |
| Field | 200–300 | | | 120–150 | 130–170 | 90–125 | 70–90 | 60–75 | 30–40 |

# 1896-O

**Optimal
Collecting Grade**
MS-63

**Circulation-
Strike Mintage**
4,900,000

**Key to Collecting Circulation Strikes:** The 1896-O is a marvelous coin for study. "No other Morgan dollar is as consistently deficient in luster, strike, and degree of surface abrasions as the 1896-O," Wayne Miller wrote. "In my opinion the 1896-O is the rarest of all Morgan dollars (even more than 1901) in truly gem condition." Of course, those who are edged out of buying a gem Mint State 1901 can wink twice and buy a Proof quickly, but the collector seeking an 1896-O has no such fallback possibility. Most of the mintage must have been released into circulation, as well-worn coins are common today and worth little premium. On the other hand, AU coins, of which there are thousands around, do have value and are a reasonable option for an example of this date, in view of the paucity of choice higher-grade pieces.

**Surface Quality:** Striking is usually below average, insipid and unattractive. This will be a problem and a challenge, as very few exceptions can be found. The luster is typically dull and lifeless. Again, cherrypicking is needed, in combination with strike, making the challenge even greater.

**Prooflike Coins:** Prooflike examples occur and are very rare, even well struck, but with dullish surfaces rendering most of them unattractive.

**Mintage and Distribution:** Delivery figures by month: January, 0; February, 500,000; March, 500,000; April, 350,000; May, 300,000; June, 300,000; July, 300,000; August, 600,000; September, 600,000; October, 600,000; November, 600,000; December, 250,000. Large quantities reached circulation. Mint State coins turned up here and there in numismatic circles and attracted no notice. By 1953 a few bags had come on the market, and dealer specialists had a nice supply. More were released in 1956. This date and mint was known for its generally unmemorable quality, and it never was a collectors' favorite. A few bags here and there came to market in the late 1950s and early 1960s, but not enough that Harry J. Forman ever owned one.

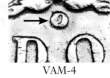
VAM-4

**Die Varieties:** Among the many die combinations, of special interest is the *1896-O Micro o Mintmark, VAM-4:* Very small o from a mintmark punch intended for a lower-denomination silver coin. Usually seen well worn. Two varieties of VAM-4 are shown to the right.

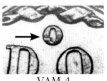
VAM-4

## Whitman Coin Guide (WCG™)

| VG-8 | F-12 | VF-20 | EF-40 | AU-50 | MS-60 | MS-63 | MS-64 | MS-65 | MS-66 | MS-67 |
|------|------|-------|-------|-------|-------|-------|-------|-------|-------|-------|
| $30 | $32 | $37 | $43 | $150 | $1,400 | $6,750 | $42,000 | $175,000 | $425,000 | – |

**AVAILABILITY**

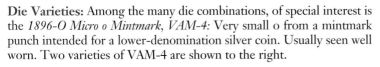

| | MS-60 | MS-61 | MS-62 | MS-63 | MS-64 | MS-65 | MS-66 | MS-67 | MS-68+ |
|---|-------|-------|-------|-------|-------|-------|-------|-------|--------|
| Certified | 319 | 724 | 952 | 428 | 36 | 4 | 2 | 0 | 0 |
| Field | | 3,000–5,000 | | 1,500–2,500 | 80–120 | 7–11 | 2–3 | 0 | 0 |
| Cert. DMPL | 2 | 2 | 3 | 1 | 1 | 0 | 0 | 0 | 0 |

# 1896-S

Optimal
Collecting Grade
MS-64

Circulation-
Strike Mintage
5,000,000

**Key to Collecting Circulation Strikes:** Although the mintage of 5,000,000 would suggest plenitude in the numismatic market today, such is not the case. Years ago the 1896-S was a key issue in all grades, and today, despite some turned loose in the Treasury releases, the 1896-S is still high on the most-wanted list. Striking varies, but is usually soft. Luster is average or somewhat shallow, not deeply frosty. Bagmarks are a problem. Accordingly, connoisseurship is needed to find a just-right example, an exception to the general rule that San Francisco Mint coins offer few problems. Mint State coins, especially true of MS-64 or higher grades, are rare. Circulated examples are scarce, but not rare. Likely, most of this generous issue went to the melting pot.

**Surface Quality:** Usually average or a bit below, but sharp pieces can be found with searching. Usually somewhat subdued, unlike most other San Francisco Mint dollars of the era.

**Prooflike Coins:** Prooflike strikes are rare but win no awards for beauty. This feature was caused by the basining process, and many raised die-swirl lines are usually seen.

**Mintage and Distribution:** Delivery figures by month: January, 0; February, 100,000; March, 100,000; April, 250,000; May, 300,000; June, 300,000; July, 600,000; August, 750,000; September, 800,000; October, 550,000; November, 800,000; December, 450,000. Probably a million pieces or so were placed into circulation, and most others melted. However, some remained stored at the San Francisco Mint. On occasion a bag or two would be turned loose, but never a flood. By the 1970s the issue was viewed as being rare in Mint State.

**Die Varieties:** Minor varieties of date and mintmark positions.

## Whitman Coin Guide (WCG™)

| VG-8 | F-12 | VF-20 | EF-40 | AU-50 | MS-60 | MS-63 | MS-64 | MS-65 | MS-66 | MS-67 |
|------|------|-------|-------|-------|-------|-------|-------|-------|-------|-------|
| $33 | $38 | $65 | $250 | $750 | $1,750 | $3,250 | $4,750 | $17,500 | $74,000 | $110,000 |

**AVAILABILITY**

|  | MS-60 | MS-61 | MS-62 | MS-63 | MS-64 | MS-65 | MS-66 | MS-67 | MS-68+ |
|--|-------|-------|-------|-------|-------|-------|-------|-------|--------|
| Certified | 50 | 186 | 507 | 683 | 596 | 75 | 6 | 2 | 1 |
| Field | | 2,500-3,500 | | 1,250-1,750 | 700-1,000 | 75-100 | 6-9 | 3-5 | 1-2 |
| Cert. DMPL | 0 | 0 | 1 | 1 | 0 | 0 | 0 | 0 | 0 |

# MORGAN SILVER DOLLARS, RARE COINS, AND LIFE IN 1897

## THE MORGAN DOLLAR SCENARIO

Throughout the year, little press ink was spent on Morgan silver dollars. Perhaps no more than a dozen collectors ordered them from the branch mints (following Heaton's advice given in his 1893 *Mint Marks* treatise).

On December 17 and 18, 1897, Ed. Frossard's sale of the John F. Bateman Collection offered a selection of silver dollars, mostly all Proofs, which brought only small premiums over face value (prices realized in parentheses):

| | | |
|---|---|---|
| 1878, 8 Tail Feathers, EF ($1.50) | 1882 Fine ($1.20) | 1888 Br. Proof ($1.20) |
| 1878-CC, 7 Tail Feathers, | 1883 Br. Proof ($1.30) | 1889 Br. Proof ($1.20) |
| VF ($1.75) | 1884 Br. Proof ($1.20) | 1890 Br. Proof ($1.20) |
| 1879 Br. Proof ($1.20) | 1885 Br. Proof ($1.20) | 1891-O, VF ($1.20) |
| 1880 Br. Proof ($1.05) | 1886 Br. Proof ($1.20) | 1892 Br. Proof ($1.20) |
| 1881 Br. Proof ($1.20) | 1887 Br. Proof ($1.20) | 1893 Br. Proof ($1.20) |

## LITTLE ACTIVITY

The American Numismatic Association was inactive, and the entire coin hobby slow, as reflected by editor Heath's comment in the January issue of *The Numismatist*:

> Auction sales have not been as numerous this winter as usual, no doubt due to the stringent times and low prices that must be realized. The advice of *The Numismatist* has been to wait if possible to sell, but at the same time those who have the spare cash would be urged to buy.

On the auction scene, the two most important American sales of the year were probably Ed. Frossard's offering of the W.H. Johnson and B.H. Collins Collections on March 2 and 3, and the Chapman brothers' M.A. Brown Collection sale of April 16 and 17.[64]

## MEANWHILE, ON THE AMERICAN SCENE IN 1897

The Sandwich Islands, today known as the Hawaiian Islands, were annexed to the United States under provisions of a treaty dated June 16. The movement was largely conducted by sugar plantation owners friendly to America.

The Klondike gold rush caused great excitement, with Portland, Oregon, becoming an important staging point to Chilkoot Pass, Skagway, and the Yukon—names that soon became familiar to newspaper readers. Among others, writer Jack London traveled north to record the event. Romantic stories aside, very few miners hit pay dirt. By year's end the Klondike district was estimated to have produced $22 million worth of gold (small compared to earlier yields); still, the Klondike excitement helped bring America out of the financial doldrums caused by the Panic of 1893.

Crises in Cuba were widely covered in the press, in particular the savage actions against Cuban citizens by Spanish soldiers. Revolutionaries established a government that was not recognized by Spain. In December, President William McKinley, in his message to Congress, stated, "This is not civilized warfare. It is extermination."

Francis Church, editor of the *New York Sun*, answered an inquiry from little Virginia O'Hanlon, age eight, who had asked if Santa Claus really exists. "Yes, Virginia, there is a Santa Claus," was his famous reply. The Library of Congress building was finished in Washington near the Capitol building. Coney Island began its journey toward becoming a magnet for millions of New York City residents and vacationers, and John Jacob Astor IV opened the Waldorf-Astoria—the most luxurious large hotel in America.

# 1897

Optimal
Collecting Grade
MS-65

Circulation-
Strike Mintage
2,822,000

Proof Mintage
731

**Key to Collecting Circulation Strikes:** The 1897 Morgan dollar in Mint State is usually well struck and has nice luster, the paradigm of a common date. AU coins can be very lustrous and attractive, and years ago many were sold as "slider Uncirculated" or, curiously, as "commercial Uncirculated." Bagmarks, while not endemic among 1897 dollars, can be unsightly on lower-grade Mint State pieces. What is available or even common in a later era of Morgan dollar collecting could have been rare earlier. Such is the case with 1897, examples of which were hardly ever seen in circulation as late as 1925, a quarter century after their release.

**Surface Quality:** Usually an above-average strike. Usually lustrous and frosty.

**Prooflike Coins:** Prooflike coins are seen, but are only a fraction of the overall population.

**Mintage and Distribution:** Delivery figures by month: January, 772,000; February–May, 0; June, 600,000; July–August, 0; September, 100,000; October, 100,000; November, 450,000; December, 800,000. Although it was considered to be a scarce date, large quantities were later released, ending the drought. In the 1950s, banks in the East were deluged with them, an annoyance to numismatists. Many more bags came out in the Treasury release of 1962 through 1964, some popping up as far west as California and Nevada.

**Die Varieties:** The Mint reported that 13 obverse and 12 reverse dies were destroyed at year's end, these being the number "used" during the year. However, it is likely that for this year and others, certain reverse dies, undated and capable of coining if they are not cracked or damaged, were not destroyed, but were kept on hand for further use.

## 1897, PROOFS

**Mintage:** 731. Delivery figures by month: January–February, 0; March, 250; April–May, 0; June, 101; July–August, 0; September, 50; October–November, 0; December, 330.

**Key to Collecting Proofs:** Well struck. Deep cameo contrast.

## Whitman Coin Guide (WCG™)

| VG-8 | F-12 | VF-20 | EF-40 | AU-50 | MS-60 | MS-63 | MS-64 | MS-65 | MS-66 | MS-67 | PF-60 | PF-64 | PF-65 | PF-66 | PF-67 |
|------|------|-------|-------|-------|-------|-------|-------|-------|-------|-------|-------|-------|-------|-------|-------|
| $28 | $29 | $34 | $37 | $41 | $48 | $75 | $115 | $310 | $1,050 | $9,000 | $1,300 | $3,900 | $6,100 | $9,750 | $15,500 |

### AVAILABILITY

| | MS-60 | MS-61 | MS-62 | MS-63 | MS-64 | MS-65 | MS-66 | MS-67 | MS-68+ |
|---|-------|-------|-------|-------|-------|-------|-------|-------|--------|
| Certified | 55 | 316 | 2,007 | 8,460 | 10,464 | 2,863 | 414 | 25 | 0 |
| Field | 300,000–500,000 | | | 60,000–100,000 | 30,000–50,000 | 5,000–7,500 | 1,500–2,500 | 30–45 | 1–5 |
| Cert. DMPL | 0 | 18 | 45 | 105 | 125 | 35 | 2 | 0 | 0 |
| | PF-60 | PF-61 | PF-62 | PF-63 | PF-64 | PF-65 | PF-66 | PF-67 | PF-68+ |
| Certified | 20 | 28 | 69 | 69 | 73 | 41 | 41 | 25 | 7 |
| Field | 250–350 | | | 135–160 | 120–150 | 60–90 | 50–70 | 40–55 | 10–15 |

# 1897-O

**Optimal Collecting Grade**
MS-63

**Circulation-Strike Mintage**
4,004,000

**Key to Collecting Circulation Strikes:** The 1897-O is a cherrypicker's dream. Most are poorly or lightly struck, and on most the luster is below par as well. However, there are exceptions. While others buy certified coins of blah quality, you can track down a nice one—say, a hand-picked MS-63. A choice MS-64 or a gem MS-65 is expensive, and not easily ordered just anywhere! The 1897-O is not a key date and not much attention is paid to it by the average collector. At least, if you spend a handsome sum for a gem Proof 1895 dollar (a heck of a lot cheaper than a gem 1897-O), others at your local coin club will share your excitement.

**Surface Quality:** Strike ranges from poor to below average, not a good sign, but enough sharp pieces exist that with searching one can be found. The luster on 1897-O usually is dull and lifeless, mounting a challenge to be combined with searching for a sharp strike.

**Prooflike Coins:** Prooflike coins are rare, and when seen are usually extensively bagmarked.

**Mintage and Distribution:** Delivery figures by month: January, 240,000; February, 540,000; March, 600,000; April, 600,000; May, 600,000; June, 400,000; July–September, 0; October, 220,000; November, 450,000; December, 354,000. Mint State specimens of the 1897-O dollar are seen now and then on the market from bags paid out much earlier than 1962. From the Treasury Building in Washington, DC, bags were distributed in the late 1940s and early 1950s, but there was hardly any investor interest, and most went here and there. To investors in dollars during the 1950s and 1960s we all need to express thanks, in retrospect, for saving millions of Morgan dollars that might otherwise have gone to Nevada casinos or into general circulation.

**Die Varieties:** Minor varieties of date and mintmark positions from 22 die pairs shipped to New Orleans.

## Whitman Coin Guide (WCG™)

| VG-8 | F-12 | VF-20 | EF-40 | AU-50 | MS-60 | MS-63 | MS-64 | MS-65 | MS-66 | MS-67 |
|------|------|-------|-------|-------|-------|-------|-------|-------|-------|-------|
| $29 | $31 | $34 | $41 | $110 | $725 | $4,750 | $16,500 | $60,000 | $100,000 | $145,000 |

**AVAILABILITY**

| | MS-60 | MS-61 | MS-62 | MS-63 | MS-64 | MS-65 | MS-66 | MS-67 | MS-68+ |
|--|-------|-------|-------|-------|-------|-------|-------|-------|--------|
| Certified | 327 | 819 | 926 | 463 | 63 | 12 | 5 | 3 | 0 |
| Field | | 5,000–7,500 | | 700–1,100 | 125–175 | 15–25 | 12–18 | 5–8 | 0 |
| Cert. DMPL | 2 | 4 | 10 | 1 | 3 | 0 | 0 | 0 | 0 |

# 1897-S

Optimal
Collecting Grade
MS-64

Circulation-
Strike Mintage
5,825,000

**Key to Collecting Circulation Strikes:** Here we are, back again to a really top-notch dollar in terms of availability, strike, luster, and all else good. The 1897-S is usually all of these, and adding one to your collection can be done on just about any budget. The entire situation of 1897-S is reminiscent of the memorable-quality, but inexpensive, S Mint coins of the early years of the series.

**Surface Quality:** Usually seen well struck, decent strikes being the rule, not the exception, for San Francisco coins of this era—in contrast to those of New Orleans. Usually lustrous and attractive.

**Prooflike Coins:** Prooflike coins are fairly plentiful, but are often lightly struck and with little eye appeal. However, sharp and attractive coins can be found here and there.

**Mintage and Distribution:** Delivery figures by month: January, 800,000; February, 800,000; March, 800,000; April, 800,000; May, 800,000; June, 475,000; July–September, 0; October, 300,000; November, 600,000; December, 450,000. It's the same old story, San Francisco procedures redux. Many were stored at the Mint and were kept there for decades (although notice must be taken that the Mint "moved"—i.e., that things were relocated to a modern building in 1937). In the 1950s and 1960s the Mint was a great source for "cartwheels," as some called dollars, for the gaming tables of Nevada, by which time old-line Reno had yielded its laurels as a tourist destination to Las Vegas, what with the glittering Strip lined with casinos. Many dollars also went to coin dealers and investors (a nod to LaVere Redfield and those of like mind), providing the source for those that numismatists enjoy today.

**Die Varieties:** Minor varieties of date and mintmark positions from 38 die pairs made (but not all necessarily used).

## Whitman Coin Guide (WCG™)

| VG-8 | F-12 | VF-20 | EF-40 | AU-50 | MS-60 | MS-63 | MS-64 | MS-65 | MS-66 | MS-67 |
|------|------|-------|-------|-------|-------|-------|-------|-------|-------|-------|
| $28 | $29 | $34 | $37 | $45 | $68 | $120 | $165 | $575 | $1,375 | $5,350 |

**AVAILABILITY**

| | MS-60 | MS-61 | MS-62 | MS-63 | MS-64 | MS-65 | MS-66 | MS-67 | MS-68+ |
|---|-------|-------|-------|-------|-------|-------|-------|-------|--------|
| Certified | 52 | 354 | 1,582 | 4,457 | 4,908 | 1,717 | 318 | 31 | 2 |
| Field | | 30,000–50,000 | | 15,000–25,000 | 10,000–15,000 | 2,000–3,000 | 350–500 | 40–60 | 3–5 |
| Cert. DMPL | 5 | 13 | 41 | 95 | 182 | 72 | 11 | 1 | 0 |

# MORGAN SILVER DOLLARS, RARE COINS, AND LIFE IN 1898

## THE MORGAN DOLLAR SCENARIO

Morgan silver dollars continued to appear now and again in auctions, typically with little editorial comment attached. It was not unusual for some pieces to sell for face value, as in Ed. Frossard's sale of the New Jersey Collection, March 8, 1898, when quite a few different Proofs failed to attract bids above a dollar! However, the consignor made up the difference with other pieces that brought handsome prices for the time. The rarity of the 1895 Proof was beginning to be recognized, as no circulation strikes were made. The 1895 fetched $2.15, while other Proofs of the era brought no premium at all.

## COIN DESIGNS FOUND WANTING

Not only were silver Proofs out of favor, but gold Proof coins had little in the way of an aftermarket. Many collectors who purchased silver and gold Proofs in the 1880s and early 1890s simply spent them in the waning years of the 1890s and in the early 20th century. As Dr. Heath had suggested in *The Numismatist* in 1897, it was a good time to buy coins, not a good time to sell. It seemed that padlocks were put on many checkbooks.

Probably a good part of the malaise for gold and silver Proofs lay in the view that Barber's dime, quarter, and half dollar were perceived as being unattractive, and ditto for the Liberty Head or Coronet gold coins.

> The designs on some of our coins are not artistic or beautiful. On some the significance and appropriateness of the design has been destroyed in an unsuccessful effort to improve its appearance. On most of them there is too much work, the devices are too elaborate and the effort for artistic effect is overdone. The designs could well be simplified and their beauty be thus increased, and the coins remain brighter and afford less chance for the accumulation of dirt.
>
> France has recently paid large sums of money to some of her most eminent artists for new designs for her coins. It is submitted as proper that the Secretary of the Treasury should have the authority to seek new and more attractive designs for our coins, but not to be adopted until first submitted to Congress for its approval.

Of course, by now there had been many complaints about the Morgan dollar—and "experts" agreed that the motif was inappropriate. However, production went on, and on, and on, and the design never was changed!

In February 1898, George E. Roberts was named director of the Mint, succeeding Robert E. Preston, who had been in the post since November 1898. Roberts would serve through July 1907.

## MEANWHILE, ON THE AMERICAN SCENE IN 1898

Early in the year the battleship *Maine* was sent to the harbor of Havana, Cuba, to protect American interests in the island, which was in a wild state of insurrection. New York newspaper publisher William Randolph Hearst dispatched well-known painter Frederic Remington (his depictions of cowboys, Indians, and other Western scenes were particularly admired) to Cuba to record on canvas different war scenes. The artist sent a telegram stating that everything was quiet and there was no war, and Hearst gave the famous reply, "You furnish the pictures and I'll furnish the war."

Then came the defining moment: a mysterious explosion and subsequent sinking of the USS *Maine* in Havana harbor on February 15. Two days later Hearst's *New York Journal* offered a $50,000 reward for "the conviction of the criminals who sent 258 American sailors to their death. Naval officers are unanimous that the ship was destroyed on purpose." Eager to stir up events and be on hand for the proceedings, Hearst anchored his private yacht in Havana harbor.

Hearst and others whipped the public into a frenzy, and the phrase "Remember the Maine!" was the rallying cry. Thousands of young American men were eager to fight, perhaps to emulate the heroism of their fathers in the Civil War. Since 1865 the only "wars" of significance conducted by American troops had been against essentially defenseless Indian men, women, and children—not much opportunity for glory and honor, although General George Armstrong Custer had been praised to the skies posthumously for giving his life for his country in the Battle of the Little Big Horn on June 25, 1876.

War was declared against Spain on April 25. In time, American newspaper readers were enthralled by tales of glory, as when Commodore George Dewey headed a fleet that steamed into the Bay of Manila in the Philippines. His flagship, the USS *Olympia*, arrived late at night on April 30; the Battle of Manila Bay commenced on May 1 at 5:40 a.m., when Dewey said to the captain of the Olympia, "You may fire when you are ready, Gridley," a phrase that became popular with Americans for a long time afterward. About seven hours later a cease-fire was ordered, by which time the entire Spanish squadron of 10 ships had been destroyed. No Americans were killed, and eight were slightly wounded. On May 11 Dewey was promoted to rear admiral.

On July 1, Lieutenant Colonel Theodore Roosevelt and his Rough Riders, on foot, charged Kettle Hill in the direction of San Juan Hill, as part of an invasion that had commenced in June. Roosevelt captured the elevation, extensive articles praised him in the press, and his popularity with the public went up another notch.

On August 12, 1898, a peace settlement was signed with Spain, and on December 10 the Treaty of Paris brought a formal end to the war. Spain ceded the Philippine Islands, Puerto Rico, and Guam to the United States, and withdrew from Cuba, giving that country its freedom under the watchful eye of America. Many Americans became excited at the prospect of imperialism—controlling foreign lands in the manner that Great Britain, Germany, France, Spain, and other European powers had done for a long time and in some instances were still doing, particularly in the domination of areas in South America, Africa, and the Far East.

In Springfield, Massachusetts, the Indian brand motorcycle was first made by Hendee Manufacturing Company. It was a specifically designed vehicle vastly improving on earlier devices, which were simply bicycles with attached engines. Large-scale production of the Indian would commence in 1902, and in the following year, 1903, the Harley-Davidson would set a new standard. In the meantime, in 1898 the development of automobiles forged ahead, and commercial production reached the 1,000 mark, up from about only 100 in 1897. Pneumatic tires became popular during the decade, and in 1898 in Akron, Ohio, the Goodyear Tire and Rubber Company was founded to make such accessories.

This was also the glory year of the Klondike, following up on the gold discovery made on August 16, 1896. Beginning in a large way in 1897, continuing through the winter of early 1898 and then into the warmer months, well over 20,000 prospectors visited the area. It was estimated that no more than one in a hundred people who went to the Klondike ever found enough gold to make the trip even slightly worthwhile.

In Davenport, Iowa, Daniel David Palmer, characterized as a "magnetic healer," opened the Palmer School of Chiropractic to teach others how to improve the health and well-being of patients by manipulating the spine and other joints.

The National Biscuit Company was formed by the consolidation of more than 100 regional bakeries, comprising the majority of the larger commercial firms. The Uneeda Biscuit, one of the first new products, consisted of mass-marketed soda crackers, which had largely been sold in barrels before. Large UNEEDA BISCUIT signs were painted on the sides of buildings, a popular way of advertising (already, MAIL POUCH CHEWING TOBACCO advertisements were emblazoned on hundreds of barns in America).

# 1898

Optimal
Collecting Grade
MS-65

Circulation-
Strike Mintage
5,884,000

Proof Mintage
735

**Key to Collecting Circulation Strikes:** The 1898 Morgan dollar is plentiful in any and all grades, from worn (though usually in VF or EF, toned gray) to gem Mint State. Most are well struck and have good luster. Many Proofs exist in remarkably high grades. Perhaps due to the semimoribund state of the coin hobby (see yearly narratives for 1897 and 1898), not as many people were cleaning coins!

**Surface Quality:** Usually seen well struck. Usually with attractive mint frost.

**Prooflike Coins:** Many prooflike coins exist, one sided as well as two sided, but are not deeply mirrored. DMPL coins with cameo contrast are rare indeed.

**Mintage and Distribution:** Delivery figures by month: January, 650,000; February, 582,000; March, 600,000; April, 184,000; May, 520,000; June, 172,000; July, 100,000; August, 948,000; September, 800,000; October, 450,000; November, 572,000; December, 306,000. Similar to certain other high-mintage Philadelphia Mint dates, the dollars of 1898 were scarce in and after the time they were made, but later became exceedingly common. Many bags were paid out in the mid-20th century, with more appearing in the late 1950s and early 1960s. Out in Nevada, LaVere Redfield, dollar hoarder par excellence, got his hands on an estimated 16 to 18 bags, and many were held by other investors.

**Die Varieties:** Minor varieties of date position from 30 pairs of dies prepared for circulation strikes. In addition, two obverses and three reverses were made for Proofs.

## 1898, PROOFS

**Mintage:** 735. Delivery figures by month: January, 0; February, 225; March, 75; April–May, 0; June, 100; July–August, 0; September, 75; October–November, 0; December, 260.

**Key to Collecting Proofs:** Proofs typically have nice cameo contrast, and in recent years the certification services have been noting such on their labels. In addition, they are well struck. Michael Fuljenz: "This date was probably the best made in the entire series."[65]

## Whitman Coin Guide (WCG™)

| VG-8 | F-12 | VF-20 | EF-40 | AU-50 | MS-60 | MS-63 | MS-64 | MS-65 | MS-66 | MS-67 | PF-60 | PF-64 | PF-65 | PF-66 | PF-67 |
|------|------|-------|-------|-------|-------|-------|-------|-------|-------|-------|-------|-------|-------|-------|-------|
| $28 | $29 | $34 | $37 | $41 | $48 | $65 | $90 | $235 | $675 | $6,500 | $1,300 | $3,900 | $6,100 | $9,750 | $15,500 |

### AVAILABILITY

| | MS-60 | MS-61 | MS-62 | MS-63 | MS-64 | MS-65 | MS-66 | MS-67 | MS-68+ |
|---|---|---|---|---|---|---|---|---|---|
| Certified | 57 | 326 | 2,190 | 9,485 | 13,067 | 4,562 | 1,055 | 48 | 0 |
| Field | | 200,000–300,000 | | 50,000–80,000 | 30,000–50,000 | 10,000–15,000 | 1,000–1,500 | 25–40 | 1–5 |
| Cert. DMPL | 6 | 19 | 71 | 200 | 245 | 94 | 16 | 1 | 0 |
| | PF-60 | PF-61 | PF-62 | PF-63 | PF-64 | PF-65 | PF-66 | PF-67 | PF-68+ |
| Certified | 17 | 22 | 40 | 60 | 94 | 46 | 31 | 16 | 11 |
| Field | | 125–175 | | 150–250 | 200–250 | 110–130 | 80–120 | 35–50 | 20–30 |

# 1898-O

Optimal
Collecting Grade
MS-65

Circulation-
Strike Mintage
4,440,000

**Key to Collecting Circulation Strikes:** The 1898-O is the first of the "big three" rarities released from a long-sealed vault in November 1962 to ignite the great Treasury-release treasure hunt. Previously, in Mint State the 1898-O was a rarity. Today, the 1898-O is plentiful in all grades, including gem Mint State. Striking varies, and some are lightly defined. However, enough sharp pieces are on hand that you'll find one easily. Considering their numismatic history and their beauty, it is easy to fall in love with an 1898-O dollar. In fact, for a sense of numismatic tradition, I suggest that you acquire Mint State pieces of each of the big three in the limelight in the 1962 release—this plus the 1903-O and 1904-O.

**Surface Quality:** Striking of the 1898-O ranges from poor to sharp, but is usually above average. Usually lustrous and attractive. Prooflike pieces are seen on occasion.

**Prooflike Coins:** Prooflike coins range from "semi" to full and are not rare. DMPL coins with good cameo contrast are also fairly plentiful and are popular, but become harder to find as the years slip by.

**Mintage and Distribution:** Delivery figures by month: January–April, 0; May, 500,000; June, 600,000; July, 210,000; August, 750,000; September, 30,000; October, 1,000,000; November, 450,000; December, 900,000. In late 1962 and early 1963, the 1898-O and the 1904-O dollar were released in quantities of thousands of Uncirculated bags. The 1904-O is slightly the more available of the two. Earlier, both the 1898-O and the 1904-O were very rare.

**Die Varieties:** Minor varieties of date and mintmark positions from 30 pairs of dies. As always, the possibility exists that new, interesting varieties may be found. The latest edition of the VAM book is significantly expanded from the first one.

## Whitman Coin Guide (WCG™)

| VG-8 | F-12 | VF-20 | EF-40 | AU-50 | MS-60 | MS-63 | MS-64 | MS-65 | MS-66 | MS-67 |
|------|------|-------|-------|-------|-------|-------|-------|-------|-------|-------|
| $28 | $29 | $34 | $37 | $41 | $48 | $65 | $85 | $165 | $385 | $1,850 |

### AVAILABILITY

| | MS-60 | MS-61 | MS-62 | MS-63 | MS-64 | MS-65 | MS-66 | MS-67 | MS-68+ |
|---|-------|-------|-------|-------|-------|-------|-------|-------|--------|
| Certified | 43 | 270 | 3,404 | 28,413 | 55,149 | 22,635 | 3,620 | 324 | 1 |
| Field | 250,000–400,000 | | | 200,000–300,000 | 150,000–250,000 | 40,000–60,000 | 5,000–7,500 | 250–400 | 35–50 |
| Cert. DMPL | 3 | 15 | 81 | 277 | 471 | 217 | 55 | 3 | 1 |

# 1898-S

**Optimal Collecting Grade MS-64**

**Circulation-Strike Mintage 4,102,000**

**Key to Collecting Circulation Strikes:** The 1898-S is sometimes seen softly struck, so some searching is needed to find a choice one. Luster is subtle, even satiny. There are enough 1898-S dollars around that an MS-63 is easily enough found, and an MS-64 coin is within reach. Gem MS-65 and higher pieces are in the minority, but are not rarities.

**Surface Quality:** Usually seen well struck, but there are exceptions. As always, a good eye helps form a good collection. Usually lustrous and attractive.

**Prooflike Coins:** Some are prooflike, but they usually have low contrast.

**Mintage and Distribution:** Delivery figures by month: January, 600,000; February, 450,000; March, 500,000; April, 500,000; May, 276,000; June, 44,000; July–September, 0; October, 552,000; November, 380,000; December, 800,000. Much of the mintage of the 1898-S went into storage at the San Francisco Mint. Large numbers of bags were paid out in the 1920s, when there was little numismatic interest, and nearly all went into circulation. More bags were released in the 1940s and 1950s, with many going to Nevada casinos, although some were picked up by dealers and investors. By time of the 1962 through 1964 Treasury release, most had long since fled from the vaults.

**Die Varieties:** Many varieties of date and mintmark positions from 20 obverse and 15 reverse dies shipped. Among the varieties, VAM-6 has a sharply doubled mintmark, with the first and lighter mintmarks appearing lower. This particular variety also has a slightly doubled date. VAM-10 of 1898-S has the S mintmark tilted dramatically to the right, quite interesting to observe.

## Whitman Coin Guide (WCG™)

| VG-8 | F-12 | VF-20 | EF-40 | AU-50 | MS-60 | MS-63 | MS-64 | MS-65 | MS-66 | MS-67 |
|------|------|-------|-------|-------|-------|-------|-------|-------|-------|-------|
| $35 | $37 | $40 | $50 | $95 | $250 | $440 | $600 | $2,050 | $5,250 | $22,000 |

**AVAILABILITY**

|  | MS-60 | MS-61 | MS-62 | MS-63 | MS-64 | MS-65 | MS-66 | MS-67 | MS-68+ |
|--|-------|-------|-------|-------|-------|-------|-------|-------|--------|
| Certified | 62 | 288 | 841 | 1,612 | 1,722 | 496 | 75 | 2 | 2 |
| Field | | 12,500–17,500 | | 7,500–12,500 | 5,000–8,000 | 800–1,200 | 60–75 | 3–5 | 3–5 |
| Cert. DMPL | 0 | 3 | 16 | 47 | 51 | 8 | 0 | 0 | 0 |

# MORGAN SILVER DOLLARS, RARE COINS, AND LIFE IN 1899

## THE MORGAN DOLLAR SCENARIO

An article in the June 1899 issue of *The Numismatist* advised readers that some two million regular-issue silver dollars of earlier dates, being stored in vaults in Philadelphia, were

> rusty and moldy, having been wet by water which percolated through the vaults of the Mint years ago, and caused the bags in which they were stored to rot. This might seem a serious matter were it not for the fact that the dollars are not really intended for circulation. They are simply held to give value and security to the Silver Certificates issued against them, and for this reason they will not be cleaned, not being needed for circulation, but will be allowed to continue to rust and grow tarnish in the splendid big vaults of the new Mint.

In the September issue of the same magazine, editor Heath replied to A.W. Reeves, a Chicago reader who asked how to clean tarnished coins: "If Mr. Reeves will obtain at his grocer's some 'Putz Pomade' and use it as directed he may yet be happy. For cleaning silver (even Proof coins) it is, in the editorial mind, the cleaner and polisher par excellence."

Unfortunately for later numismatists, during this era countless lightly toned silver coins, including many Proof and other Morgan dollars, were subjected to "cleaners and polishers par excellence," and their values diminished sharply. Even the silver coins in the Mint Cabinet were brightened with silver polish!

The *Annual Report of the Director of the Mint*, 1899, told this:

> The Carson City Mint was reduced officially at the end of the fiscal year to an assay office authorized by Congress in the act carrying the appropriation of the maintenance of the institution. Thus, the Carson City Mint was a mint until June 30, 1899, although no coins had been struck there since 1893. After that it was an assay office.

Soon, a bunch of Morgan dollar dies with the CC mintmark would be realized to be completely useless in Nevada, and conservation measures would taken to extract some value from them by fitting them up with an O mintmark for service elsewhere. Five million Morgan dollars, each with a little CC below the eagle's tail, would be shipped from the Carson City Mint to other destinations, including the Treasury Building in Washington, DC, where in time they would form the bulk of the fabulous GSA silver dollar sales of the 1970s.

## HOBBY NEWS AND NOTES

Joseph Hooper, newly elected president of the still somewhat sluggish American Numismatic Association, promised that he would follow "in the footsteps of illustrious predecessors," a phrase taken from an 1837 Hard Times token satirical toward Martin Van Buren, a reflection of the great and still growing interest in tokens of all kinds. Meanwhile, Dr. Benjamin P. Wright's series of articles on tokens continued in *The Numismatist*.

Per the opinion of historian John W. Adams, there were no "A"-quality auctions held in 1899;[66] there were seven B-rated auctions. Ed. Frossard's first sale (No. 161 as he continued his father's numbering sequence) was not among them, nor did the Chapman brothers make the cut. Five of the seven were conducted by the estimable Lyman H. Low, while the other two were conducted under the aegis of the New York Coin & Stamp Co.

Veteran dealer Édouard Frossard died. "What loss to the numismatic world," lamented editor Heath in the April issue of *The Numismatist*, who continued, "twas not a transition from life to death, but rather one from death to life eternal." In the next month it was announced that his son, also named Ed. Frossard, would continue the business. Unfortunately, by early 1902 the younger Frossard had proved to be a crook, a poor successor to his father, and in April of that year *The Numismatist* related, "We are informed that civil and criminal warrants have been issued for his arrest as soon as he can be located."

It remained a good time to buy federal silver and gold coins, including mintmarked issues, as these series were out of the limelight. Among the leading collectors of the time was Virgil M. Brand, wealthy Chicago brewer, who endeavored to collect as many different United States and world coins as possible, although he had not been inspired by Heaton's *Mint Marks* treatise, and concentrated on year dates. Brand could discuss with equal facility minor copper coins of Europe, the territorial gold of Clark, Gruber & Co., and Seasons medals dated 1796 and later used in the Lewis and Clark expedition.

In Pennsylvania, oilman John M. Clapp continued to be an avid buyer, eagerly devouring just about anything offered to him that he did not already possess. Each year he ordered coins from the various mints (Philadelphia, New Orleans, and San Francisco) while at the same time he employed bankers to look through stocks of gold coins for desirable dates and mintmarks.

One of the "quietest" collectors of the era was Colonel James W. Ellsworth, who had served on the board of the World's Columbian Exposition in 1892 and 1893, and in recent times had been president of the Chicago National Bank. Over a period of time Ellsworth acquired Nova Constellatio pattern coins of 1783, a 1787 gold Brasher doubloon, a Class I and a Class III 1804 dollar, and many other treasures. Many of these later went to Ambassador John Work Garrett, a son of T. Harrison Garrett, the Baltimore numismatist.

## MEANWHILE, ON THE AMERICAN SCENE IN 1899

At noon on January 1, 1899, the American flag was raised in front of the public buildings in Cuba. Throughout the island there were many demonstrations for "Cuba Libre" (Free Cuba). A treaty was perfected in which Spain turned over the sovereignty of Cuba, Puerto Rico, Guam, and the Philippine Islands to the United States, which agreed to pay $20,000,000 to Spain as indemnity for expenses for public benefit in the Philippines. The transition in government control from Spain to the United States in the Philippines was not as easy as in Cuba, and in those islands there was much domestic unrest and resentment of the American forces. Soon, as an aid to local commerce, quantities of 1898-S dimes, quarters, and half dollars would be on their way to the Philippines. The annexation of the Philippine Islands was fraught with many problems, and on February 14, 1899, two American soldiers fired on Filipino soldiers in Manila, precipitating military battles and skirmishes that would last nearly four years.

The United Mine Workers of America was formed by consolidating workers' groups and another union, and would become a powerful commercial and political influence for years to come. Mines were very poorly regulated at the time, safety measures were few, and many workers, including teenage boys, were killed in accidents, with scarcely anyone in management taking notice.

In Berwick, Pennsylvania, the American Car and Foundry Company was established to manufacture railroad equipment. Numismatist William H. Woodin became important in the company, which contributed to his family fortune. In the same year the International Paper Company was formed by merging over two dozen smaller firms. The American Smelting & Refining Company combined the interests of different copper producers to form a trust, and the United Fruit Company was incorporated. United Fruit had extensive interest in Central America, giving rise to the term *banana republic* for a country whose prime business was exporting fruit to America.

In Philadelphia, G.H.K. Curtis appointed George Horace Lorimer as editor in chief of the somewhat sleepy *Saturday Evening Post,* a magazine with a circulation of less than 2,000. In coming years Lorimer would build Curtis Publishing into an empire; the *Saturday Evening Post* would attract more than three million subscribers, and in its pages would appear the works of many American writers and artists—making it the leading magazine of the coming generation.

In 1899 Coca-Cola was sold as a bottled beverage for the first time, earlier having been dispensed as a soda-fountain syrup to be added to carbonated water. By this time, crimped metal caps (Crown cork seal caps) were replacing spring-loaded rubber stoppers in beverage bottles.

# 1899

**Optimal
Collecting Grade
MS-64**

**Circulation-
Strike Mintage
330,000**

**Proof Mintage
846**

**Key to Collecting Circulation Strikes:** Despite its low mintage, the 1899 Morgan dollar is rather plentiful on the market, causing several well-known authorities to doubt the mintage total. Circulated coins are scarce, but the demand for them is muted by the wide availability of Mint State coins. Apparently, few 1899 Morgan dollars were released into circulation at that time, for years later in 1925 a serious specialist could not find one, despite a lot of searching through quantities of dollar coins. Wonder what he would say now!

**Surface Quality:** The striking varies from below average to sharp, usually average or above. The luster is usually satiny and attractive.

**Prooflike Coins:** Prooflike coins are in the distinct minority, and when seen they usually have low contrast.

**Mintage and Distribution:** Delivery figures by month: January, 0; February, 76,000; March–April, 0; May, 214,000; June–November, 0; December, 40,000. At the time these low-mintage dollars were coined, few were paid into circulation. Collectors wanting one had to buy a Proof. Then came the silver rush, and bags were paid out in the 1950s, with dealer Harry J. Forman nabbing about 10 bags of these coins from—of all places—Las Vegas. Probably from 50,000 to 100,000 Mint State 1899 dollars were released in that decade, followed by others later, including bags in Montana in early 1962 and thereafter, in California and Nevada.

**Die Varieties:** Minor varieties of date/mintmark position from three obverse dies made. New reverses were also made, but others were on hand from earlier times.

## 1899, PROOFS

**Mintage:** 846. Delivery figures by month: January–February, 0; March, 301; April–May, 0; June, 73; July–August, 0; September, 145; October–November, 0; December, 327.

**Key to Collecting Proofs:** Proof dollars of 1899 are fairly good contrast but not as "cameo" as certain immediately preceding years. There is no universally accepted definition of *cameo* in the trade, and opinions vary, as do labels affixed to holders.

## Whitman Coin Guide (WCG™)

| VG-8 | F-12 | VF-20 | EF-40 | AU-50 | MS-60 | MS-63 | MS-64 | MS-65 | MS-66 | MS-67 | PF-60 | PF-64 | PF-65 | PF-66 | PF-67 |
|---|---|---|---|---|---|---|---|---|---|---|---|---|---|---|---|
| $145 | $155 | $165 | $185 | $205 | $255 | $290 | $375 | $925 | $2,050 | $6,750 | $1,300 | $3,900 | $6,100 | $9,750 | $15,500 |

**AVAILABILITY**

| | MS-60 | MS-61 | MS-62 | MS-63 | MS-64 | MS-65 | MS-66 | MS-67 | MS-68+ |
|---|---|---|---|---|---|---|---|---|---|
| Certified | 94 | 563 | 2,216 | 5,796 | 6,240 | 1,629 | 269 | 21 | 0 |
| Field | 40,000–60,000 | | | 25,000–40,000 | 9,000–12,000 | 2,500–4,000 | 250–400 | 25–40 | 1–5 |
| Cert. DMPL | 1 | 6 | 43 | 83 | 132 | 66 | 19 | 0 | 0 |
| | PF-60 | PF-61 | PF-62 | PF-63 | PF-64 | PF-65 | PF-66 | PF-67 | PF-68+ |
| Certified | 17 | 32 | 59 | 86 | 87 | 36 | 36 | 20 | 7 |
| Field | 200–300 | | | 160–210 | 125–175 | 60–90 | 55–70 | 35–50 | 10–12 |

# 1899-O

**Optimal Collecting Grade**
MS-65

**Circulation-Strike Mintage**
12,290,000

**Key to Collecting Circulation Strikes:** The 1899-O was another star in the great Treasury release of autumn 1962, but not of the fame of the 1898-O, 1903-O, and 1904-O, those three being acknowledged as rarities before the deluge. Although the striking quality varies, sharp pieces can be found without much problem among the large numbers on the market. The usual 1899-O is sparkling and beautiful to behold.

**Surface Quality:** Striking varies from below average to sharp, but is generally above average. Still, discrimination is advised when buying a specimen. Most 1899-O dollars are lustrous and attractive.

**Prooflike Coins:** Prooflike coins are scarce. DMPLs with cameo contrast can be of stunning beauty in high grades.

**Mintage and Distribution:** Delivery figures by month: January, 1,200,000; February, 1,100,000; March, 1,350,000; April, 1,350,000; May, 1,500,000; June, 700,000; July, 360,000; August, 830,000; September, 870,000; October, 1,000,000; November, 950,000; December, 1,080,000. In Mint State the 1899-O was elusive in early years. In 1947 and 1948, and continuing into the early 1950s, a few bags emerged from hiding in the Treasury Building in Washington, DC, and were shipped to banks, although thousands went to collectors and dealers. In November 1962 a Niagara of 1899-O dollars cascaded from the famous long-sealed (since 1929) vault in the Philadelphia Mint. Today, Mint State coins are abundant.

**Die Varieties:** There are many die varieties of this year from 85 pairs prepared, most with medium O mintmark, with some exceptions. *1899-O "Micro o" variety, VAM-4, 5, and 6:* small mint letter. Elusive; although some Mint State coins exist, they sell for a sharp premium if identified.

VAM-4

VAM-5

VAM-5

VAM-6

## Whitman Coin Guide (WCG™)

| VG-8 | F-12 | VF-20 | EF-40 | AU-50 | MS-60 | MS-63 | MS-64 | MS-65 | MS-66 | MS-67 |
|------|------|-------|-------|-------|-------|-------|-------|-------|-------|-------|
| $28 | $29 | $34 | $37 | $40 | $48 | $65 | $95 | $190 | $440 | $2,250 |

**AVAILABILITY**

| | MS-60 | MS-61 | MS-62 | MS-63 | MS-64 | MS-65 | MS-66 | MS-67 | MS-68+ |
|--|-------|-------|-------|-------|-------|-------|-------|-------|--------|
| Certified | 56 | 391 | 4,531 | 28,303 | 42,178 | 14,167 | 2,202 | 192 | 1 |
| Field | 300,000–500,000 | | | 175,000–250,000 | 125,000–200,000 | 20,000–30,000 | 1,750–2,250 | 120–160 | 5–10 |
| Cert. DMPL | 1 | 5 | 27 | 73 | 134 | 65 | 25 | 4 | 0 |

# 1899-S

**Optimal
Collecting Grade**
MS-64

**Circulation-
Strike Mintage**
2,562,000

**Key to Collecting Circulation Strikes:** The 1899-S is of medium scarcity. The typical Mint State coin is well struck and has excellent luster. Bagmarks are slight and not a problem with most 1899-S dollars, a pleasant aspect. Most coins in the MS-63 to MS-65 range are attractive indeed. Circulated coins, while not among the commonest, attract little market interest.

**Surface Quality:** Usually seen quite well struck. Finding an example will be no problem at all. Usually with rich, frosty luster.

**Prooflike Coins:** Often seen prooflike, but not with high contrast.

**Mintage and Distribution:** Delivery figures by month: January, 336,000; February, 336,000; March, 550,000; April, 284,000; May, 500,000; June, 510,000; July, 46,000; August– December, 0. Following the same script used for many other San Francisco dollars, those of 1899-S were scarce in early times, but later were paid out in quantity from Mint vaults. Most were released from about 1942 to the mid-1950s, with many going to collectors and dealers, but vastly more reaching general circulation and the gaming tables of Nevada. By the early 1960s most bags were gone.

**Die Varieties:** Minor varieties of date and mintmark positions from 20 pairs of dies. At least two styles of mintmark punches were used, one being "narrow and medium" and the other being wide.

## Whitman Coin Guide (WCG™)

| VG-8 | F-12 | VF-20 | EF-40 | AU-50 | MS-60 | MS-63 | MS-64 | MS-65 | MS-66 | MS-67 |
|------|------|-------|-------|-------|-------|-------|-------|-------|-------|-------|
| $30 | $33 | $45 | $65 | $120 | $375 | $450 | $775 | $1,900 | $3,400 | $20,000 |

### AVAILABILITY

| | MS-60 | MS-61 | MS-62 | MS-63 | MS-64 | MS-65 | MS-66 | MS-67 | MS-68+ |
|-----------|-------|-------|-------|-------|-------|-------|-------|-------|--------|
| Certified | 47 | 211 | 696 | 1,635 | 1,836 | 549 | 129 | 8 | 0 |
| Field | | 10,000–15,000 | | 6,000–9,000 | 3,500–5,000 | 600–900 | 125–175 | 12–16 | 0 |
| Cert. DMPL | 0 | 3 | 10 | 25 | 43 | 5 | 4 | 0 | 0 |

# MORGAN SILVER DOLLARS, RARE COINS, AND LIFE IN 1900

## THE MORGAN DOLLAR SCENARIO

In *The Numismatist*, March 1900, editor George F. Heath included this:

> Did you ever try to pick out United States mintmarked dollars by examining the edge? Did you know that the dollars in the Philadelphia Mint are broader than those from New Orleans and San Francisco? They are, as can readily be determined by driving two pins in a board so that a mintmarked dollar will pass easily between them, at the same time touching both; now try to pass the Philadelphia dollar between the pins and it will be found appreciably larger.
>
> Take a stack of dollars and note that some have an edge with rounded corners, the milling being plain in the center of the edge but not reaching the corners; these are all Philadelphia coinage. The others, from branch mints, were struck with a slightly smaller collar, with the result that the milling shows across the whole edge, the corners being sharp.

Today, in the early 21st century, some numismatists are concerned with the edges of Morgan dollars and such technicalities that Heath mentioned, but the subject is hardly popular. In addition, the number of vertical edge-reeds varies on certain Morgan dollars, the Van Allen–Mallis text exploring this in depth. However, with the popularity of certified coins in "slabs," few collectors today have the opportunity to examine edges at all.

## RESTYLED SILVER DOLLAR REVERSE

In 1900 an alteration was made to the reverse design, and hubs and master dies now were slightly different than the style in use since the Reverse of 1879 (SAF). The new style, known by variety collectors as C4, has a larger space between the eagle's neck and the wing edge to the right of the neck (eagle's left wing), and less detail on the feathers of the eagle's breast. This new hub was used to produce dies first used for coinage in 1900 at the Philadelphia and San Francisco mints, while the New Orleans Mint continued to use old dies on hand. At the Philadelphia Mint, where all dies were made, some existing reverses stamped with the old reverse were overpunched with the new. The features overlapped for the most part, but not completely, and "new hub over old hub" reverses have two olives connected above the branch, with the uppermost one being shallow.

A mixture of die styles was used through 1904, sometimes all three (old hub, new hub over old, and new hub) within a single year. The aspect is very technical, and not even *The Top 100 Die Varieties* study addresses it today. However, abundant details will be found in *The Comprehensive Catalogue and Encyclopedia of Morgan and Peace Dollars*, by Leroy C. Van Allen and A. George Mallis, now in its fourth edition.

## MEANWHILE, ON THE AMERICAN SCENE IN 1900

In the year 1900 the United States population stood at 75,994,575, per the decennial census. Roman Catholics numbered 12 million, compared to 6 million Methodists, 5 million Baptists, 1.5 million Lutherans, 1.5 million Presbyterians, 1 million Jews, 700,000 Episcopalians, 350,000 Mormons, 80,000 Christian Scientists, and 75,000 Unitarians. About 76 million people were natives of the United States, with 10.3 million being of foreign birth. About 9 million were black or of mixed blood, about 237,000 were American Indians or partly Indian, about 90,000 were Chinese, and about 24,000 were Japanese. The typical life expectancy for an American white male was about 48 years and for a female, 51 years. During the ensuing decade, formally beginning in 1901, about 9 million immigrants would arrive in the United States.

Telephone systems continued to expand. By 1900, most important business offices and stores in larger cities were connected, including most of the larger rare coin dealers, but fewer than one residence in a dozen had such a device. Relatively few homes in villages and small towns had indoor plumbing, and across America just one house in seven had a bathtub.

In towns and cities commercial baths served to help with cleanliness, although it was not at all unusual for people to go weeks at a time without bathing, particularly in the colder months. Privies were standard in backyards in towns and villages.

In 1900 the economy was fast showing signs of new prosperity, and in many areas of the country the hard times of the 1890s were history. Americans reveled in their victory in the Spanish-American War. There was enthusiasm in the air. The presidential campaign pitted incumbent William McKinley against his losing 1896 challenger, William Jennings Bryan, he of "Cross of Gold" speech fame. McKinley's slogan, "The full dinner pail," was intended to reflect the well-being of working people. Bryan attempted to reignite the "free silver" excitement of the 1896 campaign, but few voters were interested now, and in November he gained just 155 electoral votes as opposed to McKinley's 292. McKinley's running mate was none other than Theodore "Teddy" Roosevelt, sportsman, author, raconteur, lover of the "strenuous life," and the hero of the battle of San Juan Hill.

In Chicago the Everleigh Club opened at 2131 Dearborn Street under sisters Minna and Ada Everleigh, who used a $40,000 inheritance to equip a bordello with ornate fixtures and amenities, including musicians on the ground floor. In the meantime, in New Orleans on Basin Street a two-block section known as Storeyville, approved by the town aldermen, was set aside for houses of pleasure, and in Kansas City there were nearly 150 such establishments. Such were not a "big deal" in the eyes of most Americans, and the age of social reform had yet to arrive.

On June 3, 1900, the International Ladies Garment Workers Union was formed in New York City. By this time, only 3.5% of the American work force was organized. Young children continued to be a large segment of labor in mines and factories, and were considered expendable by many employers. Most workers had no benefits, and if injured were simply laid off or fired—no more "full dinner pail" for them.

On November 10, at Madison Square Garden in New York City, the National Automobile Show opened to the public, the first such event. On view were 19 different brands of gasoline vehicles, six powered by electricity, seven steam-operated ones, and two hybrids. The Stanley Steamer in particular was highly acclaimed for its power and durability. The automobile industry continued to expand by leaps and bounds, and by December 31 there were 13,824 registered cars in the United States. During the year the Packard, Stearns, Peerless, Franklin, Auburn, and White marques were introduced, among others. In years to come dozens of manufacturers, some set up in garages, others with facilities in sprawling factories, would produce hundreds of makes and models, until in the 1920s when consolidation occurred on a large scale.

In Camden, New Jersey, the Consolidated Talking Machine Company, owned by Eldridge Johnson, used a trademark consisting of a fox terrier, "Nipper," with his head cocked to listen to a phonograph horn, with the slogan "His master's voice." During the decade, phonographs of the cylinder and disc types would become increasingly popular, and most communities would have at least one store with a display of Edison, Victor, Columbia, and other brands.

A decade earlier, in 1890, the "Gibson Girl," drawn in pen and ink by Charles Dana Gibson, age 22, had made her debut in *Life*, a humorous weekly magazine. Gibson, who studied for a short time under Augustus Saint-Gaudens, initiated a movement for the "ideal American girl," which caught the public's fancy. In the first decade of the 20th century, the ideal American Girl would be further developed by many other artists, Harrison Fisher and Philip Boileau prominent among them. An entire genre of stories and novels arose accordingly, often depicting an American girl of modest means who marries a wealthy financier and enjoys the trappings of society or, better yet, becomes a member of royalty in a foreign country (such as the mythical Graustark). Gibson himself fared well financially, until the St. Nicholas Bank, New York City, failed in the Panic of 1907, and he lost most of his fortune.

In 1900, L. Frank Baum's novel *The Wizard of Oz* was published. The Tin Man and Dorothy would endure to enchant future generations.

# 1900

Optimal
Collecting Grade
MS-65

Circulation-
Strike Mintage
8,830,000

Proof Mintage
912

**Key to Collecting Circulation Strikes:** A new reverse hub was introduced this year. Coins struck from dies made from this hub have less definition to the eagle's breast feathers, introducing another aspect into grading techniques—as now a coin can be a full strike but not have full feathers! However, some old reverse dies continued in use in the next several years, alongside the new ones. Dollars of the 1900 date range from well struck to poorly defined, and from lustrous and frosty to dull and insipid. They are common enough, and although some discrimination is needed when buying, opportunities will abound.

**Surface Quality:** Striking is usually below average. Sharp pieces can be found but require some searching. Luster varies from dull and unattractive to somewhat pleasing. Again, cherrypicking is advised. More than just a few have raised die striae (tiny parallel raised lines) in the fields, from the basining process, probably using too large a grit size.

**Prooflike Coins:** Occasionally prooflike pieces are seen, but the contrast is not sharp.

**Mintage and Distribution:** Delivery figures by month: January, 0; February, 440,000; March, 1,600,000; April, 1,422,000; May, 56,000; June–August, 0; September, 1,500,000; October, 2,002,000; November, 1,322,000; December, 488,000. In the 1950s, dollars of 1900 were released in quantities to banks, and such pieces became very common. For years, more bags were distributed. Most were gone by the early 1960s.

**Die Varieties:** Many varieties from the old hub, the new (introduced this year) hub over the old hub. For this year 66 obverse and 61 reverse dies were prepared.

## 1900, PROOFS

**Mintage:** 912. Delivery figures by month: January–February, 0; March, 377; April–May, 0; June, 135; July–August, 0; September, 100; October–November, 0; December, 300. Two pairs of dies were made for Proofs.

**Key to Collecting Proofs:** Usually a decent strike. Contrast varies from average to cameo. Most are cameos, and, increasingly, many are being certified as such.

## Whitman Coin Guide (WCG™)

| VG-8 | F-12 | VF-20 | EF-40 | AU-50 | MS-60 | MS-64 | MS-65 | MS-66 | MS-67 | PF-60 | PF-64 | PF-65 | PF-66 | PF-67 |
|------|------|-------|-------|-------|-------|-------|-------|-------|-------|-------|-------|-------|-------|-------|
| $28 | $29 | $34 | $37 | $40 | $48 | $65 | $85 | $185 | $535 | $7,750 | $1,300 | $3,900 | $6,100 | $9,750 | $15,500 |

### AVAILABILITY

| | MS-60 | MS-61 | MS-62 | MS-63 | MS-64 | MS-65 | MS-66 | MS-67 | MS-68+ |
|---|-------|-------|-------|-------|-------|-------|-------|-------|--------|
| Certified | 67 | 284 | 2,771 | 15,192 | 25,411 | 7,606 | 1,117 | 61 | 0 |
| Field | 200,000–300,000 | | | 100,000–125,000 | 60,000–100,000 | 15,000–25,000 | 1,000–1,500 | 32–40 | 5–10 |
| Cert. DMPL | 0 | 0 | 0 | 1 | 4 | 5 | 0 | 0 | 0 |

| | PF-60 | PF-61 | PF-62 | PF-63 | PF-64 | PF-65 | PF-66 | PF-67 | PF-68+ |
|---|-------|-------|-------|-------|-------|-------|-------|-------|--------|
| Certified | 10 | 32 | 49 | 94 | 117 | 53 | 31 | 9 | 6 |
| Field | 300–400 | | | 200–300 | 150–250 | 80–120 | 45–60 | 20–25 | 12–16 |

# 1900-O

**Optimal Collecting Grade**
MS-65

**Circulation-Strike Mintage**
11,390,000
(estimated)[67]

**Key to Collecting Circulation Strikes:** 1900-S dollars are plentiful in Mint State. However, the striking quality can vary widely, and it will pay to do some picking and choosing. The luster is usually excellent, but quite a few have prominent planchet striations—from the drawing-bench process before planchets were punched out. Avoid these.

**Surface Quality:** The strike varies from weak to quite sharp, but enough sharp pieces exist that the search will not be long. All New Orleans dollars this year are from the old-style die with well-defined breast feathers (which may or may not be sharply struck on a given coin). The mint luster is typically frosty and attractive.

**Prooflike Coins:** Prooflike coins are for the most part unattractive, and deeply prooflike coins are rare. Many have raised die swirls from the basining process. Few have cameo contrast.

**Mintage and Distribution:** Delivery figures by month: January, 1,550,000; February, 1,500,000; March, 2,000,000; April, 1,500,000; May, 1,500,000; June, 1,000,000; July, 630,000; August, 400,000; September, 1,000,000; October, 0; November, 1,140,000; December, 370,000. While many 1900-O dollars were paid out in the early years, quantities remained in storage in such places as the Treasury Building in Washington, DC, and Philadelphia. The Treasury Building paid out many from the 1930s to the early 1950s, and perhaps later as well. Enough remained that hundreds of sealed 1,000-coin bags were part of the 1962 through 1964 Treasury release.

**Die Varieties:** Many varieties exist, mostly from the old hub, at least one with new hub (introduced in 1900) over old hub, and with some slight features of the undertype visible. Among the more than three dozen die varieties described for this year, the O/CC overmintmarks are the most important (and are described separately in the present book). VAM-29A has a very dramatic die crack on the obverse, an unusual feature for any Morgan dollar.

There are many mintmark positions of this year, most with medium O mintmark, with some exceptions.

## Whitman Coin Guide (WCG™)

| VG-8 | F-12 | VF-20 | EF-40 | AU-50 | MS-60 | MS-63 | MS-64 | MS-65 | MS-66 | MS-67 |
|------|------|-------|-------|-------|-------|-------|-------|-------|-------|-------|
| $28 | $29 | $34 | $37 | $40 | $48 | $65 | $85 | $185 | $450 | $5,000 |

**AVAILABILITY**

| | MS-60 | MS-61 | MS-62 | MS-63 | MS-64 | MS-65 | MS-66 | MS-67 | MS-68+ |
|---|-------|-------|-------|-------|-------|-------|-------|-------|--------|
| Certified | 65 | 317 | 2,884 | 18,973 | 33,033 | 12,045 | 1,819 | 105 | 0 |
| Field | 200,000–300,000 | | | 125,000–175,000 | 100,000–150,000 | 20,000–30,000 | 1,400–1,800 | 65–95 | 5–10 |
| Cert. DMPL | 1 | 1 | 4 | 14 | 42 | 24 | 1 | 0 | 0 |

# 1900-O/CC

**Optimal
Collecting Grade
MS-64**

**Circulation-
Strike Mintage
1,200,000
(estimated)[68]**

**Key to Collecting Circulation Strikes:** The 1900-O/CC is one of the more fascinating varieties in the series, and by all means you should have one, preferably Uncirculated, such as a nice MS-63 to MS-65. Most are decently struck and have good luster. A few years after the Treasury releases of the early 1960s I bought a bag of 1900-O dollars from a Montana source, and upon sorting through them found that about a third were O/CC, although this was probably an above average number in relation to those found elsewhere. Even though the variety had been known since the 1920s, there was little demand for it, and hence the market premium was small. Then came a greatly expanded interest in Morgan dollars, along with reference guides and listings in the Red Book, and, in time, this became a "must have" variety.

**Surface Quality:** The strike is usually average, but sharp ones can be found. The sharpness of the under-CC depends more on the die and its state (period of its use, sharper on earlier impressions, less distinct on later ones) than on striking. The luster is good, indeed usually excellent.

**Prooflike Coins:** Although some have prooflike surface, no DMPL pieces have been reported.

**Mintage and Distribution:** The 1900-O/CC dollars constituted a small fraction of the total mintage for 1900-O, probably over 10%, but not much. Except for a full bag of overmintmarks obtained by Dwight Manley (could the coins have been picked out from other bags?), most have been found mixed with regular 1900-O/CC dollars.

**Die Varieties:** At least seven CC reverses were overmintmarked with an O. The sharpness of the under-mintmark CC varies from variety to variety and coin to coin, depending on die use. Check VAM and *The Top 100 Morgan Dollar Varieties.* All are of the old-style hub, as the CC dies were made years earlier.

## Whitman Coin Guide (WCG™)

| VG-8 | F-12 | VF-20 | EF-40 | AU-50 | MS-60 | MS-63 | MS-64 | MS-65 | MS-66 | MS-67 |
|------|------|-------|-------|-------|-------|-------|-------|-------|-------|-------|
| $38 | $48 | $65 | $105 | $175 | $325 | $725 | $950 | $1,800 | $5,500 | $24,000 |

**AVAILABILITY**

| | MS-60 | MS-61 | MS-62 | MS-63 | MS-64 | MS-65 | MS-66 | MS-67 | MS-68+ |
|---|-------|-------|-------|-------|-------|-------|-------|-------|--------|
| Certified | 39 | 194 | 917 | 2,188 | 2,571 | 868 | 90 | 3 | 0 |
| Field | | 25,000–35,000 | | 12,500–17,500 | 7,000–10,000 | 1,500–2,500 | 85–95 | 5–7 | 0 |
| Cert. DMPL | 0 | 0 | 0 | 0 | 0 | 0 | 0 | 0 | 0 |

# 1900-S

Optimal
Collecting Grade
MS-64

Circulation-
Strike Mintage
3,540,000

**Key to Collecting Circulation Strikes:** The 1900-S dollar is readily available in Mint State, although it is hardly a common date. Most are very lustrous. Actual striking sharpness ranges from flat to quite good, but perceived sharpness is affected on this and many other dollars from now through 1904, from the use of the new hub with lightly defined breast feathers.

**Surface Quality:** The strike varies from weak to sharp, with most being above average. The element of new hub use now needs to be factored into evaluating die sharpness versus striking sharpness, this general rule holding for coins of the next several years from the three mints. The luster is usually frosty and rich.

**Prooflike Coins:** Prooflike pieces are occasionally seen and have low contrast.

**Mintage and Distribution:** Delivery figures by month: January–February, 0; March, 500,000; April–August, 0; September, 1,000,000; October, 1,000,000; November, 0; December, 1,040,000. Following the by-now-familiar routine, many dollars of this issue were stored at the San Francisco Mint. Beginning in a significant way in the 1930s, many bags were paid out, continuing to the 1950s. While thousands went into numismatic hands, more were circulated in commerce and in casinos. However, many bags remained and were paid out during the great Treasury release of 1962 through 1964.

**Die Varieties:** Many varieties exist, mostly of the old hub, but at least one with new hub (introduced in 1900) over old hub, and with some slight features of the undertype visible. There were 35 die pairs made. Among the varieties, VAM-3A is particularly interesting and shows a wide, small mintmark boldly overpunched with a tall, narrow mintmark. This reverse die with the small mintmark was used for coinage, and many were struck from it. That small mintmark has slight repunching. Then the small mintmark, repunched as noted, was overpunched by a tall, narrow S mintmark, for additional coinage, perhaps not as many as before the larger mintmark was overpunched. Somehow, *The Top 100 Morgan Dollar Varieties* missed this.

## Whitman Coin Guide (WCG™)

| VG-8 | F-12 | VF-20 | EF-40 | AU-50 | MS-60 | MS-63 | MS-64 | MS-65 | MS-66 | MS-67 |
|------|------|-------|-------|-------|-------|-------|-------|-------|-------|-------|
| $28 | $29 | $35 | $45 | $75 | $275 | $360 | $600 | $1,450 | $3,000 | $15,000 |

### AVAILABILITY

| | MS-60 | MS-61 | MS-62 | MS-63 | MS-64 | MS-65 | MS-66 | MS-67 | MS-68+ |
|---|-------|-------|-------|-------|-------|-------|-------|-------|--------|
| Certified | 56 | 238 | 923 | 2,212 | 2,389 | 680 | 120 | 2 | 0 |
| Field | | 15,000–25,000 | | 10,000–15,000 | 6,000–10,000 | 1,400–1,600 | 120–150 | 1–5 | 1–5 |
| Cert. DMPL | 0 | 0 | 3 | 8 | 7 | 3 | 0 | 0 | 0 |

# MORGAN SILVER DOLLARS, RARE COINS, AND LIFE IN 1901

## THE MORGAN DOLLAR SCENARIO

As to whether Morgan-design coins were involved is left to the imagination in this account of good fortune:[69] "In tearing off the roof of an old farm house north of Eldora, Iowa on May 30th, Marvin Finister found a barrel of money, and to his astonishment was almost buried by the rain of silver dollars. It is believed that some old miser at an early date hid the money as the dates on some of them are quite old."

In Denver, plans were underway for a mint, but at present there was a budget shortfall. In Philadelphia in June the new Mint building was occupied for the first time, with coinage beginning in October. The *American Journal of Numismatics* gave this view:[70]

### The New Mint

[The new Philadelphia Mint] is of gray granite, and in style is pure Italian Renaissance. It is 318 feet long, and, including terraces, 395 feet; its width between Spring Garden and Button-wood streets is 208 feet. It is fronted by a high granite wall, supporting terraces which run the entire length of the building, and these will be laid out as ornamental gardens, though beneath them are some of the largest vaults in the building. There are two interior court yards, and between them a structure extending north and south joining the sections in the centre.

The basement has shipping and express offices. Much of the Spring Garden front of the basement is occupied by vaults. That for silver dollars, 96 by 52 feet in size, holds $100,000,000. The bullion vault is 72 by 92 feet. Extending under the terraces on the north side are other large vaults for nickel and bronze storage, subsidiary coin storage, etc.

## MINT COLLECTION ON VIEW

The *Annual Report of the Director of the Mint*, 1902, covering the fiscal year that commenced on July 1, 1901, gave these details of the storage vaults, including information that would be the key to a later numismatic treasure trove:

For the storage of bullion, coin, blanks, dies, etc., the Mint is provided with 20 steel-lined vaults, 8 of which are located in the basement and are as follows: The silver-dollar vault, which is 100 feet long, 52 feet wide, and 101/2 feet high, has a capacity of storing $112,000,000 in silver dollars, packed in boxes.

The cashier's working vault, measuring 80 feet long, 52 feet wide, and 10 1/2 feet high, is used for storing the various denominations of coin prior to shipment. The remaining 6 vaults in the basement are 122 feet long, 21 feet wide, and 10 1/2 feet high, and are provided with four entrances, all opening into the main corridor. These are utilized for the storage of gold and sil-ver bullion, bars, etc. These vaults are all of the most approved modern construction. The com-bined weight of steel used in their construction is approximately 3,250,000 pounds. . . .

The two largest vaults are divided into several compartments, which, after filling, are locked and sealed so as to avoid, as much as possible, the necessity of reweighing and recounting.

The foundation of vaults is of concrete, the walls of hard bricks laid in cement 21/2 feet thick; the linings are from 2 to 3 inches thick, consisting of steel construction which has passed through a special purpose. The doors are 6 inches thick and there are three for each vault; the front door, weighing about 8 tons, is mounted on ball bearings; the other two doors are arranged in one set and are somewhat lighter than the front door. Four combination locks are used, which can be adjusted to independent combination. The remaining vaults throughout the building are of lighter construction are used only for storage of metal in the process of coinage.

Key to the numismatic treasure alluded to was the new method of locking and sealing vaults so that their contents would not need to be inspected. Years later, in 1929, millions of brilliant Uncirculated Morgan dollars were moved from the New Orleans Mint building (not used for coinage since 1909 and not for minting dollars since 1904) to Philadelphia, and there placed in sealed vaults and forgotten. In November 1962 they were discovered, yielding a king's ransom in erstwhile rarities!

## MEANWHILE, ON THE AMERICAN SCENE IN 1901

*The Octopus*, a novel by Frank Norris, was published in 1901 and chronicled the oppression of the Southern Pacific Railroad against wheat farmers in central California.

Theodore Roosevelt, vice president of the United States, was widely quoted in the press, what with his love for adventure and his readiness to give opinions regardless of how they would be interpreted. In a speech on September 2, 1901, he included the phrase "speak softly and carry a big stick," which later translated into policy when he became president of the United States and, to demonstrate America's military might, sent the Great White Fleet of battleships on an around-the-world tour.

On September 6, while visiting the Temple of Music at the Pan-American Exposition in Buffalo, President McKinley was shot twice in the stomach. The gunman was Leon Czolgosz, an anarchist. Infection set in, and on September 14 McKinely died at the Milburn house, where he had been confined. Thomas L. Elder, the telegrapher stationed there, sent the news to the world. Roosevelt became president at age 42, the youngest in American history. Soon, Elder would decide to become a professional numismatist.

J.P. Morgan supervised the consolidation and underwriting that led to the formation of the United States Steel Company, including paying $492,000,000 to steelmaker Andrew Carnegie for his holdings. Carnegie, already a philanthropist of renown, would expand his benevolence and create many Carnegie Library buildings in small and medium-sized towns across America. In the meantime U.S. Steel controlled about 65% of American capacity for producing that metal and became a formidable factor in commerce.

In Beaumont, Texas, on January 10, the Spindletop oil gusher first produced a virtual river of oil, launching what became a forest of derricks in the area, one of the richest fields in history. Spindletop flowed uncontrolled at the rate of an estimated 110,000 barrels per day until it was capped and controlled nine days later. Although oil had been taken from Texas soil before, this was the major launch of what would become a fantastic source for wealth in the Lone Star State, generating many millionaires, perhaps incorrectly typified decades later by Edna Ferber in her novel *Giant* (later made into a film).

The automobile industry continued its expansion, with products including Ransom E. Olds's curved-dash Oldsmobile Runabout. During the decade, Olds's initials were used on REO brand cars and the REO Speedwagon. Other introductions included the Pierce Motorette and the Apperson. In Germany in this year, Gottlieb Daimler introduced a car with the Mercedes nameplate, after an 11-year-old daughter of the Austrian consul at Nice, France. Cars were still a novelty in most rural areas of the United States. In the cities, gasoline vehicles were a frequent sight, but horses remained dominant. Electric street cars and interurban lines continued their expansion and were fixtures just about everywhere.

Alfred B. Nobel, who made a fortune in the manufacturing of dynamite, and who stated, "Inherited wealth is a misfortune which merely serves to dull a man's faculties," established Nobel prizes, which in 1901 were awarded for the first time.

On December 12, 1901, in Newfoundland, Guglielmo Marconi received the first transAtlantic wireless message, sent from Cornwall, England. In 1903 the first commercial transAtlantic wireless service would be instituted, and in coming years radio transmitters would be fitted to many ships, including, famously, the *Titanic* in 1912.

In an era in which mansions on Fifth Avenue, New York City, were being demolished in the area below Central Park, new private palaces rose on higher-numbered streets, including one on the corner of 78th Street for tobacco millionaire Benjamin N. Duke and another at 92nd Street for Andrew Carnegie. In the meantime development began in the general area north of Central Park known as Harlem, which soon became a popular area for housing workers and professional people.

# 1901

**Optimal Collecting Grade**
MS-60

**Circulation-Strike Mintage**
6,962,000

**Proof Mintage**
813

**Key to Collecting Circulation Strikes:** Among circulation-strike coins in the Morgan series, the 1901 is second only to the 1896-O in terms of absolute rarity at the gem level. Among 1901 dollars, lower-grade Mint State coins exist with some frequency; I recommend holding off on a Mint State coin until you become acquainted with the Morgan series in depth, after which you can make an informed decision. Circulated coins are as common as can be and are worth only a slight premium. Proofs beckon to fill the void created by the paucity of top-grade circulation strikes.

**Surface Quality:** 1901 was a transitional year, and those with the earlier-style hub, called the C3 reverse by Van Allen–Mallis, are typically decently struck, although there are exceptions. The later pieces with the C4 are usually lightly struck. Numismatists seeking but a single 1901—and here, indeed, is a rarity in Mint State—would do well to go with the earlier, sharply struck variety.

**Prooflike Coins:** Prooflike coins are very rare. No DMPL coins have been reported at the MS-65 level.

**Mintage and Distribution:** Delivery figures by month: January, 360,000; February, 500,000; March, 42,000; April, 0; May, 824,000; June, 1,462,000; July, 400,000; August, 1,514,000; September, 1,740,000; October, 86,000; November, 0; December, 34,000. Most 1901 dollars were distributed early in the 20th century or were melted under the Pittman Act of 1918. In the 1950s a number of dealers had BU pieces on hand for low prices, so perhaps some small quantities filtered out here and there. Likely, most Mint State pieces existing today in lower ranges were found in mixed bags.

**Die Varieties:** Many varieties exist, some from the old hub, some with new hub (introduced in 1900), and still others with new hub over old hub, and with some slight features of the undertype visible; check VAM for details.

## 1901, PROOFS

**Mintage:** 813. Delivery figures by month: January–February, 0; March, 350; April–May, 0; June, 100; July–August, 0; September, 85; October–November, 0; December, 278.

**Key to Collecting Proofs:** Strike is usually good. Some from the new hub over the old one show slight doubling. **Contrast** is medium cameo, not deeply frosty.

## Whitman Coin Guide (WCG™)

| VG-8 | F-12 | VF-20 | EF-40 | AU-50 | MS-60 | MS-63 | MS-64 | MS-65 | MS-66 | MS-67 | PF-60 | PF-64 | PF-65 | PF-66 | PF-67 |
|------|------|-------|-------|-------|-------|-------|-------|-------|-------|-------|-------|-------|-------|-------|-------|
| $37 | $42 | $50 | $100 | $285 | $2,300 | $15,750 | $45,000 | $375,000 | – | – | $1,600 | $4,100 | $7,100 | $12,000 | $17,000 |

### AVAILABILITY

| | MS-60 | MS-61 | MS-62 | MS-63 | MS-64 | MS-65 | MS-66 | MS-67 | MS-68+ |
|---|-------|-------|-------|-------|-------|-------|-------|-------|--------|
| Certified | 136 | 404 | 412 | 226 | 39 | 6 | 0 | 0 | 0 |
| Field | | 1,200–1,400 | | 200–300 | 40–60 | 7–10 | 0 | 0 | 0 |
| Cert. DMPL | 0 | 1 | 0 | 0 | 0 | 0 | 0 | 0 | 0 |
| | PF-60 | PF-61 | PF-62 | PF-63 | PF-64 | PF-65 | PF-66 | PF-67 | PF-68+ |
| Certified | 13 | 41 | 65 | 100 | 151 | 50 | 39 | 17 | 3 |
| Field | | 200–500 | | 150–250 | 175–250 | 50–70 | 50–60 | 20–30 | 3–5 |

# 1901-O

Optimal
Collecting Grade
MS-65

Circulation-
Strike Mintage
13,320,000

**Key to Collecting Circulation Strikes:** The 1901-O dollar is typical for a New Orleans product—quality varies all over the place, and if you were to be blindfolded and pick one from a pile, chances are it would be a poor strike and with many bagmarks, although the luster might be decent, sort of satiny. Dollars of 1901-O were released in immense quantities in the early 1960s, and because of this you will have ample opportunity to choose. It is easy to forget—or not to know in the first place—how lucky we are to have so many O Mint dollars available in Mint State today—a couple of generations ago, most were rarities in Mint State.

**Surface Quality:** Most are below average or average, with sharp pieces being the distinct minority. However, with some searching a decent strike can be found. The luster is generally satiny and quite attractive.

**Prooflike Coins:** Prooflike coins are known and do not have great contrast.

**Mintage and Distribution:** Delivery figures by month: January, 1,500,000; February, 620,000; March, 1,100,000; April, 1,550,000; May, 1,500,000; June, 1,100,000; July, 800,000; August, 200,000; September, 1,550,000; October, 1,000,000; November, 900,000; December, 1,500,000. Until about the 1930s an Uncirculated 1901-O in the hands of a numismatist was a rare situation. Then, bags began to filter into the market, accented by an especially large release in 1953, after which time they were truly plentiful. In the 1962 surprise distribution from a long-sealed vault at the Philadelphia Mint, bags of this date played a just-below-the-headlines role.

**Die Varieties:** Many varieties exist, some from the old hub, some with new hub (introduced in 1900), and still others with new hub over old hub, and with some slight features of the undertype visible; check VAM for details.

## Whitman Coin Guide (WCG™)

| VG-8 | F-12 | VF-20 | EF-40 | AU-50 | MS-60 | MS-63 | MS-64 | MS-65 | MS-66 | MS-67 |
|------|------|-------|-------|-------|-------|-------|-------|-------|-------|-------|
| $28 | $29 | $34 | $37 | $41 | $48 | $68 | $87 | $185 | $600 | $14,000 |

**AVAILABILITY**

|  | MS-60 | MS-61 | MS-62 | MS-63 | MS-64 | MS-65 | MS-66 | MS-67 | MS-68+ |
|--|-------|-------|-------|-------|-------|-------|-------|-------|--------|
| Certified | 34 | 237 | 2,466 | 17,099 | 26,486 | 7,045 | 872 | 15 | 0 |
| Field | | 125,000–200,000 | | 50,000–75,000 | 32,500–37,500 | 8,000–12,000 | 550–750 | 15–25 | 1–5 |
| Cert. DMPL | 0 | 1 | 8 | 53 | 59 | 33 | 1 | 0 | 0 |

# 1901-S

Optimal
Collecting Grade
MS-64

Circulation-
Strike Mintage
2,284,000

**Key to Collecting Circulation Strikes:** The 1901-S is quite scarce in the context of the series, the most elusive San Francisco Mint dollar since 1896, although it is hardly as rare as the 1896-S. Striking varies from poor to quite good, but the luster is usually satisfactory. MS-63 and MS-64 coins, if carefully selected, offer good values on the market. MS-65 coins are, of course, nicer yet, but the price is substantially more—due to true rarity and also from demand by investors who have been conditioned to believe that "investment grade" begins at MS-65 (but who are often clueless on matters of striking and luster). There is a reflected glory on the 1901-S in that in other silver series, especially the 1901-S Barber quarter, this is a key date.

**Surface Quality:** Usually lightly struck or of medium sharpness, not often well detailed. Weak pieces often show parallel planchet striations from the drawing-bench process, these often on the face of Miss Liberty for all the world to see. Those from the new hub reverse are usually struck better than those from the old hub—the opposite of what might be expected. The luster is usually satisfactory.

**Prooflike Coins:** Some prooflikes exist but the fields are not sharply contrasted with the designs. According to Wayne Miller: "Virtually all prooflikes are very unappealing, with plentiful abrasions, poor contrast, and unappealing gray luster."

**Mintage and Distribution:** Delivery figures by month: January, 338,000; February, 500,000; March, 400,000; April, 400,000; May, 210,000; June–July, 0; August, 218,000; September, 218,000; October–December, 0. Quantities of these coins in storage became a stock-in-trade at the San Francisco Mint, and bags were paid out to answer requests as early as 1925, if not before. From then until the 1950s many hundreds more bags were paid out. However, they did not play to a wide numismatic audience, as dealer specialists were few and far between. For a professional such as Norman Shultz or Bebee's in the early 1950s to have a "nice stock" of a given date and mint might mean 20 to a few hundred pieces. By the 1970s, Bebee's tried to have a backlog stock of precisely 100 of each common to somewhat scarce date, buying more when levels dropped below. A few bags turned up in the early 1960s, including two in Idaho.

**Die Varieties:** Many varieties exist, some from the old hub, some with new hub (introduced in 1900), and still others with new hub over old hub, and with some slight features of the undertype visible; check VAM for details. Made for the coinage were 25 die pairs.

## Whitman Coin Guide (WCG™)

| VG-8 | F-12 | VF-20 | EF-40 | AU-50 | MS-60 | MS-63 | MS-64 | MS-65 | MS-66 | MS-67 |
|------|------|-------|-------|-------|-------|-------|-------|-------|-------|-------|
| $30 | $34 | $45 | $65 | $190 | $475 | $725 | $1,050 | $3,000 | $12,500 | $38,500 |

**AVAILABILITY**

| | MS-60 | MS-61 | MS-62 | MS-63 | MS-64 | MS-65 | MS-66 | MS-67 | MS-68+ |
|---|-------|-------|-------|-------|-------|-------|-------|-------|--------|
| Certified | 46 | 217 | 702 | 1,398 | 1,435 | 312 | 35 | 1 | 0 |
| Field | | 10,000–15,000 | | 6,000–9,000 | 3,000–4,000 | 500–750 | 30–45 | 1–5 | 1–5 |
| Cert. DMPL | 1 | 0 | 3 | 2 | 2 | 1 | 1 | 0 | 0 |

# Morgan Silver Dollars, Rare Coins, and Life in 1902

## The Morgan Dollar Scenario

Production of Morgan dollars continued apace at the three active mints—Philadelphia, New Orleans, and San Francisco—with each crossing the million mark. Numismatic interest remained quiet, and, as before, those collectors who acquired Morgan dollars were usually content with Proofs. Mintmarks remained generally ignored.

In the Medal Department of the Philadelphia Mint, where Proofs were made, someone decided to polish the recessed parts of Proof dies, including the image of Miss Liberty, ending the cameo frost contrast so admired on Proofs by collectors today and, presumably, by collectors at that time.

The *Annual Report of the Director of the Mint*, 1902, related that the amount of pressure required for stamping a silver dollar was 160 tons. In comparison 35 tons was needed for a quarter eagle, 155 tons for a double eagle, 98 tons for a half dollar, 35 tons for a dime, and 40 tons for a cent. A large coining press at the mint was driven by a 7.5-horsepower electric motor running at 950 revolutions per minute and could strike 90 coins per minute. A small coining press was run by a 3-horsepower motor at 1,050 revolutions per minute and could strike 100 pieces per minute. If a large press was hooked to a 15-horsepower motor belted to a countershaft, 80 pieces per minute could be struck.

## The Collecting Scene

The past year had been "a prosperous one for the [American Numismatic] Association," reported George Heath in an editorial. Further:

> 119 new members have joined our ranks, and if indications point to anything they are a class that may be depended upon to stick by us. Of 112 of this number we have more or less complete data. The total of their ages is 4,824 years, or an average of about 38 1/2. The fascination of our science is no respecter of age, it delights the young and, as the years go by it only finds its votaries more firmly bound with its charms. Our youngest this year is 13 and our oldest is 69. Fourteen are 50 or a year over in years.[71]

The coin market was perking up, and it seemed that good times were on the way, aided by an increasingly robust economy, the nationwide enthusiasm for President Theodore Roosevelt in the White House, and other factors. Increased activity inspired thoughts of profits: "According to reports there is an effort being made to corner the market on encased postage stamps. Many will remember, no doubt, a similar effort made about a year ago on the 1856 Flying Eagle cent, and we think this should be a warning."[72]

However, time and again "corners" on certain rare coins proved to be very profitable to those involved.

Still, little respect was given numismatically or anywhere else for the current Barber-design dime, quarter, and half dollar, and few would admit to collecting such things. Editor Heath's comment in *The Numismatist*, January, was simply the latest in a long line of numismatically unfavorable comments, contrasting Barber's eagle with the flying bird created by Gobrecht:

> Our United States coinage [has] many errors of taste. . . . The heraldic eagle on recent dates of silver is but a witless imitation of the two-headed crowned eagles of old and absolute empires of Eastern Europe which typify double or triple sovereignty. What business have we, in our young and united great republic of equality and freedom, with a flayed eagle or with its hints of heraldry and imperialism?
>
> If we must need to have the rapacious and autocratic bird as an emblem, let him be restored, as on the dollars of 1838 and 1839, and on the copper-nickel cents, to life and impressive speed and power, or to his natural watchful dignity in repose.

## MEANWHILE, ON THE AMERICAN SCENE IN 1902

The recently organized United Mine Workers went on strike under John Mitchell, and 147,000 workers in the anthracite mines left the pits. Coal became in tight supply, and the market price more than doubled. While striking coal miners ultimately benefited, the rising price of coal wreaked havoc with the meager budgets of many householders and businessmen. Finally, five months later, President Roosevelt arranged a settlement.

Increased attention began to be given to labor conditions, although largely unregulated child labor was still endemic in America, and one attraction for establishing new textile factories in various states was the realization that certain states had lax laws and permitted children to work longer hours, such information being disseminated in print throughout the textile industry.

Roosevelt was feeling vigorous, and through Attorney General Philander C. Knox set about "trust busting," or breaking apart monopolies in an effort to lower prices to consumers and lessen restrictions on workers. His efforts were sped along by the popularity of Ida Tarbell's series of articles in *McClure's* magazine, later in book form, *History of the Standard Oil Company*, which noted, among other things, that John D. Rockefeller and his associates controlled 90% of the oil-refining capacity in the United States.

On June 15, 1902, the Twentieth Century Limited passenger express train went into service on the New York Central Railroad, connecting New York and Chicago. With "palace" cars featuring drawing rooms and staterooms to enjoy, passengers made the trip in about 20 hours, averaging about 49 miles per hour over the 980-mile route. On the next day, June 16, the Pennsylvania Railroad set its Broadway Limited train to connect to the same two cities, on a slightly shorter route of 904 miles, but running about the same time of 20 hours.

On May 4 in the *New York Herald* the cartoon character Buster Brown, by Richard F. Outcault (he of *Yellow Kid* cartoon fame), made its debut. Buster Brown was a typical American boy, and the strip told of his adventures accompanied by his pet dog Tige. The teddy bear made its debut in the marketplace as a stuffed toy, manufactured by Mr. and Mrs. Morrich Michtom, who had been amused by a cartoon by Clifford Berryman in the *Washington Evening Star*, November 18, showing Roosevelt refusing to shoot a bear. The story went that Roosevelt, who loved to hunt big game, was out for sport for the day, but was not successful. Meanwhile, near camp, a bear cub was captured and tied to a tree, waiting for the president to return and shoot it. The little creature's life was spared.

In 1902 the Flatiron building was finished at the southwest corner of Madison Square, New York City. Considered a marvel of modern architecture, and located in a particularly prominent spot, the 20-story structure attracted many visitors.[73]

In Philadelphia the first Horn & Hardart Automat opened for business, dispensing food, visible behind glass, upon receipt of a nickel. In the background, employees of the automat continually refilled empty compartments. Soon, automats spread to many other American cities. The nickel was becoming dominant in American life, spurred by the need to use them in a vast proliferation of coin-operated devices ranging from music boxes and pianos to gambling machines to pay telephones.

In Bretton Woods, New Hampshire, in the heart of the White Mountains, the huge Mount Washington Hotel opened for business. It joined dozens of other mountain resorts in upstate New York, New Hampshire, Maine, and elsewhere, which drew tourists and visitors during the warm summer months, in a time in which those who could afford it would often send their families away from the warm city for the duration.

For some time the Panama Canal Company, based in France, had been projecting a waterway crossing the Isthmus in Central America to capture and increase the commerce largely taken care of by the Panama Railroad (opened in 1855). On June 28, 1902, the U.S. Congress passed the Isthmian Canal Act to authorize the acquisition of the French interests and also to formulate an agreement with the government of Columbia, which controlled the district. The decades-old argument that crossing through Nicaragua to the north would save time, even though it would be more expensive, was revived, and many thought that Nicaragua would provide a viable alternative.

# 1902

Optimal
Collecting Grade
MS-64

Circulation-
Strike Mintage
7,994,000

Proof Mintage
777

**Key to Collecting Circulation Strikes:** The 1902 Philadelphia Mint dollar, while not in the common-date category, is still quite plentiful. Striking is apt to be indifferent or down-right poor, but fairly sharp examples exist. Luster is subdued and satiny, not at all deeply frosty, probably due as much to die preparation procedures as to striking.

**Surface Quality:** The strike is usually above average, but as all are from the new hub, the feather detail is not what it was in the years prior to 1900. The luster can be satiny or somewhat dull, not deeply frosty.

**Prooflike Coins:** Some prooflikes exist but are of low contrast.

**Mintage and Distribution:** Delivery figures by month: January, 800,000; February, 786,000; March, 750,000; April, 1,000,000; May, 500,000; June, 586,000; July, 500,000; August, 778,000; September, 1,054,000; October, 0; November, 726,000; December, 514,000. While 1902-dated Morgan dollars were hardly ever encountered in circulation in the early days, this changed in the 1940s when bags were paid out, followed by many more in the 1950s.

**Die Varieties:** Many varieties exist, some with new hub (introduced in 1900), and others with new hub over old hub, and with some slight features of the undertype visible; check VAM for details. For this year 80 obverse and 67 reverse dies were prepared.

## 1902, PROOFS

**Mintage:** 777. Delivery figures by month: January–February, 0; March, 312; April, 65; May, 0; June, 60; July–August, 0; September, 60; October–November, 0; December, 280.

**Key to Collecting Proofs:** The strike is usually average at best, but some employee, perhaps new on the job, decided this year to polish the portraits on the various Proof dies, and to *really* polish them in 1903—doing away with cameo contrast.

## Whitman Coin Guide (WCG™)

| VG-8 | F-12 | VF-20 | EF-40 | AU-50 | MS-60 | MS-63 | MS-64 | MS-65 | MS-66 | MS-67 | PF-60 | PF-64 | PF-65 | PF-66 | PF-67 |
|---|---|---|---|---|---|---|---|---|---|---|---|---|---|---|---|
| $28 | $29 | $34 | $37 | $45 | $55 | $120 | $155 | $475 | $1,000 | $6,500 | $1,300 | $3,900 | $6,450 | $10,000 | $15,500 |

**AVAILABILITY**

| | MS-60 | MS-61 | MS-62 | MS-63 | MS-64 | MS-65 | MS-66 | MS-67 | MS-68+ |
|---|---|---|---|---|---|---|---|---|---|
| Certified | 24 | 115 | 710 | 2,545 | 4,816 | 2,311 | 592 | 38 | 0 |
| Field | | 70,000–100,000 | | 20,000–30,000 | 12,500–17,500 | 5,000–7,500 | 450–700 | 30–45 | 1–5 |
| Cert. DMPL | 0 | 0 | 0 | 3 | 2 | 1 | 0 | 0 | 0 |

| | PF-60 | PF-61 | PF-62 | PF-63 | PF-64 | PF-65 | PF-66 | PF-67 | PF-68+ |
|---|---|---|---|---|---|---|---|---|---|
| Certified | 9 | 30 | 61 | 79 | 142 | 63 | 53 | 15 | 7 |
| Field | | 250–350 | | 175–250 | 125–200 | 100–150 | 60–90 | 12–16 | 7–10 |

# 1902-O

Optimal
Collecting Grade
MS-65

Circulation-
Strike Mintage
8,636,000

**Key to Collecting Circulation Strikes:** Some Mint State pieces are lustrous and attractive, but there is no reason to alter what Wayne Miller wrote in 1982: "Typically among the poorest struck of the late New Orleans dollars. Most are flatly struck with horrible luster." That said, where to from here? Is there hope? Yes there is, and cherrypicking can be done to great advantage. The 1902-O came out of the floodgates during the great Treasury release of November 1962 and later, and virtually countless pieces are in the marketplace.

**Surface Quality:** Generally the 1902-O is lightly struck at the centers. Some concentrated effort is needed to find sharp pieces, but, again, the advantage is that certification services take no notice, and such can be yours for the finding while 90% or more of your competitors in the market simply don't care. Some Mint State piece are lustrous and attractive, but most are not (see introductory comments).

**Prooflike Coins:** Some prooflikes exist but are not of high contrast, although there are exceptions.

**Mintage and Distribution:** Delivery figures by month: January, 1,500,000; February, 750,000; March, 750,000; April, 500,000; May, 1,000,000; June, 320,000; July, 550,000; August, 1,000,000; September, 1,200,000; October, 500,000; November, 500,000; December, 66,000. Dollars of the 1902-O variety were paid out in circulation over a long period of time. In the late 1950s and in the early 1960s enough bags were released that dealers were well supplied. In 1962 hundreds of thousands more were distributed from storage at the Philadelphia Mint.

**Die Varieties:** Many varieties exist, some with new hub (introduced in 1900), and others with new hub over old hub, and with some slight features of the undertype visible; check VAM for details. For use this year, 140 obverse and 107 reverse dies were made. Most 1902-O dollars have a medium-sized mintmark. *1902-O Micro o variety, VAM-3:* Small mint letter, rare, and typically seen well worn.

VAM-3

## Whitman Coin Guide (WCG™)

| VG-8 | F-12 | VF-20 | EF-40 | AU-50 | MS-60 | MS-63 | MS-64 | MS-65 | MS-66 | MS-67 |
|---|---|---|---|---|---|---|---|---|---|---|
| $28 | $29 | $34 | $37 | $42 | $50 | $65 | $80 | $170 | $450 | $6,500 |

**AVAILABILITY**

| | MS-60 | MS-61 | MS-62 | MS-63 | MS-64 | MS-65 | MS-66 | MS-67 | MS-68+ |
|---|---|---|---|---|---|---|---|---|---|
| Certified | 70 | 485 | 5,872 | 33,535 | 44,579 | 10,092 | 1,001 | 29 | 0 |
| Field | 200,000–300,000 | | | 125,000–175,000 | 100,000–150,000 | 12,500–17,500 | 700–1,000 | 20–30 | 12–16 |
| Cert. DMPL | 0 | 3 | 25 | 72 | 85 | 15 | 1 | 0 | 0 |

# 1902-S

Optimal
Collecting Grade
MS-64

Circulation-
Strike Mintage
1,530,000

**Key to Collecting Circulation Strikes:** The 1902-S is plentiful enough in Mint State that you will have your choice among many. However, most are lightly struck, and some also have parallel die striations located, well, where else but the most prominent place on the coin: on Miss Liberty's face. Luster is usually satiny, sometimes dull, and nearly always without much life. Most from the Treasury releases are in grades MS-60 to MS-62, often baggy, sometimes MS-63, but not often MS-64 or finer.

**Surface Quality:** Typically shallowly struck or of medium sharpness, seldom sharp, and it can be that several hundred pieces can be examined and not a sharp specimen found. Cherry-picking is the order of the day, and get set for extensive effort. The luster of the 1902-S is typically quite good, somewhat satiny.

**Prooflike Coins:** Some dies are prooflike but have little contrast. DMPL coins are very rare, are known only in low grades, and win no awards or even favorable mention for eye appeal.

**Mintage and Distribution:** Delivery figures by month: January–August, 0; September, 500,000; October, 510,000; November, 520,000; December, 0. From the outset, 1902-S dollars were paid into circulation, furnishing a supply for anyone interested. Others went into storage at the San Francisco Mint. Bag quantities were released in the late 1920s, again in the 1940s and early 1950s, and at a few other times. However, in later years, when investing and trading in bags became popular in numismatic circles, few quantities were to be found.

**Die Varieties:** Many varieties exist, some with new hub (introduced in 1900), and others with new hub over old hub, and with some slight features of the undertype visible; check VAM for details. For this year, 20 obverse and 7 reverse dies were prepared.

## Whitman Coin Guide (WCG™)

| VG-8 | F-12 | VF-20 | EF-40 | AU-50 | MS-60 | MS-63 | MS-64 | MS-65 | MS-66 | MS-67 |
|------|------|-------|-------|-------|-------|-------|-------|-------|-------|-------|
| $90 | $100 | $135 | $165 | $245 | $365 | $575 | $800 | $2,650 | $7,500 | $16,500 |

AVAILABILITY

| | MS-60 | MS-61 | MS-62 | MS-63 | MS-64 | MS-65 | MS-66 | MS-67 | MS-68+ |
|--|-------|-------|-------|-------|-------|-------|-------|-------|--------|
| Certified | 54 | 190 | 935 | 2,107 | 2,120 | 387 | 40 | 4 | 0 |
| Field | | 12,500-17,500 | | 7,500-12,500 | 4,000-6,000 | 600-900 | 35-50 | 6-9 | 1-5 |
| Cert. DMPL | 1 | 0 | 2 | 0 | 0 | 0 | 0 | 0 | 0 |

# MORGAN SILVER DOLLARS, RARE COINS, AND LIFE IN 1903

## THE MORGAN DOLLAR SCENARIO

The mintage of Morgan dollars continued in 1903, with 4,652,000 turned out at the Philadelphia Mint and mostly bagged and stored, 4,450,000 at New Orleans with the same destination, and 1,241,000 in San Francisco.

The 1903-O coins in particular went into hiding in storage. Then in 1918, when the Pittman Act was passed and 270,232,722 silver dollars were melted, the melt included most of the 1903-O coins. Numismatists in 1903 yawned at the prospect of collecting mintmarks, and few were saved at the time of issue—although examples could have been ordered directly from the New Orleans Mint. When collectors woke up decades later, most of the 1903-O dollars were gone, save for a stray worn piece found now and then in circulation. Mint State coins were virtually unknown, the stuff of which numismatic legends are made. By 1962 a Mint State 1903-O was cataloged in the *Guide Book of United States Coins* for $1,500, or 10 times the price of an 1889-CC.

Today, as you read these words early in the 21st century, one of those Mint State 1889-CCs, if gem, is worth over $300,000, but a gem 1903-O has not maintained the same ratio and is not a million-dollar coin. Therein lies a story, the linchpin of the 1962 Treasury release.

## MARKET STRENGTH

The coin hobby continued to build strength, and the American Numismatic Association could be proud that in the most recent year 111 new members joined, and only 7 resigned. It was a time of discovery, and such byways as tokens, medals, encased postage stamps, and obsolete currency were eagerly explored, while old standbys such as colonials and copper half cents and cents continued to play to wide audiences. The activity was noted elsewhere, even in a publication about stamp collecting, when the *Metropolitan Philatelist* was moved to comment:[74]

> The specimens of U.S. coins are rapidly appreciating in value. Cents which could be bought for $10 a few years ago now demand twice that amount. A dealer lately showed us an 1809 cent which he sold four years ago for $2.50 and which he had now purchased at $5.
>
> Gold of the rarer dates and mints in Fine condition is in great demand, while the territorial gold is practically unobtainable, and, strange to say, the more prices advance, the greater demand of amateurs.

Farran Zerbe emerged as a numismatic entrepreneur who enjoyed investigating obscure avenues of the hobby and sharing his findings with readers of *The Numismatist*. In the meantime he was laying plans to market the first-ever issue of United States commemorative gold dollars, to be made in 1903 to commemorate the centennial of the Louisiana Purchase. He was enthusiastic about the prospect of an issue of 250,000 coins, evenly divided into two types, one with the portrait with Thomas Jefferson and the other with William McKinley. However, few others in the hobby shared his optimism, as most collectors had been disillusioned by Columbian half dollars, originally selling at $1 each, now worth little more than face value, and 1900-dated Lafayette silver dollars now available for less than the $2 issue price, with one collector reporting that he had recently purchased some for $1.10 each.

## CLEANING COINS

The peripatetic Farran Zerbe told of a visit to the Mint Collection in Philadelphia, admiring many items on display, but commenting:

> I found many of the silver Proof coins of late years partially covered with a white coating. On inquiry I learned that an over zealous attendant during the last vacation months when the numismatic room was closed took it on himself to clean the tarnished coins, purchase some

metal polish at a department store, and proceed with his cleaning operation. Later a coating of white appeared on the coins, which was now slowly disappearing.

I expressed my displeasure at this improper treatment of Proof coins, and the custodian explained, "that is nothing. I have been here eight years and they have been cleaned three or four times in my time."

Zerbe noted that if this practice continued, in the future there would not be much left except plain discs or badly worn coins! The caretakers of the Mint Collection were hardly alone. All across America many collectors routinely brightened their coins by dipping them in acidic or other compounds, or polishing them with paste intended to keep tableware gleaming. Today, collectors of Uncirculated Morgan dollars can be thankful that most of these coins were safe in Treasury storage during this era. However, Proofs were indeed in the hands of numismatists, and over a period of time the majority of pieces lost the superb gem quality they had when first struck.

## Way Down in Texas

Tucked away on page 382 of the December issue of *The Numismatist* was an advertisement titled "For Sale." Offered were items for mail bidding, the sale to close on December 25. Among the pieces offered were well-worn (Very Good to Fine) Columbian half dollars of 1892 and 1893, probably taken from pocket change. The notice was signed "B. Max Mehl, 1211 Main St., Fort Worth, Texas."

During the next half century, Mehl's business would grow and prosper beyond anyone's expectations and no doubt beyond Mehl's own dreams. Through advertising in magazines, newspapers, and, eventually, in the new medium of radio, he would sell copies of his *Star Rare Coin Encyclopedia*, offering premiums for scarce and rare coins. In the meantime he would have another side to his business—buying and selling from serious numismatists. In the process some of the largest and finest of all American collections would come his way.

## Meanwhile, on the American Scene in 1903

On February 14, 1903, Congress voted to establish the Department of Commerce and Labor, a position on the president's cabinet. On April 27, the U.S. Supreme Court upheld a provision in the Alabama Constitution denying black people the right to vote.

Alexander Winton, manufacturer of the Winton Motor Car, drove one of his cars at a breakneck 68 miles per hour on the water-dampened hard sand at Daytona Beach. The Winton factory employed 1,200 people. On June 16, 1903, the Ford Motor Company was incorporated for $28,000. Its first popular product was the model A at $750 (different from the vehicle of the same designation marketed a quarter century later). On May 23 a Packard automobile departed San Francisco and 52 days later arrived in New York City, the first crossing of the continent by an automobile entirely using its own power.

On December 17, 1903, at Kitty Hawk, North Carolina, brothers Orville and Wilbur Wright were able to achieve a 59-second flight covering 852 feet, rising to 15 feet in altitude. Whether the Wright brothers were the first in the world to fly a powered aircraft, apart from balloons and related devices, may never be ascertained, but in time they received most of the credit. However, in December 1903 just three newspapers reported the happening, not at all a media event.

Joseph Pulitzer, publisher of the *New York World*, set up an endowment at Columbia University for what became known as the Pulitzer Prizes.

On December 30, flames rushed through the large Iroquois Theatre in Chicago, and 602 people died in an effort to escape, many finding that exit doors were locked. The interior was soon refurbished, and the establishment was renamed Hyde & Beaman's New Music Hall and opened to the public. The tragedy would forever remain the largest theater disaster in America.

The first World Series championship contest was conducted this year, pitting the Boston team of the American league against the Pittsburgh team of the National league. Boston won five of the eight games.

# 1903

**Optimal
Collecting Grade**
MS-65

**Circulation-
Strike Mintage**
4,652,000

**Proof Mintage**
755

**Key to Collecting Circulation Strikes:** The 1903 Philadelphia Mint silver dollars were well made, with nice striking quality and bright luster, although more with a satiny sheen, sort of "greasy" (but attractive), than with a deep frost. I recall in the 1950s getting a large quantity of these that popped up in a holiday release in the northeastern section of Pennsylvania. Each coin looked as if it had been minted an hour earlier! Many coins are in the marketplace, and choice and gem pieces await your consideration.

**Surface Quality:** Usually fairly well struck, but there are exceptions. Satiny and brilliant, but not deeply frosty. Raised die striae are seen on many coins, from the die preparation process.

**Prooflike Coins:** Prooflike pieces are seen at widely scattered intervals and do not have high contrast.

**Mintage and Distribution:** Delivery figures by month: January, 500,000; February, 1,000,000; March, 526,000; April, 428,000; May, 0; June, 2,000,000; July–October, 0; November, 64,000; December, 134,000. Quantities of Uncirculated 1903 dollars were scarce in numismatic circles until multiple bags were released in 1955. Quantities surfaced here and there, and in the 1960s a dealer in Salinas, California, had the remarkable quantity of 50 bags. However, elsewhere bags of this date were scarcely seen.

**Die Varieties:** All from new-style hub (introduced in 1900). Coinage was accomplished from some or all of 46 obverse and 40 reverse dies prepared.

## 1903, PROOFS

**Mintage:** 755. Delivery figures by month: January–February, 0; March, 325; April–May, 0; June, 120; July–August, 0; September, 75; October–November, 0; December, 235.

**Key to Collecting Proofs:** Medium to subpar strike plus no cameo contrast. The portraits and certain other recessed parts of the die were polished—what student of the series Michael Fuljenz calls "the chrome look."

## Whitman Coin Guide (WCG™)

| VG-8 | F-12 | VF-20 | EF-40 | AU-50 | MS-60 | MS-63 | MS-64 | MS-65 | MS-66 | MS-67 | PF-60 | PF-64 | PF-65 | PF-66 | PF-67 |
|---|---|---|---|---|---|---|---|---|---|---|---|---|---|---|---|
| $45 | $48 | $50 | $55 | $65 | $78 | $90 | $120 | $270 | $575 | $3,000 | $1,300 | $3,900 | $6,100 | $9,750 | $15,500 |

**AVAILABILITY**

| | MS-60 | MS-61 | MS-62 | MS-63 | MS-64 | MS-65 | MS-66 | MS-67 | MS-68+ |
|---|---|---|---|---|---|---|---|---|---|
| Certified | 44 | 252 | 1,301 | 4,583 | 8,597 | 4,937 | 1,302 | 158 | 2 |
| Field | | 100,000–200,000 | | 40,000–60,000 | 20,000–30,000 | 10,000–15,000 | 1,250–1,750 | 120–125 | 1–5 |
| Cert. DMPL | 0 | 1 | 1 | 8 | 12 | 6 | 0 | 0 | 0 |
| | PF-60 | PF-61 | PF-62 | PF-63 | PF-64 | PF-65 | PF-66 | PF-67 | PF-68+ |
| Certified | 11 | 37 | 57 | 119 | 136 | 68 | 54 | 33 | 6 |
| Field | | 200–300 | | 160–200 | 140–180 | 90–140 | 60–90 | 35–50 | 3–5 |

# 1903-O

Optimal
Collecting Grade
MS-65

Circulation-
Strike Mintage
4,450,000

**Key to Collecting Circulation Strikes:** The 1903-O is one of my favorite coins in all of American numismatics. In one book, *More Adventures With Rare Coins,* I devoted a chapter to it. In brief, by 1962 the 1903-O was viewed as being the great rarity among Mint State Morgan dollars, valued at 10 times the price of an 1889-CC. No matter; even at the $1,500 listing none were available. In my nearly decade of dealing in coins by that time I had never owned one! Then in November 1962 a storage vault in the Philadelphia Mint, sealed since 1929, was opened to gain access to some dollars for holiday distribution. They turned out to be mint-fresh 1903-Os, and hundreds of thousands of them! The numismatic world has not been the same since. Today, there are many 1903-O dollars around, usually well struck and nearly always with brilliance and luster. Enjoy!

**Surface Quality:** Usually fairly well struck. Typically seen brilliant and lustrous.

**Prooflike Coins:** Some prooflike pieces exist, are of light contrast, and are fairly elusive.

**Mintage and Distribution:** Delivery figures by month: January, 1,000,000; February, 350,000; March, 500,000; April, 500,000; May, 500,000; June, 1,250,000; July–November, 0; December, 350,000. This is the ultimate "story coin" of the Morgan series. Releases were small in the early 20th century, and it seems that no more than a dozen or so were saved by interested numismatists. Years later, in the 1930s when numismatics became popular, it was realized that 1903-O dollars were rare and that Mint State coins were especially so. The explanation was simple: they had been melted under the 1918 Pittman Act. And, probably the majority were. Then in 1962 many thousands were released from a long-sealed vault in the Philadelphia Mint, setting off the treasure hunt that led to the depletion of bank and Treasury reserves of nearly all dollars. How many 1903-O dollars were found? Estimates have ranged to the long side of a million. I guess that 200,000 to 350,000 might be in the ballpark.

**Die Varieties:** Many varieties exist, all from the new hub (introduced in 1900).

## Whitman Coin Guide (WCG™)

| VG-8 | F-12 | VF-20 | EF-40 | AU-50 | MS-60 | MS-63 | MS-64 | MS-65 | MS-66 | MS-67 |
|------|------|-------|-------|-------|-------|-------|-------|-------|-------|-------|
| $275 | $290 | $300 | $325 | $345 | $375 | $400 | $440 | $550 | $875 | $3,250 |

**AVAILABILITY**

|  | MS-60 | MS-61 | MS-62 | MS-63 | MS-64 | MS-65 | MS-66 | MS-67 | MS-68+ |
|--|-------|-------|-------|-------|-------|-------|-------|-------|--------|
| Certified | 48 | 288 | 1,417 | 4,168 | 6,275 | 3,263 | 926 | 103 | 0 |
| Field |  | 125,000–175,000 |  | 40,000–60,000 | 15,000–25,000 | 5,000–8,000 | 750–1,250 | 75–125 | 1–5 |
| Cert. DMPL | 1 | 0 | 10 | 25 | 43 | 15 | 5 | 0 | 0 |

# 1903-S

**Optimal Collecting Grade**
EF-40

**Circulation-Strike Mintage**
1,241,000

**Key to Collecting Circulation Strikes:** The 1903-S remains a rare issue in the Morgan dollar series, and Mint State coins are desirable at all levels. Most are well struck and very attractive, and bagmarks are often minimal. If you can afford it, an MS-63 coin, hand picked for quality, is well worth owning. For many collectors the 1903-S will be one of those varieties for which a nice VF or EF coin is acquired, requiring some effort to find one of nice quality.

**Surface Quality:** Usually seen well struck, lustrous, and attractive.

**Prooflike Coins:** Prooflike coins are hardly ever seen, and on those blue-moon occasions it will be noticed that contrast is low.

**Mintage and Distribution:** Delivery figures by month: January–May, 0; June, 500,000; July, 0; August, 74,000; September, 108,000; October, 232,000; November, 99,000; December, 228,000. In July 1903 *The Numismatist* commented, "Up to April 6th the San Francisco Mint had coined in silver only half dollars. Quarters and dimes will probably be struck later in the year, but it is quite likely that no dollars will be issued at this mint during 1903." However, dollars were indeed issued. Many were stored in the San Francisco Mint and distributed over a long period of years. In November 1953 several bags were released, causing a stir at the time. Now and again other bags would be paid out, including one obtained by California dealer John Skubis. By the late 1950s virtually all had been paid out. I am not aware of any bags coming to light after that time.

**Die Varieties:** Many varieties exist, some with new hub (introduced in 1900), and others with new hub over old hub, and with some slight features of the undertype visible; check VAM for details. *1903-S "Small s," VAM-2:* Mintmark much smaller than the regular, larger S. Possibly intended for use on quarter dollar dies. Usually seen in worn grades when seen at all. Rare.

VAM-2

## Whitman Coin Guide (WCG™)

| VG-8 | F-12 | VF-20 | EF-40 | AU-50 | MS-60 | MS-63 | MS-64 | MS-65 | MS-66 | MS-67 |
|------|------|-------|-------|-------|-------|-------|-------|-------|-------|-------|
| $75 | $115 | $180 | $335 | $1,600 | $3,900 | $6,250 | $7,500 | $10,750 | $15,500 | $42,500 |

**AVAILABILITY**

| | MS-60 | MS-61 | MS-62 | MS-63 | MS-64 | MS-65 | MS-66 | MS-67 | MS-68+ |
|------|-------|-------|-------|-------|-------|-------|-------|-------|--------|
| Certified | 6 | 20 | 96 | 220 | 340 | 167 | 42 | 4 | 0 |
| Field | | 1,000–1,500 | | 800–1,000 | 600–900 | 200–300 | 45–50 | 7–9 | 0 |
| Cert. DMPL | 0 | 0 | 0 | 0 | 0 | 0 | 0 | 0 | 0 |

# Morgan Silver Dollars, Rare Coins, and Life in 1904

## The Morgan Dollar Scenario

At the three mints the production of Morgan dollars continued in 1904, until the supply of silver ran out. The *Annual Report of the Director of the Mint* for the fiscal year ended June 30, 1905, told the story: "The stock of silver bullion purchased under the Act of July 14, 1890, is now exhausted, and the coinage of the dollar piece is at an end unless Congress at some future time shall provide for its resumption."

End of the Morgan dollar series, or so it was thought at the time. In view of this, some years later, in 1910, the hubs, master dies, and other production items were destroyed, as hundreds of millions of coins remained in storage—and who would ever need to have more?

Summary of Morgan dollar coinage and legislation through 1904:

- Act of February 28, 1878 (Bland-Allison Act): 378,166,793 silver dollars minted
- Acts of July 14, 1890, etc. (Sherman Silver Purchase Act and related later acts): 187,027,345
- Act of March 3, 1891 (recoinage of trade dollars): 5,078,472
- Grand total: 570,272,610

(Not including Proof coins for collectors)

## Morgan Dollars at Auction

The Chapman brothers' sale of the Ralph Barker Collection, July 7 and 8, 1904, contained a run of Philadelphia Mint dollars, each described as brilliant Proof, save for two. No longer were Proofs selling at or near face value, although prices remained nominal.

By this time most numismatists realized that despite a published Mint Report listing 12,000 circulation strikes for the 1895, if they wanted examples of this date they had to buy Proofs. Accordingly, the price of the 1895 stood head and shoulders above the others:

| | | |
|---|---|---|
| 1878, 7 Tail Feathers (sold for $2.10) | 1887 ($1.20) | 1895 ($6.10) |
| 1880 ($1.35) | 1888 brilliant Proof with light hairmark on obverse ($1.35) | 1895-S EF ($1.35) |
| 1881 ($1.35) | 1889 ($1.31) | 1896 ($1.35) |
| 1882 ($1.35) | 1890 ($1.31) | 1897 ($1.35) |
| 1883 ($1.15) | 1891 ($1.31) | 1898 ($1.50) |
| 1884 ($1.20) | 1892 ($1.31) | 1899 ($1.50) |
| 1885 ($1.30) | 1893 ($1.20) | 1900 ($1.20) |
| 1886 ($1.20) | 1894 ($1.20) | 1902 ($1.35) |
| | | 1903 ($1.35) |

## Hobby and Market Notes

The rare coin market continued to be strong, indeed dynamic, in 1904. Nearly all series and specialties were in demand by buyers, save perhaps for the silver Barber coinage and large-denomination gold. There was a brisk trade in gold dollars in any and all grades, a combined demand by jewelers and numismatists, and $3 pieces also found a ready market.

A March 1903 advertisement by F.H. Stewart, of Grand Rapids, Michigan, offered 1856 Flying Eagle cents for sale: brilliant Proof $11, Uncirculated $10, Very Fine (nearly Uncirculated) $9, Very Fine $8.50, Fine $8, Very Good $7.50, and Good $7. Stewart had been hoarding these pieces for the best part of a decade and, presumably, had well over a hundred on hand.[75]

Thomas L. Elder, who in Pittsburgh had worked as a telegrapher and also as a meat packer while dealing in coins as a sideline, moved to New York City in 1904 and set up shop at 32

East 22nd Street. In time, Elder would produce many auction catalogs and become the leading dealer in the city.

In Baltimore on February 7 and 8 a huge fire swept through the city, destroying well over a thousand buildings across 75 blocks. A small part of the Garrett coin and medal collection was stored downtown (while most of it was on display at Princeton), and certain of the numismatic items were reduced to molten blobs. King C. Gillette, an enthusiastic numismatist in his off-hours, patented his thin-blade razor this year, the latest product in the Gillette line. Using replaceable blades, the device eventually attracted millions of users.

## ACROSS THE AUCTION BLOCK

The year 1904 was a fine one for rare coin auction sales, the best in recent times. The Chapman brothers' presentation of the cabinet of John G. Mills, of Albany, New York, from April 27 through 29 drew wide attention, including an enthusiastic article in the *New York Times*. When all was said and done the nearly 2,000 lots realized the impressive total of about $15,000.

On October 11, Lyman H. Low's sale No. 93 featured Part I of the H.G. Brown Collection, followed on November 16 by Part II. The cabinet was a stunning one and comprised many rarities in the American and world coin series. The highlight was an 1804 dollar, recently the subject of several comments in *The Numismatist*. Brown had paid $2,000 for his, but at the auction it laid an egg and sold for a disappointing $1,100, perhaps proving that even in the most active sales there are often bargains for alert buyers—for never again would an 1804 dollar cross the block at such a low figure.

Among other auctioneers, Geoffrey Charlton Adams, in New York City, turned out a stream of catalogs and attracted favorable notice.

## MEANWHILE, ON THE AMERICAN SCENE IN 1904

The presidential contest of 1904 saw incumbent Theodore Roosevelt challenge the Democratic contender, Judge Alton B. Parker. By this time Roosevelt was immensely popular with the majority of American citizens, and the outcome reflected this—with 336 electoral votes to Roosevelt, compared to just 140 for Parker.

The dissolution of trusts took a giant step forward when the Supreme Court ruled that the Northern Securities Company, formed in 1901 by consolidation of major railroads, was in violation of the Sherman Anti-Trust Act of 1890, and ordered that the trust be disbanded.

The automobile industry continued its rapid expansion, in 1904 adding the Cadillac, Pierce Arrow, and Maxwell brands, among others. In the first part of the 20th century, the phonograph, both cylinder versions (as favored at first by Edison) and disk versions, achieved fantastic popularity. Available recordings included the voice of Teddy Roosevelt, the march music of John Philip Sousa, and countless toe-tapping "rags," as ragtime tunes were known.

The *New York Times* relocated to a new 25-story building at 42nd Street facing Longacre Square, which was soon renamed Times Square. The *Ladies' Home Journal* began a series on exposing puffery and quackery in the sale of patent medicines, a widely circulated feature that became a foundation stone in the Pure Food and Drug Act of 1906 (effective January 1, 1907). In 1904 there were absolutely no restrictions on the claims that could be made for cure-alls, and the public was widely victimized. Drugs such as opium, easily available without prescription at apothecary shops, were not a social problem in the United States (but were in China). However, alcoholism was endemic, and in the warmer months drunks sleeping on benches, at railroad stations, and in doorways were a common sight just about everywhere.

By this year a scattering of so-called nickelodeon theaters opened across the United States, typically consisting of rented storefronts. Inside were chairs or benches where patrons sat to watch one-reel films projected on a small screen in the front. A nickel was the typical admission, giving rise to the name of the genre.

# 1904

**Optimal Collecting Grade**
MS-64

**Circulation-Strike Mintage**
2,788,000

**Proof Mintage**
650

**Key to Collecting Circulation Strikes:** As the curtain rings down on the production of Morgan dollars, and the dies and hubs are about to be put into storage, the swan song at the Philadelphia Mint is off-key. Most coins seen today are poorly to indifferently struck and with poor luster—all in all, rather sorry looking. If you want quality, some intense cherry-picking is called for. Nice coins do exist, but if choice or gem and well struck they can be expensive. Most such coins are from old-time collections or holdings (such as a group that Dr. Richard A. Bagg unearthed in Florida years ago) and are lightly, often attractively, toned. The Treasury-release coins are usually subpar.

**Surface Quality:** The strike varies and is usually of only medium quality. According to Wayne Miller, "Most 1904 dollars give the appearance of being poorly struck. It is hard to believe that the same mint that produced the very beautiful 1903 dollar could, one year later, produce such an inferior dollars as the 1904." Sharp pieces can be found, but some searching is required. The luster is usually fairly shallow, not at all deep or flashy. To find a deeply lustrous, sharp 1904 will be a challenge.

**Prooflike Coins:** Some prooflikes exist but are not of high contrast.

**Mintage and Distribution:** Delivery figures by month: January, 2,200,000; February, 66,000; March–May, 0; June, 522,000; July–December, 0. Although it is likely that many 1904 dollars were stored by the Treasury Department, no record has been found of a particularly spectacular release. Some bags came out in the early 1940s, others in the 1950s, and a few more in the early 1960s, but few turned up in dealers' hands.

**Die Varieties:** All are from the new hub (style of 1900).

## 1904, PROOFS

**Mintage:** 650. Delivery figures by month: January–February, 0; March, 275; April–May, 0; June, 65; July–August, 0; September, 10; October–November, 0; December, 300. At least two obverse dies were used.

**Key to Collecting Proofs:** Some lightness at the centers. Undesirable chrome look to the motifs.

## Whitman Coin Guide (WCG™)

| VG-8 | F-12 | VF-20 | EF-40 | AU-50 | MS-60 | MS-63 | MS-64 | MS-65 | MS-66 | MS-67 | PF-60 | PF-64 | PF-65 | PF-66 | PF-67 |
|------|------|-------|-------|-------|-------|-------|-------|-------|-------|-------|-------|-------|-------|-------|-------|
| $31 | $34 | $40 | $47 | $55 | $95 | $260 | $525 | $2,850 | $11,000 | – | $1,300 | $3,900 | $6,100 | $9,750 | $15,500 |

### AVAILABILITY

|  | MS-60 | MS-61 | MS-62 | MS-63 | MS-64 | MS-65 | MS-66 | MS-67 | MS-68+ |
|--|-------|-------|-------|-------|-------|-------|-------|-------|--------|
| Certified | 74 | 395 | 1,545 | 2,829 | 2,120 | 286 | 24 | 0 | 0 |
| Field |  | 30,000–50,000 |  | 8,000–12,000 | 3,500–5,000 | 300–500 | 18–24 | 0 | 1–5 |
| Cert. DMPL | 0 | 0 | 1 | 0 | 1 | 1 | 0 | 0 | 0 |
|  | PF-60 | PF-61 | PF-62 | PF-63 | PF-64 | PF-65 | PF-66 | PF-67 | PF-68+ |
| Certified | 19 | 39 | 102 | 129 | 152 | 72 | 49 | 24 | 4 |
| Field |  | 125–300 |  | 175–225 | 150–180 | 80–120 | 60–70 | 20–30 | 3–5 |

# 1904-O

**Optimal
Collecting Grade
MS-65**

**Circulation-
Strike Mintage
3,720,000**

**Key to Collecting Circulation Strikes:** The 1904-O is the last and also the most plentiful today of the big-three former New Orleans Mint rarities that launched the Treasury release and resultant pandemonium in November 1962, the others being the 1898-O and the marvelous and ultra-rare 1903-O. Today, many 1904-O dollars exist, usually very brilliant and very attractive. Striking sharpness is another matter entirely, and on this count you may have to look at several pieces before finding one that is just right.

**Surface Quality:** The strike is usually average or a bit below average, although with some searching sharp pieces can be found. The luster is usually attractive—in fact, especially so. Wow, what a contrast to the insipid Philadelphia Mint dollars of this year!

**Prooflike Coins:** Prooflike coins, some deeply mirrored, are abundant. The contrast is usually low and there is usually some light striking at the centers.

**Mintage and Distribution:** Delivery figures by month: January, 1,000,000; February, 1,000,000; March, 1,200,000; April, 520,000; May–December, 0. The scenario for the 1904-O parallels those of 1898-O and 1903-O. This was a very rare variety, hardly ever seen in Mint State, until over a million coins were released from the Philadelphia Mint. These had been shipped from New Orleans in 1929 and placed in a sealed vault. Today, the 1904-O dollar is the most plentiful Mint State New Orleans dollar after 1885.

**Die Varieties:** All are from the new hub (style of 1900). VAM-2 and VAM-13 exist with rotated reverse dies.

## Whitman Coin Guide (WCG™)

| VG-8 | F-12 | VF-20 | EF-40 | AU-50 | MS-60 | MS-63 | MS-64 | MS-65 | MS-66 | MS-67 |
|------|------|-------|-------|-------|-------|-------|-------|-------|-------|-------|
| $28 | $29 | $34 | $37 | $41 | $48 | $65 | $80 | $185 | $400 | $4,250 |

**AVAILABILITY**

| | MS-60 | MS-61 | MS-62 | MS-63 | MS-64 | MS-65 | MS-66 | MS-67 | MS-68+ |
|---|-------|-------|-------|-------|-------|-------|-------|-------|--------|
| Certified | 107 | 910 | 10,449 | 66,195 | 100,740 | 25,517 | 2,163 | 120 | 0 |
| Field | 500,000–750,000 | | | 350,000–500,000 | 200,000–300,000 | 45,000–65,000 | 3,000–5,000 | 100–150 | 15–20 |
| Cert. DMPL | 0 | 10 | 60 | 334 | 519 | 196 | 27 | 1 | 0 |

# 1904-S

Optimal
Collecting Grade
MS-65

Circulation-
Strike Mintage
2,304,000

**Key to Collecting Circulation Strikes:** The 1904-S dollar is one of the key issues in the series, and in comparison to the demand for them, Mint State pieces are elusive. When found, the strike is apt to be shallow and the luster average or poor. In contrast, price-wise, there are many nice VF and EF pieces around, also requiring careful selection, that can be just right for those who do not want to invest in Mint State coins.

**Surface Quality:** The strike is typically about average. Sharp pieces exist but must be sought out, which is not particularly easy to do as Mint State pieces are somewhat elusive. Most Mint State pieces are usually below average in this respect, but there are some notable exceptions.

**Prooflike Coins:** Prooflike coins exist but have low contrast. DMPL coins are very rare.

**Mintage and Distribution:** Delivery figures by month: January, 1,252,000; February, 216,000; March, 0; April, 576,000; May, 260,000; June–December, 0. 1904-S dollars were distributed into circulation over a long period of time. In addition to bags stored at the San Francisco Mint, others were shipped to the Treasury Building in Washington, DC, from which depot many were paid out in the 1930s and 1940s. In 1941 and 1942 multiple bags came out, filling numismatic channels to the extent that 1904-S was considered to be a plentiful issue. Although scattered supplies remained for a long time, and in the 1950s the 1904-S was not expensive, none were to be had in San Francisco. Dealer John Skubis recalled that the only full bags of S-Mint dollars he never handled were 1892-S, 1893-S, and 1904-S. No mention of quantities of 1904-S dollars has been found in connection with either the Treasury release of 1962 through 1964 or the Redfield hoard (1976).

**Die Varieties:** Many varieties exist, some with new hub (introduced in 1900), others with new hub over old hub, and with some slight features of the undertype visible; check VAM for details.

## Whitman Coin Guide (WCG™)

| VG-8 | F-12 | VF-20 | EF-40 | AU-50 | MS-60 | MS-63 | MS-64 | MS-65 | MS-66 | MS-67 |
|------|------|-------|-------|-------|-------|-------|-------|-------|-------|-------|
| $40 | $50 | $90 | $190 | $525 | $1,400 | $3,650 | $4,750 | $9,750 | $23,500 | $46,500 |

**AVAILABILITY**

| | MS-60 | MS-61 | MS-62 | MS-63 | MS-64 | MS-65 | MS-66 | MS-67 | MS-68+ |
|--|-------|-------|-------|-------|-------|-------|-------|-------|--------|
| Certified | 18 | 103 | 320 | 566 | 610 | 146 | 14 | 3 | 0 |
| Field | | 4,000–6,000 | | 1,750–2,500 | 1,250–1,750 | 150–250 | 12–15 | 4–6 | 0 |
| Cert. DMPL | 0 | 0 | 0 | 1 | 1 | 0 | 0 | 0 | 0 |

# MORGAN SILVER DOLLARS, RARE COINS, AND LIFE IN 1921

## THE MORGAN DOLLAR IS REVIVED

The original hubs for Morgan dollars were destroyed in 1910, at which time millions of coins were in storage, and no one dreamed that more would ever be needed. Then came new legislation, following the melting of hundreds of millions of coins under the Pittman Act of 1918. Now, in 1921, there was a hurry-up call for more coins, to act as backing to Silver Certificates.

An actual silver dollar of the 1878 style with 7 Tail Feathers and with Reverse of 1878 (parallel arrow feather) was used to create a model, and then, by adjustment and the changing of some details and the lowering of relief, the hubs for the new dollars were made. Although the design and lettering were the same, the overall appearance of the 1921 dollar was one of a shallow, flatly struck, and somewhat unappealing coin.

Concerning this design, Van Allen–Mallis wrote years later, "The eagle's breast is flat and the feathers have little detail. Aesthetically, the 1921 design is not pleasing to most people."[76]

The Philadelphia, Denver (for the first time), and San Francisco mints struck Morgan dollars in 1921. The D and S branch mint coins had tiny mintmarks, smaller than any used for dollars of earlier years.

## STRIKING THE NEW MORGAN DOLLARS

In February 1921 silver dollars were coined for the first time since 1904. During that month 56,000 were struck, but none were paid out. In March a further 2,310,000 were made. All coins were made in Philadelphia. Amazingly, although these figures were published in *The Numismatist*, there were absolutely no news articles or explanations of the new coinage!

## NEWS AT LAST

Finally, in June, *The Numismatist* enlightened its readers by reprinting an article from the *Colorado Springs Gazette*, April 20:

> The first American silver dollars ever manufactured in Denver will be coined at the local mint beginning next Thursday, it was announced today, following the receipt of more than 1,000,000 ounces of silver. The silver has been received in small amounts over a period of 30 days from western mining camps. Silver dollars were last stamped by the Philadelphia Mint in 1904, until the resumption of their mintage in that city last month, officials said.
>
> The manufacture of Denver's first silver dollars will continue several months, and the work will be handled by a double shift of employees, working day and night. Mint employees have been busy for two weeks installing new machinery in preparation for the manufacture of dollars. Special dies are being made under supervision of experts from Washington.
>
> The new dollars are to be made under a provision of the Pittman Act to replace silver dollars melted during the war and shipped in bars to India. All mints in the country will make silver dollars until 208,000,000 have been made.
>
> The San Francisco Mint will begin making dollars within 30 days, it was said. Hundreds of thousands of dollars' worth of silver has been hauled through Denver's streets in unpretentious wagons during the last few days, unknown to the thousands of people by whom it passed.

The raison d'être for making new silver dollars was explained months later in the October issue of *The Numismatist*, the editor of which, Frank G. Duffield, was hardly a newshound:

> The Philadelphia Mint is cutting down the interest-bearing debt of the United States $5 million a month. Each day the Mint is cutting $5,000 from the annual interest on paper held against the United States. All of that comes about because of the concentration of the work of the three United States mints on the coinage of silver dollars to replace 350 million dollars that were melted down during the war to sell to the English as bullion.

When all those dollars were melted the United States had to call in all the silver certificates—the $1, $2, and $5 "bills," to speak in common lingo—representing the dollars that were deposited in the vaults of the mints. Under the law of the land the Treasury must hold a silver dollar for each dollar silver certificate issued. So with the melting of the silver dollars the silver certificates had to be recalled. To cover that loss in currency, the government issued short-term certificates of indebtedness bearing 2% interest. The silver dollars now being coined allow for the issuance of new silver certificates which are being used in calling in those certificates of indebtedness.

There are three mints—Philadelphia, Denver, and San Francisco. The Philadelphia Mint is equal in output to those in Denver and San Francisco combined. Last April all three plants were started on the making of the silver dollars. They were put on 24-hour working days for six days of the week. Two shifts of 12 hours each are now working in the Philadelphia Mint. Until a few weeks ago there were three shifts of eight hours each. But when Freas Styer succeeded Adam Joyce as superintendent of the mint the third shift was put to work counting the money in the vaults in the making of an audit due to the change in administration.

In the four months since April, 20 million silver dollars have been coined. There remains on hand to be pressed into coin of the land 30 million ounces of silver, which will make approximately 35 million silver dollars. Robert Clark, superintendent of the coinage in the Philadelphia Mint, says that the greatest production in the history of the plant is now being obtained. The daily average in production for the last month has been 260,000 silver dollars. In some days it has run as high as 275,000. That rate will be maintained until the present supply of silver is exhausted, and then the Mint for a time will go back to the coining of the smaller coins.

On October 21, 1921, Secretary of the Treasury Andrew W. Mellon wrote to Director of the Mint Raymond T. Baker:[77]

> I have noted with great satisfaction the increased coinage of standard silver dollars at the mints, and wish to congratulate you, and through you the superintendents of the coinage mints, on the energy and efficiency which have made it possible to bring up the aggregate coinage to $1,000,000 a day and to maintain it at that rate.
>
> This will soon take up the accumulation of silver bullion purchased under the Pittman Act, which has heretofore been carried as a dead asset in the general fund, and thereby permit the Treasury to reduce the amount of outstanding Pittman Act certificates, with a corresponding reduction in the public debt and the interest thereon. This is an achievement of which the Mint service has a right to be proud.

## Meanwhile, on the American Scene in 1921

The present text left off in 1904, since no silver dollars had been struck in the meantime. This span of 16 years had encompassed the World War (1914–1918); widespread adoption of the automobile, the player piano and phonograph, and the telephone; innovations in aviation and the transmission of radio signals; the addition of Arizona and New Mexico as states; and the presidencies of William Howard Taft (1909–1913), Woodrow Wilson (1913–1921), and, since his inauguration in March 1921, Warren G. Harding.

Great advances had been made on the labor front: children no longer worked long hours in factories, many safety conditions had been introduced, and wages were significantly higher than in 1904. The Pure Food and Drug Act, effective in 1907, drove out the most egregious swindles in patent medicines, and adulterated foods were minimal. Nationwide prohibition had been in effect since January 16, 1920, and hard liquor was no longer sold. Bootlegging arose, speakeasies opened, and opportunities for profit beckoned to the criminal element. Drug stores boosted their business by prescribing alcoholic beverages for medical purposes.

Dramatic changes had taken place in American coinage. In 1909 the Lincoln cent replaced the Indian Head cent (introduced in 1859), and in 1913 the Liberty Head nickel (used since 1883) was replaced by the Buffalo design. In 1916 the "Mercury" dime, Liberty Walking half dollar, and Standing Liberty quarter dollar supplanted the Barber designs for those denominations.

# 1921

**Optimal Collecting Grade**
MS-65

**Circulation-Strike Mintage**
44,690,000

**Proof Mintage**
25–30 (estimated)

**Key to Collecting Circulation Strikes:** The 1921 Morgan dollar is far and away—by a country mile—more plentiful than any other coin in the entire series. Many millions exist in Mint State. However, finding one with eye appeal can be a challenge. Made from different hubs with shallow relief, 1921 dollars of all mints are different in appearance from those of the years 1878 through 1921.

**Surface Quality:** The nature of the dies is that even the best 1921 Morgan dollars are apt to be somewhat shallow. That said, on most there is additional weakness, due to striking, on the reverse among the lower wreath leaves. Examples with this feature sharp are in the minority. The die faces are "plane," not basined, on all 1921 Morgan dollars from the several mints. Luster is typically satiny rather than deeply frosty, but quite a few are grainy or dull.

**Prooflike Coins:** Prooflike pieces are seen on occasion, and have a mirrorlike quality to the fields, which are not completely "plane" but show distortions in the mirror surface near the lettering and other features. Such pieces can have a very nice strike (for a 1921 dollar). Pieces called Zerbe Proofs are simply circulation strikes with a semi-prooflike character, not as nice as on the earlier-noted prooflike pieces, struck from dies that were slightly polished, but that retained countless minute striae and preparation lines. In the view of the writer, Zerbe Proofs have no basis in numismatic fact or history, although opinions differ on the subject. It seems highly unlikely that these were produced as Proofs for collectors. If indeed they were furnished to Farran Zerbe, a leading numismatic entrepreneur of the era, it is likely that they were simply regular production pieces. Zerbe had a fine collection and certainly knew what a brilliant Proof should look like, and he never would have accepted such pieces as mirror Proofs.

**Mintage and Distribution:** Distribution of the 1921 Morgan dollars seems to have been more or less continuous from the 1920s onward. Soon, these became very common in areas in which dollars circulated, and in bags of mixed dollars in banks in other locations. By early 1964, most dollars seen on Nevada gaming tables were of this date, mostly Philadelphia issues, but many of Denver and San Francisco as well. Bags of 1921 dollars were a drag on the market, and dealers in bags often posted buying prices for bulk "except 1921."

**Die Varieties:** The dies of the early issues have 17 berries on the right reverse wreath. Later, 16 berries appear on the right wreath, this also being the style used for Denver and San Francisco Mint 1921 Morgan dollars. For the 1921 Philadelphia version, both berry types are plentiful. Unlike earlier Morgan dollar dies, those used to coin 1921 dollars of all mints were not basined. Some varieties of the 1921 Morgan dollars, all mints, have small raised dots. On the Philadelphia Mint versions, VAM-8 and 9 each show a raised dot in the field. It has been suggested that these are marks from a Rockwell punch used to test the hardness of the dies. Others have suggested they may have been gas bubbles in the blank die face before it was impressed with the hub. The standard edge-reed count is 189 for the 1921 Morgan dollar, but some with the 17-berry count (e.g., VAM-2 and 4) have only 157 reeds. VAM-3 is known with the reverse die misaligned 45°.

## 1921, "CHAPMAN PROOFS"

**Mintage:** Unknown, estimated to be fewer than 30; Breen (*Proof Coin Encyclopedia*, p. 220) positively states 12. Sometimes called Chapman Proofs today, as Philadelphia dealer Henry Chapman advertised Proofs as early as spring 1922, a few months after they were coined. The number of Chapman Proofs certified, as given below, is surprisingly large. I have only ever seen a handful in 60 years that I would call mirrored Chapman Proofs.

**Key to Collecting Proofs:** Most are nearly of the same highly polished deep mirror surfaces characteristic of 19th century Proof Morgan dollars, but sometimes with slight tinges of graininess near the rims. Contrast is average.

### Whitman Coin Guide (WCG™)

| VG-8 | F-12 | VF-20 | EF-40 | AU-50 | MS-60 | MS-63 | MS-64 | MS-65 | MS-66 | MS-67 | PF-60 | PF-64 | PF-65 | PF-66 | PF-67 |
|---|---|---|---|---|---|---|---|---|---|---|---|---|---|---|---|
| $28 | $29 | $32 | $35 | $36 | $43 | $58 | $75 | $170 | $700 | $11,000 | $16,500 | $35,000 | $67,500 | $90,000 | – |

**AVAILABILITY**

|  | MS-60 | MS-61 | MS-62 | MS-63 | MS-64 | MS-65 | MS-66 | MS-67 | MS-68+ |
|---|---|---|---|---|---|---|---|---|---|
| Certified | 127 | 853 | 12,130 | 52,830 | 54,806 | 11,193 | 843 | 14 | 0 |
| Field | 4,000,000–7,000,000 | | | 750,000–1,500,000 | 200,000–300,000 | 30,000–50,000 | 2,500–4,000 | 50–100 | 15–20 |
| Cert. DMPL | 2 | 9 | 34 | 68 | 58 | 7 | 0 | 0 | 0 |
|  | PF-60 | PF-61 | PF-62 | PF-63 | PF-64 | PF-65 | PF-66 | PF-67 | PF-68+ |
| Certified | 1 | 2 | 8 | 16 | 11 | 1 | 3 | 1 | 0 |
| Field | | 2–4 | | 5–10 | 5–10 | 4–6 | 5–10 | 1–2 | 0 |

# 1921-D

Optimal
Collecting Grade
MS-65

Circulation-
Strike Mintage
20,345,000

Detail of
"micro" mintmark
on 1921-D.

**Key to Collecting Circulation Strikes:** Dollars of the 1921-D variety are common in Mint State today (although not nearly as plentiful as Philadelphia pieces), but some searching is needed to find an example with good eye appeal. Prooflike coins exist, and DMPL pieces are rare; these coins have little eye appeal. All have a tiny or "micro" D mintmark.

**Surface Quality:** The 1921-D, from shallow dies to begin with, usually is lightly struck on the wreath leaves. Sharply struck pieces are in the distinct minority and will require extensive cherrypicking to find. The luster ranges from dull to somewhat frosty, with frosty pieces being plentiful.

**Prooflike Coins:** Prooflike coins exist but are very elusive. Such pieces are nearly always weakly struck and with poor eye appeal.

**Mintage and Distribution:** Morgan dollars were first struck at the Denver Mint on May 9, 1921, an important occasion as silver dollars had never been made there before. The first 100 pieces were set aside and were later hand-engraved in the obverse fields, creating souvenirs, such inscription indicating the number of the coin and its significance, as in this example: 7TH DOLLAR RELEASED FROM 1ST 100 EVER COINED AT DENVER MINT THOMAS ANNEAR, SUPT. The first of these is now in the Colorado Historical Society collection. Millions of 1921-D dollars were put into storage, and in time, many if not most were released, including to gambling parlors and casinos in Nevada. Some remained to be paid out during the Treasury releases of 1962 through 1964, but this was not one of the more plentiful varieties.

**Die Varieties:** All reverses have 16 berries in the right-hand-side reverse wreath. Some dies have raised dots, thought by some to be from the point of a hardness-testing gauge, and by others to be from gas bubbles in the die blank. These dots occur on dollars from all three mints.

## Whitman Coin Guide (WCG™)

| VG-8 | F-12 | VF-20 | EF-40 | AU-50 | MS-60 | MS-63 | MS-64 | MS-65 | MS-66 | MS-67 |
|------|------|-------|-------|-------|-------|-------|-------|-------|-------|-------|
| $28 | $29 | $32 | $35 | $37 | $48 | $65 | $140 | $290 | $1,250 | $7,000 |

**AVAILABILITY**

| | MS-60 | MS-61 | MS-62 | MS-63 | MS-64 | MS-65 | MS-66 | MS-67 | MS-68+ |
|---|-------|-------|-------|-------|-------|-------|-------|-------|--------|
| Certified | 120 | 521 | 2,292 | 7,304 | 9,955 | 3,349 | 489 | 13 | 1 |
| Field | 600,000–800,000 | | | 200,000–400,000 | 50,000–75,000 | 8,000–12,000 | 800–1,250 | 25–50 | 5–10 |
| Cert. DMPL | 1 | 1 | 1 | 6 | 9 | 4 | 0 | 0 | 0 |

# 1921-S

Optimal
Collecting Grade
MS-64

Circulation-
Strike Mintage
21,695,000

Detail of
"micro" mintmark
on 1921-S.

**Key to Collecting Circulation Strikes:** Following suit with the other varieties of this year, the 1921-S Morgan is common in all grades including Mint State. Most are poorly struck. Again, there is opportunity for connoisseurship. The 1921-S, although plentiful, is seen less often than its Philadelphia and Denver counterparts. All have a tiny or "micro" S mintmark.

**Surface Quality:** Most are somewhat shallowly struck on Miss Liberty's hair and on the reverse. "A fully struck piece with good luster is very rare," note Van Allen and Mallis, and raises a challenge for the collector who, in the word of the late Frank Archer, is in any way "particular." The strike varies, but is often unattractive.

**Prooflike Coins:** Prooflike coins are very rare. As none of the 1921 dies of this or the other two mints were basined (a process that in the 1878–1904 era often imparted prooflike character to the dies), this feature is seldom seen.

**Mintage and Distribution:** It seems that the 1921-S dollars were fairly scarce in the 1920s, as when dollars were needed the Treasury Department and the San Francisco Mint paid out other coins. Beginning in a large way in the 1930s, millions were released, many going to Nevada. In 1939 a torrent of these coins entered local commerce in San Francisco. In 1942, many may have been melted under legislation that reduced 50,000,000 coins to bullion. Unlike certain dollars of other dates, bags of 1921-S coins were viewed with disdain, and few were kept. Today, few bulk lots survive in any one place. These coins are seen much less often than are 1921 dollars of the other two mints.

**Die Varieties:** All reverses have 16 berries in the right-hand-side reverse wreath. Some dies have raised dots, thought by some to be from the point of a hardness-testing gauge, and by others to be from gas bubbles in the die blank. These dots occur on dollars from all three mints.

## Whitman Coin Guide (WCG™)

| VG-8 | F-12 | VF-20 | EF-40 | AU-50 | MS-60 | MS-63 | MS-64 | MS-65 | MS-66 | MS-67 |
|------|------|-------|-------|-------|-------|-------|-------|-------|-------|-------|
| $28 | $29 | $32 | $35 | $37 | $48 | $75 | $150 | $1,000 | $9,500 | $26,000 |

**AVAILABILITY**

| | MS-60 | MS-61 | MS-62 | MS-63 | MS-64 | MS-65 | MS-66 | MS-67 | MS-68+ |
|---|-------|-------|-------|-------|-------|-------|-------|-------|--------|
| Certified | 44 | 288 | 1,810 | 6,604 | 8,062 | 1,480 | 82 | 1 | 0 |
| Field | 400,000–600,000 | | | 100,000–150,000 | 20,000–30,000 | 3,500–5,000 | 200–300 | 1–2 | 0 |
| Cert. DMPL | 1 | 0 | 0 | 0 | 0 | 0 | 0 | 0 | 0 |

# MORGAN SILVER
# DOLLAR PATTERNS

lthough the pattern coins that led up to the adopted design of the Morgan silver dollar in 1878 are discussed in chapter 3, it is appropriate to delineate some of the most important varieties here. In 1877, Chief Engraver William Barber and assistant engraver George T. Morgan, along with several others, prepared extensive half-dollar pattern proposals—a gallery of interesting obverse and reverse motifs. These are delineated in *United States Pattern Coins: Experimental and Trial Pieces* (J. Hewitt Judd, edited by Q. David Bowers; Atlanta, Georgia, Whitman Publishing), the source of "Judd numbers" used to catalog U.S. patterns.

In 1877, more than two dozen pattern half dollars were created by several different artists, including Chief Engraver William Barber, assistant engravers Charles E. Barber and George T. Morgan, and Anthony Paquet (a local engraver who had worked at the Mint earlier). An example of Judd 1509, the 1877 half dollar that most closely resembles the 1878 Morgan dollar, is shown here. This copper pattern by George T. Morgan served as the inspiration for what became the Morgan silver dollar of 1878.

Several half dollars of 1877 and four varieties of silver dollars of 1878 depict the portrait of Miss Liberty as adopted for regular use on the Morgan dollar, first struck for circulation in March of the latter year. The obverse is said to have been modeled by Miss Anna Willess Williams (see further discussion in chapter 3), while several designs for the reverse eagle were created—stylistic, not from life.

Today, all of these patterns are rare, and some are extremely so. Descriptions below are by Judd numbers. They include the four die combinations with the famous Miss Liberty portrait (other combinations of reverse dies, etc., can be found in the Judd text). Certified population numbers are combined from pieces encapsulated by NGC and PCGS.

The first three of the following die combinations exist in both silver and copper versions and are similar to the adopted design, save for differences as explained. The fourth, Judd 1731, was made only in copper. Struck in 1884, years after the Morgan design was adopted, it was likely struck for placement in numismatic cabinets. All of the patterns below have reeded edges.

J-1509

## J-1550A AND J-1550B (1878)

This variety's obverse, the motif featuring the portrait of Miss Williams, is the same design as that adopted for regular coinage. On some pieces, the obverse bears the raised initial M on Liberty's neck, while on others the M is incuse. The reverse design is somewhat similar to the one adopted, but with heavier wings on the eagle and with just three leaves on the olive branch.

J-1550a

| Auction Record | | | | | | | | | | |
|---|---|---|---|---|---|---|---|---|---|---|
| Judd No. | Metal | Year | Pop. | Firm | Date | Amount | Grade | 60 | 63 | 65 |
| 1550a | Silver | 1878 | 19 | Stack's Bowers | 8/2010 | $12,650 | PCGS65Cam | $4,000 | $6,300 | $12,500 |
| 1550b | Copper | 1878 | 1 | Heritage | 1/2009 | $23,000 | NGC67RB | $3,850 | $6,100 | $11,500 |

# J-1550 and J-1551 (1878)

The obverse design is similar to Judd 1550a and b, but at least two other dies were used, differing from each other slightly. The initial M is incuse. The reverse is also similar to that of Judd 1550a and b, except there is a notch or indentation at the bottom of each wing where it joins the body. Three leaves are on the branch.

J-1551

Pattern researchers, including Bob Julian and, later, Roger W. Burdette, have studied Mint archives regarding Judd 1550a, 1550b, 1550, and 1551. Their research shows that 50 pieces were produced in silver between December 1, 1877, and January 2, 1878. It is not known in what sequence the different die combinations were used.

| Judd No. | Metal | Year | Pop. | Auction Record | | | | 60 | 63 | 65 |
| --- | --- | --- | --- | --- | --- | --- | --- | --- | --- | --- |
| | | | | Firm | Date | Amount | Grade | | | |
| 1550 | Silver | 1878 | 19 | Heritage | 12/2009 | $7,475 | NGC63 | $5,000 | $8,000 | $13,500 |
| 1551 | Copper | 1878 | 13 | Heritage | 7/2008 | $10,350 | NGC65RD | $4,750 | $7,500 | $16,000 |

# J-1611 and J-1612 (1879)

Although the 1878 "Morgan" dollar in circulation seems to have satisfied most everyone, in 1879 George T. Morgan made several patterns featuring other designs. This combines the standard silver dollar obverse with a reverse featuring an eagle with especially large wings, a style created by Morgan and used on the reverse of certain pattern $5 coins of 1878.

J-1612

| Judd No. | Metal | Year | Pop. | Auction Record | | | | 60 | 63 | 65 |
| --- | --- | --- | --- | --- | --- | --- | --- | --- | --- | --- |
| | | | | Firm | Date | Amount | Grade | | | |
| 1611 | Silver | 1879 | 13 | Heritage | 10/2010 | $27,600 | NGC68Cam | $6,000 | $10,000 | $17,000 |
| 1612 | Copper | 1879 | 11 | Stack's Bowers | 6/2010 | $8,912 | NGC64BN | $2,750 | $4,500 | $9,000 |

# J-1731 (1884)

On a regular basis, the Mint used regular Proof silver dollar dies to strike copper impressions, as here. Although some have suggested these were made to "test the press," in actuality they seem to have been struck as special pieces for numismatic cabinets. Only a few were produced.

J-1731

| Judd No. | Metal | Year | Pop. | Auction Record | | | | 60 | 63 | 65 |
| --- | --- | --- | --- | --- | --- | --- | --- | --- | --- | --- |
| | | | | Firm | Date | Amount | Grade | | | |
| 1731 | Copper | 1884 | 1 | Superior | 7/2003 | $19,838 | NGC62BN | $18,000 | $30,000 | N/A |

# MISSTRUCK AND ERROR
# MORGAN DOLLARS

The U.S. Mint is a powerhouse factory—an awe-inspiring model of accurate and precise high-speed production. In recent decades the Mint has produced *billions* of coins every year, for collectors and, more significantly, to facilitate everyday commerce. Even in the era of the Morgan dollar, more than 100 years ago, the nation's mints were cranking out coins by the millions annually. With production reaching such numbers, it is understandable that a few irregular pieces (of all denominations) would escape inspection and inadvertently be released, usually in original (mint-sewn) bags or rolls of new coins. To err is human, it is said, and to forgive divine; for coin collectors, for the Mint to err is divine—no forgiveness needed! Today, Morgan dollar mint errors, elusive as a class, are eagerly sought, not only for the light they shed on minting techniques but also as fascinating variations from normal date-and-mintmark collecting.

Morgan dollar errors are decidedly uncommon. Nicholas P. Brown, David J. Camire, and Fred Weinberg, writing in *100 Greatest U.S. Error Coins*, note that "Because of the large size of silver dollars, error coins . . . were easily spotted by the mint personnel who inspected coins after striking." Describing a Peace dollar struck on a quarter dollar planchet (the coin ranked number 5 in their book), they write, "The fact that there are no other Morgan or Peace dollar off-metal or wrong-planchet errors in existence is a testimony to the effectiveness of the Mint's inspection process for silver dollar coins."

Most Morgan errors have been found by dealers and collectors opening original bags, as opposed to having entered circulation and being noticed in the course of a transaction. The most common errors in the Morgan series are laminations (a flaw whereby a fragment of metal peels off the coin's surface), strike-throughs (often caused by grease clogging a die, with the effect that some design details are missing), and planchets with small clips.

A multiple-struck coin occurs when a finished coin is not ejected properly from the press, but remains in place, perhaps slightly off orientation, and is struck again with the same dies. About a half dozen double-struck Morgan dollars are known to exist. Values for such coins start around $10,000, while a dramatic example like the one pictured could be worth about $50,000 to a collector.

**Double-struck 1887 Morgan dollar
Ranked no. 6 among the *100 Greatest
U.S. Error Coins*. (Shown enlarged.)**

An off-center coin is one that was struck out of collar and incorrectly centered, with the result that part of the design is missing. Off-center Morgan dollars are rare, with Brown, Camire, and Weinberg estimating 15 to 20 in existence. The example pictured—an 1880-S struck 40% off center at exactly 12:00—first came to light at the 1979 American Numismatic Association Convention in St. Louis. It brought a then-record price for an off-center Morgan dollar: $2,000. Of course, markets change over time, and the hobby community's interest in error coins has skyrocketed since then; today this high-grade, dramatically off-centered coin might easily fetch $75,000 at auction. Most off-center Morgan dollars are dated 1921 and were struck at Philadelphia or San Francisco. A handful are known from the Denver, New Orleans, and Carson City mints. Most Morgan dollar off-center errors are minor, having been struck only 5% to 10% off kilter. They typically command values of $1,500 for a circulated 10% off-center coin to $10,000 for one struck 50% off center.

Collectors should be aware that many Morgan dollar errors listed as "off center" are actually only uncentered broadstrikes, and are worth far less than a true off-center example. On a broadstruck coin, none of the design is missing, although the coin is slightly off center and spread out larger than a regular dollar (again, the result of having been struck without being contained in the retaining collar die). Broadstrikes lack the normal reeded edge of a finished coin.

**Examples of typical
off-center Morgan dollars
Most vary from 5% to 10% off center.**

Off-center 1880-S Morgan dollar
Ranked no. 22 among the *100 Greatest
U.S. Error Coins.* (Shown enlarged.)

Off-center 1921-S Morgan dollar
Ranked no. 23 among the *100 Greatest
U.S. Error Coins.* (Shown enlarged.)

# GLOSSARY

**Act of March 3, 1887** (Trade Dollar Redemption Act)—Also called the Act of February 19, 1887, although March 3, 1887, was the final date on the legislation. Provided for the redemption of trade dollars with silver dollars and other silver coins. The redemption privilege was to extend for only six months following the passage of the act, after which trade dollars would once again be worth only bullion or meltdown value. Redemptions of trade dollars under the Act of March 3, 1887, eventually amounted to 7,689,036 pieces, equal to about 20% of the number coined.

**Act of July 14, 1890**—See *Sherman Silver Purchase Act.*

**Act of March 3, 1891** (Trade Dollar Recoinage Act)—Directed that the secretary of the Treasury, "as soon as practicable, coin into standard silver dollars the trade dollar bullion and trade dollars now in the Treasury, the expense thereof to be charged to the silver profit fund."

**Act of June 12, 1898**—See *War-Revenue Bill of June 12, 1898.*

**Act of 1918**—See *Pittman Act of 1918.*

**Act of 1941**—Implemented in 1942 to provide silver for the Manhattan Project and other wartime uses. Provided for the melting of 50,000,000 "uncurrent" silver dollars then being stored by the Treasury Department, various mints, and other facilities. No accounting was kept of the Morgan and Peace silver dollars destroyed.

**adjustment marks**—Marks left on a formerly overweight planchet that was filed down to the proper standard.

**branch-mint Proof**—A coin struck at a branch mint.

**Baker, Raymond T.**—Director of the Mint from March 15, 1917, to March 6, 1922. Was responsible for effecting the coinage of 1921 Morgan dollars.

**Bland dollar**—Name used by some, especially circa 1878 through the 1940s, for what is generally known as the Morgan dollar today; style minted from 1878 through 1921.

**Bland-Allison Act of February 28, 1878**—Provided for the coinage of silver dollars (known today as Morgan dollars) and authorized Silver Certificates.

**cameo**—A coin that has high contrast between frosty or lustrous designs and letters in relation to the surrounding field.

**Carson City Mint**—Branch mint in the capital of Nevada; completed in 1869, it struck its first coin for circulation in 1870. Morgan silver dollars were produced there from 1878 continuously through 1885, and again from 1889 to 1893. The Mint was later closed, and in 1942 it became the home of the Nevada State Museum.

**Chapman Proof**—A term that has arisen to describe a 1921 Proof Morgan dollar with deep mirror fields, in the style of Proofs of 1878 through 1904.

**choice**—An adjective, choice Uncirculated, now the equivalent of MS-63 (more or less), although no precise definitions are in place.

**circulation strike**—A Morgan dollar struck for commercial use, acceptable for the channels of commerce, and made available at face value.

**Coinage Act of January 18, 1873**—Set the standard of the silver dollar at 412 grains, 90% silver (371 grains pure silver).

**commercial Uncirculated**—An unofficial term particularly popular in the 1970s and 1980s, describing a piece advertised as Uncirculated, often at a bargain price; upon inspection, such coins would often be found by a knowledgeable collector to have some wear and thus to be About Uncirculated.

**condition rarity**—A coin that is easily available in low grades, but that, at a particularly high Mint State level, becomes very hard to find.

**Denver Mint**—U.S. Mint facility in Denver, Colorado; opened for business in a new building in 1906 and struck Morgan dollars in only one year, 1921. The 1921-D dollars bear a very tiny D mintmark.

**fine; fineness**—Degree of purity of silver, expressed in thousandths.

**gem**—An Uncirculated coin of above-average quality, generally MS-65 or finer on the numerical scale.

**ingot**—In the context of Morgan dollars, a heavy (usually) billet or bar of silver from a refinery, or from the refining process within a mint, from which a thin strip of metal is rolled, and from which planchets are cut.

**luster**—The "frost" or "flash" on a coin minted for circulation—a coruscating effect that sometimes changes as a coin is turned, and light reflects at different angles into an observer's eye.

**Morgan, George T.**—Designer of the Morgan dollar.

**New Orleans Mint**—Branch mint in New Orleans, Louisiana; opened for business in 1838, then closed in 1861, the first year of the Civil War. In 1879 it reopened for coinage, and from that year through 1904, Morgan dollars were struck there. Production of Morgan dollars was often casual, with the resultant pieces being below average in sharpness and often with unsatisfactory luster. Many were prooflike, although not necessarily well struck. The reason for the low quality may be due to most pieces' being struck, bagged, and taken out of circulation, rather than being used in commerce. There was no particular incentive to make "nice" pieces.

**ounce; Troy ounce**—System of weights used by the Mint for silver and gold. A Troy ounce contains 480 grains. There are 12 Troy ounces to a pound. In contrast, under the avoirdupois system used for nearly all other goods, materials, and products, there are 437.5 grains per ounce, and 16 ounces to a pound. The dual systems have been confusing for a long time.

**Philadelphia Mint**—U.S. Mint facility in Philadelphia, Pennsylvania. Morgan silver dollars were first coined at the second Philadelphia Mint, the cornerstone of which was laid on July 4, 1829, the building being occupied for coinage in January 1833. Within the Philadelphia Mint were all facilities for making dies, including for branch mints; the Engraving Department, in which the chief engraver and assistants worked; refining and assaying equipment; planchet-making devices; coin presses; and storage facilities. The second Philadelphia Mint building was used until 1901, when it was replaced by the third Philadelphia Mint, in use through the end of the Morgan dollar series (1921) and onward until replaced by the fourth Philadelphia Mint (1969). Morgan silver dollars were coined continuously at the Philadelphia Mint from 1878 through 1904 and again in 1921.

**Pittman Act of 1918**—This curious piece of legislation provided simultaneously for the melting of hundreds of millions of existing silver dollars and their replacement by the minting of millions more. Eventually, 270,232,722 silver dollars of earlier dates were melted and converted to bullion, much of which was shipped to India.

**Redfield hoard**—A quantity of 407,576 silver dollars from the estate of LaVere Redfield, of Nevada, who died in 1974.

**San Francisco Mint**—U.S. Mint facility in San Francisco. The second San Francisco Mint, the cornerstone of which was laid in 1870, opened for business in 1874 and was the site at which Morgan silver dollars were coined continuously from 1878 through 1904 and again in 1921. Within its large and modern facilities, the San Francisco Mint produced Morgan dollars of generally high quality, admired today for their sharpness of detail and luster. In April 1906 the Mint was the only building in its district to survive the earthquake and fire.

**Sherman Silver Purchase Act; Act of July 14, 1890**—Bears the name of Senator John Sherman, former secretary of the Treasury (1877–1881). Replaced the Bland-Allison Act and set new rules for the government purchase of silver. The act became effective 30 days after it was made final.

**standard dollar**—Regular silver dollar, as the Morgan type. Term used to differentiate the 412.5-grain silver dollar from the 420-grain trade dollar.

**Treasury hoard**—Generally a term referring to hundreds of millions of dollars held by the U.S. Treasury Department from the 19th century through the early 20th century. Most coins in the hoard were distributed from 1962 through 1964, after which only about three million remained, to be sold by the General Services Administration.

**Trade Dollar Recoinage Act**—See *Act of March 3, 1891.*

**Trade Dollar Redemption Act**—See *Act of March 3, 1887.*

**Treasury release**—Term usually employed in connection with the dispersal of long-stored silver dollars from Treasury reserves from 1962 through 1964.

**VAM variety**—Denotes specific die varieties of Morgan dollars defined by Leroy Van Allen and A. George Mallis.

**War-Revenue Bill of June 12, 1898**—Provided for the additional coinage of silver dollars.

**white surface**—The surface of a brilliant silver dollar that has no trace of toning anywhere.

**Zerbe Proof**—A Morgan silver dollar with fields that are slightly prooflike but that mainly have countless die-finishing marks, and that, when held at an angle to the light, show some reflectivity. In the writer's opinion these are simply circulation strikes that are slightly prooflike, nothing more.

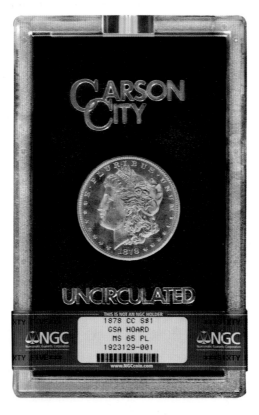

# NOTES

## CHAPTER 2

1. Noted scholar R.W. Julian was of great help with that book, as was the late Walter Breen. Mark Borckardt assisted with technical descriptions of dollars from 1794 through 1803.
2. The legal tender status of Spanish milled dollars was ended by the act of February 21, 1857, which, given an extension, became effective in 1860. By that time the Philadelphia, New Orleans, and San Francisco mints had struck many United States silver dollars.
3. As cited in the *Annual Report of the Director of the Mint*, 1895.
4. For these and other patterns mentioned in the text see Andrew W. Pollock III, *United States Patterns and Related Issues*, 1993; and Dr. J. Hewitt Judd, *United States Pattern Coins, Experimental and Trial Pieces*, 8th edition, 2003.
5. *Fractional Money.*
6. *Annual Report of the Director of the Mint*, 1878.

## CHAPTER 3

1. *Annual Report of the Director of the Mint*, 1877.
2. Certain items from Mint correspondence are from Neil Shafer, *The Morgan Silver Dollars of 1878–1921: A Study of Major Die Varieties, The Whitman Numismatic Journal*, November 1964; Don Taxay, *U.S. Mint and Coinage*, 1966; Cornelius Vermeule, *Numismatic Art in America*, 1971; and Leroy C. Van Allen and A. George Mallis, *Comprehensive Catalogue and Encyclopedia of Morgan and Peace Dollars*, various editions to 1997.
3. As quoted in *Harper's Weekly*, March 9, 1878.
4. Walter Breen, quoted by Neil Shafer, 1964.
5. The variety known today as VAM-9, noted by Leroy C. Van Allen and A. George Mallis, *Comprehensive Catalogue and Encyclopedia of U.S. Morgan and Peace Dollars*, 1997, p. 142, as having been first attributed in this regard by Pete Bishal.
6. At the time, all gold coins were worth a premium in terms of paper money. Apparently, the Treasury thought that there would be sufficient excitement on the part of the public that citizens would pay a premium. This did not materialize.
7. These were Silver Certificates of the Series of 1878, made only in high denominations, $10 to $1,000, and never released in quantity. It was not until the Series of 1886 that large-scale distribution of Silver Certificates commenced.
8. *Chicago Daily Tribune*, March 12, 1878, as cited by Leroy C. Van Allen and A. George Mallis, *Comprehensive Catalogue and Encyclopedia of Morgan and Peace Dollars*, 1997, p. 85, from the original furnished by *Numismatic News*.
9. This reiterates Secretary Sherman's earlier statement.
10. This is hype from either a Mint spokesperson or an imaginative writer. There is no government record of requests from "store keepers" for any such quantities.
11. A reference to the dollar containing just 92 cents' worth of silver.
12. The organization was known as the American Numismatic Society from 1858 to 1864, as the American Numismatic and Archaeological Society from 1864 to 1907, and since then, as the American Numismatic Society once again. Founded in New York City by teenage collector Augustus B. Sage and his friends in 1858, the group has always been domiciled in that city.
13. The editor apparently admired the Flowing Hair design used on silver dollars of 1794 and 1795.
14. The 1907 Saint-Gaudens Indian $10 coins with wire and rounded rims, and the MCMVII coins, were all made from basined dies, and all show raised swirl marks on the finished coins. The grit used to make the 1907 coins was coarse and produced not a hint of prooflike character.
15. Reprinted in December 1879, *Mason's Coin Collectors' Herald, Vol. I.*, p. 21. The sittings would have taken place before the preparation of certain 1877 pattern half dollars.

16. For a long time in numismatics as well as the popular press after 1878, early silver dollars from 1794 through 1873, and, in particular, Liberty Seated dollars from 1840 through 1873, were referred to as the "dollars of our daddies," to immediately distinguish them from the new Morgan dollars.

17. Cornelius Vermeule, *Numismatic Art in America*, 1971, pp. 74–79, citing "From the Mint Archives," *The Numismatic Scrapbook Magazine*, March 1966, p. 730.

18. Ibid.

19. "Engravers of the U.S. Mint in Philadelphia," *The Numismatist*, July 1940.

20. Certain information from Ted Schwarz, "The Morgan and Peace Silver Dollars," *The Numismatist*, November 1975; also R.W. Julian and other sources.

## CHAPTER 4

1. As someone would surely catch me on this, I mention that Pathé, the French manufacturer, made some center-start phonograph records—the opposite of the Berliner style as used in America (by everyone—Edison, Columbia, Decca, etc.).

2. Before being used for coinage, a die other than a Morgan dollar die (to give a view of the process) was typically placed against a grinding device that smoothed the surfaces, then a polishing device to remove the grinding lines. If the die was not polished, then grinding lines, called die striae, remained. During the Civil War in particular (but also at other times) working dies were sometimes made in haste, and nearly all Mint State examples of silver dollars of the early 1860s show die striae, in the form of minute raised lines on the finished coins.

3. Elsewhere in numismatics, edge styles differed. Many early United States coins had lettered edges, as did some later ones (e.g., the Saint-Gaudens double eagles of 1907–1933). In the Morgan dollar series an 1885 pattern was made with E PLURIBUS UNUM in raised letters on the edge, illogical as the motto duplicated the inscription on the obverse of the coin. Other denominations had plain edges.

4. There are many interesting early sources on die making during and before the Morgan dollar era. In particular, see Franklin Peale's report in the Proceedings of the American Philosophical Society, Philadelphia, January–April 1855; and the *Report of the Director of the Mint*, 1896. Over a period of time, including during the 1878 through 1921 span of Morgan dollar coinage, techniques varied, and no single account, including the preceding text in this book, can cover all situations.

5. Chester West in "Chester West Tells It As It Is—Of Federal and State Government Regulations," in *The Comprehensive U.S. Silver Dollar Encyclopedia*.

## CHAPTER 6

1. Details of the Pittman Act may be found in appendix B.

2. Again, see the appendix for details.

3. Information from *The Numismatist*, October 1937.

4. Author's conversation with Boosel, August 13, 1992. (Harry X Boosel's middle initial required no period, as it was not an abbreviation for a longer name, a situation similar to that with Harry S Truman's middle initial.)

5. In the 1930s Frank Dunn, of Lexington, Kentucky, had charge of the distribution of the Boone Centennial commemorative half dollars. He issued phony press releases, said that certain low mintage issues had been "sold out" when they had not been, etc. The complete story is related in the author's 1992 study, *Commemorative Coins of the United States: A Complete Encyclopedia*.

6. Author's conversation with Boosel, August 13, 1992.

7. Beginning in 1934, Whitman produced such boards for J.K. Post of Neenah, Wisconsin. Later, Whitman bought Post's rights.

8. Gold coins were first minted by the federal government in 1795. From then until 1933, production continued for most years (exceptions being 1816, 1817, and 1917–1919). In 1933 President Franklin D. Roosevelt halted the payment of gold coins by the Treasury Department, fearing a further disruption of an already precarious economy in the depth of the Depression. During the next several years, gold coins in circulation were called in, and circa 1937 most on hand were melted and converted into ingots (mostly stored today at Fort Knox, Kentucky).

9. Leading makers of slot machines in the second quarter of the 20th century included Mills, Watling, Jennings, and Caille. Slot machines for gambling first became widely popular in the very early 20th century, with perhaps the most widely known model being the Mills Dewey, named after Admiral George Dewey, hero of the Battle of Manila Bay in 1898. The writer has never seen an early slot machine that used silver dollars.

10. Reprinted with permission of *Coin World*, Beth Deisher, editor.

11. QDB note: No dealer had a "heavy stock" of Mint State coins at the time. However, many had supplies of rare and expensive circulated grades, such as VF and EF.

12. Stephen D. Ruddel told of a Midwestern dealer who sold a bag in his local market for $3 to $4 per coin. Dean Tavenner recalled $7 as the lowest price ever paid by one of the leading dealers at the time (cf. Dean Tavenner, "My Numismatic Memories," 1992).

13. Interview with the author, May 12, 1992.

14. From *The Coin Dealer Newsletter*, December 27, 1963, adapted from *International Coin Investors*, December 1963.

15. Copy provided by Charles Huff.

16. Certain parts of this account of gold and silver are adapted from the writer's "Joys of Collecting," Coin World, 2003.

17. Relative to the number in existence, Proofs have a much higher submission and resubmission rate to certification services, with the result that in some future year, for many Proof issues there have been more "certification instances" than there were coins minted.

## CHAPTER 7

1. Leroy C. Van Allen and A. George Mallis, *Comprehensive Catalogue and Encyclopedia of U.S. Morgan and Peace Dollars*, 1997, p. 99.

## CHAPTER 8

1. *ANA Grading Standards*, pp. 268–271, slightly adapted. Photographs not from the ANA text, but gathered for the present work.

2. Comment to author, September 14, 2003. (For all of his inaccuracies, the cumulative works of Walter Breen remain valuable for study, for general information, for specific citations from Mint reports, etc., and for such historical information that can be independently verified elsewhere.)

3. *The Morgan and Peace Dollar Textbook*, p. 208.

4. The reference is to *Breen's Encyclopedia of United States and Colonial Proof Coins*, 1977.

## CHAPTER 9

1. George W. Rice today is an unsung hero of numismatic research. He was among the first collectors to take an interest in mintmarked silver coins, joining such figures as W.M. Friesner, John M. Clapp, Edward Goldschmidt, and, of course, Augustus G. Heaton. In *The Numismatist*, February 1895, his article "Restrikes of U.S. Half Cents" was published—then an arcane topic that was confusing to even the most experienced dealers. An article in the October 1897 issue of the same magazine, "The Unexplained rarity of Certain U.S. Coins," stated that a certain cent reverse die was used in its perfect state with an obverse dated 1803, but in its cracked or later state with an obverse dated 1802. "It will thus be seen that it would be possible to have a large coinage recorded without a piece being struck bearing a corresponding date; and the recorded coinage of cents for 1799 may have been largely from dies of 1798 or 1800, and that of 1804 may have been dated 1803 or 1805, or perhaps both." Such comments were unusual for the era. His other contributions were numerous and valuable. In the meantime, he enjoyed hoarding 1856 Flying Eagle cents and amassed hundreds of them. In 1918 he died at the age of 66.

2. *The Numismatist*, October 1913.

3. A detailed discussion by Leroy C. Van Allen concerning his studies of dollar varieties, aspects of publishing, and work with A. George Mallis, is found on pp. v–vii of the fourth edition of the *Comprehensive Catalogue and Encyclopedia*.

4. *Comprehensive Catalogue and Encyclopedia of Morgan and Peace Dollars*, 1997, pp. 91, 99.

## CHAPTER 10

1. *Fractional Money.*
2. The total mintage of all varieties combined was 10,009,000 coins. The estimates by varieties are approximate, as it is not known when certain dies were retired.
3. Michael Fuljenz, *Proof Morgan Dollars*, 1992, was especially useful in the present study of Proof characteristics.
4. Michael Fuljenz, *Proof Morgan Dollars*, 1992.
5. *Walter Breen's Encyclopedia of United States and Colonial Proof Coins 1722–1989*, pp. 161, 162.
6. *The Morgan and Peace Dollar Textbook*, 1982, p. 83.
7. As quoted by Leroy C. Van Allen and A. George Mallis, *Comprehensive Catalogue and Encyclopedia of Morgan and Peace Dollars*, 1997, p. 91.
8. Quoted by E.A. Link in advertisements for the Link coin-operated piano, circa 1920, which was equipped with a nickel slot.
9. *Walter Breen's Encyclopedia of United States and Colonial Proof Coins 1722–1989*, p. 163.
10. Recollection of San Francisco dealer John Skubis, to author.
11. John W. Highfill, "The Carson City Mint: A Branch Mint Profile," 1992; William E. Spears, "The Mystique of the Carson City Silver Dollar," 1992.
12. Wayne Miller, *The Morgan and Peace Dollar Textbook*, 1982, p. 86; modified by John Kamin, publisher of *The Forecaster*, to the author, October 29, 1992.
13. For a dissertation on this variety and some opinions, see John W. Highfill (with Walter Breen), *The 1879-S Reverse of '78 Morgan Dollar*, 1992.
14. Estimate of John Kamin in *The Forecaster*, September 15, 1971. Kamin was one of the more active dealers in bags and other quantities of Mint State dollars.
15. *The Morgan and Peace Dollar Textbook*, 1982, p. 88.
16. The total mintage of 1880-CC, both varieties combined, was 591,000, but 96,000 were melted, leaving a net mintage for distribution of just 495,000.
17. As quoted by Chester West in "Chester West Tells It As It Is—Of Federal and State Government Regulations."
18. John W. Adams, *United States Numismatic Literature*, Vol. I, p. 129. In that era, December 25, if it fell on a weekday, was a normal day for labor and commerce. Christmas was widely regarded as mainly a papal holiday observed by Roman Catholics.
19. Cf. his Bowdoin sale catalog (March 21–April 2, 1879); Ferguson Haines catalog (October 13–16, 1880), and Clogston catalog (April 8–9, 1881), among others.
20. *The Morgan and Peace Dollar Textbook*, 1982, p. 95.
21. John W. Highfill, "The Carson City Mint: A Branch Mint Profile," 1992; William E. Spears, "The Mystique of the Carson City Silver Dollar," 1992.
22. Years ago, in the early 1980s, the American Numismatic Association Grading Service used a more logical "split grade" system and assigned one number or description to the obverse and another to the reverse. Often the numbers were the same for both sides, but there were many coins with each side graded with a different number.
23. As quoted by Chester West in "Chester West Tells It As It Is—Of Federal and State Government Regulations."
24. *Fractional Money*, 1930, p. 268.
25. *Walter Breen's Encyclopedia of United States and Colonial Proof Coins 1722–1989*, p. 171.
26. *The Numismatist*, October 1926.
27. Advertisement in *The Numismatist*, January 1964. On another occasion Ruddel obtained unsold remainders of Booker T. Washington and Washington-Carver commemoratives and sold them into the coin market. (His mother was Elizabeth Rudel [sic] Smith, who served as treasurer of the United States from 1961 to 1962; her signature appeared on currency.)
28. John W. Highfill, "The Carson City Mint: A Branch Mint Profile," 1992; William E. Spears, "The Mystique of the Carson City Silver Dollar," 1992.
29. *The Morgan and Peace Dollar Textbook*, p. 97.
30. "Haymarked" was a popular term in the late 19th and early 20th centuries for what numismatists call "hairlined" today.
31. *Walter Breen's Encyclopedia of United States and Colonial Proof Coins 1722–1989*, p. 174.

32. John W. Highfill, "The Carson City Mint: A Branch Mint Profile," 1992; William E. Spears, "The Mystique of the Carson City Silver Dollar," 1992.

33. As is true in most instances, for the number of dies said to have been made for coinage, many fewer have been identified by specialists today. Part of the explanation may be that not all die pairs were used.

34. As quoted by Chester West in "Chester West Tells It As It Is—Of Federal and State Government Regulations."

35. *History of the First National Bank of the United States: A History of the First National Bank of Davenport, Iowa.* Chicago, IL: Rand McNally & Company, 1913; and other sources.

36. The phrase "mind your p's and q's" is said to have come from typesetting by hand, during which process lowercase "p" and "q" letters could be easily confused.

37. By mistake the official invitations sent to dignitaries were misdated February 21, 1885.

38. *The Morgan and Peace Dollar Textbook*, 1982, p. 107

39. See advertisement by Steve Ruddel in *The Numismatist*, January 1964.

40. John W. Highfill, "The Carson City Mint: A Branch Mint Profile," 1992; William E. Spears, "The Mystique of the Carson City Silver Dollar," 1992.

41. *The Morgan and Peace Dollar Textbook*, 1982, p. 105.

42. Ibid., 106

43. [Original footnote in *Mint Report*]: "Since this report was put in press Superintendent Fox has reported that the only vault in the Mint with a combination lock was on the 21st of October filled to repletion with coin consisting mainly of standard silver dollars, even to filling up its passages. Relief, however, was then daily expected from the completion of the work of preparing for the reception of silver specie—two empty vaults connecting with the vacant apartments originally designed for occupation by the Sub-treasury at Philadelphia in the new United States (Post-office) building of that city. At the insistence of the Department these vaults have been supplied with time-locks and metallic lattice work, and consigned to use by the Superintendent of the Mint at Philadelphia for the storage of silver coins, in excess of what can be kept at the Mint, and the delivery of which to the Treasury or Sub-treasury has not yet been called for. The anomaly is thus presented that, after passing out of its immediate custody, beyond the walls of the Mint, the output of the Mint must, for some time to come, remain in the care of that institution. As no other appropriation is available, the expense of police and watch will have to be defrayed out of the regular appropriations of the Mint at Philadelphia, the cost of transportation only between the Mint and the vaults referred to being payable out of the Silver Profit Fund." Director Burchard added that silver dollars were put up, 1,000 coins each in 8-ounce duck-cloth bags. To store one million dollars' (face value) worth required 250 cubic feet. On the other hand, to store one million dollars of other silver coinage (half dollars and smaller denominations) took 150 cubic feet, and to store one million dollars' worth of gold coins, in $5,000 groups in 8-ounce duck bags, took nearly 17 cubic feet. The space occupied by a bag of standard silver dollars, piled snugly en mass, is 12 inches long, 9 wide, and 4 deep. Small silver (subsidiary) packs better than dollars. The weight of a thousand dollars in subsidiary silver being 56 ounces less than that of an equal value in standard silver dollars, the spaces occupied by each vary but little from each other.

44. In *The Numismatist*, July 1925, E.S. Thresher stated that although he had been searching through quantities of dollars for six years, eight coins remained missing from his collection: 1884-CC, 1885-CC, 1889-S, 1892, 1893-S, 1894, 1897, and 1899.

45. John W. Highfill, "The Carson City Mint: A Branch Mint Profile," 1992; William E. Spears, "The Mystique of the Carson City Silver Dollar," 1992.

46. Quoted by Chester West in "Chester West Tells It As It Is—Of Federal and State Government Regulations."

47. *Collecting American Coins in England*, p. 82.

48. In 1887, 1/55 of the mintage equaled 368,909 (give or take), the average use of a die pair—but it is not known whether all dies made for this year were employed. The estimated populations given here for Mint State coins show a greater rarity than 1/55 of the surviving 1886 dollars. More remains to be learned through study and observation.

49. Letter to the author, November 29, 1992.

50. Less an allowance for 1887/6, one of 55 obverse dies used this year; 1/55 of the total mintage equals 368,909 (give or take).
51. In any event, a fraction of 11,550,000 total for the year.
52. *The Morgan and Peace Dollar Textbook*, 1982, p. 117.
53. Although Proskey was held in low esteem by certain of his competitors, in their time *The Coin Collector's Journal* included much worthwhile information. Together with the privately issued *Numisma* and the institutional *American Journal of Numismatics*, it provides a window on the collecting scene of the period.
54. Until 2003, when an outside consultant was hired to "improve" the magazine, after which *The* was dropped, as were popular columns and in-depth research articles.
55. Specimen, presumably a Proof, struck for inclusion in the Mint Cabinet; footnote on p. 155 of the *Report of the Director of the Mint*, 1888, not included in numismatic listings giving 832 as the total.
56. Per Wayne Miller in 1982.
57. Coinage to and including this figure under the 1878 Bland-Allison Act; other, later monthly totals under the 1890 Sherman Silver Purchase Act. These cannot be distinguished.
58. John W. Highfill, "The Carson City Mint: A Branch Mint Profile," 1992; William E. Spears, "The Mystique of the Carson City Silver Dollar," 1992.
59. Wayne Miller, *The Morgan and Peace Dollar Textbook*, 1982, p. 134.
60. To a present-day reader, amazing insight! Decades later Uncle Sam would do precisely this—and buy up countless tons of cheese, peanuts, wheat, corn, you name it.
61. In 1903 Hershey would commence building a factory in what would become known as Hershey, Pennsylvania, complete with Cocoa and Chocolate avenues.
62. This is not true. The Flying Eagle design was dropped after 1858 as the motif was difficult to strike up properly.
63. Adapted from *The Numismatist* and the present writer's 1991 book, *The American Numismatic Association Centennial History 1891–1991*.
64. The only two sales of 1897 to earn an "A" rating in John W. Adams, *United States Numismatic Literature*, Vol. I.
65. Michael Fuljenz, *Proof Morgan Dollars*, 1992.
66. John W. Adams, *United States Numismatic Literature*, Vol. 1.
67. Estimated distribution: probably 10 to 20% of the 12,590,000 mintage of 1900-O (approximately 1,250,000–2,500,000 coins).
68. See note 67.
69. *The Numismatist*, August 1901.
70. July 1902. Excerpt from the article "The New United States Mint and Its Predecessors." Subtitles added.
71. *The Numismatist*, January 1902.
72. Contribution by Albert R. Frey to *The Numismatist*, May 1902.
73. A few years later, dealer and auctioneer Geoffrey Charlton Adams would set up offices there. Still later, he would disappear à la Ed. Frossard (the younger), owing a string of people a lot of money.
74. Quoted in *The Numismatist*, July 1903.
75. Many of the Stewart coins went to John Beck, a Pittsburgh collector who was in the wholesale salt business, and who, during his lifetime was to amass the remarkable quantity of 531 pieces. Beck died on January 27, 1924. In 1931 his Flying Eagle cents were inventoried by George H. Clapp of Pittsburgh. In the same era the R.B. Leeds Collection, auctioned November 27 and 28, 1906, by Henry Chapman (on his own, following the dissolution in the same year of the partnership with his brother) included a hoard of 106 Flying Eagle cents.
76. *Comprehensive Catalogue and Encyclopedia of Morgan and Peace Dollars*, 1997, p. 388.
77. Letter quoted in the 1922 *Assay Commission Report*. Copy furnished by Roger W. Burdette.

# BIBLIOGRAPHY

Adams, Edgar H. and William H. Woodin. *U.S. Pattern, Trial and Experimental Pieces.* New York: American Numismatic Society, 1913.

Adams, John Weston. *United States Numismatic Literature. Volume I. Nineteenth Century Auction Catalogues.* Mission Viejo, CA: George Frederick Kolbe Publications, 1982.

———. *United States Numismatic Literature. Volume II. Twentieth Century Auction Catalogues.* Crestline, CA: George Frederick Kolbe Publications, 1990.

Amspacher, Bruce. "Morgan Dollars: An Analysis of Condition Rarity." Monthly Summary, *The Coin Dealer Newsletter,* November–December 1979, January 1980.

Amspacher, Bruce and Wayne H. Miller. "Prooflike Dollars." *The Comprehensive U.S. Silver Dollar Encyclopedia.* Broken Arrow, OK: Highfill Press, Inc., 1992, pp. 657–676.

Block, Victor. "How the Government Will Sell Those Silver Dollars." *COINage Magazine,* February 1970.

Bodway, George E., Ph.D. "The 'Bodway Set' of Morgan Dollars." *The Comprehensive U.S. Silver Dollar Encyclopedia.* Broken Arrow, OK: Highfill Press, Inc., 1992, pp. 337–346.

Bolles, Albert S. *The Financial History of the United States from 1774 to 1885.* 3 vols. New York, 1879–1894.

Bowers, Q. David. "Silver Dollars: A Personal Reminiscence." *The Comprehensive U.S. Silver Dollar Encyclopedia.* Broken Arrow, OK: Highfill Press, Inc., 1992, pp. 21–24.

———. "The Silver Dollar Treasure Hunt: One Dealer's Discoveries About Fabled U.S. Coin Hoards." *COINage Magazine,* Aug. 1979.

———. *The American Numismatic Association Centennial History.* 2 vols. Wolfeboro, NH: Bowers and Merena Galleries, Inc., 1991.

———. *The History of United States Coinage.* Los Angeles, California: Bowers and Ruddy Galleries, Inc. 1979; later printings by Bowers and Merena Galleries, Inc., Wolfeboro, NH.

———. *Silver Dollars and Trade Dollars of the United States: A Complete Encyclopedia.* 2 vols. Wolfeboro, NH: Bowers and Merena Galleries, Inc., 1992.

———. *American Coin Hoards and Treasures.* Wolfeboro, NH: Bowers and Merena Galleries, Inc., 1997.

———. *More Adventures With Rare Coins.* Wolfeboro, NH: Bowers and Merena Galleries, Inc., 2002.

Boyd, James P. *Men and Issues of 1900.* No place or publisher, 1900.

Breen, Walter H. *Walter Breen's Encyclopedia of U.S. and Colonial Proof Coins, 1792–1977.* Albertson, New York: FCI Press, 1977. Updated edition published by Bowers and Merena Galleries, Wolfeboro, NH, 1987.

———. *Walter Breen's Complete Encyclopedia of U.S. and Colonial Coins.* Garden City, NY: Doubleday, 1988.

Bressett, Kenneth and Q. David Bowers. *The Official American Numismatic Association Grading Standards for United States Coins.* 6th ed. Atlanta: Whitman Publishing, LLC, 2005.

Brown, Robert L. *Central City and Gilpin County, Then and Now*. Caldwell, ID: The Caxton Printers, Ltd., 1994.

Burdette, Roger W. *Renaissance of American Coinage, 1916–1921*. Manuscript of work in progress, copy provided to the author.

Byars, William Vincent, editor. *"An American Commoner": The Life and Times of Richard Parks Bland*. Copyright 1900 by E.W. Stephens. No publisher or location.

Carothers, Neil. *Fractional Money*. New York: John Wiley & Sons, 1930.

Carter, Mike. *The 1921 Morgan Dollars: An In-Depth Study*. Beverly Hills, CA: Advance Coin & Stamp Co., 1986.

*Certified Coin Dealer Newsletter*, Torrance, CA Various issues of the 1980s and 1990s.

*Coin Dealer Newsletter*, Torrance, CA, various issues 1963 to date.

*Coin World*. Sidney, OH: Amos Press, et al., 1960 to date.

*Coin World Almanac*. 6th ed. Sidney, OH: Amos Press, 1990.

*Coinage Laws of the United States 1792–1894*. Modern foreword to reprint by David L. Ganz. Wolfeboro, NH: Bowers and Merena Galleries, Inc., 1991.

*Coinage of Gold and Silver. Collection, amounting to 491 printed pages, of documents, testimonies, etc., before the House of Representatives, Committee on Coinage, Weights, and Measures, 1891*. Washington, DC: Government Printing Office, 1891.

Crowell, Drew R. "Common Date Uncirculated Silver Dollars." *The Comprehensive U.S. Silver Dollar Encyclopedia*. Broken Arrow, OK: Highfill Press, Inc., 1992, pp. 525–527.

DeLorey, Thomas. "Collectors' Clearinghouse." *Coin World*, May 1975.

DesRochers, Euclide C. Jr., D.M.D. "Morgan Dollar Die Varieties." *The Numismatist*, Aug. 1966.

Deters, Richard T. "How Many Morgan Dollars Are Out There???" *COINage Magazine*, Sept. 1972.

———. "The Great Silver Dollar Mystery." *COINage Magazine*, May 1973.

———. "The Missing Morgan Dollars: Here's The Evidence. Decide For Yourself If There Is An 1896 Over 4 Variety." *COINage Magazine*, Oct. 1976.

———. "The Unwanted '21 Morgan." *COINage Magazine*, Jan. 1974.

Emerson, Edwin, Jr. *A History of the Nineteenth Century Year by Year*. New York: P.F. Collier & Son, 1901.

Evans, George G. *Illustrated History of the United States Mint*. Philadelphia, PA: published by the author, editions of 1883, 1885, 1889, 1893.

Fey, Michael S. and Jeff Oxman. *The Top 100 Morgan Dollar Varieties: The VAM Keys*. NJ, Morris Plains: Rare Coin Investments, 1997.

Fivaz, Bill and J.T. Stanton. *The Cherrypicker's Guide to Rare Die Varieties*. 2nd ed. Savannah, GA: Published by the authors, 1991.

Fivaz, Bill and J.T. Stanton. *The Cherrypicker's Guide to Rare Die Varieties*. 4th ed. Atlanta, GA: Whitman Publishing, 2006.

Fox, Les and Sue. *Silver Dollar Fortune Telling*. Closter, NJ: Carson City Associates, 1987.

Fuljenz, Michael. "Proof Morgan Dollars." *The Comprehensive U.S. Silver Dollar Encyclopedia*. Broken Arrow, OK: Highfill Press, Inc., 1992, pp. 677–696.

Glaser, Lynn. "The Origin of the Bland Dollar." *Numismatic Scrapbook*, June 1962.

Heaton, Augustus G. *A Treatise on the Coinage of the United States Branch Mints*. Washington, DC: published by the author, 1893.

Hepburn, A. Barton, LL.D. *A History of Currency in the United States and the Perennial Contest for Sound Money*. New York: The Macmillan Company, 1903.

———. *A History of Currency in the United States*. New York: The Macmillan Company, editions of 1915 and 1924.

Herbert, Alan. "Coin Clinic." *Numismatic News*, Sept. 11, 1990.

———. "Denver Dollars Not Engraved at Mint." *Numismatic News*, Nov. 28, 1989.

Hettger, Henry T. "Were Business Strike 1895 Dollars Made? *Rare Coin Review*, no. 99. Wolfeboro, NH: Bowers and Merena Galleries, Inc.

Hickson, Howard. *Mint Mark CC: The Story of the United States Mint at Carson City, Nevada*. Carson City: The Nevada State Museum, 1972, 1990.

Highfill, John W. "The Redfield Hoard." *The Comprehensive U.S. Silver Dollar Encyclopedia*. Broken Arrow, OK: Highfill Press, Inc., 1992, pp. 93–96.

———. "The 1879-S Reverse of '78 Morgan Dollar." *The Comprehensive U.S. Silver Dollar Encyclopedia*. Broken Arrow, OK: Highfill Press, Inc., 1992, pp. 111–114.

———. "World's Finest Collections and Prices Realized." *The Comprehensive U.S. Silver Dollar Encyclopedia*. Broken Arrow, OK: Highfill Press, Inc., 1992, pp. 279–336.

———. "The Carson City Mint: A Branch Mint Profile." *The Comprehensive U.S. Silver Dollar Encyclopedia*. Broken Arrow, OK: Highfill Press, Inc., 1992, pp. 65–84.

———. *The Comprehensive U.S. Silver Dollar Encyclopedia*. Broken Arrow, OK: Highfill Press, Inc., 1992.

Highfill, John W. and Walter H. Breen. "Morgan Dollars—A Date by Date Analysis." *The Comprehensive U.S. Silver Dollar Encyclopedia*. Broken Arrow, OK: Highfill Press, Inc., 1992.

———. "The 1879-S Reverse of '78 Morgan Silver Dollar." *The Comprehensive U.S. Silver Dollar Encyclopedia*. Broken Arrow, OK: Highfill Press, Inc., 1992, pp. 111–114.

Hodder, Michael and Q. David Bowers. *The Norweb Collection: An American Legacy*. Wolfeboro, NH: Bowers and Merena Galleries, Inc., 1987.

Howe, Dean F. *Morgan Dollars: An In Depth Study*. 2nd ed. Sandy, UT: Published by the author, 1993.

Ivy, Steve and Ron Howard. *What Every Silver Dollar Buyer Should Know*. Dallas, TX: The Ivy Press, 1984.

Judd, Dr. J. Hewitt. *United States Pattern, Experimental and Trial Pieces*. Racine, WI: Whitman Division of Western Publishing Company, 1959 and later editions (through the 7th edition); 8th edition, 2003, edited by Q. David Bowers, Whitman Publishing, Atlanta, GA.

Judd, Dr. J. Hewitt. *United States Pattern Coins: Complete Source for History, Rarity, and Values*. 9th ed. Atlanta, GA: Whitman Publishing, 2005

Julian, R.W. "The Silver Proof Coinage of 1878." *The Numismatist* Dec. 1986, pp. 2493–2498.

Klaes, Francis X. *Die Varieties: of Morgan Silver Dollars*, 1963. Northampton, MA: Self published.

Laughlin, J. Laurence, Ph.D. *The History of Bimetallism in the United States*. New York: D. Appleton & Company, 1900.

Love, John B. "Old Timer Stories." *The Comprehensive U.S. Silver Dollar Encyclopedia*. Broken Arrow, OK: Highfill Press, Inc., 1992, pp. 37–42.

Mansfield, Sen. Mike et al. "The Silver Dollar—Vanishing Americana." *Congressional Record*, March 21, 1964.

Manley, Dwight N. "Knowledge Is King." *The Comprehensive U.S. Silver Dollar Encyclopedia*. Broken Arrow, OK: Highfill Press, Inc., 1992, pp. 25–28.

Martin, Lee. "Surplus Silver Dollars." *COINage Magazine*, Nov. 1968.

———. "The Great Silver Dollar Drain." *COINage Magazine*, June 1970.

Miller, Wayne H. *The Morgan and Peace Dollar Textbook*. Metairie, LA: Adam Smith Publishing Co., 1982.

———. *The Comprehensive U.S. Silver Dollar Encyclopedia*. Broken Arrow, OK: Highfill Press, Inc., 1992.

Morano, Anthony J. and Dazelle. "Philadelphia 1880 Over 79 Silver Dollar." *Numismatic Scrapbook*, Dec. 1964.

Morano, Anthony J. and Dazelle. "The 1878 Silver Dollar Story." *Numismatic Scrapbook*, Feb. 1965.

*NGC Census Report*. Sarasota, FL: Numismatic Guaranty Corporation of America, various issues.

*Numismatic News*. Krause Publications, Iola, WI. Various issues 1950s to date.

*Numismatic Scrapbook Magazine*. Lee F. Hewitt, Chicago, IL; Amos Press, Sidney, OH. Various issues 1935 to 1976.

*Numismatist, The*. Dr. Geo. F. Heath, Farran Zerbe, American Numismatic Association, 1888 to date. Currently published in Colorado Springs, CO.

Osbon, James B. *Jim Osbon's Silver Dollar Encyclopedia*. Richmond, VA: Headquarters Publishing Company, 1976.

Oxman, Jeff G. "Die Varieties in the Morgan Dollar Series." *The Comprehensive U.S. Silver Dollar Encyclopedia*. Broken Arrow, OK: Highfill Press, Inc., 1992, pp. 133–144.

*PCGS Population Report, The*. Newport Beach, California: Professional Coin Grading Service, Inc. Various issues, 1980s and 1990s.

Pollock, Andrew W. *United States Pattern Coins and Related Pieces*. Wolfeboro, NH: Bowers and Merena Galleries, 1994.

Pollock, Andrew W., III and Q. David Bowers. "George T. Morgan, Ambrose Swasey, and the 1921 Proof Morgan Dollars." *The American Numismatic Association Centennial Anthology*. Wolfeboro, NH: Bowers and Merena Galleries, Inc., 1991.

Samuelson, Clark A. and Leon P. Hendrickson. "The Continental-Illinois Bank Deal." *The Comprehensive U.S. Silver Dollar Encyclopedia*. Broken Arrow, OK: Highfill Press, Inc., 1992, 97–104.

Shafer, Neil. "The Morgan Silver Dollars of 1878–1921: A Study of Major Die Varieties." *The Whitman Numismatic Journal*, Nov. 1964.

Sherman, John. *John Sherman's Recollections of Forty Years in the House, Senate and Cabinet, An Autobiography*. 2 vols. The Werner Company, 1895.

*Silver and Gold, or Both Sides of the Shield, A Symposium of the Views of all Parties on the Currency Question. . . .* John Sherman, William B. Allison, et al. Philadelphia and Chicago: P.W. Ziegler & Co., 1895.

Smith, A.M. *Illustrated History of the U.S. Mint*. Philadelphia: A.M. Smith, 1881.

Spears, William E. "The Mystique of the Carson City Silver Dollar." *The Comprehensive U.S. Silver Dollar Encyclopedia*. Broken Arrow, OK: Highfill Press, Inc., 1992, pp. 85–92.

Tavenner, Dean. "My Numismatic Memories." *The Comprehensive U.S. Silver Dollar Encyclopedia*. Broken Arrow, OK: Highfill Press, Inc., 1992, pp. 29–36.

Taxay, Don. *United States Mint and Coinage*. New York: Arco Publications, 1966.

Trager, James. *The People's Chronology*. New York: Henry Holt & Company, Inc., 1994.

Travers, Scott A., editor. *Official Coin Grading and Counterfeit Detecting.* New York: House of Collectibles, The Ballantine Publishing Group, 1997.

United States House of Representatives. Various documents c. 1877–1921.

United States Mint, Bureau of the Mint, et al. *Annual Report of the Director of the Mint.* Philadelphia, PA, c. 1877–1921.

Van Allen, Leroy C. "1878 7/8 Tail Feathers Silver Dollar: How and Why." *Numismatic Scrapbook,* April 1965.

———. "Total Uncirculated Silver Dollars Remaining." *The Comprehensive U.S. Silver Dollar Encyclopedia.* Broken Arrow, OK: Highfill Press, Inc., 1992, pp. 765–772.

Van Allen, Leroy C. and A. George Mallis. *Comprehensive Catalogue and Encyclopedia of U.S. Morgan and Peace Dollars.* New York: FCI Press, 1976; Revised edition, *Comprehensive Catalog and Encyclopedia of Morgan and Peace Dollars.* Virginia Beach, VA: DLRC Press, 1992; Fourth Edition, Worldwide Ventures, Inc., Orlando; Bob Paul, Inc., Philadelphia, 1997.

Vermeule, Cornelius. *Numismatic Art in America,* 2nd edition. Atlanta, GA: Whitman Publishing, 2008.

Wallechinsky, David and Irving Wallace. *The People's Almanac.* Garden City, NY: Doubleday and Company, 1975.

———. The People's Almanac #2. New York: Bantam Books, 1978.

West, Chester. "Chester West Tells It As It Is—Of Federal and State Government Regulations." *The Comprehensive U.S. Silver Dollar Encyclopedia.* Broken Arrow, OK: Highfill Press, Inc., 1992, pp. 561–572.

White, Horace. *Money and Banking.* Boston: Ginn & Company, 1896.

White, Trumbull, editor. *Silver and Gold, or Both Sides of the Shield.* No location, no publisher, 1896.

*World Almanac and Book of Facts, The.* Rahway, NJ: Funk & Wagnall's, various editions.

Yeoman, R.S. *A Guide Book of United States Coins.* Kenneth, E. Bressett, editor. Whitman Publishing Company (and Western Publishing Company, Inc.), Racine, Wisconsin: various editions 1946 to date, current publisher, Whitman Publishing, Atlanta, GA.

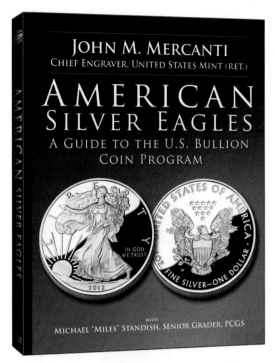

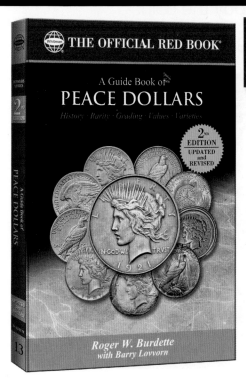